CREATING IRELAND

"Whereas the Irish people is by right a free people:"

Declaration of Independence

CREATING IRELAND

THE WORDS AND EVENTS THAT SHAPED US

PAUL DALY

HACHETTE
BOOKS
IRELAND

To Finbarr O'Malley

First published in 2008 by Hachette Books Ireland
A division of Hachette Livre UK Ltd

A CIP catalogue record for this title is available from the British Library.

ISBN 978-0-340-97732-3

Typeset in 11 point Bembo
Cover and text design by Anú Design, Tara
Printed and bound in Italy by L.E.G.O. SpA - Vicenza

Hodder Headline Ireland's policy is to use papers that are natural, renewable and recyclable products and made from wood grown in sustainable forests. The logging and manufacturing processes are expected to conform to the environmental regulations of the country of origin.

Hachette Books Ireland
8 Castlecourt Centre
Castleknock
Dublin 15
Ireland

A division of Hachette Livre, 338 Euston Road, London NW1 3BH, England

Contents

Introduction   **vi**

About this Book   **vii**

1919—1922   Struggling for the Soul of Ireland   **1**

1922—1932   Men of Destiny   **31**

1932—1948   The Return of the Old Gospel   **59**

1948—1957   Turmoil and Torpor   **93**

1957—1973   Let Lemass Lead On   **117**

1973—1982   On the Road to God Knows Where   **159**

1982—1992   Debt, Divorce, Dessie and Dick   **195**

1992—2002   Peace, Prosperity and Perdition   **235**

2002—2008   The End of an Era?   **277**

Conclusion   **309**

Acknowledgements   **312**

Permission Acknowledgements   **312**

Introduction

People are initially attracted to politics for a myriad of reasons. For some, it's family history, for others it's a desire to shape the future, for a minority it's the sheer elixir of power. In my case it was a much more mundane reason – I didn't really like school all that much.

Not that the Sacred Heart Boys National School in Ballygall in the early 1980s was a bad school. We had fine teachers, a green nearby to play football on and, once, Arsenal star and former pupil Dave O'Leary came to visit. Heady days indeed.

But for some reason sitting in a dilapidated prefab with thirty other kids waiting on the free bottle of milk that mysteriously arrived every day just didn't fire the imagination. For me, there was nothing better than an unexpected day off. Invariably, though, rumours of burst pipes in the winter or extra holidays to allow the youth of the nation top up on Vitamin D after a lousy summer came to naught.

However, if your school also served as a polling station in 1981–1982, you quickly learned that you could depend on politicians. Every couple of months these kind, generous people would ensure that kids like me could leave the school bag in the corner, have a lie-in and then spend a glorious day watching the TV while the adults in the house trudged off to schools across the country to try elect a government that might last more than a couple of months.

My dad used to take me with him to vote and, for some reason, I was fascinated by the whole event. At that time, the environs of polling stations resembled an exotic bazaar where all sorts of strange political types used the final hours of the campaign to sell voters their wares as they went to cast their ballots. As if this wasn't exciting enough, the following day, election results came with all the bells and whistles that RTÉ could muster at the time, all brilliantly anchored by a man in a dicky bow.

For that time on, I was a political junkie. I was hooked on the drama, the personalities and the game. Over time, I learned to appreciate how politics can change society and correspondingly how nothing will change if people don't engage in the political process.

Over the decades, Dáil Éireann has been the forum for vital debates on the future of our country and this book gives an insight into the role the Dáil has played in shaping modern Ireland, at a time when perhaps more and more people are minded to dismiss the institution. Many forces have shaped Irish society since the Declaration of Independence was adopted by the First Dáil and politics has been central to the direction we have taken as a society since 1919. Yet, the role played by Dáil Éireann in that process is quite often ignored. This book provides an accessible, comprehensive overview of the key events in modern Irish political history – including the Treaty debates, the ascent to power of Fianna Fáil and the battle over the liberal agenda – to give an insight into the debate, division and dilemmas they provoked in Dáil Éireann.

Speaking during a Dáil debate in April 1932, West Cork TD Eamon O'Neil recalled the words of a former Home Rule MP, poet and writer when describing Irish politics:

> The late Tom Kettle described the vagaries of some of our politicians. He once used the phrase that we were endeavouring to create an impossible future out of an imaginary past.
>
> *(29 April 1932)*

Kettle died on the Western Front in 1916 at the age of just thirty-six and never got to witness Ireland's efforts to overcome the legacy of history he described. In the following pages light is cast on the role Dáil Éireann played in that journey.

Paul Daly, August 2008

Note on the text:

The extracts from the Dáil debates have been accessed from the excellent historical archive on the Houses of the Oireachtas website www.oireachtas.ie and doubled-checked against the printed record in cases where syntax or spelling had to be clarified. The extracts of the debates have not been amended so there may be some grammatical difference, such as the capitalisation of certain words, between the extracts and the narrative text. In most cases, every effort has been made to retain as much of the original extract as possible, but some editing has been necessary, which I hope in no way distorts or misrepresents the original import of the quotation.

In relation to the proceedings of the First Dáil many comments are not reported verbatim. Much of the proceedings were recorded in 'note-taking' style where a synopsis of the main points made by each speaker was taken, which in itself is a remarkable achievement given the atmosphere within which the First Dáil met. Indeed, the minutes of the meeting of Dáil Éireann on 11 April 1919, the fifth day the Dáil sat, were lost with the printed record stating: 'The minutes of the Proceedings of this day were destroyed owing to enemy action. The following is a Press report taken from *The Irish Independent* of the 12 April 1919.'

Anyone with comments or queries in relation to the extracts from the Dáil debates or any other material in this book is welcome to contact me at: creatingireland@gmail.com.

'Peace with England, alliance with England to some extent, and, under certain circumstances, confederation with England; but an Irish ambition, Irish hopes, strength, virtue and rewards for the Irish.'

Signing the Treaty, 6 December 1921.
Seated from left: Arthur Griffith,
E.J. Duggan, Michael Collins;
Robert Barton. Standing Robert
Erskine Childers, George Gavan
Duffy and John Chartres.

Whereas the Irish people is by right a free people

1919-1922

Struggling for
the Soul of Ireland

'Deserters all! We will now call
the Irish people to rally to us.
Deserters all! ... Deserters all to
the Irish nation in her
hour of trial. We will stand by her.'

'Deserters all! We wi[ll] ... [rally] to
to us. Deserters all! ... [rally] ... to
the Irish nat[ion] ... [her hour] no[t]
of trial. We will stand by her.'
rally to us. Deserters all! ...Deserters all to
the Irish nation in her hour of trial.

1919-1922

No politician relishes the prospect of a December election, and that was never more true than for members of the Irish Parliamentary Party in 1918. The party of Isaac Butt, Charles Stewart Parnell and John Redmond, which had dominated Irish politics since the 1870s, now faced extinction at the hands of Sinn Féin.

Under John Redmond's leadership, the Irish Parliamentary Party had won eighty of the 105 Irish seats in Westminster at the 1910 general election. Despite strong Unionist opposition, the party's goal of Home Rule – a limited form of self-government for Ireland – was finally achieved in September 1914 only for the measure to be put on hold with the outbreak of the First World War.

Believing, like many others, that the war would be short-lived, Redmond encouraged his supporters to join Irish regiments of the British army and hasten the day when a Home Rule parliament would be established in Ireland.

Redmond's call to enlist was heeded by thousands of Irishmen of military age. The campaign for Home Rule had produced a military organisation, the Irish Volunteers, and the vast majority of its 180,000 members followed Redmond's policy of supporting the British war effort. In the first year of the war, over 75,000 Irishmen joined the British army and, though estimates vary, at least 35,000 were to lose their lives in the trenches over the four years of bloody conflict

A minority of Irish Volunteers, numbering around 12,000, disagreed with Redmond's approach. More nationalist in outlook, they refused to join the British war effort and a minority set themselves the goal of achieving Irish independence through force. A core group, including names that would resonate in subsequent years – such as Eamon de Valera, Michael Collins, W.T. Cosgrave and Cathal Brugha – participated in the Easter Rising in 1916.

While the 1916 Rising failed from a military point of view, it did manage to plant the idea of an independent Irish republic in the public mind. The harsh British response to the Rising – the execution of fifteen men, the imposition of martial law and the rounding up of 4,000 people suspected of republican sympathies, of whom approximately 1,800 were interned without trial – created sympathy for Sinn Féin, which, until then, had been a marginal presence in Irish politics.

In the aftermath of the Rising, nationalist opinion was radicalised, and the prospect of Home Rule, which was greeted with widespread delight in 1914, increasingly failed to satisfy the aspirations of a growing section of the population, with Sinn Féin playing a key role in this shift in public opinion.

1919

1 January
In Germany, socialist demonstrations in Berlin turn into an attempted communist revolution. Rosa Luxemburg and Karl Liebknecht, two of the socialist elite, are killed as a result of the uprising two weeks later.

6 January
In Scotland, HMS *Iolaire* sinks after hitting rocks drowning 205 men.

6 January
Theodore Roosevelt, the twenty-sixth president of the United States, dies at his home at Oyster Bay, Long Island.

11 January
Romania annexes Transylvania.

13 January
German workers meet to end the general strike.

15 January
In Boston, a wave of molasses sweeps through the city, killing twenty-one people and injuring 150 others.

18 January
The Paris Peace Conference opens in Versailles to discuss German reparations for the First World War.

18 January
Bentley Motors is founded.

31 January
In Glasgow, demonstrations by strikers for a shorter working week are crushed by the army in what becomes known as the Battle of George Square.

3 February
Soviet troops occupy the Ukraine.

23 February
In Italy, Benito Mussolini founds the Fascist Party.

De Valera speaks, 1917. Eamon de Valera speaking from O'Connell's monument in Ennis, County Clare, whilst campaigning in the 1917 by-election.

The growing popular appeal of the party was demonstrated in 1917 when it won by-election victories in Roscommon, Longford, Kilkenny and Clare, the latter contest seeing Eamon de Valera winning the seat previously held by the Irish Parliamentary Party's Willie Redmond, a brother of John Redmond, who had been killed in action on the Western Front that year.

In 1918, the situation for the Irish Parliamentary Party continued to decline. Its leader, John Redmond, died in March and John Dillon took over the leadership. In the spring, as the carnage of the First World War continued, British government plans to introduce conscription across Ireland handed Sinn Féin its greatest political weapon. Conscription was resisted across all sections of nationalist Ireland, and Sinn Féin was in the forefront of the campaign. The plan was eventually shelved but the controversy had sidelined the Irish Parliamentary Party and had given Sinn Féin a major propaganda victory.

The First World War was finally brought to an end in November 1918, and a general election to the Westminster Parliament was held in December. Sinn Féin contested the election, pledging that its candidates would boycott Westminster and establish an Irish parliament. In advance of the election, the Labour movement decided not to field candidates, thus ensuring that the campaign outside the Unionist-dominated northeast of the country was effectively a contest between Sinn Féin and the more moderate voice of the Irish Parliamentary Party.

Critically, the 1918 election saw a huge expansion in the Irish electorate, with many women over thirty and most men over twenty-one being entitled to vote for the first time. The number of voters increased threefold, with nearly 2 million people entitled to cast a ballot, many of them younger, first-time voters for whom the grand old men of the Irish Parliamentary Party held little appeal.

The election, held on 14 December, proved to be a triumph for Sinn Féin. It won seventy-three of the 105 seats available and, in the process, delivered a mortal blow to the Irish Parliamentary Party, reduced to just six seats. The remaining twenty-six seats were won by Unionist candidates.

Following the election, Sinn Féin moved to establish the Irish parliament it promised in its manifesto and called a meeting of all those elected in Ireland at the December election. Unsurprisingly, those elected for the Irish Parliamentary Party and the Unionists ignored the formation of an independent national parliament, and so the first meeting of Dáil Éireann, held on 21 January 1919 in the Mansion House in Dublin, was comprised exclusively of Sinn Féin members.

The Dáil met at 3.30 p.m and in the roll-call of those elected, forty Sinn Féin members were either declared 'fe ghlas ag gallaibh' ('jailed by the foreigner') or 'ag dibirt ag gallaibh' ('deported by the foreigner'). Among those in prison were the Sinn Féin president Eamon de Valera, Arthur Griffith and Countess Markievicz. Only twenty-eight of the seventy-three Sinn Féin representatives elected were present for the historic first meeting of the Dáil, but its actions that day left no doubt of the intentions of those gathered.

The new parliament adopted four important documents, the first was the simplest: the Constitution of Dáil Éireann. The short document was evidence that far from instituting a revolutionary government, the newly declared parliament of Ireland would closely follow the theory and practices of the Westminster parliament of whose control over Irish affairs Sinn Féin members so dearly wished to rid themselves. In the constitution, the Dáil was vested with full legislative powers. The document also provided for an executive to be formed and established the position of Ceann Comhairle, or chairperson of parliament, who would preside over Dáil business and enforce the rules of debate, which were borrowed from the 'foreigners' in Westminster.

25 February
In America, Oregon puts a 1 cent per litre tax on gasoline – the first state to do so.

28 February
Amanullah Khan becomes King of Afghanistan.

2 March
First Communist International meets in Moscow.

12 April
Henri Désiré Landru is arrested in Paris. Between 1914 and 1918, he duped at least eleven women into giving him access to their funds by promising marriage. He then murdered the women and, reportedly, burned their bodies in his kitchen.

14 April
The Emperor of Austria goes into exile in Switzerland.

25 April
In the Weimar Republic, Walter Gropius founds the Bauhaus movement, combining function and form.

25 April
ANZAC Day is celebrated for the first time in Australia and New Zealand.

28 April
In America, pipe bombs are posted to thirty prominent citizens in a two-month period.

5 May
The League of Red Cross Societies is founded in Paris.

25 May
In Java, Indonesia, 16,000 people are killed when the volcano Kelut erupts.

15 June
John Alcock and Arthur Brown arrive in Clifden, Galway, having flown non-stop from Newfoundland in Canada.

In comparison to the Dáil constitution, the other documents adopted that day – the Declaration of Independence, the Message to the Free Nations of the World and the Democratic Programme – were more visionary in both language and tone. Both the Declaration of Independence and the Message to the Free Nations of the World were read in Irish, English and French, the use of the latter highlighting the hope that the new parliament placed on the post-war Paris Peace Conference that would draw a new map of Europe.

The Declaration of Independence was a tour de force of Irish nationalist sentiment, it stated:

Whereas the Irish people is by right a free people:
And Whereas for seven hundred years the Irish people has never ceased to repudiate and has repeatedly protested in arms against foreign usurpation:

And Whereas English rule in this country is, and always has been, based upon force and fraud and maintained by military occupation against the declared will of the people:

And Whereas the Irish Republic was proclaimed in Dublin on Easter Monday, 1916, by the Irish Republican Army acting on behalf of the Irish people: …

And Whereas at the threshold of a new era in history the Irish electorate has in the General Election of December, 1918, seized the first occasion to declare by an overwhelming majority its firm allegiance to the Irish Republic:

Now, therefore, we, the elected Representatives of the ancient Irish people in National Parliament assembled, do, in the name of the Irish nation, ratify the establishment of the Irish Republic and pledge ourselves and our people to make this declaration effective by every means at our command:

We ordain that the elected Representatives of the Irish people alone have power to make laws binding on the people of Ireland, and that the Irish Parliament is the only Parliament to which that people will give its allegiance:

(*19 January 1919*)

The Message to the Nations of the Free World was couched in similar language to the Declaration of Independence and appealed especially to those assembling in Paris for the Peace Conference to recognise the legitimacy of the Irish Republic.

The final document adopted at the first sitting of Dáil Éireann attracted the most attention in later years. The Democratic Programme was a statement of social and economic intent, giving a distinctly left-wing hue to the new parliament. The

" ... at the threshold of a new era in history the Irish electorate has ... seized the first occasion to declare by an overwhelming majority its firm allegiance to the Irish Republic ... "

Declaration of Independence, 19 January 1919

document declared that the right to private property must be subordinated to the public good, it established the right of citizens to a share in the wealth of the nation and stated that the first duty of government was to the physical, mental and spiritual well being of the country's children.

The Democratic Programme was, in part, a payback to the Labour movement for not contesting the December election. Intent on securing as much popular support for the new Dáil as possible, Sinn Féin invited the leader of the Labour Party, Thomas Johnson, to draft text for the Democratic Programme before the Dáil met. Johnson's early version, which included a reference to the 'elimination of the class in society which lives upon the wealth produced by the workers but gives no useful service in return' was deemed too radical, and the final text, prepared by future president Seán T. O'Kelly, was less strident in both tone and ambition.

The Democratic Programme of the First Dáil was regularly invoked in subsequent years to highlight the State's failings in terms of social policy, especially towards children. However, it is clear that the First Dáil, and indeed subsequent parliaments, viewed the document as little more than an aspirational form of words rather than the foundation stone of social policy, a point that de Valera made clear to the Dáil four months after the Democratic Programme was adopted:

> Mr. DE VALERA, replying, said that it was quite clear that the democratic programme, as adopted by the Dáil, contemplated a situation somewhat different from that in which they actually found themselves. They had the occupation of the foreigner in their country, and while that state of affairs existed, they could not put fully into force their desires and their wishes as far as their social programme was concerned … He had never made any promise to Labour, because, while the enemy was within their gates, the immediate question was to get possession of their country.
>
> (*11 April 1919*)

At the same time as the twenty-eight Sinn Féin representatives were mapping out the democratic future of the country in the Mansion House, their colleagues in the emerging IRA embarked on a course that would also leave a mark on modern Irish history. The day the Dáil met, a group of IRA men killed two members of the Royal Irish Constabulary (RIC) escorting explosives in Soloheadbeg in Tipperary. The ambush marked the start of the War of Independence.

Many of those involved in the Sinn Féin movement were also involved in military resistance to Britain and, following the establishment of the First Dáil, this armed organisation eventually became known as the Irish Republican Army or the IRA.

Despite the close relationship and crossover in membership between Sinn Féin and the IRA, the military wing maintained its own command structure and, in theory, owed loyalty only to its own leadership. During 1919, the IRA carried out a number of raids on RIC barracks throughout the country in an attempt to seize arms and ammunition, and, as the military action continued, the government moved to bring the IRA under the authority of the Dáil. In August 1919, the Dáil adopted an Oath of Allegiance that would be taken by all TDs, officials in Dáil Éireann and, most importantly, the IRA. The oath stated:

> I, _____ do solemnly swear (or affirm) that I do not and shall not yield a voluntary support to any pretended Government, authority or power within Ireland hostile and inimical thereto, and I do further swear (or affirm) that to the best of my knowledge and ability I will support and defend the Irish Republic and the Government of the Irish Republic, which is Dáil Éireann, against all enemies, foreign and domestic, and I will bear true faith and allegiance to the same, and that I take this obligation freely without any mental reservation or purpose of evasion, so help me, God.

Eamon de Valera, the most senior surviving 1916 commander, had been elected President of Dáil Éireann on 1 April 1919, following his escape from Lincoln Prison. The following day, de Valera appointed seven government ministers, including Michael Collins in Finance, Arthur Griffith in Home Affairs, Cathal Brugha in Defence, W. T. Cosgrave in Local Government and Countess Markievicz in Labour.

Born in London, Countess Markievicz's wealthy Anglo-Irish family, the Gore-Booths, owned a large estate at Lissadell in County Sligo. She married a Polish Count, Casimir Markievicz, thus acquiring the title countess, but the couple separated before the outbreak of the First World War. Markievicz was actively involved in the labour movement and joined the Irish Citizen Army, a small force formed to protect workers from the police during the 1913 Lockout. The Irish Citizen Army took part in the 1916 Rising and Markievicz was second-in-command of those fighting in St Stephen's Green. She was sentenced to death for her role in the Rising but this was later commuted to life imprisonment and she served thirteen months before being released in a general amnesty in 1917. Elected for Sinn Féin in the 1918 general

19 August
Afghanistan gains independence from Britain.

31 August
The America Communist Party is founded.

8 October
Sixty-three planes take off from San Francisco and New York in the first transcontinental air race in the United States.

30 October
Because of Prohibition in America, thousand of gallons of 'plain' spirits from America are dumped in Dublin, causing many problems for Irish whiskey distillers.

28 November
American-born Nancy Astor is the first woman in British history elected to a seat in the House of Commons.

1920

election, Countess Markievicz was the first woman appointed to a government post in Europe. However, those who thought that this initiative would mark out the emerging Irish democracy as a progressive forum for women's representation would be proved wrong. It would take another sixty years until a woman served in cabinet again.

On 10 April 1919, the Dáil adopted a proposal by de Valera that RIC and British army personnel be ostracised by the Irish people. The motion was strongly supported by Dáil deputies, with Tipperary South TD Patrick Moloney declaring:

> I think it should go out to the Irish people from An Dáil that those tools who allow themselves to be made use of for such deeds deserve to be ostracised completely and made to feel that there can be no place for them in the free Ireland of to-morrow. And the Power that is responsible for such terrorism and encourages such offences against humanity, we can hold up to the world as a hypocrite and despot, whose claim to be the champion of the rights and liberties of weak nations is but a mockery and an insult to liberty.
>
> (*10 April 1919*)

The ostracisation policy was part of a strategy to wrest the administration of the country from Britain. In June 1919, the Dáil passed a decree that established its own justice system, called the Dáil Courts, which arbitrated on local disputes. Local elections held twelve months later delivered Sinn Féin control of twenty-nine of the thirty-three county councils, and these bodies gave their allegiance to Dáil Éireann, further eroding the capacity of the British authorities to govern effectively.

In addition to putting in place a system of government and administration, the First Dáil worked hard to promote Ireland's case abroad. One of the Dáil's first acts was to appoint two TDs – Seán T. O'Kelly and Dr Pat McCartan – as representatives to Paris and Washington respectively.

America was, of course, the most important foreign audience for the new Irish government. The Dáil was determined to secure support for Irish independence from the Paris Peace Conference, and the backing of US President Woodrow Wilson was critical in that regard. Prospects for a US initiative regarding Irish independence received a boost when the American Senate passed a motion on 6 June calling for an Irish delegation to be given a hearing at the conference.

De Valera left Ireland for America in June 1919 to bolster support for the new Republic and was not to return until December 1920. In his absence,

Black and Tans, 1921. A convoy of Black and Tans arrives at the junction of Middle Abbey Street and O'Connell Street, Dublin, during the War of Independence.

Arthur Griffith was appointed Deputy President by Dáil Éireann on 17 June. De Valera's mission to the USA raised substantial funds and gained significant publicity for the emerging Irish state, with Griffith, for example, informing the Dáil in October of the reception the President of Dáil Éireann received in Cleveland:

> Our President opened a big campaign on 29th September, and has since addressed meetings in a very large number of cities in America.
>
> He visited Cleveland within a day of the visit of the King of the Belgians to that city. The King of the Belgians was accorded the courtesy due to his position, but President de Valera was received with a salute of 21 guns, and was accompanied by a procession headed by the Police and Military.
>
> (*27 October 1919*)

However, de Valera failed in his main aim of securing recognition for the Dáil from the American political establishment, despite exerting significant pressure on both the Republican and Democratic parties.

The War of Independence intensified during de Valera's absence. In September, the British government banned Dáil Éireann and Sinn Féin, effectively driving the entire parliament and the government underground. While Cathal Brugha remained Minister for Defence, the organisation and execution of the war were

9 January
In New York, thousands of onlookers watch as George Polley, the 'Human Fly', scales the Woolworth Building. He reaches the thirtieth floor before he is arrested for climbing without a permit.

10 January
The League of Nations is established in the hope of preventing another world war.

16 January
The First World War Allies demand that the Netherlands extradite Kaiser Wilhelm II of German. The Netherlands government refuses and the kaiser lives in the country until his death in 1941.

24 January
Percy French, the entertainer and artist dies in Liverpool. His song, 'Are You Right there, Michael, are You Right?' which was based on the west Clare railway, provoked a libel action.

26 January
Rathmines Catholic church is destroyed by fire. The damage is estimated at £30,000.

29 January
In America, prohibition becomes federal law across the country having previously been in effect in thirty-six states.

1 February
The Royal Canadian Mounted Police is founded.

17 February
A woman named Anna Anderson tries to commit suicide in Berlin and is taken to mental hospital, where she claims she is Anastasia, daughter of the executed Czar Nicholas II.

19 March
The United States Senate refuses to ratify the Treaty of Versailles for the second time; the United States does not join the League of Nations.

largely managed by two other Dáil deputies who held pivotal positions in the IRA – Michael Collins, the organisation's Director of Intelligence, and Chief-of-Staff Richard Mulcahy. During 1916, Mulcahy had fought in Ashbourne, County Meath, one of the few battles that took place outside Dublin. Interned after the Rising, he played a key role in the War of Independence on his release.

Collins and Mulcahy devised a system of modern urban guerrilla warfare that played to the strengths of the new republic's military capacity. Flying columns of IRA men carried out attacks on RIC patrols and barracks throughout the country, forcing the police from rural areas. In addition to the flying-column attacks, Collins established a network of informers within the British administration and formed a unit of loyal gunmen, called 'the Squad' who assassinated army and police intelligence officers.

The British government responded to the deteriorating situation with both political and military initiatives. In December 1919, the Government of Ireland Bill was introduced in the House of Commons. The legislation established two parliaments with limited powers in Ireland: one in the six northeastern, Unionist-dominated counties and another in Dublin to administer the remaining twenty-six counties. The measure resulted in the opening of a parliament in Belfast in June 1921.

The terms of the British legislation were unacceptable to those fighting for an independent Irish republic. To counter IRA attacks, the British deployed two new forces in Ireland in 1920: the Black and Tans and the Auxiliaries, both composed of former British army soldiers and officers. The arrival of these forces marked the widespread use of reprisal tactics by British forces, with the sacking and burning towns including Balbriggan, Cork and Tuam.

The Dáil, banned by the British authorities, met only three times during 1920 – in June, August and September. In August, the British government introduced the Restoration of Order in Ireland Act, which gave sweeping powers of arrest and detention to the military. The intensification of the war was evidenced by a decree passed by Dáil Éireann that same month prohibiting emigration, without the prior approval of the government. Not surprisingly, the decree, like many future debates on emigration that would take place in Dáil Éireann, had little effect.

November 1920 was to prove one of the bloodiest months of the war. It began with the execution of teenager Kevin Barry following his arrest during a botched IRA operation that resulted in the deaths of three British soldiers. Barry's execution created outrage, both nationally and internationally, but worse was to follow.

On Sunday 21 November, a day that became known as Bloody Sunday, Collins'

'Squad' assassinated fourteen British servicemen, many of whom were involved in counter-insurgency work. Later that day, British forces carried out a reprisal attack, firing into the crowd attending a football match between Dublin and Tipperary in Croke Park, killing twelve civilians, including Tipperary player Michael Hogan, after whom the Hogan Stand is named. The same day saw the shooting of three republicans detained in Dublin Castle: Conor Clune, Peadar Clancy and the IRA's commander in Dublin, Dick McKee. The official version claimed they were shot as they tried to escape.

The escalating bloodshed, and particularly the events of Bloody Sunday, provoked one Sinn Féin TD, Roger Sweetman of north Wexford to publicly call for negotiations to halt the violence, much to the outrage of his colleagues in Dáil Éireann. However, Sweetman's actions reveal the wide breadth of nationalist opinion that the Sinn Féin organisation had attracted under its umbrella since 1916, and, while most TDs fervently supported the armed campaign against British rule, a minority were repulsed by the worsening violence. Two months later, Sweetman explained his actions to the Dáil and is recorded as saying:

> He was quite certain at the time, and was still certain, that a number of things like that Sunday would bring destruction to the Irish cause. Such actions had a reactionary and unfortunate effect in America. He refused to be put down as an utter pacifist, but he wanted to see nothing done which they as moderate men could not stand over in the main … He thought it was absolutely necessary to call off that form of activity which culminated in the events of that Sunday.
>
> (*25 January 1921*)

Sweetman wasn't the only person seeking an end to the conflict, and, as 1920 came to a close, the Clare-born Archbishop of Perth, Joseph Clune, an uncle of Conor Clune, one of the men shot in Dublin Castle on Bloody Sunday, held discussions with British Prime Minister David Lloyd George.

The attempts by Archbishop Clune to negotiate a truce failed over the issue of weapons. After initial progress, Lloyd George – aware of Sweetman's stance and other appeals for a truce – formed the opinion that Irish resistance was close to collapse and insisted on a surrender of arms as part of the truce deal. When the Dáil debated the failed truce negotiations, Michael Collins informed the Houses of the Prime Minister's changing attitude during the talks:

29 March
In Britain, Sir William Roberston, who enlisted in the British army in 1877, becomes a field marshal. He is the first to rise to this rank from private.

4 April
In Jerusalem, violence between Arabic and Jewish residents in Jerusalem. The governor declares the state of siege.

9 April
The short-lived Far Eastern Republic is founded in Siberia.

16 May
In Rome, 30,000 people, including 140 descendants, gather in St Peter's Basilica for the ceremony to mark Joan of Arc's canonisation.

17 May
The Dutch airline, KLM, makes its first flight from Amsterdam to London.

17 May
French and Belgian troops leave the cities they have occupied in Germany since the end of the First World War.

24 May
The beatification of the Venerable Oliver Plunkett takes place in Rome. He was executed for treason in 1681.

13 June
In America, the Post Office Department rules that children may not be sent via parcel post.

15 June
In a new border treaty between Germany and Denmark, northern Schleswig is given to Denmark.

1 July
Germany declares its neutrality in the Soviet–Polish War.

There was one official intermediary who came to them by request of the English Prime Minister … The formula for a truce was agreed upon and the intermediary was surprised at the sweet reasonableness of the people whom he was led to believe were frightful ruffians. He returned to the Prime Minister of England and the latter had three things in his hand, a letter from the Deputy for North Wexford taken from the Press, a telegram from Father O'Flanagan, and a resolution which was bogus from the Galway County Council. "Now, Dr. Clune," he said, "this is the white feather, and we are going to make these fellows surrender."

(*25 January 1921*)

The moves to establish a truce resulted in de Valera returning from his eighteen-month mission to America in December 1920. On his return to Ireland, de Valera immediately sought to reassert his authority over the Dáil, Sinn Féin and the IRA, chiefly at the expense of Michael Collins, whose influence and standing had increased immeasurably whilst de Valera had been in America.

On the same day as Collins informed the Dáil of a breakdown in negotiations, de Valera alluded to a strange fact that marked the Irish War of Independence: it had never formally existed in so far as the Dáil, as a sovereign parliament, had never passed a declaration of war:

They were in a very curious position. The question was whether it was feasible for them to accept formally a state of war that was being thrust on them, or not. The balance was pretty even. If they declared war just now it might give the impression of a small boy asking a six-footer to come out and fight, and his position would be regarded as ridiculous. But if, on the other hand, the small boy was being kicked about and defending himself to the best of his ability, then he would have public opinion supporting him. Taking the situation as a whole, he did not think it advisable to take that step at present.

(*25 January 1921*)

Two months later, de Valera returned to the issue:

There was one important question for them to decide … the acceptance of full responsibility for the acts of the Army … He thought it absolutely necessary that the Dáil should let the world know that they took full responsibility

The Custom House, 1921. The Custom House on fire after an IRA attack.

for all the operations of their Army. That would practically mean a public acceptance of a State of War.

(*11 March 1921*)

The Dáil agreed with the president's request and so, twenty-six months after the beginning of hostilities, the country was officially at war with Britain.

One of the main reasons behind de Valera's proposal regarding a state of war was that, in his view, it legitimised the conflict, especially on the international stage. De Valera was also of the view that the guerilla-war tactics employed by the IRA, were not in keeping with its status of a national army. He wanted the IRA to embark on large-scale engagements with British forces, a strategy that Collins knew would be disastrous and would result in near-total defeat.

Collins' resistance to de Valera's demands was largely successfully however, one spectacular attack on the Custom House in Dublin was undertaken on 25 May 1921. While the symbolism of an attack on a key institution of British administration generated significant publicity, the venture was a military failure, resulting in the deaths of five IRA men and the capture of more than eighty.

The First Dáil was to meet for the final time on 10 May 1921. Elections to the two parliaments in Belfast and Dublin established by the Government of Ireland Act were due later that month.

31 July
The French government prohibits the sale or prescription of contraceptives.

4 September
In Spain, *El Tercio de Extranjeros*, the 'Regiment of Foreigners' (modern-day Spanish Legion) is inaugurated.

16 September
In New York, a hi cordell bomb in a horse wagon explodes in front of the J.P. Morgan building on Wall Street, killing thirty-eight people and injuring 400 others.

22 September
The Flying Squad is formed in London.

29 September
In America, the first domestic radio sets go on sale. The Westinghouse radio costs $10.

Members of Dáil Éireann decreed that the elections in the twenty-six counties would be deemed an election to a new Dáil. Sinn Féin candidates stood unopposed in 124 seats, the four remaining seats in the Trinity College constituency returned unionist-leaning candidates. As the Sinn Féin candidates were unopposed, no actual vote took place, and among those elected to the Dáil for the first time in 1921 were Mary MacSwiney, the sister of Thomas MacSwiney, IRA commander and Lord Mayor of Cork who had died on hunger strike the previous year, Kathleen Clarke, wife of executed 1916 leader Tom Clarke, and Margaret Pearse, whose two sons Pádraig and Willie were also executed following the 1916 Rising.

When the Second Dáil met for the first time on 16 August 1921, the political situation had changed dramatically. At the opening of the new Unionist-dominated Northern Ireland parliament in Stormont on 22 June that year, King George V extended an olive branch to the Dáil government, calling for 'all Irishmen to pause, to stretch out the hand of forbearance and conciliation, to forgive and to forget, and to join in making for the land they love a new era of peace, contentment, and good will'.

Three days later, Lloyd George offered talks with de Valera, and, following a flurry of diplomatic effort, a truce finally came into force on 11 July 1921.

When the Dáil met on 26 August, de Valera was unanimously re-elected president, with Richard Mulcahy paying the following tribute:

> It is because he is a youth among youths with them, because at every stage in that fight he has epitomised what we would wish to be, and out of pride in him and the love we have for him, and out of the knowledge and appreciation that we are to-day grown to the stature to which we are grown simply by his example, that it is with something more than pleasure that I ask that this Dáil select as President of the Irish Republic a man who has been so much to us personally and a man who has been so much to our nation, Eamonn de Valera.
>
> (*26 August 1921*)

Within four months, de Valera and Mulcahy would take opposing sides on the Anglo-Irish Treaty, and the glowing words used in August would be quickly forgotten.

Over the next weeks, arrangements for the peace negotiations in London were made, and, critically, de Valera decided that he would not join the delegation, insisting that his place was in Ireland.

Since January 1919, people had fought and died for the Irish Republic established in Easter 1916 and ratified in the Declaration of Independence adopted by the First Dáil. Now, however, as the reality of negotiations loomed, it was clear that Britain would never accede to recognition of an Irish republic.

Whatever deal was reached in London, it would undoubtedly fall short of the rhetoric that had sustained the independence struggle of the previous two years. Many suspected de Valera's decision to exempt himself from the talks delegation was specifically because he wanted to distance himself from the political conse-quences of negotiating away the dearly held, if by now unachievable, concept of the Republic. Arthur Griffith later told the Dáil:

> And when I was going to London Mr. de Valera said to me "There may have to be scapegoats." There is a member here on the Opposition side who heard that remark. I said I was willing to be a scape-goat to save him from some of his present supporters' criticism; and Mr. Collins and myself were willing to be scapegoats so long as Mr. de Valera got what he wanted and so long as Mr. de Valera's face was saved. That is the inner history of what happened.
>
> *(27 April 1922)*

On 14 September, the Dáil met to ratify the delegation that would negotiate the Treaty in London. It consisted of Arthur Griffith, Michael Collins, Robert Barton, Eamonn Duggan and George Gavan Duffy. The delegation left for London in November, basing themselves at 22 Hans Place, near Harrods in Knightsbridge. Michael Collins' reputation as the driving force behind the War of Independence preceded him, and the words 'Collins the Murderer' were whitewashed on the pavement outside the house.

In the tortuous negotiations that followed, the Irish delegation dealt with a British team which included Prime Minister Lloyd George, Winston Churchill and Lord Birkenhead. For the Irish side, Griffith and Collins conducted most of the negotiations, regularly returning to Dublin to brief de Valera and the cabinet on the emerging deal that was on offer.

Finally, on 6 December, under intense pressure and facing a threat from Lloyd George to return to war if an agreement wasn't concluded, the Irish delegation signed the Anglo-Irish Treaty.

The Treaty granted Ireland dominion status within the British Empire, a status shared by Canada, Australia and New Zealand, and the new Irish Free State would have control over domestic affairs – but its parliamentarians would have to sign an oath of allegiance to the crown.

15 December
The Brussels Conference establishes the timetable for the German payment of war reparations. It is agreed that payments will be extended over forty-two years, ending in 1962.

16 December
180,000 are killed by and earthquake measuring 8.6 on the Richter scale in Gansu Province, China.

23 December
Britain and France ratify the border between French-held Syria and British-held Palestine.

1921

2 January
The Spanish liner *Santa Isabel* sinks off Villa Garcia, killing 244 people.

IRA Volunteers, 1921. IRA Volunteers take a break during the War of Independence.

Far from gaining recognition of the Irish Republic, the Treaty stipulated that the British monarch would be the head of state, with a governor-general representing the monarch in Ireland. British forces would withdraw from Ireland, but Britain would retain control over three Irish ports – Cobh, Lough Swilly and Berehaven – for defensive purposes. The Treaty also effectively recognised the separate existence of the Northern Ireland parliament and proposed a boundary commission to decide on the final border between the Free State and Northern Ireland.

The Treaty fell far short of republican hopes but was regarded as the best available deal by the signatories, especially given the alternative of a renewal of hostilities.

Robert Barton, a reluctant signatory of the Treaty, was later to tell the Dáil of the immense pressure that the delegation faced in the final hours of negotiation:

Speaking for himself and his colleagues, the English Prime Minister with all the solemnity and the power of conviction that he alone, of all men I met, can impart by word and gesture – the vehicles by which the mind of one man oppresses and impresses the mind of another – declared that the signature and recommendation of every member of our delegation was necessary or war would follow immediately. He gave us until 10 o'clock to make up our minds, and it was then about 8.30. We returned to our house to decide upon our answer.

The issue before us was whether we should stand behind our proposals for external association, face war and maintain the Republic, or whether we should accept inclusion in the British Empire and take peace.

Arthur Griffith, Michael Collins, and Eamonn Duggan were for acceptance and peace; Gavan Duffy and myself were for refusal – war or no war. An answer that was not unanimous committed you to immediate war, and the responsibility for that was to rest directly upon those two delegates who refused to sign. For myself, I preferred war. I told my colleagues so, but for the nation, without consultation, I dared not accept that responsibility. The alternative which I sought to avoid seemed to me a lesser outrage than the violation of what is my faith. So that I myself, and of my own choice, must commit my nation to immediate war, without you, Mr. President, or the Members of the Dáil, or the nation having an opportunity to examine the terms upon which war could be avoided. I signed, and now I have fulfilled my undertaking I recommend to you the Treaty I signed in London.

(19 December 1921)

The cabinet split when it discussed the Treaty on 8 December, with de Valera, Cathal Brugha and Austin Stack against and those who had signed – Griffith, Collins and Barton – standing by the agreement. The crucial vote fell to W.T. Cosgrave, who recommended acceptance.

The division in cabinet was replicated in Dáil Éireann, the IRA and in the country at large, leading to the bloody civil war which began the following year. Divisions over the Treaty formed the most durable fault line in Irish politics that lasts to this day, with Fianna Fáil and Fine Gael both tracing their roots back to the stance their predecessors took on the Treaty signed on 6 December 1921.

The Treaty came before the Dáil for ratification on 14 December, and the debate continued until 7 January. The opening discussions centred on the authority of the delegation to conclude an agreement in London and were followed by de Valera's efforts to gain support for a renewed round of negotiations based on the idea of 'external association'. De Valera's initiative failed.

7 May
In Palestine, a week of rioting ends with forty-seven Jews and forty-eight Arabs dead.

8 May
The death penalty is abolished in Sweden.

14 May
In Egypt, violent anti-European riots occur in Cairo and Alexandria that last three days.

19 May
In America, Congress passes the Emergency Quota Act, establishing immigration quotas.

1 June
In Dublin, the Football Association of Ireland is formed when Shelbourne refuses to play its match against Glenavon in Belfast.

1 July
The Communist Party of China is officially founded.

Finally, on 19 December, the debate on the Treaty began. Arthur Griffith proposed the motion seeking Dáil approval, arguing that the agreement ended the conflict between Britain and Ireland and heralded a new relationship between the two countries:

> The prophet I followed throughout my life, the man whose words and teachings I tried to translate into practice in politics, the man whom I revered above all Irish patriots was Thomas Davis. In the hard way of fitting practical affairs into idealism I have made Thomas Davis my guide. I have never departed in my life one inch from the principles of Thomas Davis, and in signing this Treaty and bringing it here and asking Ireland to ratify it I am following Thomas Davis still … Thomas Davis said: "Peace with England, alliance with England to some extent, and, under certain circumstances, confederation with England; but an Irish ambition, Irish hopes, strength, virtue and rewards for the Irish."
>
> That is what we have brought back, peace with England, alliance with England, confederation with England, an Ireland developing her own life, carving out her own way of existence, and rebuilding the Gaelic civilisation broken down at the battle of Kinsale. I say we have brought you that. I say we have translated Thomas Davis into the practical politics of the day … Let us stand as free partners, equal with England, and make after 700 years the greatest revolution that has ever been made in the history of the world – a revolution of seeing the two countries standing not apart as enemies, but standing together as equals and as friends. I ask you, therefore, to pass this resolution.
>
> (*19 December 1921*)

De Valera was the first speaker to oppose the Treaty, stating his opposition in unequivocal terms:

> I wanted, and the Cabinet wanted, to get a document we could stand by, a document that could enable Irishmen to meet Englishmen and shake hands with them as fellow-citizens of the world. That document makes British authority our masters in Ireland … you have an oath to the Irish Constitution, and that Constitution will be a Constitution which will have the King of Great Britain as head of Ireland. You will swear allegiance to that

"Peace with England, alliance with England to some extent, and, under certain circumstances, confederation with England; but an Irish ambition, Irish hopes, strength, virtue and rewards for the Irish."

Arthur Griffith, 19 December 1921

21 September
At least 500 people are killed when there is an explosion at BASF's nitrate factory in Oppau, Germany.

Constitution and to that King; and if the representatives of the Republic should ask the people of Ireland to do that which is inconsistent with the Republic, I say they are subverting the Republic. It would be a surrender which was never heard of in Ireland since the days of Henry II.; and are we in this generation, which has made Irishmen famous throughout the world, to sign our names to the most ignoble document that could be signed …

I am as anxious as anyone for the material prosperity of Ireland and the Irish people, but I cannot do anything that would make the Irish people hang their heads. I would rather see the same thing over again than that Irishmen should have to hang their heads in shame for having signed and put their hands to a document handing over their authority to a foreign country. The Irish people would not want me to save them materially at the expense of their national honour.

(19 December 1921)

19 October
In Portugal, a massacre in Lisbon claims the lives of Portuguese Prime Minister António Granjo and other politicians.

9 November
Albert Einstein is awarded the Nobel Prize in Physics.

De Valera's arguments against the Treaty focused on its failure to deliver complete independence to the Irish nation over its affairs. This failing was best symbolised by the Oath of Allegiance to the British monarch that members of a future Irish parliament were required to take. For many who opposed the Treaty, its contents were irreconcilable with the oath they had sworn to the Republic in August 1919.

One notable fact about the Treaty debates is the relative lack of concern about the effective recognition of partition that the Treaty also contained. Anti-Treaty speakers declared the Oath of Allegiance, the relationship with the British Empire and the concession in relation to port facilities unacceptable, but little was made of the Treaty's institutionalisation of partition which, to all intents and purposes, had become a reality with the establishment of the Stormont parliament earlier in June, or the fate of the nationalist minority now living in what would become an overtly sectarian state.

Michael Collins spoke the same day, urging acceptance of the Treaty:

1 December
Rising prices cause riots in Vienna.

6 December
In Canada, Agnes Macphail becomes the first woman MP.

In my opinion it gives us the freedom, not the ultimate freedom that all nations desire and develop to, but freedom to achieve it …

The history of this nation has not been, as is so often said, the history of a military struggle of 750 years; it has been much more a history of peaceful penetration of 750 years. It has not been a struggle for the ideal of freedom for 750 years symbolised in the name Republic. It has been a story of slow,

13 December
The Four Power Treaty on Insular Possessions results in Japan, America, Britain and France maintaining the status quo in the Pacific.

steady, economic encroach by England. It has been a struggle on our part to prevent that, a struggle against exploitation, a struggle against the cancer that was eating up our lives …

Our aspirations, by whatever term they may be symbolised, had one thing in front all the time, that was to rid the country of the enemy strength. Now it was not by any form of communication except through their military strength that the English held this country. That is simply a plain fact which, I think, nobody will deny. It wasn't by any forms of government, it wasn't by their judiciary or anything of that kind. These people could not operate except for the military strength that was always there. Now, starting from that, I maintain that the disappearance of that military strength gives us the chief proof that our national liberties are established …

(19 December 1921)

Those in favour of the Treaty followed Griffith's and Collins' appeal to face political reality, to accept that the agreement reached in London, while imperfect, was the best accommodation available – it gave Ireland the potential to control its own affairs – and that the alternative, a return to war, would spell disaster for the country, with Richard Mulcahy bluntly reminding the Dáil of the military capacity of the national army:

I am not afraid of the influence of the King, or the influence of the King exerted through some supposedly corrupt court of his representative here. I am not afraid of that power interfering with the power of the Irish people; because, if we have control it is full control over legislation, over order, over peace, over the whole internal life and resources of the country. As to our ports, we are not in a position of force, either military or otherwise, to drive the enemy from our ports. We have not … been able to drive the enemy from anything but from a fairly good-sized police barracks …

(22 December 1921)

Against the pragmatic arguments in favour of the Treaty, many speakers opposing the motion refused to accept an agreement that failed to secure the Republic proclaimed in 1916 and for which hundreds had died for during the War of Independence, with Kathleen Clarke making a moving contribution:

5 January
On South Georgia Island, as he is about to embark on a scientific study in Antartica, Ernest Shackleton suffers a fatal heart attack and dies at the age of forty-seven.

22 January
Pope Benedict XV dies.

23 January
Fourteen-year-old Leonard Thompson becomes the first person to be successfully treated with insulin for diabetes.

24 January
In America, Danish immigrant Christian K. Nelson patents the Eskimo Pie, a chocolate-covered vanilla ice cream bar wrapped in foil. It is the first such dessert sold in the country.

1 February
Forty-nine-year-old,
Hollywood actor
William Desmond
Taylor, who was
born in County
Carlow, is murdered.
It is one of the first
sensational crimes
in Hollywood and
remains officially
unsolved.

2 February
James Joyce's
Ulysses is published
in its entirety for the
first time.

5 February
The first edition
of *Readers' Digest*
is published in
America.

6 February
Achille Ratti
becomes Pope Pius
XI, the 259th pope.

1 March
The British Civil
Aviation Authority
is established.

I rise to support the motion of the President to reject this Treaty. It is to me the simple questions of right and wrong. To my mind it is a surrender of all our national ideals. I came to the first meeting of this Session with this feeling strong upon me, and I have listened carefully to all the arguments in favour of the Treaty. But the only thing I can say of them is: maybe there is something in them; I can't see it … if this Treaty is ratified the result will be a divided people; the same only division will go on; those who enter the British Empire and those who will not, and so England's old game of divide and conquer goes on. God, the tragedy of it …

I heard big, strong, military men say here they would vote for this Treaty, which necessarily means taking the Oath of Allegiance, and I tell those men there is not power enough to force me, nor eloquence enough to influence me in the whole British Empire into taking that Oath, though I am only a frail scrap of humanity. I took an Oath to the Irish Republic, solemnly, reverently, meaning every word. I shall never go back from that. Like Deputy Duggan, I too can go back to 1916. Between 1 and 2 o'clock on the morning of May 3rd I, a prisoner in Dublin Castle, was roused from my rest on the floor, and taken under armed escort to Kilmainham Jail to see my husband for the last time. I saw him, not alone, but surrounded by British soldiers. He informed me he was to be shot at dawn. Was he in despair like the man who spoke of him on Tuesday? Not he. His head was up; his eyes flashing; his years seemed to have slipped from him; victory was in very line of him. "Tell the Irish people," he said, "that I and my comrades believe we have saved the soul of Ireland. We believe she will never lie down again until she has gained absolute freedom." And, though sorrow was in my heart I gloried in him, and I have gloried in the men who have carried on the fight since; every one of them … I have sorrow in my heart now, but I don't despair; I never shall. I still believe in them.

(22 December 1921)

The Dáil broke for the Christmas holiday that day and reconvened on 3 January. During the Christmas recess, twenty-four county councils passed resolutions backing the Treaty, and the hierarchy of the Catholic Church made its support for the Treaty clear, reflecting widespread, but by no means overwhelming, acceptance among the people for the agreement.

While mainly focused on the merits or otherwise of the Treaty, personal differences between those who had fought together over the previous years inevitably came to

The Second Dáil, 7 January 1922. The Treaty was approved sixty-four votes to fifty-seven. Within months, the country was plunged into Civil War.

a head during the debate, with Minister for Defence Cathal Brugha, whose dislike of Michael Collins and his role in the IRA was palpable, attempting to debunk the popular image of the IRA's Director of Intelligence that had emerged:

> While the war was in progress I could not praise too highly the work done by the Head Quarters' Staff. The Chief of Staff and each of the leaders of the subsections were the best men we could get for the positions; each of them carried out efficiently, so far as I know, the work that was entrusted to him

20 March
In America the USS *Langley* is commissioned. It is the first US navy aircraft carrier.

3 April
Josef Stalin is appointed General Secretary of the Central Committee of the Soviet Communist Party.

10 April
In Italy, the representatives of thirty-four countries convened at the Genoa Conference to discuss monetary economics in the wake of the First World War.

13 April
In America, the state of Massachusetts opens all public offices to women.

16 April
The Treaty of Rapallo marks a rapprochement between the Weimar Republic and Bolshevik Russia.

12 May
In America, a
twenty-ton
meteorite lands
near Blackstone
in Virginia.

they worked conscientiously and patriotically for Ireland without seeking any notoriety, with one exception; whether he is responsible or not for the notoriety I am not going to say (cries of "Shame" and "Get on with the Treaty"). There is little more for me to say. One member was specially selected by the Press and the people to put him into a position which he never held; he was made a romantic figure, a mystical character such as this person certainly is not; the gentleman I refer to is Mr. Michael Collins …

(7 January 1922)

66 As a **protest** against the election as President of the Irish Republic of the Chairman of the Delegation, who is bound by **the Treaty conditions** to set up **a State** which is to subvert the Republic, and who, in the interim period, instead of using the office as it should be used — **to support the Republic** — will, of necessity, have to be taking action which will tend to its **destruction**, I, while this vote is being taken, as one, am going to leave the House. **99**

Eamon de Valera, 10 January 1922

The Dáil vote on the Treaty took place on 7 January, and the agreement was approved by seven votes, sixty-four in favour and fifty-seven against. Following the vote, de Valera immediately signalled his intention to resign as president and broke down after an exchange with Michael Collins. One of the final voices heard in the Dáil that day was that of fervent anti-Treaty deputy, Mary MacSwiney:

You may talk about the will of the Irish people, as Arthur Griffith did; you know it is not the will of the Irish people; it is the fear of the Irish people …

30 May
In Washington DC,
the Lincoln Memorial
is dedicated.

2 June
The first edition of
the newspaper
*Poblacht na
hÉireann* is
published by anti-
Treaty supporters.

24 June
German nationalists
assassinate foreign
minister Walther
Rathenau, a German
Jew, in response to
his policy of paying
reparations for
Germany's role in
the First World War.

27 June
In Dundalk, 105
Irregular prisoners
escape from jail.

26 CREATING IRELAND

and tomorrow or another day when they come to their senses, they will talk of those who betrayed them today … Make no doubt about it. This is a betrayal, a gross betrayal; and the fact is that it is only a small majority, and that majority is not united; half of them look for a gun and the other half are looking for the fleshpots of the Empire. I tell you here there can be no union between the representatives of the Irish Republic and the so-called Free State.

(7 January 1922)

"Deserters all! We will now call the Irish people to rally to us. Deserters all! … Deserters all to the Irish nation in her hour of trial. We will stand by her."

Michael Collins, 10 January 1922

MacSwiney's prediction that the Treaty vote would produce an irreconcilable split in Sinn Féin proved right, and, following the approval of the Treaty and de Valera's resignation, the Dáil met on 10 January to elect Arthur Griffith as president and head of a new provisional government that would exist until the new Free State parliament officially came into existence the following December.

Griffith was proposed by Michael Collins, but, before the vote was taken, de Valera led his supporters out of Dáil Éireann, declaring:

As a protest against the election as President of the Irish Republic of the Chairman of the Delegation, who is bound by the Treaty conditions to set up a State which is to subvert the Republic, and who, in the interim period, instead of using the office as it should be used – to support the Republic – will, of necessity, have to be taking action which will tend to its destruction, I, while this vote is being taken, as one, am going to leave the House.

(10 January 1922)

11 July
In America, the Hollywood Bowl opens.

9 August
Clerys opens its new building on O'Connell Street, six years after the original building was destroyed in the 1916 Rising.

28 August
Japan agrees to withdraw its troops from Siberia.

13 September
In Smyrna, Turkey, fire breaks out killing nearly 100,000 citizens.

31 October
At the age of thirty-nine, Benito Mussolini becomes the youngest premier in Italian history.

1 November
The ancient Ottoman Empire is abolished and the last sultan, Mehmed VI Vahdettin, abdicates.

1 November
In Britain, a broadcasting licence fee of ten shillings is introduced.

To which Collins retorted:

> Deserters all! We will now call the Irish people to rally to us. Deserters all! …
> Deserters all to the Irish nation in her hour of trial. We will stand by her.
>
> (*10 January 1922*)

4 November
British archaeologist Howard Carter discovers the tomb of Pharaoh Tutankhamun in Luxor, Egypt.

De Valera and his supporters returned to the Dáil following the vote, but the symbolic walkout confirmed the deep divisions that now existed within Sinn Féin. In effect, these divisions created two parties, one swearing allegiance to the Republic declared in 1916, the other insistent that the Treaty arrangements had received the democratic approval of the representatives of the Irish people.

Within a week of the Dáil approving the Treaty, the symbol of British influence in Ireland, Dublin Castle, was handed over to the new government, with Michael Collins presiding over the ceremony.

14 November
In Britain, the British Broadcasting Corporation (BBC) begins its radio service.

Despite the departure of British troops, the divisions in Sinn Féin were replicated in the IRA over the following months. Attempts to prevent a split proved futile with anti-Treaty units in the IRA seizing arms and raiding banks and post offices. In early April, leading anti-Treaty IRA commander Rory O'Connor occupied the Four Courts in Dublin.

15 November
In Britain, the Conservatives win an overall majority in the general election.

Speaking in the Dáil the following September, Mayo TD William Sears gave an indication of the fear that existed throughout the country at the time:

> Widespread brigandage made its appearance. Banks were robbed. Post Offices were raided … and there only remained one further crowning insult when the Four Courts was seized by a handful of foolish young men, whose brains were fired by the word-spinning of the Dáil. That building, the Four Courts, perhaps was selected because that building, more than any other, stood for orderly Government, for fair and just administration. I say that was the darkest hour for Ireland. It seemed that our country had escaped from the throttling hand of England only to perish by suicide. We were near the very edge, and if at that moment there were feeble hands at the helm the ship of State would have foundered on the rocks.
>
> (*12 September 1922*)

28 November
In New York, Captain Cyril Turner of the RAF gives a skywriting exhibition. He spells out, 'Hello USA, Call Vanderbitt 700' and over 47,000 people telephone in.

Collins worked tirelessly to prevent the slide into civil war. In drawing up a draft constitution for the new Free State, he attempted to remove or neuter those aspects of the Treaty most repugnant to republicans, such as the Oath of Allegiance to the crown. However, these attempts encountered strong opposition from Downing Street and ultimately failed.

An election was held on 16 June, and attempts orchestrated by de Valera and Collins to present a united Sinn Féin ticket to the electorate with a proportional balance between pro- and anti-Treaty sides collapsed.

In announcing the election on 19 May 1922, Arthur Griffith, as President of the Dáil, was in no doubt that the election would not only decide the people's view on the Treaty but, as fears of civil war grew with each passing day, it would also decide whether the democratic will of the Irish people was paramount:

> There is nothing more insolent in the history of this country, or in the history of modern civilization, as it appears to me, than the claim that any body of men, or any minority of this country, should tell the Irish people that they have no right to decide upon an issue which affects their whole future and affects the destiny of the country. I thought when this issue of "Treaty or no Treaty" was being placed before the people, it was the biggest issue that could be placed before them. But a greater issue has arisen now—an issue that strikes at every right we struggled for, every conception of nationalism we ever had, and every right of a civilised people. The issue that is before the people is that they have no right in their own country to determine their own future. If that is so, all of us who have been all our lives struggling against England, have been a pack of fools.
>
> (*22 May 1922*)

The election result endorsed the Treaty with those in favour of the agreement gaining fifty-eight seats compared to thirty-six for its opponents. The Labour Party, contesting its first election, having remained on the sidelines in 1918 and 1921, returned seventeen deputies, and the Farmers' Party, Independents and Unionists elected to the Trinity College constituency also gained seventeen seats in total.

After the election, the government, under pressure from London, moved against Rory O'Connor and the anti-Treaty Four Courts garrison, and the Civil War began in earnest. It would engulf the country over the summer months before the recently elected pro-Treaty TDs assembled in Dublin in September for the first session of what would be the Third Dáil. It was an assembly which, for different reasons, would be deprived of the talents of three of the leading figures in the fight for independence – Arthur Griffith, Michael Collins and Eamon de Valera.

18 November
French novelist Marcel Proust dies in Paris aged fifty-one. His most famous work *À la recherche du temps perdue* (often translated as *Remembrance of Things Past*) is considered a seminal work of twentieth-century fiction and was first published in seven parts between 1913 and 1927.

6 December
The first domestically designed 2d stamps are issued, depicting a map of Ireland and inscribed 'Éire'.

11 December
All existing British postage stamps are issued with the overprint 'Saorstát Éireann 1922'.

30 December
Russia, Ukraine, Belarus and Transcaucasia form the Union of Soviet Socialist Republics (USSR).

I am almost forced to say you
have killed the new

'Two days have elapsed since
there was a formal proclamation
announcing the birth of this
new State. It was hoped that
the course of law would be in
operation henceforth.

W.T. Cosgrave addresses
an election rally.

At this moment
this country is fighting
for its life

1922-1932

Men of Destiny

'When a man has his hand at your throat and his knee on your chest you do not lie there and tell yourself that force settles nothing.'

wo days have elapsed sin

formal proclamation

nouncing the ant o

. It was hoped that the

parated

raw

were the leaders, and to

whom we looked, as the leaders of the future

1922-1932

On 9 September 1922, *The Man of Destiny* was staged at the Abbey Theatre and, perhaps, some TDs gathering in Dublin that day for the first sitting of the Third Dáil identified with the title of George Bernard Shaw's play.

Over the summer, the pro-Treaty side emerged dominant from the major military confrontations, and, by the beginning of September, anti-Treaty forces had abandoned most towns and cities and were forced to retreat to remote areas of the country and adopt guerrilla-war tactics.

Despite this initial military success, the nascent Free State suffered two major blows during August 1922. Arthur Griffith died on 12 August, aged fifty. His death was ascribed to the exhaustion and strain he suffered over the previous eight months in particular. Ten days later, Michael Collins was killed by anti-Treaty forces in an ambush at Béal na mBláth, near Clonakilty, County Cork. The deaths of Griffith and Collins cast a shadow over TDs assembling for the Dáil sitting.

Anti-Treaty TDs didn't recognise or attend the new Dáil and many, such as Austin Stack and Cathal Brugha, joined the war against the new state. Brugha had been killed in the fighting in Dublin in July.

Mary MacSwiney and Kathleen O'Callaghan were the only two women elected to the Dáil in June 1922, and refused to take their seats in the new parliament, resulting in an exclusively male national assembly.

Following the death of Griffith and Collins, the first task of the new parliament was to elect a president who would also serve as chairman of the Provisional Government until the Irish Free State formally came into existence on 6 December 1922. In proposing W. T. Cosgrave in the Dáil that day, Richard Mulcahy, who at the time also commanded the pro-Treaty army, invoked the legacy of Griffith and Collins:

> Since the last Dáil separated we have lost the two people who were the leaders, and to whom we looked, as the leaders of the future—one of them the greatest sower who lived in Ireland while we have been here, and the other the greatest reaper the country has ever had. Now in this country, without these two great leaders, we are faced with greater responsibilities thrown upon each particular Member of this Dáil, and very great responsibilities indeed thrown, upon certain Members who have to undertake the work which would have been taken up by the two great Chiefs whom we have lost.
>
> *(9 September 1922)*

11 January
Troops from France and Belgium occupy the Ruhr area of Germany to force the German government to make its reparation payments from the First World War.

2 March
Time magazine debuts as a weekly news review.

18 June
Mount Etna in Sicily erupts making nearly 60,000 people homeless.

20 July
Former Mexican revolutionary Pancho Villa is shot and killed by members of the Herrera family.

2 August
The President of America, Warren Harding, dies and is succeeded by Calvin Coolidge.

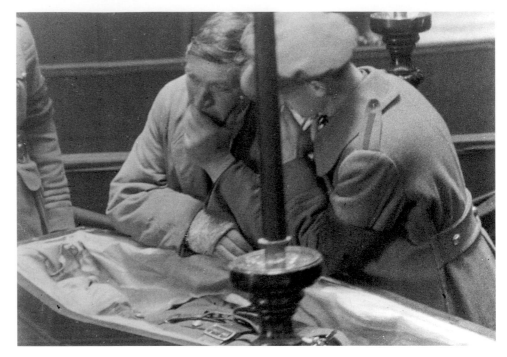

Death of the Big Fellow, 1922. Seán Collins stands by the coffin of his brother, who was killed by anti-Treaty republicans in an ambush near Béal na mBláth in County Cork.

13 August
Gustav Stresemann becomes the chancellor of the coalition government in the Weimar Republic, Germany.

1 September
The Great Kanto Earthquake kills 142,807 people in Japan.

10 September
Ireland joins the League of Nations.

13 September
In a military coup in Spain, Miguel Primo de Rivera takes power and establishes a dictatorship. He bans trade unions for ten years.

17 September
In America, a major fire destroys hundreds of homes near the University of California in Berkely.

6 November
The USSR adopts an experimental calendar with five day 'weeks'.

W.T. Cosgrave was one of the most experienced politicians elected to the Third Dáil. A strong proponent of the Treaty, he spoke strongly in favour of it during the Dáil debate in December 1921, when he also managed to damn with faint praise his former 1916 comrade in arms, the Minister for Defence and implacable opponent of compromise, Cathal Brugha:

> To my mind, when I first saw this instrument, it appeared that there were potentialities in it undreamt of in this country up to this time. If as a result of the successful working and administration of this Act that that gradual improvement that has been outlined in a semi-prophetic fashion by the Minister of Finance was brought about and the ideals this country struggled for for generations should come to pass, it might possibly be within the bounds of certainty that a reconciliation would be effected between the new world and the old; that these two great countries would be able to keep the peace not only of themselves but the world, working for the best interests of Humanity …

I know the Minister for Defence. My own conviction is that except for war he is not worth a damn for anything else, but that he is a great man for war I bear witness to, because even when the spark of life was practically gone out of him he was as full of fight as when he was going into it.

(*21 December 1921*)

Cosgrave appointed a cabinet that included Kevin O'Higgins as Minister for Home Affairs, Richard Mulcahy as Minister for Defence and Desmond FitzGerald, father of future Taoiseach Garret FitzGerald, as Minister for External Affairs. For the remainder of 1922, that government was preoccupied with two main concerns: the establishment of the Free State and the continuing Civil War which raged in the country.

The Constitution of Saorstat Éireann Bill was introduced in September and provided a constitutional framework for the Free State. Despite Collins' earlier efforts, the Free State Constitution reflected key aspects of the Treaty: it included the Oath of Allegiance to the British crown, vested ultimate executive authority in the monarch and gave constitutional status to the governor-general, the monarch's representative in Ireland.

It also contained some innovative approaches to modern parliamentary democracy. It established a second chamber called Seanad Éireann and ensured that the first Seanad would include representatives of the Unionist tradition in the South.

Significantly, the constitution also provided for a degree of direct democracy with provision made for citizens to initiate legislation or amendments to the constitution by way of petitions. However, the imaginative approach to parliamentary democracy contained in the constitution proved illusory. It could be amended by a simple vote of the Dáil and Seanad and, in subsequent years, political circumstances resulted in the abandonment of the more progressive democratic aspects of the constitution with power being concentrated within the executive, similar to the cabinet system of government in Westminster.

During the Dáil debate on the constitution, the inclusion of controversial aspects of the Treaty, such as the Oath of Allegiance, attracted criticism from the opposition benches. For Kevin O'Higgins, the Minister for Home Affairs, the rehearsing of these old arguments held little water:

… if this Parliament wishes to secure for the country the benefits of the Treaty settlement, the Constitution it draws up must be within the four corners

8 November
In Munich, Adolf Hitler leads the Nazis in an unsuccessful attempt to overthrow the German government. Police and troops crush the attempt, which becomes known as the Beer Hall Putsch, the next day. Hitler is sentenced to five years in prison, but serves only nine months.

15 November
Hyperinflation in Germany reaches its height. One American dollar is worth 4,200,000,000,000,000 Papiermark (4.2 quadrillion). Gustav Stresemann, the chancellor of the Weimar Republic, abolishes the currency. It will be replaced by the Deutschmark.

14 November
W.B. Yeats is awarded the Nobel Prize for Literature.

23 November
Gustav Stresemann's government collapses.

1924

of that Treaty . . . There is no use in people getting up to present their sentimental objections to His Majesty. These objections were all thrashed out last December ... it is merely waste of time, particularly of a Parliament which has very serious duty and very serious responsibility upon it, to get up here and talk mere sentimental poetry. The position is a little too grave and a little too urgent for that.

(21 September 1922)

Aside from the constitution, the other main concern of the government, the prosecution of the Civil War, provoked considerable opposition in the new parliament.

On 27 September, the government proposed a motion on public safety, designed to give sweeping powers to military courts to try and punish anyone suspected of subversion. It was a move that provoked a furious response from the Labour Party, led by Thomas Johnson. The government ignored the outcry, believing that the measures, which included the death penalty, were necessary to combat the continuing resistance to the authority of the Dáil by republican forces, with Minister for Foreign Affairs Desmond FitzGerald summing up the government's position:

At this moment this country is fighting for its life in a way possibly that it never did before, because its life is threatened more imminently now than at any time of its history ... All over the country ruin is being spread, and the longer that continues the more disastrous the state the whole country gets into. On an occasion like the present there is no opportunity, and there is no justification, for any quibbling about legality or anything else ... We are faced with the grim fact, and legal quibbles or humanitarian catch-cries and things like that have no meaning and no place in the present situation.... It is no good for Deputies—if they propose doing so—to get up here with pious emendations and restrictions. We are sitting here and sending men out to face death, and it is up to us to give these men every protection and put every possible weapon in their hands, and we propose to do so.

(27 September 1922)

The motion was passed, forty-eight votes to eighteen, but the actions legitimised by that vote would convulse the Dáil, and the nation, over the coming months.

The first executions under the new powers took place on 17 November. Four rank-and-file IRA men, arrested in possession of weapons – an offence punishable by death under the new public safety regime – were executed by a firing squad. Earlier that week, Erskine Childers, a significant anti-Treaty figure, had been arrested in possession of a revolver. Childers, whose son would later be president, was executed at dawn on 24 November at Beggars Bush Barracks in Dublin.

These executions were condemned in Dáil Éireann by Thomas Johnson and George Gavan Duffy. The IRA also issued a response – though it used more than words to attack the government. A week after the first executions, the IRA issued a directive ordering the execution on sight of TDs who had supported the public order legislation. The directive also listed judges and editors, among others, as legitimate targets.

On 7 December, the day after the Free State came into existence, IRA gunmen assassinated Seán Hales, a leading pro-Treaty TD and close colleague of Michael Collins in Dublin. In reprisal, the government of the new Free State approved the execution of four IRA members, including Liam Mellows and Rory O'Connor, who had been detained in Mountjoy Prison since June when the Four Courts Garrison collapsed.

Again, Thomas Johnson expressed his outrage at the executions in the Dáil, declaring:

> Two days have elapsed since there was a formal proclamation announcing the birth of this new State. It was hoped that the course of law would be in operation henceforth. It was hoped that there would be some rehabilitation of the idea of law; and almost the first act is utterly to destroy in the public mind the association of the Government with the idea of law. I am almost forced to say you have killed the new State at its birth …
>
> *(8 December 1922)*

Kevin O'Higgins was unmoved by the criticism. He felt the legitimate government of the people was under assault and was entitled to use all means at its disposal to protect itself:

> The safety and preservation of the people is the highest law. It is at any rate the only law, for laws are not made or written down in a book to guide men when a state of war exists, for war is anarchy, and there are no rules and no laws to guide men.
>
> The Treaty was signed; the Treaty was endorsed by Parliament; the Treaty was wanted by the Nation; the Provisional Government was set up to carry it out. Now something vital is challenged—the majority right to decide political

5 February
A radio time signal is broadcast for the first time from the Royal Greenwich Observatory in London.

12 February
George Gershwin's 'Rhapsody in Blue' is performed for the first time at the Aeolian Hall in New York.

14 February
IBM (International Business Machines) is founded in America.

25 March
Greece proclaims itself a republic.

3 June
Franz Kafka dies in Vienna, Austria. His death is attributed to starvation, brought on by tuberculosis.

5 June
Ernst Alexanderson sends the first fax from America to Europe (to his father in Sweden).

"Two days have elapsed since there was a formal **proclamation** announcing the birth of this new **State.** It was hoped that the **course of law** would be in operation henceforth It was hoped that there would be some **rehabilitation** of the idea of law; and almost **the first act** is utterly to destroy in the public mind the **association** of the Government with the idea of law. I am almost forced to say you have killed **the new State** at its birth ..."

Thomas Johnson, 8 December 1922

issues. Mankind learned that lesson in blood and chaos long ago. We must learn it again here, apparently, and we are learning it, and by the time this thing is over that lesson will be burned bitterly into Ireland's brain, that when you depart from that great fundamental principle you step into sheer anarchy.

People took that step quite deliberately, in the early part of this year. They did get a lot of silly, neurotic women to back them in that course and a lot of silly neurotic young boys to do likewise … The thing came on and boiled over in June. We have been grappling since June, not with any political creed but with sheer anarchy. It is all right for people … to stand up here and preach sermons about the principle that force settles nothing. When a man has his hand on your throat and his knee on your chest you do not lie there and tell yourself that force settles nothing.

(8 December 1922)

O'Higgins went on to reject claims that the executions had been ordered out of spite or personal bitterness:

The thing that was decided on last evening was decided on after the coldest of cold discussions … we will not acquiesce in gun-bullying, and we will take very stern and drastic measures to stop it. Personal spite, great heavens! Vindictiveness! One of these men was a friend of mine.

(8 December 1922)

The friend O'Higgins refers to was Rory O'Connor, who had been the best man at his wedding the previous year and who was one of the four men executed on 7 December. This poignant vignette sums up the tragedy and horror of the Civil War, which tore families and communities asunder.

The IRA's violent campaign against the Free State continued, and O'Higgins' father was among those murdered by the IRA in the following months as the war dragged on.

By the early summer of 1923, the IRA was all but a spent force. Poorly armed, lacking a unified command, condemned by the Catholic hierarchy and unable to rely on widespread popular support, it had been decisively beaten by the Free State Army. De Valera and Frank Aiken, IRA Chief-of-Staff, issued the order to dump arms on 24 May. The Civil War was over, and the existence of the Free State assured. However, the legacy of bitterness and division it left in its

4 August
The Tailteann Games open.

14 August
The Royal Dublin Society transfers its headquarters to its showgrounds in Ballsbridge, having sold Leinster House to the government.

30 September
Truman Capote, the American author who popularised the true crime genre with his book *In Cold Blood*, is born.

1925

3 January
Benito Mussolini pronounces himself dictator of Italy.

10 April
F. Scott Fitzgerald's *The Great Gatsby* is published. It will become one of the most important novels of the twentieth century.

5 May
In Dayton, Tennessee in the US, biology teacher John Scopes is arrested for teaching Darwin's Theory of Evolution. After an eight-day trial his is fined $100. The legislation prohibiting the teaching of evolution is not abolished until 1968.

19 May
Pol Pot the future leader of the Khmer Rouge and dictator of Cambodia, is born. During his dictatorship nearly a quarter of Cambodia's population die from malnutrition and slave labour working conditions in collective farms, which became known as the Killing Fields.

26 June
The Gold Rush, Charlie Chaplin's epic comedy, opens to critical and popular acclaim.

10 July
Meher Baba, the Indian mystic and spiritual leader, starts his 'silence'. He dies forty-four years later in 1969, without speaking again.

wake would dominate politics in the Dáil, and in the country, for decades to come.

It is estimated that 4,000 people were killed in the Civil War, and, at the end of hostilities, more than 11,000 republican prisoners were in jail. In addition to the terrible human cost, the Civil War had caused enormous damage to the already weak economy of the Free State. The financial strain the war placed on the new administration was substantial, and Cosgrave's economically conservative government preferred to balance the books rather than embark on expensive reconstruction efforts.

The 1926 census revealed the poverty in the country, with 800,000 people living in overcrowded conditions, many in the slum tenements of inner-city Dublin. In this area of acute deprivation, for every hundred children born, nearly three would die before they reached the age of five.

Ireland was a predominately rural country, with over 60 per cent of the population living on the land and with half of these earning a meagre living off holdings of thirty acres or less. Emigration remained high during the 1920s – at the start of the decade, 43 per cent of all Irish-born men and women were living abroad, the majority in the USA, Britain and Australia.

Despite the chronic social conditions, politics was still dominated by the issue at the heart of the Civil War dispute. Those opposed to the Treaty continued to boycott Dáil Éireann and so parliamentary opposition to the Cosgrave government was provided in the main by the Labour Party. Labour deputies articulated the concerns of their constituencies, raising issues such as unemployment, emigration and industrial dispute to little avail. Responding to a Labour motion on unemployment in October 1924, the Minister for Industry and Commerce, Patrick McGilligan, outlined the laissez-faire philosophy of the cabinet:

> It is said that the Government has failed to adopt effective means to find useful work for willing workers. I can only answer that it is no function of Government to provide work for anybody. They can try and develop tendencies, and can try and set the pace a bit, but it is not the function of the government to provide work.
>
> (*30 October 1924*)

One area where the Free State government did show a willingness to intervene was on the issue of censorship.

In the mid-1920s, there were 150 cinemas in the country, and Kevin O'Higgins informed the Dáil that, every day, approximately 20,000 people sought solace and escape in front of the silent movies on the silver screen. There was widespread

"One of these men was a friend of mine."

Kevin O'Higgins, 8 December 1922

Posting bills, August 1923. Men pasting posters on the walls of the Sinn Féin Election Committee Headquarters, exhorting voters to vote for Sinn Féin leader Eamon de Valera in the forthcoming election.

18 July
The first volume of *Mein Kampf* is published in Germany.

27 October
The American dance troupe, La Revue Negre, starring Josephine Baker, sensationalises Paris with the dancers' risqué costumes.

agreement in the Dáil that the citizens of the country, especially young citizens, needed to be protected from 'vile pictures'. A speech by Independent TD Professor William Magennis caught the mood of the time:

I think the Minister deserves the highest credit … for providing the Saorstát with an agency like this, which helps to realise our Gaelic traditions. Purity of mind and sanity of outlook upon life were long ago regarded as characteristic of our people. The loose views and the vile lowering of values that belong to other races and other peoples were being forced upon our people through the popularity of the cinematograph … and this is in an indirect way securing the protection of the growing citizens of the Free State from the unhealthy influence of the outside world. In that way it is helping all the objects of the Gaelic League, because it is exactly like gardening. You have to attend to the pests and plagues that beset your growing vegetation as well as to cultivate the ground.

(*10 May 1923*)

Casablanca, Gone With the Wind and *The Graduate* were among the films that would fall foul of the censor in future years and, having saved the youth of the country from the evils of cinema, it did not take long before the government turned its attention to the dangers presented by 'evil literature'.

Censorship aside, the Third Dáil introduced legislation that paved the way for the establishment of An Garda Síochána, provided a framework for democratic elections and extended the functions of the Land Commission, which, under the direction of Minister for Agriculture Patrick Hogan, would transfer significant holdings from landlords to tenants – a process that would continue until the 1980s.

Another development, not unknown to some of our more recent parliamentarians, also emerged during this period. In March 1924, the Dáil was informed that Henry Coyle, a TD for Mayo North, had been arrested in a fraud investigation. Coyle was convicted of cheque fraud, involving the sum of £450, and was sentenced to three years in prison. Given the length of the sentence, Coyle was disqualified from membership of Dáil Éireann, the only TD ever to suffer this fate.

The Third Dáil was dissolved on 9 August 1923, and an election was held on 27 August. The eleven months of its existence had witnessed the most bloody and violent period in Irish history. Yet, as TDs left to campaign in the election, the course of parliamentary politics in Ireland was firmly established: Dáil Éireann would be the legitimate, democratic seat of the Irish people.

The number of seats contested in the election had increased from 128 at the previous election to 153, and most parties made gains at the election. Pro-Treaty TDs, led by W.T. Cosgrave, contested the 1923 election under the Cumann na nGaedheal banner, a party that had been formed the previous April. In its first electoral outing, the party won sixty-three seats, ensuring its return to power.

Sinn Féin, led by de Valera, won forty-four seats but maintained its abstentionist policy and refused to take its seats in the Free State parliament. The Farmers' Party, founded the previous year to represent agricultural interests, and Independent TDs increased their representation, with the Labour Party being the only group to suffer a loss, returning fourteen TDs to the Fourth Dáil.

Richard Mulcahy proposed W.T. Cosgrave as President of the Executive

30 October
John Logie Baird creates Britain's first television transmitter.

26 December
The entirety of the Sphinx is finally displayed after excavations.

1926

1 January
Douglas Hyde opens the State's broadcasting service in Dublin.

12 February
In chaotic scenes at the Abbey Theatre, a production of *The Plough and the Stars* by Sean O'Casey is halted by protesters objecting to the play's portrayal of those who fought in the 1916 Rising.

22 March
The Free State soccer team plays its first international match against Italy. Italy wins 3–0.

3 May
Britain's General
Strike begins in
support of coal
miners who had
stopped working on
1 May. The strike
lasts nine days –
though miners would
remain on strike till
October – and martial
law is declared to
control crowds of
striking workers.
King George V gave
his support to the
strike saying,
'Try living on their
wages before you
judge them.'

Council when the Dáil met on 19 September. The ghosts of Griffith and Collins again populated Mulcahy's thoughts, as he commended Cosgrave to the new parliament and, perhaps, inadvertently, gave an indication of the private doubts some had about the president's ability when Cosgrave was first elected to the office:

> Twelve months ago we found ourselves meeting here, a Parliament of the Irish people, in days of very great sorrow and very great stress … We had lost the two leaders that we had been depending on for a very long time, the two leaders that we had hoped would be our strength and our guidance in shouldering the great responsibilities that came on the shoulders of the Irish people, the responsibilities of their own government … we were not able to say, or we could not have said, of Liam T. MacCosgair then that, like Arthur Griffith, he had been a light and a guidance and a teacher to us for many years, or that like Michael Collins he had been, as it were, a legend among us … we could say that he had been for years a very faithful servant of those who were foremost in the work of building up our country and in fighting for its liberty. We did ask one who was to us then a faithful servant of others to take on the responsibilities of leadership. Any doubts that were in our hearts at that time as to whether we had or had not amongst us a national leader have passed.
>
> (*9 September 1923*)

6 August
The Warner Brothers
studio gives the
first public exhibition
of their Vitaphone
system for showing
talking motion
pictures.

The new government continued in its task of building up the administrative capacity of the Free State, reforming the judicial system, establishing a radio broadcasting service and initiating the Shannon Hydro-Electric Scheme, one of the few examples of significant state investment in infrastructure.

The passage of legislation on reform of the jury system in May 1924 provoked a significant disagreement regarding the role of women in the Free State and demonstrated the deep conservatism, if not outright sexism, of the times.

6 August
American Gertrude
Ederle becomes the
first woman to swim
the English Channel
from France to
England.

Until 1919, women were exempted from jury service, when an Act of the British parliament made them liable equally with men. Under the Juries (Amendment) Act 1924, the Oireachtas decided that women could apply for automatic exemption from jury service. Explaining the reasoning behind this move, Kevin O'Higgins said:

> This section has been inserted in order to get rid of the unwilling woman juror. In this country the number of women who desire to serve on juries is very small, and in practice the insertion of women's names in the Jury Book

leads to nothing but trouble; the women do not turn up, or they get themselves excused, or they are objected to.

(*5 March 1924*)

The move was resisted on equality grounds chiefly by the Labour Party. According to the Minister for Home Affairs:

There is a perfectly honest difference of opinion on this matter, but I am very well satisfied that a majority opinion in the country would favour my view rather than that put forward by Deputy Johnson … He puts forward abstract principles about the equality of the sexes. I admire Deputy Johnson on abstract principles … but no matter what abstract principles may be enunciated, there remains the fact that the woman juror has not been an outstanding success, and that this abstract principle has broken down in practice.

(*13 March 1924*)

The Labour leader interjected and asked:

Has the woman voter been an outstanding success?

To which O'Higgins responded:

I would not like to pronounce an opinion on it in public …

The social conservatism of the government was mirrored by a similar approach to economic measures. In 1924, the government cut the old-age pension, with Finance Minister Ernest Blythe informing the Dáil:

It is necessary, owing to the state in which we find ourselves financially, that a great reduction shall be made in expenditure. That reduction it will be very difficult to effect in full. There is no way of avoiding it, however. We cannot afford to increase taxation in this country. … We cannot, if we have any prudence at all, contemplate any increase in taxation. The only thing left for us is to effect whatever cuts we can effect.

(*21 February 1924*)

18 August
A weather map is televised for the first time when images are sent from NAA Arlington to the Weather Bureau Office in Washington DC.

23 August
There is mass hysteria in America when the death of the movie star Rudolph Valentino at the age of thirty-one is announced.

29 August
P.D. Mehigan (also known as 'Carbery') commentates on the Galway v. Kilkenny All-Ireland senior hurling final from Croke Park in what is acknowledged as the first broadcast sports commentary on a field game in Europe.

31 October
Magician Harry Houdini dies of peritonitis which has developed after his appendix ruptured.

5 December
The French
impressionist painter
Claude Monet dies at
the age of eighty-six.

10 December
The Nobel Prize
for Literature is
awarded to George
Bernard Shaw.

25 December
Twenty-five-year-
old Crown Prince
Hirohito is declared
the new Emperor
of Japan.

1927

Unsurprisingly, the old–age pension cut proved deeply unpopular and was used as a stick to beat the government by its opponents over the coming years.

The constitutional and practical impact of the Treaty also continued to loom large. Britain still held control of key ports around the country, including Spike Island, County Cork. In March 1924, an IRA unit, dressed in the uniform of the Free State army, opened fire on a party of unarmed British soldiers as they disembarked at Cobh. One soldier was killed and twenty others were wounded in the attack. In the Dáil, Cosgrave condemned the attack and used the opportunity to laud the new relationship that was developing between Britain and Ireland:

> It is impossible to find words to describe this dastardly outrage … The murderers could have had only one motive in their murderous minds—that of embroiling our people in a struggle with Great Britain. The generosity of the British Nation … to the crime, and their sympathy to our country in the disgrace and humiliation which this abominable outrage has cast upon us is a comforting assurance of the strength of the friendship between our peoples which has followed the Treaty between the nations.
>
> *(25 March 1924)*

However, the strength of friendship between Britain and Ireland that Cosgrave alluded to was put under severe strain the following year when the issue of the border between the Free State and Northern Ireland provoked a political and public outcry.

The Treaty included a provision to establish a Boundary Commission to decide where the border between Northern Ireland and the Free State should fall.

The three-man commission to decide the issue was appointed in 1924, and its report a year later, which proposed minimal changes to the existing border and effectively emasculated a proposed all-island Council of Ireland, caused outrage across all sections of nationalist Ireland.

In the Dáil, Professor William Magennis, who was born in the North, and, until then, was a strong supporter of Cosgrave, was incensed by the government's handling of the issue.

> What do we get? The border as it was … That is what we have got out of this superb settlement. What has Ulster got? A boundary of its own choice— a boundary line as its gladiators and champions had it drawn for them by a

prejudiced British Ministry in 1920 … It has also got rid of what irritated them so exceedingly—the prospect of the Council of Ireland.

(*7 December 1925*)

A related issue at the time was the extent of the payment the Free State would make under the terms of the Treaty as a contribution towards Britain's public debt.

Following negotiations, Ireland's obligation to the debt issue was wiped out and, in his defence of the government's handling of the Boundary Commission, Cosgrave put great store on this fact. However, suspicion that the government had accepted the border deal in exchange for financial concessions was rife. Many northern nationalists had looked to the Free State as a protector following partition, and the deal Cosgrave concluded now offered these people scant consolation, despite his insistence that:

The question as to how a minority should be protected has been very often asked. I believe that there is only one real security for minorities, and that is the good will and neighbourly feeling of the people among whom they live.

(*7 December 1925*)

Over the coming decades, little 'good will' or 'neighbourly feeling' would be extended to northern nationalists by the new administration in Belfast as it evolved into, in Prime Minister James Craig's words, 'a Protestant Parliament, and a Protestant State'.

The refusal of the republican movement to recognise the State and continuing IRA violence, caused the government to continue to rely on repressive public order legislation throughout the lifetime of the Fourth Dáil.

However, change was afoot amongst those targeted by the government and de Valera, increasingly frustrated at his self-imposed exclusion from power, split from the militant republicans in Sinn Féin and the IRA. The split resulted in the foundation of Fianna Fáil in 1926. The party espoused the republican creed, with the unification of the state, economic self-sufficiency and the restoration of the Irish language among its founding principles, arguing that these aims could be advanced through the ballot box rather than by force of arms.

Fianna Fáil also successfully appealed beyond its core republican base and attracted those who had become disillusioned with Cosgrave's government. Economic austerity had undermined the popularity of the government, though Cumann na nGaedheal went about its business with little thought of the electoral implications, as illustrated by its approach to the licensing laws.

7 April
The Bell Telephone Company transmits an image of Commerce Secretary Hoover in the first successful long distance demonstration of television.

4 May
The American Academy of Motion Picture Arts and Sciences is founded in Hollywood.

20 May
US aviator Charles Lindbergh takes off from New York in his single-engine aircraft, the *Spirit of St Louis*. He completes the first non-stop solo transatlantic flight when he lands in Paris after thirty-three and a half hours.

6 October
The Jazz Singer, starring Al Jolson, debuts in New York. It is the first 'talkie'.

1928

31 January
Leon Trotsky is sent into internal exile in the USSR.

12 April
The first transatlantic flight from Ireland to America leaves Baldonnel Aerodrome. The *Bremen* is piloted by a two-man, Irish and German crew.

15 May
The Royal Flying Doctor Service begins in Australia.

2 July
In Britain, the Representation of the People Act becomes law. It extends the right to vote to all women in the UK.

27 August
The Kellogg-Briand Pact is signed in Paris. It is the first international agreement to ban aggressive war. All major countries – sixty-one in total – sign the pact.

A short number of months before the June 1927 election, O'Higgins introduced the Intoxicating Liquor Bill, which infuriated publicans and discommoded the persistent tippler. The legislation prohibited the opening of licensed premises on Christmas Day, Good Friday and St Patrick's Day. The Act also heralded the introduction of the 'holy hour' whereby pubs were required to close in the afternoon, a measure O'Higgins thought necessary because:

> It sends the long sitter about his business for a couple of hours. It sends him away to get a meal or to attend to his affairs … Then we are asked what about the long sitter, what about the man who is ruining his health and his business by spending his entire days in the publichouse? … What are we here for? Is it not to legislate, as we believe, in the best interests of the State and its people? Do any of us believe that a twelve hours' drinking day is in the best interests of the State and the people — a twelve hours' drinking day without a break?
>
> (*16 February 1927*)

Far from emptying the pubs, O'Higgins' initiative was to lead to clandestine mid-afternoon 'lock-ins' in premises throughout the country until it was finally abolished in 2000.

Fianna Fáil's growth was rapid. It attacked the government mercilessly at every opportunity, portraying itself as the advocate of the small farmer, the worker and those who strived to build a republic. The new party also had access to considerable finances following a fundraising tour of the USA undertaken by de Valera in the spring of 1927.

Cosgrave dissolved the Fourth Dáil on 20 May and called an election for 9 June 1927. Referring to a minor disagreement regarding the election date, Cosgrave explained to the Dáil that nothing could be done 'as the calendar is against us'. Labour TD, Daniel Morrissey retorted, 'There is more than the calendar against you.'

Morrissey's assessment was correct. The election proved a triumph for de Valera and Fianna Fáil. In its first electoral outing, the party won forty-four seats and practically wiped out its former irredentist colleagues in Sinn Féin, who secured just five seats. What is more, the election saw Cumann na nGaedhael lose sixteen seats, returning with just three seats more than de Valera's democratic neophytes. Fianna Fáil was on the brink of power.

One significant hurdle remained though. Fianna Fáil TDs, while prepared to use the Free State institutions, still refused to take their seats in Dáil Éireann because of the Oath of Allegiance to the British crown.

Following the election Fianna Fáil deputies attempted to enter Dáil Éireann without taking the oath, only to be disbarred by the clerk of the Dáil. They then embarked on a campaign to remove the oath by popular vote of the people, a campaign which was stopped in its tracks, ironically by the bullets fired from a republican gun.

On 10 July, just a month after the election, Kevin O'Higgins was assassinated by republican gunmen in Booterstown, Dublin. Aged just thirty-five, O'Higgins had been one of the most dynamic, industrious and hardline members of the Free State government. His defiance in the face of IRA violence and his willingness to introduce draconian measures to deal with the threat had made him a hate figure within republican circles. His murder deprived the State of a remarkable, if controversial, talent. An emotional Cosgrave paid tribute to O'Higgins in the Dáil two days after the assassination:

> With all that he had accomplished, and for all the cold determination and iron will which seemed to the public to be his principal characteristics, Kevin O'Higgins was essentially modest because essentially sincere. He had in a high degree that self-command which he showed so wonderfully in those last-terrible moments. But to those of us who were privileged to be admitted to a more intimate acquaintance with the man there was revealed a softness, a charm, and a kindness which made him the more dear to us, as we knew what he must have suffered in mastering himself to give what was required of him by his lofty ideal of public duty.
>
> The crime which has been committed is grievous beyond words. We are bereft of a colleague loyal, steadfast, of rare ability; the nation is robbed of a statesman invaluable in council, of unswerving purpose, who knew not fear or weakness, a very exemplar of public virtue. This crime has not been committed by private individuals against Kevin O'Higgins. It is the political assassination of a pillar of the State.
>
> (*12 July 1927*)

O'Higgins' assassination provoked an immediate response from the government. Among the measures proposed was legislation which required election candidates to pledge to take the oath and occupy their seats in Dáil Éireann. In one move, de Valera's objection to the oath was rendered redundant in practical terms, and, declaring the oath 'an empty formula', he led his TDs into Dáil Éireann. It was the

28 July
The Olympic Games are officially opened in Amsterdam. During the tournament, Coca-Cola appears in Europe for the first time.

30 July
Dr Pat O'Callaghan wins Ireland's first ever Olympic gold medal at the games in Amsterdam, for his hammer throwing.

30 August
Indian nationalist Jawarhalal Nehru organises the Independence of India League to challenge British rule in India.

15 September
Scottish bacteriologist Sir Alexander Fleming notices a bacteria-killing mould growing in his laboratory. The mould will later be developed into penicillin.

1929

Kevin O'Higgins, February 1923. Kevin O'Higgins speaks to crowds from the back of a truck during the Civil War.

first, but by no means the last, time that republicans formerly associated with violence would come in from the cold and accept a constitutional, democratic path.

With Fianna Fáil now in parliament, Cumann na nGaedheal's hold on power became increasingly tenuous. On 16 August, the Labour Party placed a motion of no confidence in the government before the Dáil. The combined voting strength of Labour, Fianna Fáil and the National League Party was enough to oust Cosgrave from power and to install an alternative coalition. The National League Party, led by William Redmond, a son of Irish Parliamentary Party leader John Redmond, had won eight seats at the June election garnering much of its support from ex-servicemen. With power in sight, it was now prepared to throw its weight behind Labour and de Valera.

Cosgrave's government was facing defeat and was saved only through the intervention of two intriguing figures, Major Bryan Cooper TD and Bertie Smyllie. As the Dáil debated the no-confidence motion, Cooper and Smyllie waylaid John Jinks, a National League TD for Sligo–Leitrim. Both men convinced Jinks that his electorate would not appreciate his role in handing the reigns of power over to de Valera and his republican brethren. Cooper and Smyllie's analysis came accompanied by enough drink to convince Jinks of the efficacy of their argument and, rather than voting in the Dáil division, Jinks boarded the train to Sligo.

Smyllie was later to make a significant mark on the new Free State as a famed editor of *The Irish Times*, and Cooper would later join Cumann na nGaedhael. In April 1931, following Cooper's death, his widow presented Dáil Éireann with a replica of the ancient bell of Lough Lene Castle which is still used today by the Ceann Comhairle during Dáil proceedings.

Cosgrave survived the no-confidence motion by the slimmest of margins and a week later Cumann na nGaedhael won the by-elections caused by the death of Kevin O'Higgins and Countess Markievicz, who died a month after being elected for Fianna Fáil in June.

Cosgrave, buoyed up by these election triumphs, and frustrated with the tight Dáil arithmetic, called another general election for 15 September. Cumann na nGaedhael won an additional fifteen seats, with the National League Party, including Deputy Jinks, being among the largest losers.

The Sixth Dáil met on 11 October, and Cosgrave was re-elected President of the Executive Council by six votes. During the debate on Cosgrave's nomination, Seán T. O'Kelly, a 1916 veteran, founding member of Fianna Fáil and future president, delivered a trenchant attack on Cosgrave and his party. O'Kelly's speech was proof positive that despite the entry of Fianna Fáil into constitutional politics, the wounds of the Civil War were still open and that rather than just administer the machinery of state, Fianna Fáil in office would seek to radically alter the very constitutional basis on which the State existed:

> I personally take this the first opportunity that is given to me in an Assembly of this kind … to say that I would do all I could to drive out of political power and office the gentleman and the Party associated with him who have the primary, if not complete, responsibility for the tragedies, sorrows, misdeeds, poverty and suffering that make up Ireland's history in the last five years …
>
> If Deputies are satisfied that these conditions ought to continue and that they cannot be bettered, then they have nobody more fitted to run Ireland on those lines than Deputy Cosgrave and his colleagues, and they ought to vote for him. If, however, they want to give Ireland half a chance … politically and economically, they will try to find, and no doubt will find, the means of putting in power those who hope for Ireland and who stand by the old gospel that has always inspired Ireland with hope and enthusiasm.
>
> (*11 October 1927*)

14 February
Disguised as Chicago police officers and detectives, Al Capone's mobsters take out six of George 'Bugs' Moran's gang in a warehouse. The infamous event will become known as the St Valentine's Day massacre.

18 February
The first Academy Awards – the Oscars – are announced. The winner of the Most Outstanding Production is *Wings*, the First World War epic staring Buddy Rogers and Clara Bow.

22 July
The Shannon Hydroelectric Power Scheme is opened by President Cosgrave to help provide electricity to the nation.

25 July
Pope Pius XI makes the first public appearance by a pope outside the Vatican since 1870.

3 October
The name of the
Kingdom of the Serbs,
Croats, and Slovenes
is changed to
Yugoslavia as part of
King Alexander I's
attempt to end ethnic
divisions within
the country.

3 October
Gustav Stresemann,
Chancellor of
Germany, dies of a
stroke at the age
of fifty-one.

29 October
The New York stock
market crashes,
heralding the onset of
the Great Depression.

31 December
Guy Lombardo and
his Royal Canadian
Band play 'Auld Lang
Syne' for the first
time in America and it
becomes part of
the New Year's Eve
tradition.

Within five years, O'Kelly and his colleagues would finally oust Cosgrave, and begin to resurrect 'the old gospel'.

The entry of Fianna Fáil into Dáil Éireann radically changed the atmosphere of the parliament. Until then, the Labour Party had provided the main parliamentary opposition to Cosgrave's government. By and large, Labour operated as a diligent and, at times, deferential parliamentary opposition. It rarely used the Dáil as a platform to promote its agenda or to embarrass the government. For instance, in the lead-in to the June 1927 election, motions raised in the Dáil by the Labour Party included the annulment of orders related to tailors and milliners, hardly an issue to strike fear into the heart of the administration.

The September 1927 election was a significant setback for Labour. The party lost nine seats, including that of its leader Thomas Johnson, who was replaced by Mayo TD T.J. O'Connell. Labour's problems at the time extended beyond the vagaries of electoral politics. In 1923, the mercurial figure of James Larkin returned to Ireland after nearly a decade's absence. Larkin immediately embarked on a battle for control of the wider labour movement, and the turmoil that ensued divided and distracted both the Labour Party and the trade union movement for years to come.

During the Sixth Dáil, Fianna Fáil would emerge as the dominant force on the opposition benches, intent on using every avenue to challenge the Cosgrave administration and promote its own electoral fortunes.

It used its parliamentary time to solidify its standing among its core republican support. Dozens of raids by the gardaí on republican suspects, were challenged in the Dáil and the welfare of republican prisoners was brought up time and again. In March 1928, Fianna Fáil even objected to the pension made available to the family of the late Kevin O'Higgins, arguing that the sum was too high.

The party also continued its campaign against the provisions of the Treaty. Less than twelve months after entering Dáil Éireann, de Valera presented a petition, signed by over 96,000 people, aimed at removing the Oath of Allegiance under the power of initiative contained in the Free State Constitution. The move not only revealed the considerable organisational skills of Fianna Fáil but also demonstrated its determination to use the machinery of the Free State Constitution to dismantle the Treaty, step by step. The government was forced to amend the constitution to remove the right of initiative in July 1928.

However, Fianna Fáil did not confine itself to articulating the concerns of its republican base. The party also used the Dáil to promote its social programme, often claiming ownership of issues previously the bailiwick of the Labour Party.

Fianna Fáil lambasted the government over unemployment and the continuing high levels of poverty; the workers' case in industrial disputes was often raised on the floor of the Dáil by Fianna Fáil deputies; and it was de Valera's party, rather than Labour, that challenged the government over garda raids on the Irish Labour Defence League in March 1930 and the banning of left-wing newspapers such as *Workers' Voice* in December 1931.

The one issue where the main parties in Dáil Éireann could find common agreement was the issue of censorship. Following the introduction of a film censor, repeated calls were made to introduce a similar regime for books and publications and the Minister for Justice James Fitzgerald-Kenney introduced the Censorship of Publications Bill in October 1928.

The bill established a Censorship of Publications Board which would ban books, newspapers and magazines which were deemed to be indecent. It also included a special section which Minister Fitzgerald-Kenney informed the Dáil 'deals with propaganda in favour of birth control which is now such a growing force'.

The danger posed by the English press featured prominently in the Dáil debate. However, Fianna Fáil deputy Domhnall Ua Buachalla, later appointed Governor-General by de Valera, urged the new censorship regime to pay particular attention to 'cheap novels'. Speaking during the debate in October 1928, Deputy Ua Buachalla outlined his concerns:

> I do not agree at all with what has been said by many Teachtaí to the effect that the greatest harm has been done through the reading of newspapers that come into the country. It is my opinion that just as much harm is done by the cheap novels that are imported by the ton every week. They are distributed to the shops throughout the country and they are sold in an underhand way. They are bought principally by young girls, I am sorry to say, and they go into almost every cabin in the country.
>
> A short time ago I had occasion to visit a poor woman in an out-of-the-way place in County Meath … This poor woman and I were sitting by the fire in the kitchen—the roof had been taken off the bedroom—and we were chatting. I saw on a shelf inside the chimney breast a box with some books in it. "Biddy," said I to the woman. "I see you have some books here. Perhaps there may be some valuable old Irish manuscripts among them. May I have a look at them?" She said that I might.
>
> I took down the box and examined the contents. There were about ten

6 January
The first literary character licensing agreement is signed by A.A. Milne. It gives Stephen Slesinger US and Canadian merchandising rights to the Winnie the Pooh novels.

12 January
The writer Jennifer Johnston is born in Dublin.

31 January
The 3M company starts to market Scotch Tape.

18 February
The planet Pluto is discovered and, at the time, is counted as the ninth planet of the solar system. It is downgraded to a dwarf planet in 2006.

28 March
The ancient Turkish city of Constantinople changes its name to Istanbul.

18 April
In London, the BBC Radio Service reports that, today, 'There is no news.'

15 May
In America, United Airlines introduces the first stewardesses on a flight from San Francisco to Cheyenne, Wyoming.

30 July
Uruguay beats Argentina 4–2 in the first soccer World Cup.

1 December
The French start work on the Maginot Line, a line of concrete fortifications on the French–German border that its architect, General Maginot, is convinced will ensure that France is never invaded by its neighbour again.

copies of the "Irish Rosary" and just as many copies of these filthy novels, novels with attractively coloured covers, with their suggestive, immoral, filthy stories. I looked through one of them to see what they were like, and then I asked her where she got them. She said she got them to read from girls in the neighbourhood. Now, what happened there is happening throughout the country, and, as I said before, these books are bought principally by young girls. The result is that the girls are getting a taste for that sort of thing, and their morals are being destroyed. Therefore, I say that at least as much attention should be paid to the importation of these books as to the importation of newspapers …

(*19 October 1928*)

The Censorship of Publications Board did indeed heed the deputy's advice. In 1942, in an impassioned critique of the board, Sir John Keane informed Seanad Éireann that 1,600 books had been banned, including works by John Steinbeck, Graham Greene, Ernest Hemingway, D.H. Lawrence, Benedict Kiely, Kate O'Brien, Frank O'Connor and Seán Ó Faoláin.

Conflict, rather than consensus, however, was the dominant theme of the Dáil between 1927 and 1932, and the level of old-age pensions proved one of the most divisive topics. In March 1930, Fianna Fáil tabled a bill to roll back on the government's reductions in the pension, legislation that gained the support of the Labour Party and some Independents. Despite the government's arguments that the measure would cost £300,000 extra per year, the initiative narrowly passed, by two votes, on 27 March. Having lost the vote, Cosgrave resigned the following day and the Dáil met on 2 April to resolve the dilemma, with Cosgrave seeking re-election.

The brief unity of purpose shown by Fianna Fáil and Labour was short-lived. The debate on the election of a new president was marked not by a co-ordinated attempt to remove the Cumann na nGaedhael government but, rather, by mutual distrust and bitterness between Fianna Fáil and Labour.

After entering Dáil Éireann in 1927, Fianna Fáil had used the parliament effectively to advance its political agenda. However, the party's republicanism was still central to its philosophy, and it refused to wholeheartedly endorse the constitutional legitimacy of the parliament, with de Valera stating in a debate in 1929:

We are asked to state clearly what our attitude towards this House is. I have on more than one occasion said exactly what our attitude was. I still hold that our right to be regarded as the legitimate Government of this country is faulty, that this House itself is faulty. You have secured a de facto position. Very well … We are all morally handicapped because of the circumstances in which the whole thing came about. The setting up of this State put a moral handicap on every one of us here … I for one, when the flag of the Republic was run up against an Executive that was bringing off a coup d'état, stood by the flag of the Republic, and I will do it again.

(14 March 1929)

Labour's T.J. O'Connell launched a ferocious attack on Fianna Fáil, quoting de Valera's speech of March 1929 and questioning the party's commitment to democracy, stating:

Any person who denies or questions, or even doubts the sovereignty of this Parliament, who denies or questions or even doubts its moral right to make and administer the laws of this State, and to insist on the strict observance of these laws, is not, in my humble opinion, a suitable person to be entrusted with the control of the powers which are inherent in this Parliament. That I lay down as my first essential … So long as these views are held by Deputy de Valera, no vote of mine will be cast to enable him to become head of a Government chosen by this House.

If the action of the Labour Party to-day and the reasons which I have given for that action, have the effect of bringing Deputy de Valera and his followers to realise that what the country earnestly wants is an end to the barren controversies of the past eight years and the substitution therefore of what is sometimes disparagingly called a "bread and butter" policy, then Labour will … have rendered valuable and lasting service to the national interest.

(2 April 1930)

Not to be outdone, Seán Lemass replied to O'Connell in trenchant terms with a damning assessment of Labour's contribution to politics since the foundation of the State:

We cannot forget that the Constitution was framed in London and imposed by threats upon the Irish people. We cannot accept that document as sacred in consequence of that knowledge. We will not be prepared to accept it as sacred until it has been freely revised and amended by the elected representatives of the Irish people …

I have said already that the outstanding characteristic of the Labour Party

12 February
Radio Vaticana, the official voice of the Vatican, broadcasts for the first time.

3 March
The US Senate adopts 'The Star Spangled Banner' as America's national anthem.

2 May
The Empire State Building is opened in New York.

15 May
In an encyclical, Pope Pius XI tells Catholics that they cannot also be socialists.

5 September
The first edition of Fianna Fáil's newspaper, the *Irish Press*, is printed and sells 200,000 copies.

Cosgrave has the key, 11 June 1929. W.T. Cosgrave officially reopens Dublin's General Post Office, which is finally restored thirteen years after being destroyed during the 1916 Rising.

is that it is the most respectable Party in this State. The members of that Party desire to be respectable above everything else. So long as they cannot be accused of being even pale pink in politics they seem to think they have fulfilled their function towards the Irish people.

(2 April 1930)

Cosgrave was comfortably re-elected by fifteen votes and would remain President of the Executive Council for the remainder of the Sixth Dáil.

Despite the social and economic conservatism of his administration, Cosgrave's decade in power laid the foundations of the emerging Irish State. His tenure as President of the Executive Council saw the formation of an unarmed police force, the establishment of an impartial and fair judicial system and other institutional developments crucial to the effective working of a modern democracy.

The decade in power also witnessed significant diplomatic successes for the Free State. Ireland joined the League of Nations in 1923 and registered the Treaty with the organisation the following year, promoting it as an agreement between two sovereign nations rather than an internal British Commonwealth matter.

Ireland also worked effectively with other members of the Commonwealth to secure the passage of the Statute of Westminster in 1931. This law introduced a new degree of equality between Britain and its former colonial possessions and ensured that the decisions of national parliaments established in Ireland, Canada and other parts of the Commonwealth could not be overruled or declared void by the British parliament. It was a vital constitutional development that confirmed Michael Collins' assertion that the Treaty gave Ireland the freedom to achieve freedom. Ironically, it was de Valera who would grasp the opportunity created by the Statute of Westminster to radically alter the nature of the Free State in the 1930s.

Perhaps the lasting achievement of Cosgrave's period in power was the wide-spread acceptance of Dáil Éireann as the legitimate democratic forum of the Irish people. The willingness of Cosgrave's governments in the 1920s to use emergency legislation to crack down on continuing subversive action by republicans is open to criticism, but the passion and commitment that leading members of Cumann na nGaedheal demonstrated in defending the State against attack was crucial in establishing the rule of democracy amid the mayhem and bitterness that followed the Civil War. By the early 1930s, the strength of democratic institutions was sufficient to enable the smooth transition of power to the republicans in Fianna Fáil.

Arguably the most fitting tribute paid to Cosgrave's decade in power came from an unlikely source, his bitter rival Eamon de Valera. In his book *Ireland in the Twentieth Century*, author and historian Tim Pat Coogan recounts a story told to him by de Valera's son, Vivion. In the early 1930s, after Fianna Fáil came to power, the young Vivion launched into a trenchant attack on the record of Cumann na nGaedheal but was stopped in his tracks by his father, who said, 'Yes, yes, yes. We said all that … but when we got in and saw the files … they did a magnificent job, Viv.'

21 May
Amelia Earhart becomes the first woman to fly solo across the Atlantic, when she arrives in Ireland from Newfoundland, Canada.

22 June
The thirty-first Eucharistic Congress opens at the Pro-Cathedral in Dublin.

30 June
The Tailteann Games open in Croke Park in the presence of Cardinal McRory.

8 November
Franklin D. Roosevelt becomes the thirty-second president of the United States. He will serve a record four terms as president before dying, in office, in 1945.

27 December
BBC World Service begins broadcasting as the British Empire Service.

'So far as the Labour Party is concerned, so far as the plain people of this country are concerned, they can bid adieu to the outgoing Government with no feeling of regret whatever and with no kind wishes for their early return.'

Taoiseach elect, 1932.
Eamon de Valera shortly after his election victory.

We do not believe in coalition governments. We think they are a bad system of government.

1932-1948

The Return
of the Old Gospel

'We must all be brothers in one
in one holy cause, and
no voice if dissension
should be heard amongst us.'

are expected, in that st
to work ourselves up t
thusiasm over *Surely*
charge, as
Government of this country,

is the happiness of our own people.

1932-1948

The February 1932 election was to prove a milestone for

Fianna Fáil, ushering de Valera to power, where he would remain as Taoiseach until 1948.

The election itself became a battle between the two largest parties, with Fianna Fáil fighting a vigorous campaign, focusing on social and economic development, along with radical constitutional reform and loyally supported by the *Irish Press*, the newspaper de Valera had founded the previous year.

Cumann na nGaedhael, on the other hand, went into the election in defensive mode. An increase in IRA activity in the preceding years, and a rather exaggerated threat of communist subversion, had led to the introduction of new emergency legislation in October 1931, with Cosgrave claiming at the time:

> Foul murders have been committed, acknowledged and gloried in by certain organisations. Young men are being taught that murder is a legitimate instrument for the furtherance of Communist or political aims. They are being taught that the Christian Church around which our whole history and civilisation have been built up is an instrument of tyranny for the suppression of the people …
>
> We believe that the new patriotism based on Muscovite teachings with a sugar coating of Irish extremism is completely alien to Irish tradition …
>
> The Church and the State are the only bulwarks against chaos. The present movements aim at the destruction of both … The powers, that we as a Government ask for—we ask for because we are convinced that without them it would be impossible for this or any other Government to carry on in circumstances such as now prevail.
>
> *(14 October 1931)*

Cosgrave's attitude in October was a foretaste of the Cumann na nGaedhael election campaign a few months later, with the party trying to portray the choice before the people as one between responsible, conservative Cumann na nGaedhael government or anarchy. The strategy didn't work.

Fianna Fáil won an extra fifteen seats at the polls, leaving it five seats short of an overall majority. Cumann na nGaedhael lost five seats, and the Labour Party recorded the worst election result in its history, returning just seven TDs. For the second election in a row, Labour lost its leader, with T.J. O'Connell failing to retain his seat in Mayo, resulting in the young, industrious Kildare TD, William Norton, taking up the leadership, aged just thirty-two.

1933

5 January
Work begins on constructing the Golden Gate Bridge in San Francisco.

30 January
Adolf Hitler is named Chancellor of Germany by President Hindenburg.

27 February
The Reichstag, seat of the German parliament, is set on fire.

2 March
King Kong starring Fay Wray premieres in New York.

4 March
Giving his inauguration speech, Franklin D. Roosevelt declares, 'We have nothing to fear but fear itself.'

22 March
Dachau, the first Nazi concentration camp, opens.

Despite its depleted strength, the Labour Party was to make its presence felt when the Seventh Dáil met on 9 March 1932. The party supported de Valera's nomination as President of the Executive Council, with Norton adopting a more positive stance towards Fianna Fáil than either of his predecessors and managing a sideswipe at Cumann na nGaedhael when setting out his stall:

> So far as the Labour Party is concerned, so far as the plain people of this country are concerned, they can bid adieu to the outgoing Government with no feeling of regret whatever and with no kind wishes for their early return … It is because we have hopes that the Fianna Fáil Party will live up to their declared policy, that they will endeavour to implement the promises they have given to the electors in social and economic matters, that the Labour Party is going to vote for Deputy de Valera …
>
> (*9 March 1932*)

1934

With the support of the Labour Party, and that of some Independents, de Valera was duly elected President of the Executive Council. The peaceful transfer of power from Cumann na nGaedhael to the republicans in Fianna Fáil was a remarkable achievement. Just four years earlier, Seán Lemass had famously described Fianna Fáil as a 'slightly constitutional' party. During a debate on the status of republican prisoners in March 1928, Lemass had given a less-than-ringing endorsement of the party's commitment to the Irish Free State:

> Fianna Fáil is a slightly constitutional party. We are perhaps open to the definition of a constitutional party, but before anything we are a Republican party. We have adopted the method of political agitation to achieve our end, because we believe, in the present circumstances, that method is best in the interests of the nation and of the Republican movement, and for no other reason … Our object is to establish a Republican Government in Ireland. If that can be done by the present methods we have we will be very pleased, but if not we would not confine ourselves to them.
>
> (*21 March 1928*)

Fianna Fáil wasted no time in setting about its task of dismantling those aspects of the Treaty that most offended its republican principles. Within weeks of taking power, de Valera introduced legislation to remove the Oath of Allegiance, without

Election poster, 1932. Cumann na nGaedhael poster for the 1932 election, ridiculing Fianna Fáil.

any negotiation or discussion with the British government.

Remarkably, when he introduced the legislation, de Valera invoked the 'stepping stone to independence' argument that had been used by the Michael Collins and others during the debate on the Treaty:

When the Treaty was being put before the old Dáil, one of the arguments put forward in favour of it was that it gave freedom to achieve freedom. Are those who acted on that policy now going to say that there is to be a barrier and a perpetual barrier to advancement? Let the British say that if they choose. Why should any Irishman say it, particularly when it is not true? I say then that whatever the position may have been in 1921, in the year 1932 there is no doubt whatever that we can remove Article 17 of the Constitution, and do it without violating any contractual obligation whatever that we have with Britain …

(*27 April 1932*)

The initiative to remove the oath was opposed by Cumann na nGaedhael, who argued that it was an essential part of the Treaty agreement and could not be deleted without discussion and negotiation with Downing Street but the government's majority ensured the Dáil passed the legislation. However, the Seanad was not as amenable to Fianna Fáil's agenda and attempted to delay and amend the bill, which was eventually passed in May 1933. It would not be the last clash between de

30 June
In the 'Night of the Long Knives', Adolf Hitler purges the National Socialist, or Nazi, party of its paramilitary stormtrooper wing, killing hundreds of the party's most dedicated followers.

22 September
In soccer, Stanley Matthews debuts for England, beginning a twenty-three-year international career.

27 December
Persia becomes Iran.

1935

28 January
Iceland becomes the first country to legalise abortion, on medical grounds.

1 February
The National Council for the Welfare of the Blind standardises the Gaelic Braille system.

"So far as the Labour Party is concerned, so far as the plain people of this country are concerned, they can bid adieu to the outgoing Government, with no feeling of regret whatever and no kind wishes for their early return."

William Norton, 9 March 1932

Valera's government and the Seanad, a stand-off which would eventually result in de Valera abolishing the Upper House in 1936.

Fianna Fáil's ire was also directed towards the Governor-General, James MacNeill. After taking office, the government engaged in numerous diplomatic and personal slights against MacNeill.

The stand-off involving the Governor-General continued until MacNeill decided to quit in November 1932. Domhnall Ua Buachalla, a Fianna Fáil loyalist, was subsequently installed as Governor-General, with the status and the trappings of the office greatly reduced and the position effectively consigned to a constitutional backwater.

The standing of the new Fianna Fáil government was greatly enhanced by the prominent role government members played during the Eucharistic Congress in June 1932. This huge Catholic event saw approximately a quarter of the entire population attend the final mass in the Phoenix Park. The sight of senior Fianna Fáil members hosting the great and good of the Catholic Church confirmed that the transfer of power was secure and that Fianna Fáil's attachment to 'slightly constitutional' ways was growing stronger.

De Valera came to power in 1932 advocating a strong form of economic nationalism. Fianna Fáil's economic policy envisioned an independent, self-sufficient economy protected from outside competition by high taxes on foreign imports. In the words of Seán Lemass, Minister for Industry and Commerce, when introducing the Control of Manufactures Bill in June 1932:

> The main design behind it is to secure that we will have here in the future an Irish Ireland, not merely in the cultural sense but in the economic sense as well.
>
> *(14 June 1932)*

The implementation of this policy was significantly hastened by the economic war between Ireland and Britain that broke out in summer of 1932 and lasted until 1938.

The economic war was triggered by Fianna Fáil's aggressive approach to another key policy priority, the withholding of land annuities – the payments due to the British government for the purchase and distribution of large country estates, which had occurred from the late nineteenth century.

Fianna Fáil's opposition to land annuities garnered significant support for the party among small farmers during the election, and de Valera's government quickly set about attempting to renegotiate payments with the British government. The negotiations failed, and Ireland withheld payment of annuities in July. The following

16 March
Adolf Hitler begins the rearmament of Germany.

19 May
T.E. Lawrence, the British soldier and adventurer known as Lawrence of Arabia, dies in England following a motorcycle accident.

10 June
Two recovering alcoholics, Bill W. and Dr. Bob S., found Alcoholics Anonymous in Ohio, to help each other stay sober.

16 July
The world's first parking meters are introduced in Oklahoma City.

17 July
George Russell, Æ, the well-known poet, artist and economist, dies at the age of sixty-eight.

30 July
The first set of
Penguin paperback
books is published,
an early step in
the paperback
revolution that
will take off after the
Second World War.

2 October
Italy invades Ethiopia.

5 November
The board game
Monopoly, based on
Atlantic City, is
released by the
Parker Brothers.

11 November
Nineteen people,
including seven from
one family, drown off
Aranmore in County
Donegal.

27 November
Japanese troops
have arrived in
Peking [Beijing]
having annexed
Manchuria earlier
in the year.

day, the British government imposed a punitive 20 per cent tax on all Irish imports; this was reciprocated on the Irish side; and thus began the economic war.

Within days, Minister for Finance, Seán MacEntee, explained the government's position to the Dáil:

> We have retained the land annuities because we believe ourselves to be justly, to be morally entitled to them. To hold otherwise would be to admit the justice and the rightness of the confiscations and persecutions which have characterised the relations of Great Britain with this country … We have retained them because they are the very life-blood of our economic system and because the continued payment of them would frustrate all hope of an industrial revival in this country and doom our people year by year to wastage and decay until this island might become nothing more than a cattle ranch or a bird sanctuary upon the waves of the Atlantic …
>
> … the trade relations between this country and Great Britain are such that for every penny piece which she robs from us by a tariff upon our agricultural produce we can recoup ourselves by a tariff upon her manufactures … The economic history of this country is a record of Irish industry destroyed by British legislation, but under different circumstances. When these former attempts were successful there was not a united nation to resist British policy.
>
> (*14 July 1932*)

MacEntee's assessment that the loss of agricultural exports would be cancelled out by higher tax revenues from British imports was flawed in the extreme. Britain was the market for over 90 per cent of Ireland's exports at the time, and agriculture produce, mainly cattle, accounted for the vast majority of exports. The farming sector, particularly larger farmers who traditionally supported Cumann na nGaedhael, bore the immediate consequences of the economic sanctions.

As the effects of the economic war began to bite, Cosgrave condemned the government's handling of the issue, telling the Dáil:

> By their blundering incompetence in the handling of that dispute they not alone involved this country in a terrible economic war of attrition with a rich and powerful nation but they have, by their actions, precluded themselves from seeking or making an honourable settlement. Through neglect, incapacity, lack of statesmanship, want of foresight, the Executive Council allowed

themselves and permitted the country to slip into a wholly unnecessary and wretched struggle which, in order still further to mislead the country, they tried to dignify with the name of a "war," while they were without a plan, without an intelligence staff, and without an adequate supply of war material.

Since the inception of this war their handling of both the internal and external affairs of this country has been so reckless and irresponsible that the country is now facing political and economic disaster.

(15 November 1932)

Despite the severe strain imposed by the international depression and the economic war, Fianna Fáil was intent on making good on its social commitments. Over the coming years, state-housing construction saw a significant increase, with local authorities building more than 25,000 houses between 1933 and 1937. Social-welfare provision for widows and orphans was introduced and the old-age pension was protected from the cutbacks imposed in previous years. Public spending increased significantly to pay for these initiatives, a development that was roundly criticised by Cumann na nGaedhael, which continued to espouse economic and fiscal conservatism.

Labour, on the other hand, supported these social initiatives, viewing them as payback for its support of de Valera. However, during the 1930s, Labour got little electoral benefit from this strategy, with the party struggling to retain 10 per cent of the vote during the period.

The economic war wasn't the only source of confrontation in 1932. Within days of coming to office, Fianna Fáil released IRA prisoners, which republicans marked by a triumphant march in Dublin. At the same time, the Army Comrades Association (ACA) was founded, comprising mainly of former army personnel and Cumann na nGaedhael supporters, deeply fearful of Fianna Fáil's ascent to power and the continuing existence of the IRA. Clashes between the IRA and ACA members became a regular occurrence.

As civil unrest grew throughout the country, Fianna Fáil used the occasion of a speech by a British minister which was critical of de Valera over the land annuities issue to call a snap election in December and the ensuing campaign was often marked with violent confrontations between the ACA and republican supporters of Fianna Fáil.

The election, held on 24 January 1933, gave an additional five seats to Fianna Fáil and removed de Valera's reliance on Labour support, though the party supported his

19 January
A special showing of *The Dawn* takes place for the press. It is the first talking film to be produced, directed and acted in Ireland.

27 May
The first flight by Aer Lingus – from Dublin to Bristol –takes place.

30 June
Emperor Haile Selassie I of Ethiopia appeals in vain to the League of Nations to halt the Italian invasion of his country.

30 June
Margaret Mitchell's novel *Gone With the Wind* is published. An immediate bestseller, it becomes one of the most popular novels of the twentieth century.

18 July
Led by generals
Francisco Franco and
Emilio Mola, a rebel-
lion of the army
against the Spanish
Second Republic
begins the Spanish
Civil War.

3 August
American sprinter
Jesse Owens wins the
first of his four gold
medals in the Olympic
Games in Berlin,
Germany, tying the
Olympic record of 10.3
seconds in the
100-metre dash.

6 September
The last surviving
Tasmanian Tiger dies
in Hobart Zoo.

2 November
The BBC launches
world's first, regular,
high-definition
television service.

11 December
Edward VIII of England
abdicates his throne,
enabling him to marry
the American divorcee
Wallis Simpson.

Blueshirt Rally, 1935. Irish fascist leader Eoin O'Duffy at a rally of his Blueshirts. To his right is Alfred Byrne, the Lord Mayor of Dublin.

re-election as President of the Executive Council. Cumann na nGaedhael lost ground, dropping nine seats, which was partly due to the presence on the ballot paper of the newly formed Centre Party, led by Frank McDermott and James Dillon.

When the Eighth Dáil met in February 1933, one of the first acts of the new government was to dismiss Garda Commissioner Eoin O'Duffy and replace him with Eamon Broy, Michael Collins' informant in the Dublin Metropolitan Police during the War of Independence. O'Duffy was offered the position of Controller of Prices but rejected it and turned his attention to the development of the ACA.

By July 1933, O'Duffy had become leader of the ACA, changing its name to the National Guard, though they were more popularly known as 'Blueshirts' because of the coloured shirt they adopted as part of their uniform. The uniform and the rhetoric of the Blueshirts led to inevitable comparisons with emerging fascist movements in Italy and Germany; however, support for the organisation was rooted in more parochial matters, such as disquiet among larger farmers at the consequences of the economic war and the ongoing existence of the IRA rather than a widespread enthusiasm for continental fascism.

De Valera's government took a hard line against the increasingly paramilitary Blueshirt movement. Firearm certificates were revoked and personal firearms held by Cumann na nGaedhael TDs were seized by the Gardaí. The move outraged the opposition benches, particularly as the government ignored the arsenal still held by its former comrades in the IRA, with Cumann na nGaedhael's James Fitzgerald-Kenney revealing the fears of many in the party at the suspected influence of the IRA on the new administration when he attacked the Minister for Justice, P.J. Ruttledge:

> Everybody knows that the Minister has his orders and he has obeyed his orders. He has got his orders from the I.R.A. and kindred associations. Of course these persons who have no licences and can carry guns without the slightest bit of interference, these gentlemen who can have revolvers and Thompson guns and fire at a superintendent of the Guards, or anybody else, will not be touched by the Minister. As the President tells us, they are to have their revolvers and their Thompson guns and everything else, provided they do not show them in public ... They simply tell the Minister that they do not care a button about him; that they will carry them without his permission, and down on his knees goes the Minister for Justice.

> *(1 August 1933)*

De Valera, in reply, drew a distinct difference between the IRA and the Blueshirt movement: the Blueshirts he regarded as a real and present threat to the State. His approach to the IRA, however, was noticeably different. It, in his view, needed to be cajoled into accepting the advances republicans could make through the democratic process, and with that achieved the organisation would fade away.

> Our attitude was that as time went on and as it was quite clear that many of the objects for which they were formed were being attained by action such as is being taken by this House, the reason for the I.R.A. would disappear ... My present attitude is that the moment that the Oath was removed, and it was possible for all sections of the people to be freely represented in this House, there was no excuse for anybody trying to use force or arming for the purpose of securing national freedom ... Therefore, it was simply a question

15 March
The first blood bank in the world is established in Chicago.

6 May
The German dirigible *Hindenburg*, the largest airship ever built, bursts into flames upon landing in New Jersey, killing thirty-six passengers and crew members.

13 May
A bronze statue of King George II seated on his horse, which has stood in the centre of St Stephen's Green since 1758, is blown up.

3 June
Wallis Simpson weds the Duke of Windsor, formerly King Edward VIII.

2 July
Pioneer aviator Amelia Earhart and navigator Frederick J. Noonan disappear without a trace in the South Pacific while attempting to fly around the world.

11 July
Composer George
Gershwin dies of a
brain tumor at the age
of thirty-eight.

of time until that truth had penetrated to the minds of all the people in the country, to the minds of the young people and the old people. It was penetrating very rapidly …

(*1 August 1933*)

23 September
The Hobbit, Oxford
University professor
J. R. R. Tolkien's tale
of Middle Earth, is
published.

The fault lines in Irish politics extenuated by the rise of the Blueshirts were formalised later that year when Cumann na nGaedhael and the Centre Party joined with the National Guard to form Fine Gael, with O'Duffy as its leader.

The government maintained its strong line against what it saw as a dangerous paramilitary movement and introduced legislation to ban the wearing of uniforms in public, a measure specifically aimed at the Blueshirts.

4 December
The Dandy, the
world's longest
running comic is
first published.

In introducing the legislation, Minister for Justice P.J. Ruttledge outlined similar measures which had been taken in Norway, Belgium and the Netherlands to counter right–wing organisations. Minister Ruttledge's tour of European legislative initiatives provoked the following outburst from future Taoiseach John A. Costello:

The Minister gave extracts from various laws on the Continent, but he carefully refrained from drawing attention to the fact that the Blackshirts were victorious in Italy and that the Hitler Shirts were victorious in Germany, as, assuredly, in spite of this Bill and in spite of the Public Safety Act, the Blueshirts will be victorious in the Irish Free State.

21 December
The animated motion
picture *Snow White
and the Seven
Dwarfs* premiers.

(*28 February 1934*)

1938

Costello's impetuous prediction was to prove unfounded. Despite serious clashes over the coming months, the Blueshirt movement, and O'Duffy's leadership, would eventually implode. Many within Fine Gael were appalled at O'Duffy's erratic, bombastic and politically naive leadership, and, by September 1934, he was deposed as leader and left Fine Gael only to emerge some years later leading a group of former comrades to fight for Franco in the Spanish Civil War.

3 March
Oil is discovered in
Saudi Arabia.

The Seanad emerged as one of the biggest losers from the government's crusade against the Blueshirts. Ruttledge's legislation banning the wearing of uniforms was rejected by the Seanad, and it was the final straw for de Valera who, the following day, moved to abolish the Upper House. Speaking during the debate, Lemass put the case for abolition bluntly:

16 April
The Carlton Cinema
in Dublin opens its
doors to patrons.

Here is the situation: that we have a House representative of the majority of the people who, according to the Party opposite some years ago, have a right to do anything they damn well like; but it has been unable to do so because, in another institution, set up under the Constitution of this State, the representatives of the minority are exercising a veto. That situation has only arisen since this Government came into office … If there is going to be a dictatorship in consequence of this measure, it will be a dictatorship of the majority of the Irish people. It is about time that the Irish people became masters in this country. This is a Bill to make them masters.

(18 April 1934)

Despite strong resistance to the move, the Seanad was abolished in 1936.

As the turmoil created by the rise of the Blueshirts receded, the economic conditions in the country and the effect of the economic war took centre stage in Dáil proceedings.

In a Dáil debate on the eve of the 1932 general election, de Valera estimated that there were between 60,000 and 80,000 people without work in the Free State. Four years later, official unemployment levels had risen to 130,300.

Emigration remained a permanent feature of Irish life with net migration of over 40,000 people recorded between 1934 and 1936. As the USA had introduced immigration controls following the Depression, the vast majority of Irish emigrants took the boat to Britain, from where, although life was hard, they provided a financial lifeline to those left at home. In March 1934, the Dáil was informed that emigrants' remittances were worth £4 million per year to the economy, ten times more than tourism at the time.

However, the government maintained that the economic war with Britain was not only right in principle but also assisted the country in attaining self-sufficiency. In August 1934, Lemass put forward his views on the fallacy of free trade and the foolishness of concentrating on an export market:

We are maintaining our position because we believe it will be possible at some stage to effect a real settlement of all these matters which will ensure that these problems will never again arise for us. It will help us considerably towards that end if we can succeed in our efforts to reorganise the economic life of this country so as to lessen our dependency on export markets for our prosperity. Surely we have learned in the last five years … that there is no basis for national prosperity in the maintenance of an export trade … there

1 June
Action Comics #1 is released, the first comic book featuring the Superman character created by Joe Shuster and Jerry Siegel.

24 June
A 450 ton (metric) meteorite falls to earth in an empty field near Chickora, Pennsylvania.

30 September
British and French leaders agree to allow Nazi Germany to occupy sections of the Sudeten region of Czechoslovakia. Neville Chamberlain, Prime Minister of Britain, declares there is 'peace in our time'.

22 October
American inventor Chester F. Carlson makes the first Xerox copy.

30 October
Orson Welles stirs nationwide panic with his *War of the Worlds* radio dramatisation.

1939

29 January
W.B. Yeats dies at his home in Mentone on the Cote d'Azur at the age of seventy-three.

2 March
Pope Pius XII succeeds Pope Pius XI to become the 260th pope.

13 April
Seamus Heaney is born near Castledawson, County Derry.

14 April
The Grapes of Wrath by John Steinbeck is published.

22 May
Italy and Germany sign the 'Pact of Steel'.

17 June
In Versailles, France, murderer Eugen Weidmann becomes the last person to be guillotined in public.

is no security based upon an export market and that the only way we can build up prosperity here is by making the home market the basis of our whole economic organisation. We are getting that done.

(10 August 1934)

> " ... the Minister for Industry and Commerce tells us that we are marching with heads erect towards the glorious dawn of Fianna Fáil prosperity. It is not towards the dawn of prosperity that we are marching, but towards the conflagration of ruin ... "

James Dillon, 10 August 1934

Fianna Fáil's economic vision met with condemnation and derision from the opposition benches, especially Fine Gael. Responding to Lemass, James Dillon debunked Fianna Fáil's economic strategy:

The Minister for Industry and Commerce can talk till the cows come home about his highfalutin industrial revival in this country. The hard fact remains, and it is known to every member of the Fianna Fáil Party who lives in rural Ireland, to every trader and to every banker in this country, that the agricultural community are getting progressively poorer and poorer ... the Minister for Industry and Commerce tells us that we are marching with heads erect towards the glorious dawn of Fianna Fáil prosperity. It is not towards the dawn of prosperity that we are marching, but towards the conflagration of ruin ...

(10 August 1934)

72

CREATING IRELAND

In the face of opposition, Fianna Fáil stuck rigidly to its economic plan, utilising all means at its disposal. From May 1934, only companies producing goods in the Free State were allowed to sponsor radio programmes and imports of any product that could be produced in Ireland were banned, with, for example, imports of the popular cereal Shredded Wheat outlawed in July 1935.

The economic war continued until 1938 when eventually an agreement, which included the return of the Treaty ports and a once-off payment of £10 million by Ireland to the British Exchequer, was reached.

Throughout the period, Fianna Fáil's constitutional reform continued unabated, culminating in the introduction of a new constitution in 1937. While the unswerving pursuit of this agenda represented the fulfilment of a core part of the party's agenda and, indeed, its electoral mandate, it also fortuitously deflected political debate from the dire economic and social conditions in the country. So, for instance, parliamentary business in November 1937 was dominated by legislative measures to implement the provisions of the new constitution, a document that cherished the family. Yet, the fact that infant mortality had actually increased in the previous ten years hardly raised a whimper from deputies on either side of the House when the information was provided to Dáil Éireann.

However, there can be no doubt that the introduction of the new constitution, Bunreacht na hÉireann, and its acceptance by the people, albeit rather narrowly, was a significant and lasting achievement for de Valera and his party.

During December 1936, de Valera skilfully seized upon the abdication crisis gripping the British monarchy to remove the king from constitutional provisions related to the internal affairs of the Free State, and, with no Seanad to frustrate the government's plans, the legislation to give effect to this passed in a two-day sitting of Dáil Éireann.

The monarchy conveniently removed, de Valera introduced his draft constitution to Dáil Éireann in May 1937 and effectively established a republic in all but name. Democratic legitimacy was vested solely in the Irish people, the Governor-General was replaced with a directly elected president, a new Seanad, intended to be elected on vocational lines, replaced the defunct Free State Seanad, and the ambitions of Irish nationalism were given full voice through Articles 2 and 3 of the constitution which established a territorial claim to Northern Ireland.

De Valera introduced his constitution in relatively low-key fashion, and, while his Dáil speech lasted for more than two hours, a large proportion of which was in Irish, he made no historic claims for the document, preferring instead to portray

28 June
Pan American Airways debuts the first regular transatlantic air service, flying from New York to Lisbon, Portugal, and Marseilles, France.

15 August
The film version of *The Wizard of Oz*, starring Judy Garland as Dorothy, has its premiere in Hollywood, California.

1 September
Nazi Germany begins the Second World War by invading Poland. The invasion will lead Britain and France to declare war on Germany two days later.

14 September
After many years of experimentation, Russian-born aircraft designer Igor Sikorsky flies his first successful helicopter, the VS-300.

it as a sensible, rational approach given the extensive constitutional change of previous years:

> No people more than the Opposition were so insistent in saying that the present position leaves the Government with tremendous powers and without check, and that, in the interests of the community as a whole, it would be better not to leave them these unreasonable powers. Therefore, it is that the Constitution is necessary. It is necessary also from the point of view of bringing to completion that series of step-by-step changes which, taken as a whole, have left the old Constitution a tattered and torn affair. The Draft Constitution is, therefore, necessary. The aim has been, if possible, to present the Dáil with a Draft which would be likely to get the greatest possible amount of support.
>
> (*11 May 1937*)

In framing his constitution, de Valera had consulted senior figures in the Catholic Church, and the Constitution reflected this contribution, with the special status of the Catholic Church recognised and divorce explicitly banned.

Article 41 of the Constitution gave the role of the traditional family constitutional status, acknowledged the work of women within the home and committed the State to endeavour to ensure that mothers shall not be obliged by economic necessity to engage in labour to the neglect of their duties in the home.

This latter provision, and the paternalistic attitude to women it sought to exalt, provoked some of the strongest criticism of Bunreacht na hÉireann, criticism which de Valera found difficult to comprehend:

> Let us consider this whole question of women's rights. I seem to have got a bad reputation. I do not think I deserve it. I myself was not conscious at any time of having deserved all those terrible things that I am told I am where women's rights are concerned … This Constitution has been attacked on the ground that it is taking away women's rights. What it is doing where women are concerned is that, where their rights are, they are equal. Therefore, where they are referred to here, they are referred to by way of protection and the protection which the State is bound to give. We say, therefore, that the inadequate strength of women or the tender age of children should not be abused … What is wrong about that, I should like to know?
>
> (*11 May 1937*)

---

10 February
In Dublin, a roller-skate rink is opened on Duke Street.

29 February
Gone With the Wind one of the biggest production events in film history, wins eight Oscars at the Academy Awards ceremony.

10 May
British prime minister Neville Chamberlain resigns at the request of King George VI, and Winston Churchill agrees to take over as prime minister.

14 June
German troops enter Paris.

10 July
The Battle of Britain, which lasts 114 days, begins.

There was no shortage of feminist voices eager to tell de Valera in no uncertain terms what was wrong about it, although most of the opposition was voiced outside the Dáil by, among others, the trade unionist Louie Bennett. Even the historian and ardent de Valera supporter Dorothy McCardle communicated her disappointment with the provision to its chief architect.

Criticism in the Dáil was more muted, however. When the draft constitution was introduced in May 1937, there were only three women TDs in Dáil Éireann. Helena Concannon, the sole female Fianna Fáil TD to contribute to the debate on the Constitution, was entirely supportive of de Valera's views on women in the home, declaring:

> I sincerely hope that not a comma of this noble declaration will be altered. I think it is due to women who have so bravely carried on the battle for civilisation, and who have had to bear the hardest part, that the State should give them this recognition. Do we not all know that the price of each human life is some woman's agony? Do we not know that the rearing of each child is purchased at the cost of some woman's sleepless nights and hardworking days, and are we not all aware of the life of sacrifice that each woman has to experience to launch her family on the world …
>
> It is to Irish mothers and Irish homes that we owe the fact that we have won, to the extent to which we have won it, success in the long fight we have had for our faith and nationality, and I am very glad that Article 41 has recognised the services of women in the home.
>
> (*12 May 1937*)

In addition to reflecting a distinctly Catholic ethos, the Constitution was unreservedly nationalist. The territorial claim in Articles 2 and 3 gave constitutional status to Irish nationalist aspirations to unity. Opposition to partition and demands for unity were an article of faith for Fianna Fáil members in particular. However, Frank McDermott, former leader of the Centre Party, rejected the jingoism of much nationalist rhetoric and proposed a different vision of Irish unity which, while it fell on deaf ears in 1937, would find a resonance decades later.

> Now I come to the question which interests me most, and that is the question of the unity of Ireland … It is not of course that any legislation here could immediately solve the problem of partition; that problem can only be solved

20 August
Exiled Soviet revolutionary Leon Trotsky is assassinated in Mexico City by a Spanish Communist, under the orders of Soviet leader Joseph Stalin.

7 September
The blitz begins. The Luftwaffe starts to bomb London – the bombing will continue for fifty-seven consecutive nights.

12 September
Four French teenagers, following their dog into an underground cavern near Lascaux in France, discover 17,000-year old cave paintings made by Stone Age artists.

1941

10 January
The artist Sir John Lavery dies in Kilkenny aged eighty-four.

13 January
James Joyce,
Ireland's most
controversial novelist,
dies of peritonitis at
his home in Zurich.
He was fifty-one.

14 January
Dr McQuaid is made
Archbishop of Dublin.

1 May
Citizen Kane, starring
and directed by Orson
Welles, premieres in
New York. It will be
hailed as one of the
greatest films of
all time.

1 May
In America, General
Mills' breakfast cereal
Cheerios goes on sale
as CheeriOats.

10 May
Rudolf Hess, Hitler's
deputy, parachutes
into Scotland
claiming to be on a
peace mission.

by inducing the Northern Unionists to give their first allegiance to Ireland—to put the peace, dignity and happiness of Ireland before any other loyalty. For this to be possible, we have got to offer them an Ireland in which a place can be found for their traditions and aspirations as well as for ours. Until we are willing to do this we are partitionists at heart, no matter how loudly we shout about unity … partition can only be cured when we attain some unity of heart and mind, when we are able to gather up conflicting traditions and aspirations and fuse them into one national life …

We ought to remember that there are about 1,000,000 of our people, with so many generations behind them that it is absurd to call them invaders and intruders, who have got to be conciliated if this nation is to grow to its full stature. We ought to remember the long agony of Irish history—an agony not wholly due to wrongful oppression but also in part to tragic misunderstandings, prejudices and inability to compromise … It is we who seek unity and it is on us that the burden lies of showing vision, kindliness and courage. It is because we stand at a turning point and these proposals invite us to take the wrong turning that I ask the House to reject them.

(11 May 1937)

De Valera's entire constitutional project also came in for criticism from the opposition benches, many of whom viewed the exercise as an attempt to deflect attention from the consequences of the economic war, with James Dillon stating in his own inimitable style:

We are expected, in that state of affairs, to work ourselves up to enthusiasm over a new Constitution … Is there any common sense left in this House at all?

Surely our first charge, as the temporal Government of this country, is the happiness of our own people. Everything we do here is contributing to their unhappiness and to their undoing, and the compensation we offer them is a Constitution. Surely we ought to wake up to some sense of reality … This Constitution can do nothing whatever towards that end … That is why this Constitution disgusts me. It is as irrelevant as a nursery rhyme, and it revolts me that, in the condition of our people, the mind of the country and the mind of this House should be thrust by this Government under a grotesquely irrelevant Constitution, while the people are perishing on the land.

(12 May 1937)

"We are expected, in that state of affairs, to work ourselves up to enthusiasm over a new Constitution ... Is there any common sense left in this House at all? Surely our first charge, as the temporal Government of this country, is the happiness of our own people. Everything we do here is contributing to their unhappiness and to their undoing, and the compensation we offer them is a Constitution."

James Dillon, 12 May 1937

24 May
HMS *Hood* is sunk
by the German
battleship *Bismarck*,
only three of the
1,418 crew survive.
Three days later, the
Bismarck is sunk
with the loss of all
2,300 lives.

2 June
The Second World
War comes to Dublin
when bombs fall on
the North Strand,
killing thirty people
and destroying
many houses.

3 July
After the German
invasion of Russia,
Stalin calls on
Russians to follow
a 'scorched
earth' policy.

6 September
The Nazis' legislation
requiring all Jews
to wear the Star
of David with the
word 'Jew' inscribed,
is extended to all
Jews over the age
of six in German-
occupied areas.

Despite the opposition in Dáil Éireann, the majority of people did not agree with Dillon that Bunreacht na hÉireann was 'grotesquely irrelevant', and the Constitution was narrowly accepted in referendum held on 1 July 1937.

De Valera called a general election to coincide with the referendum, and Fianna Fáil was returned to office; however, the party's hopes of an overall majority were thwarted, and the government had to rely once again on Labour support, much as in 1932.

Frustrated by this state of affairs, de Valera called a snap election eleven months later in June 1938 after losing a parliamentary vote in relation to civil service reform. The result of the election was a decisive victory for Fianna Fáil. De Valera, having just concluded an agreement with Britain which brought an end to the economic war and resulted in the return of the Treaty ports, was at the height of his popularity, and the party achieved more than 50 per cent of the popular vote and enjoyed a comfortable overall majority in the Tenth Dáil.

Accepting the nomination for Taoiseach following the 1938 election, de Valera could reflect on a remarkable political achievement. Not only had he succeeded in bringing the majority of republicans into constitutional politics, but they now reigned supreme. The hated constitutional provisions of the Treaty were effectively dismantled and replaced by a Constitution which was republican in both ethos and outlook. Fianna Fáil had developed into the most potent force in Irish politics, with a loyal base in every community dedicated to the party founded by de Valera just twelve years earlier.

However, following the 1938 election, the energy and initiative which characterised the first years of Fianna Fáil in government declined and were replaced by a conservative, insular philosophy, which, while always present in Fianna Fáil, had now gained the upper hand. This development was, of course, hastened by the darkening clouds on the Continent as Europe headed towards war.

Politics until the late 1930s was dominated by domestic concerns and the country's relationship with Great Britain. While Ireland was always an active participant in the League of Nations, international issues rarely featured prominently in parliamentary debate. However, even the largely rural, impoverished and conservative state at the far edge of Europe couldn't escape the dramatic and portentous developments occurring on the Continent.

The first international issue to merit significant debate in Dáil Éireann was the Spanish Civil War. In July 1936, a right-wing group of army officers, including General Franco, staged a *coup d'état* against the republican government elected earlier that year, beginning a bloody civil war that eventually saw Franco and his nationalist colleagues emerge victorious in April 1939.

Following the events of July, the nationalists established a rival government, which was quickly recognised by the fascist regimes in Italy and Germany.

In Ireland, propaganda from Nationalist Spain, and, in particular, accounts of republican attacks on the Catholic Church, helped to engender sympathy for Franco's cause, with more than 30,000 people attending a pro-Franco meeting organised by the Irish Christian Front in Dublin's College Green in October 1936.

In the Dáil, Fine Gael reflected this popular feeling, with Cosgrave and Dillon pressing the government to recognise Franco's regime as early as November 1936 and urging de Valera to give moral backing to its war against the godless Communists on the republican side.

De Valera, to his credit, resisted this pressure and adhered doggedly to the policy of non-intervention, an approach adopted by many European states from the outset of the conflict, with the government introducing legislation to this effect in February 1937 when de Valera told the Dáil:

> I am anxious that we should play our part in trying to shorten this conflict in Spain by preventing the export of arms to the combatants and also by preventing recruitment for the various sides who are fighting out in Spain— a fight which for most of them, at any rate, is not the sort of fight that we think it is, but is a fight for one "ism" against another.

> (*18 February 1937*)

The legislation provoked uproar on the Fine Gael benches in particular, with Dublin TD and leading member of the Irish Christian Front, Paddy Belton Snr condemning de Valera's stance on the issue:

> There is no use in the President coming into this House and saying:"Everybody knows on what side Irish sympathy is." He has not expressed that. Well, I am going to express it, and I challenge contradiction on it: 99.9 per cent of the Irish people stand for the recognition of General Franco, and there should be no equivocation about it … There is no need to paint the lily any further. Full proofs have been adduced here as to the real issues in the Spanish conflict … They have all indicated that this is a war between Christ and anti-Christ in Spain, and I do not think anybody here will attempt to deny that … I urge that the President should accept my amendment and that we should recognise the Franco Government. It is not asking much. It is only asking our Government

26 November
In America, President Roosevelt signs a bill finally establishing the fourth Thursday in November as Thanksgiving Day.

7 December
The Japanese bomb Pearl Harbor in Hawaii.

1942

1 January
Twenty-six nations sign the United Nations declaration.

6 January
The first round-the-world commercial flight is completed by Pan American Airways.

4 June
The Battle of the Midway begins in the Pacific between America and Japan.

9 July
Anne Frank's family
goes into hiding in
an attic above her
father's office in
an Amsterdam
warehouse.

to do what the people of this country want it to do, and to recognise the reign of Christianity against the reign of anti-Christianity …

(*19 February 1937*)

De Valera eventually recognised Franco's government in February 1939, as the republican resistance in Spain collapsed.

31 July
Canon Theodore
Milford founds the
Oxford Committee of
Famine Relief
(OXFAM) with the aim
of relieving the
famine in Greece
caused by the Allied
naval blockades.

TDs' fear of an even bloodier conflict erupting throughout the rest of Europe is evident in Dáil business from late 1938. Nearly a year before the outbreak of the Second World War in September 1939, William Norton questioned the steps taken by the government to protect the population from air raids.

As the threat of war loomed, there was considerable concern in both Britain and Ireland about the potential threat represented by the IRA.

Fianna Fáil's benign attitude towards the IRA had ended some years earlier, with the organisation being proscribed in 1936. The introduction of the Offences Against the State Act in June 1939 ensured that de Valera had overwhelming legal power to pursue any organisation intent on undermining the authority of the State, particularly the IRA, which initiated a bombing campaign in Britain in 1939 and, in the government's view, threatened Ireland's neutral status.

During the following years, de Valera would not hesitate to exercise these powers against the IRA and, within a year of war breaking out, 462 people were interned without trial, the vast majority of them IRA members.

By the end of the Second World War, the government had sanctioned the execution of six IRA prisoners, and another three IRA men had died on hunger strike. For a party that still excoriated Fine Gael for the state executions of IRA members in the Civil War era, it was a remarkable, and at times painful, transition for Fianna Fáil.

2 October
The British cruiser
Curaçao collides with
the liner *Queen Mary*
off the Donegal
coast and sinks, 338
people drown.

De Valera's government stuck rigidly to its internment policy. Replying to William Norton, who raised the plight of republican hunger strikers in 1943, Minister for Justice Gerald Boland wouldn't countenance compromise, and some of his comments are more akin to those of the Thatcher government faced with a similar crisis forty years later rather than that of a republican Minister for Justice.

2 December
Italian physicist
Enrico Fermi
produces the first
nuclear chain
reaction at the
University of Chicago.

I do regret that any man should die on hunger strike, but I will not take the responsibility. The responsibility is on themselves. They have been offered their food. They can get their liberty on the same terms as everybody else … the Government is determined that they will be held until they are prepared to do so … if there is any sign that these people are prepared to obey the law of the

State that will be accepted and they will be released, but that is the position.

I am very sorry to have to say that if any of these men are prepared to die on hunger strike, I cannot help it. I very much regret it, but there is no way out that I can see, and I cannot see what else we are to do.

(7 July 1943)

"Back in February last I stated in a very definite way that it was the aim of Government policy, in case of a European war, to keep this country, if at all possible, out of it."

Eamon de Valera, 2 September 1939

De Valera adopted his hardline stance against the IRA because of the threat that organisation posed to Ireland's neutrality. De Valera's determination to keep Ireland out of the impending war had been clearly signalled in the months leading up to it. Following Hitler's invasion of Poland and the declaration of war, the Dáil was recalled on 2 September and a State of Emergency declared, giving rise to the Second World War being referred to as 'the Emergency' in Ireland. De Valera outlined his policy of neutrality to the Dáil:

> Back in February last I stated in a very definite way that it was the aim of Government policy, in case of a European war, to keep this country, if at all possible, out of it. We have pursued that policy, and we intend to pursue it … It is not, as some people appear to think, sufficient for us to indicate our attitude, or to express the desire of our people. It is necessary at every step to protect our own interests in that regard, to avoid giving to any of the belligerents any due cause, and proper cause, of complaint.

(2 September 1939)

23 February
In County Cavan, a fire breaks out at St Joseph's Orphanage, killing thirty-five children and one adult.

4 March
A wall enclosing Waterford Jail collapses onto a row of terraced houses, killing nine people.

19 April
Swiss chemist Albert Hofmann self-administers the drug LSD for the first time in history, and records the details of his trip.

16 May
RAF 617 Squadron begin the Dambuster Raids on German dams.

2 August
A Japanese destroyer rams a US Navy PT boat commanded by John F. Kennedy. Kennedy and the other survivors swim for hours to a nearby island and are rescued four days later.

8 September
General Dwight D.
Eisenhower
announces the
surrender of Italy
to the Allies.

1944

25 January
Clery's opens its
new ballroom which
covers the entire
upper part of the
O'Connell Street
building.

27 January
More than two years
after it began, Soviet
forces finally lift the
siege of Leningrad.

2 March
Casablanca wins the
Best Picture Oscar
at the sixteenth
Academy Awards.

10 March
In Britain an
Education Act lifts
the ban on women
teachers marrying.

The State of Emergency and the accompanying Emergency Powers Act gave sweeping control to the government over all aspects of economic, security and communications policy.

A strict censorship regime was introduced so that news of the war and of conditions in Ireland could be controlled by the government. So severe was the regime that reports of Dáil debates, the contents of Catholic bishops' pastoral letters and death notices became victims of the censors' blue pen in the following years. Even an edition of the popular, and far from subversive, publication *Old Moore's Almanac* was seized from newsagents in 1943.

The Emergency Powers Act also gave enormous economic control to the government. Orders introduced under the measure included initiatives to impose a wage freeze, introduce rationing and control the import and export of a variety of goods. To boost the food supply, farmers were required to increase the amount, of cereals grown on their land.

Despite Ireland's neutral status, many Irish people gave their lives in the conflict. It is estimated that more than 45,000 Irish people served in the British army in the Second World War, and dozens of Irish seafarers lost their lives trying to keep trade routes open. Thousands more emigrated to Britain to work in war industries. In the twelve-month period up to September 1942, for example, the Irish government issued 50,821 travel permits to people taking up work in Britain, with women taking up 12,406 of them.

Many of those who emigrated did so to escape the poverty and hardship in Ireland during the Emergency. By February 1940, more than 117,000 people were on the live register, industrial output had dropped, and rationing would soon be a feature of everyday life.

The management of the economy during the Emergency was largely driven by Seán Lemass, who had been made Minister of Supplies at the outbreak of the war and endeavoured to ensure that essential supplies were available, despite the crisis which gripped Britain, the country's largest source of imports.

Enormous efforts were also made to utilise natural resources. As coal imports from Britain were drastically reduced, a major drive to increase turf production was embarked upon. Efforts to increase tillage were less successful but, on a smaller scale, a campaign to get homeowners to plant gardens and allotments had some impact and engendered a spirit of cooperation among many communities. The deer population of the Phoenix Park barely survived this drive for self-sufficiency, with the government sanctioning the culling of the herd, which stood at approximately 800 in 1942, leaving just forty or fifty deer which, thankfully, managed to recover in subsequent years.

For de Valera, the restrictions on international trade only served to confirm the probity of Fianna Fáil's self-sufficency policies of previous years:

> The policy which the Government have pursued in regard to our whole economic life is undoubtedly of great assistance at the moment. But we still have a good distance to go before we would arrive at such a degree of self-containedness that a war like the present one would not strike us badly. We have gone, as I have indicated already, a very great distance. It is a source of satisfaction to us to find at the present time that we have gone that distance, because going the distance we have gone is going to relieve us from many difficulties which we would otherwise have to face.
>
> *(27 September 1939)*

However, for Fine Gael, the urgent necessity to source essential imports, a key task for Lemass in his new position, only served to dispel Fianna Fáil's self-sufficiency myth, with James Dillon remarking:

> Has it ever occurred to them that the Chancellor of the German Reich has provided Fianna Fáil with that one thing which during the past seven years they have been professing to seek under the leadership of the Taoiseach? Fianna Fáil had not been able to get that one thing in a period of over seven years. But the Chancellor of the German Reich got for them self-sufficiency in a fortnight. And they do not like it. The Fianna Fáil Party has been crying out for self-sufficiency for more than seven weary years. We, on this side of the House, have been telling them that they could not get it, or that when they got it they would not like it. Now somebody else has got it for them and the welkin rings with their lamentations.
>
> *(27 September 1939)*

Despite these occasional disagreements, in general Fine Gael was supportive of the government during the Emergency, with Cosgrave in particular refusing to score party political points given the crisis that faced the country. Fine Gael objected to some of the emergency powers introduced, particularly as they affected the farming community, but never publicly raised a principled objection to the government's policy of neutrality or the more draconian security measures imposed at the time.

18 March
Mount Vesuvius in Italy erupts, killing twenty-six people and causing thousands others to flee their homes.

19 May
Germany's defence line in Italy collapses.

1 June
The BBC transmits a coded message (the first line of a poem by Paul Verlaine) to French Resistance fighters warning that the invasion of Europe is imminent.

6 June
In the largest seaborne invasion in history, known as D-Day, more than 120,000 Allied troops land on the beaches of Normandy in German-occupied northern France.

1 August
The Polish Underground Army begins battle to liberate Warsaw.

The eighteen months from the beginning of 1940 to the Nazi invasion of the Soviet Union in June 1941 was the most tense period for Ireland during the Second World War, where the threat of attack or invasion was most heightened. Plans to evacuate more than 150,000 women and children from Dublin in the event of aerial bombing were put in place.

As the situation grew increasingly tense, de Valera addressed the Dáil, proposing the establishment of a cross-party committee to meet on security matters, and urged unity among Dáil parties:

> We must all be brothers in one holy cause, and no voice of dissension should be heard amongst us. The liberties of which we in this Parliament are the trustees have been dearly bought. Let there not be found in this land anywhere one treacherous hand to give them away. We are a small people, but if we are true to ourselves, and courageously defend our rights, with God's help we shall survive the present dangers as we and our fathers survived no less grievous ones in the past.
>
> *(28 May 1940)*

Cosgrave responded for Fine Gael, pledging support for the government in the national interest:

> Fine Gael is alive to the dangers of our present situation … On certain matters united national action is now essential. It is obviously the duty of a Government with a majority support in Parliament to decide the way in which that united national action can best be brought about … We regard the national security as the supreme interest worth considering at the moment; and will withhold no assistance which we can give or can influence others to give … A situation of national danger is upon us … Fine Gael responds to that desire and is prepared to do its part.
>
> *(28 May 1940)*

The fear that Ireland would be attacked reached its height in November 1940, when Churchill made a speech deploring the Irish government for denying the Allies' use of the Treaty ports. De Valera addressed the Dáil following Churchill's speech and stoutly defended his policy of neutrality:

> We have chosen the policy of neutrality in this war because we believed that

4 August
In Amsterdam, Nazi officers arrest fifteen-year-old diarist Anne Frank and four other Jews in the annex where they have been hiding for two years. Frank will die in the Belsen concentration camp in 1945.

25 August
American troops, along with Free French and French Resistance forces, liberate Paris from German occupation.

1945

28 January
The Soviet army marches into the Nazi concentration camp Auschwitz, liberating about 7,600 prisoners abandoned there.

4 February
The Yalta Conference convenes with Roosevelt, Churchill and Stalin to formulate Allied military strategy in for the remainder of the war.

Dillon Wins, 10 July 1943. James Dillon is congratulated on his election as an Independent at Monaghan. The photograph was originally published in America in an article entitled 'Neutral Eire Returns One Supporter of the Allied Nations'

it was the right policy for our people. It is the policy which has been accepted, not merely by this House, but by our people as a whole, and nobody who realises what modern war means, and what it means particularly for those who have not sufficient air defences, will have the slightest doubt that that policy was the right one, apart altogether from any questions of sympathy on one side or the other …

There can be no question of the handing over of these ports so long as this State remains neutral. There can be no question of leasing these ports. They are ours. They are within our sovereignty, and there can be no question, as long as we remain neutral, of handing them over on any condition whatsoever.

(*7 November 1944*)

Labour, while supporting neutrality, adopted a vigorous approach to parliamentary business. It continued to harry the government over high rates of unemployment,

14 February
British and US bombers pound the ancient German city of Dresden with high explosives and incendiaries.

19 February
US Marines storm the island of Iwo Jima. Nearly 60,000 Marines went ashore the eight-square-mile volcanic island.

9 March
American B-52 bombers attack Tokyo, Japan, killing 100,000 citizens.

18 March
1,250 American bombers attack Berlin.

12 April
President Franklin D. Roosevelt, recently elected to a record fourth term in office, dies of a cerebral haemorrhage. Vice president Harry Truman is sworn in as president.

20 April
The League of Nations formally ceases to exist.

28 April
Benito Mussolini, Italian fascist dictator, is shot by the Italian Resistance in Dongo, Italy. His mistress, Clara Petacci and members of his entourage are also shot.

wage freezes, rising prices and the operation of the censorship regime. Labour objected to the continuation of the Emergency Powers Act as early as 1941, and its aggressive opposition strategy was to pay dividends at the 1943 general election when the party nearly doubled its representation in Dáil Éireann.

The one voice in Dáil Éireann to object to neutrality was that of Fine Gael's James Dillon. Dillon argued passionately for the Allied cause, telling the Dáil in 1942:

> I would give them all we had to help them in that fight, in every sense of the word, in the profound conviction that it is a fight for the survival of Ireland, as well as a fight for the survival of every free people in the world; in the profound conviction that it is a fight for the survival of the right of every man to render unto God the things that are God's and unto Caesar the things that are Caesar's. But I cannot control foreign policy in this country.
>
> (*12 May 1942*)

Dillon's views on the war and the moral duty to join the Allies resulted in his departure from Fine Gael in 1942. For the next decade, he would sit in Dáil Éireann as an Independent TD, before rejoining the party in 1953.

De Valera dissolved the Dáil in May 1943, and a general election was held in June. The election saw the entry of a new party, Clann na Talmhan, into Dáil Éireann. The party, largely based in the west of Ireland, was established to represent the interests of small farmers, accusing Fianna Fáil of abandoning this core constituency, a message that resonated with many and resulted in the party winning thirteen seats. The Labour Party also managed to gain considerable ground, winning an additional eight seats and returning with seventeen TDs.

Fianna Fáil, whose harsh wartime policies had managed to disaffect many supporters, lost six seats in the election; however, the biggest loser in the face of Labour and Clann na Talmhan gains was Fine Gael. The party lost significant support and entered the eleventh Dáil with just thirty-two TDs.

For the previous decade, following the demise of the Farmers' Party and the decision of the Centre Party to merge with others to form Fine Gael, only three parties, Fianna Fáil, Fine Gael and Labour had gained representation in Dáil Éireann, and the Labour Party had languished throughout this period. Now a revitalised Labour Party and the breakthrough of Clann na Talmhan produced a new dynamic in the parliament.

Fianna Fáil, frustrated again at having failed to secure an overall majority, dismissed any suggestion of entering a coalition government, with Lemass stating during the debate on the nomination of the Taoiseach:

> We do not believe in coalition governments … We think that in any circumstances they are a bad system of government and we consider that in present circumstances in this country a coalition government would be a source of weakness and perhaps even a source of danger. In abnormal conditions, democracy may be forced to work through coalition governments, but those who desire the preservation of democracy and the proper functioning of democratic institutions of government will endeavour to avoid the establishment of coalitions and endeavour to end them as quickly as possible. That is our view.
>
> (*1 July 1943*)

"We do not believe in coalition governments. We think they are a bad system of government."

Sean Lemass, 1 July 1943

This core principle of the Fianna Fáil party would last until 1989 when Charles Haughey was forced to share power with his nemesis and founder of the Progressive Democrats, Des O'Malley.

Both Labour and Clann na Talmhan abstained on the vote for Taoiseach, and de Valera was re-elected. However, the result of the election irked Fianna Fáil, and the first questions about changing the electoral system and replacing the proportional representation method began to arise, a measure that Fianna Fáil would unsuccessful try to introduce twice in future years.

One of the new TDs elected in 1943 was Oliver J. Flanagan. He was elected in the

30 April
German dictator Adolf Hitler marries Eva Braun in a Berlin bunker. The following day they commit suicide.

8 May
VE Day, marking the end European phase of the Second World War, is celebrated after Nazi forces surrender unconditionally to US General Dwight D. Eisenhower's army in Reims, France.

1 July
Germany is divided between the Allied occupation forces.

26 July
A landslide victory for the opposition Labour Party in the British elections near the end of the Second World War forces prime minister Winston Churchill to resign. He is succeeded by Clement Attlee.

28 July
A B-25 bomber, lost
in low clouds, crashes
into the seventy-ninth
floor of the Empire
State Building, killing
fourteen people.

Laois–Offaly constituency on a monetary reform ticket at the age of twenty-three.

Flanagan would later join Fine Gael and remain a TD for forty-three years, but his early career was marked by an outspoken republicanism and a strong anti-Semitic sentiment, an early contribution to the Dáil revealing both strands:

> I am very sorry that I cannot associate myself with this Bill or with anything relating to the public safety measures introduced by the Cumann na nGaedheal Government or by the present Fianna Fáil Government because I have seen that most of these Emergency Acts were always directed against Republicanism. How is it that we do not see any of these Acts directed against the Jews, who crucified Our Saviour nineteen hundred years ago, and who are crucifying us every day in the week? How is it that we do not see them directed against the Masonic Order? How is it that the I.R.A. is considered an illegal organisation while the Masonic Order is not considered an illegal organization ... There is one thing that Germany did, and that was to rout the Jews out of their country. Until we rout the Jews out of this country it does not matter a hair's breadth what orders you make. Where the bees are there is the honey, and where the Jews are there is the money. I do not propose to detain the House further. I propose to vote against such Orders and actions, and I am doing so on Christian principles.
>
> *(9 July 1943)*

6 August
The American
bomber *Enola Gay*
drops an atomic
bomb on Hiroshima
in Japan, destroying
a majority of the city
and killing 60,000 to
70,000 inhabitants,
according to
American estimates.

14 August
US president
Harry S. Truman
announces the
surrender of Japan,
which ends the
Second World War.

The Eleventh Dáil elected in 1943 would be short-lived and was relatively unremarkable. The most notable act was the introduction of legislation to provide for children's allowances for large-sized families.

De Valera, annoyed at the minority status of his government, availed of the earliest opportunity to seek a dissolution of the Dáil in May 1944, following a government defeat on transport legislation. The opposition parties were outraged at de Valera's action, which was judged to be based on little more than his desire to secure an overall majority, with William Norton perhaps providing the most trenchant criticism of de Valera's rush to seek a dissolution from President Douglas Hyde:

16 September
Count John
McCormack, the
world-famous tenor,
dies of pneumonia at
his home in Dublin.

7 December
The microwave oven
is patented.

> He was like an uncaged political bear last night anxious to make sure that the House would suffer the peculiar form of wrath which the Taoiseach is capable of venting on people who do anything to disturb his equanimity in political matters. We find the Taoiseach engaged in a midnight ride to the Park, arriving

there about midnight, as a political marauder, beseeching the President to dissolve the Dáil, not because the Dáil wanted to be dissolved or the people wanted a new election, but because the Taoiseach was in a temper, a temper no thermometer could measure. When the Taoiseach is in that peculiar temper, every opponent must be squashed ... High treason was committed in the Park last night. We find the Taoiseach arriving in the darkness of the night in the house of an aged man whom everyone knows to be in anything but a perfect state of health.

(*10 May 1944*)

Despite the opposition to the calling of the election, it proved to be a master stoke by de Valera, with Fianna Fáil regaining nearly all the seats lost the previous year and delivering the party an overall majority.

Fianna Fáil's success was partly due to the disarray in the opposition ranks. The previous January, W.T. Cosgrave had resigned as leader of Fine Gael; the main opposition party's new leader, Richard Mulcahy, sat in the Seanad, having lost his Dáil seat in the 1943 election; Thomas F. O'Higgins, a brother of Kevin O'Higgins, the Minister for Home Affairs assassinated in 1927, led Fine Gael's parliamentary party in the Dáil.

Internal divisions in the labour movement, caused chiefly by the long-running animosity between 'Big Jim' Larkin and Transport Union chief William O'Brien, resulted in a split in the party in advance of the general election, with TDs associated with the Transport Union forming a new party, National Labour, led by James Everett. Both factions competed against each other at the election, succeeding only in wiping out most of the gains made in 1943 with Labour returning just eight TDs and National Labour securing four seats. The split would endure until 1950.

De Valera's government, now with a secure overall majority, would continue to govern the country throughout the remainder of the Emergency until the general election of 1948.

The end of the war eventually led to the expiration of the Emergency Powers Act; however, de Valera didn't declare an end to the declared State of Emergency which would continue in existence until 1976, when it was eventually ended by Taoiseach Liam Cosgrave, only to be replaced with a similar declaration related to ongoing violence in Northern Ireland at the time.

Following the end of the Second World War, the government, and Lemass in particular, brought forward some significant legislation, such as the establishment of

1946

3 January
William Joyce, aka Lord Haw Haw, Nazi propagandist, is hanged for treason in London.

29 January
It is announced that national parks are to be established in Killarney, north Donegal, the Curragh, the Wicklow Mountains, the Clare coast, Achill Island and the Dingle Peninsula.

1947

8 February
In rugby, Ireland beats England 22–0 at Lansdowne Road.

5 June
US secretary of state George C. Marshall calls for the United States to fund a European Recovery Program (the Marshall Plan) to help European countries recover from the war.

Sean Lemass, re-elected, 10 July 1943. Sean Lemass addresses a crowd in Dublin after being elected.

15 August
Indian independence from Britain is proclaimed, with the former colony partitioned into the two nations of India and Pakistan.

duty-free status at Shannon Airport. Lemass also brought an end to wage freezes, reformed industrial relations practices and established the Labour Court in this period.

However, despite these initiatives, not all was well for the government. Its continuing draconian policy against IRA prisoners, which had seen the execution of its Chief-of-Staff Charlie Kerins on 1 December 1944 and the death on hunger strike of Seán McCaughey on 11 May 1946, created widespread public revulsion.

The degree to which many of those of a republican mindset had lost faith in Fianna Fáil was revealed in the first presidential election in June 1945. Although Fianna Fáil stalwart Seán T. O'Kelly emerged victorious, Dr Patrick McCartan, an independent republican candidate who was appointed the First Dáil's representative to Washington, won nearly 20 per cent of the vote.

The post-war years also witnessed significant labour unrest, and a seven-month strike by national teachers in 1946 undermined support for Fianna Fáil among a profession which had, up until then, given it overwhelming support.

The ending of the war brought little reduction in the hardship experienced during the Emergency: rationing continued, unemployment remained high, and emigration to find work in post-war reconstruction in Britain was the only option for thousands of Irish citizens.

In addition to these woes, allegations of financial impropriety were made against the members of the government, with tribunals established to get to the bottom of the claims. Two tribunals, one into the failed attempt to purchase Locke's Distillery in Kilbeggan by a group of shady foreign businessmen and another into fraud allegations against prominent Fianna Fáil politician Dr Con Ward, managed to take the shine off Fianna Fáil's aesthetic image. Interestingly, unlike latter tribunals of inquiry, both tribunals took about a month to complete their investigations and issue a report. Following the report of the tribunal into the allegations against Ward, de Valera demanded his resignation and established a standard for Fianna Fáil members in office, a standard that would be breached by some prominent members time and again in later years.

> The public interest demands that the highest standard of conduct be maintained by those who occupy positions of trust and responsibility in Governmental administration. The punishment for any failure to maintain this standard is necessarily severe.
>
> (16 July 1946)

The Dáil sat for the final time on 10 December 1947, and a general election was held on 4 February 1948. That election would mark the end to sixteen years of unbroken Fianna Fáil rule and bring to office Ireland's first coalition government.

14 September
The first All-Ireland football final to be held outside Ireland takes place in New York. Cavan are the winners against Kerry.

1948

15 January
Gas rationing ends in Dublin. Gas will be available twenty-four hours a day for the first time in six years.

30 January
Mahatma Ghandi is shot and killed as he walks in the grounds of his house in New Dehli.

15 March
In rugby, Ireland wins the Grand Slam for the first time with a 6–3 win over Wales in Belfast.

The Irish Times
ELECTION RESULTS

FIANNA FAIL	OTHER PARTIES
95	95
90	90
85	85
80	80
75	75
70	70
65	65
60	60
55	55
50	50
45	45
40	40
35	35
30	30
25	25
20	20
15	15
10	10
5	5

KEAN & COMPY CHARTERED ACCOUNTANTS

RYAN TROY & Co CHARTERED ACCOUNTANTS

ELECTION RESULTS: STATE OF PARTIES at 1 45

FIANNA FAIL	FINE GAEL	LABOUR	NATIONAL LABOUR	CLANN NA POBLACHTA	INDEPENDENTS	CLANN NA TALMHAN
53	24	11	2	7	7	7

SUMMARY **FIANNA FAIL 53   ALL OTHERS 58**

See to-morrows IRISH TIMES for latest results

The Irish Times.

The Irish T

M & Co PHARMACISTS

CHEMIST

Breaking news, 1948.
Latest election results are
posted at the Irish Times Building.

1948-1956

Turmoil and Torpor

'I have often heard talk about imagination ... I have heard it said that the people want a Government with imagination. Imagination is an excellent thing if it is governed by reason and prudence, but imagination can lead to rank growth.

will end, and end fore

in a simple, clear and

way this coun

man

equivocation or subtlety tht the national

and international status of this country is that

1948-1956

The main reason for de Valera's decision to to dissolve the Twelfth Dáil in 1948 and to call an early election was to counter the threat posed by a new political entity, Clann na Poblachta.

Clann na Poblachta had been founded in 1946 and, two years later, had already tapped into the growing disillusionment with de Valera's government among many Fianna Fáil supporters. It was avowedly republican and espoused the left-of-centre social radicalism that had helped to usher Fianna Fáil to power in 1932.

Led by Seán MacBride, the son of Maud Gonne and executed 1916 leader Major John MacBride, it advocated full employment, a minimum wage, an end to partition and increased social provision, particularly in health and housing.

Clann an Poblachta had high expectations heading into the 1948 general election, and the party stood enough candidates to, theoretically at least, form a majority, single-party government. However, this ambitious strategy failed to deliver the expected breakthrough, and it returned just ten deputies even with an impressive 13 per cent of the national vote. By contrast, both wings of the Labour Party managed to return nineteen TDs with a lower share of the national vote.

Fine Gael continued its poor electoral showing, polling less than 20 per cent, and returned with thirty-one TDs – though things were no better for Fianna Fáil which lost all the gains it made in 1944, winning just sixty-seven seats. However, the biggest loser in the 1948 election was Clann na Talmhan whose vote was halved from the previous election, a blow from which it never recovered, though it struggled on for another decade.

Fianna Fáil's drubbing at the polls meant that, after sixteen years, an alternative to a de Valera-led government was possible, and, when the Dáil met on 18 February 1948, an inter-party – or coalition – government took the reins of power for the first time.

The government consisted of five parties – Fine Gael, Labour, National Labour, Clann na Poblachta and Clann na Talmhan – though assembling the coalition had not been without its problems. Clann na Poblachta rejected the idea of serving in a government headed by Fine Gael leader Richard Mulcahy. Mulcahy's role as Chief of Staff of the Free State army during the Civil War still evoked revulsion amongst republicans, not least those who were the backbone of Clann na Poblachta. To ensure his party achieved power, Mulcahy agreed not to contest the position of Taoiseach and, instead, proposed his fellow Fine Gael TD, John A. Costello.

The decision to form an inter-party government had significant consequences

1949

10 January
RCA unveils the 7", 45rpm record.

11 January
Los Angeles, California, receives its first recorded snowfall.

25 January
David Ben-Gurion becomes the first prime minister of Israel.

26 January
Australian citizenship comes into being.

4 April
NATO is formed by twelve western democratic nations, including the United States and Great Britain, to safeguard against Soviet aggression.

11 May
Siam, in southeast Asia, changes its name to Thailand.

23 May
The Federal
Republic of Germany
is declared.

20 August
Phil Lynott is born
in West Bromwich
in England.

28 August
The final six surviving
veterans of the
American Civil War
meet in Indianapolis.

22 September
Ireland defeats
England 2–0 in a
soccer match at
Goodison Park. It is
the first time England
has been beaten on
its home soil by a
foreign team.

1 October
Birth of People's
Republic of China.

7 October
The Democratic
Republic of Germany
(DDR) is officially
established.

Seán MacBride, 1948. Seán MacBride speaking at a political rally.

for Irish politics. First, it rescued Fine Gael from what had been a long, slow and seemingly terminal decline. The party had lost support at each of the previous six general elections and appeared incapable of breaking this pattern even when dissatisfaction with Fianna Fáil was high. However, being in government boosted its fortunes, and it would receive an important electoral bounce after its first period in office in sixteen years.

Second, the formation of the government, combined with Fianna Fáil's aversion to the idea of coalition government, cemented the notion that electoral contests were basically a battle between Fianna Fáil and everyone else. The experience of coalition was important in proving that an alternative to Fianna Fáil was possible.

In the Dáil debate on the formation of the government, which took place on 18 February 1948, Mulcahy attributed some type of metaphysical import to the outcome of the election:

> Just as there is a harmony between the animal, the plant, the soil and the climate
> … there is a harmony between men's minds that has to be studied reverently
> and worked for as assiduously as any harmony that God established in the soil
> of the country we live in. I feel that harmony to exist because of the reactions
> that have come from the country as a result of the recent General Election
> campaign and because of the movement in people's minds that has made it
> possible for a number of Parties to say that they are willing to sit in the council
> chambers of the nation, willing to form an inter-Party Government in harmony

and in reverent thought for their responsibilities and their duties to their country, as against the ideas that have been preached contrary to that harmony during this recent election campaign. I feel we are working, with sacrifice, with goodwill, with faith and with hope to establish a fruitful harmony among men of various attainments, various callings and various outlooks for their country.

(*18 February 1948*)

Both Labour leader William Norton and Seán MacBride were more workmanlike in their utterances in support of Costello, with MacBride stating:

I am prepared to co-operate with the other Parties in this House in order to lift public life out of the rut of Party politics and to deal with the problems that threaten the very life of this part of our nation. We as a Party do not abandon, waive, mitigate or abate in any respect any portion of our policy. We merely agree to co-operate with other Parties in giving effect to those portions of our policy upon which there is common agreement. We shall do so honestly, frankly and to the best of our ability, because we believe that that is what the nation wishes us to do and because we believe that is what is best for the nation at this particular time.

(*18 February 1948*)

The new government gave Fine Gael six seats at the cabinet table, with Mulcahy serving as Minister for Education. Fine Gael also ensured that its former colleague James Dillon, expelled from the party over his opposition to neutrality, served as Minister for Agriculture. William Norton became Tánaiste and Minister for Social Welfare, and he was joined at the cabinet table by his colleague T.J. Murphy, Minister for Local Government, while their former colleagues in National Labour had one seat at government in the form of Minister for Posts and Telegraphs, James Everett. Clann na Talmhan also held one cabinet seat with leader Joseph Blowick serving as Minister for Lands. Clann na Poblachta held two cabinet positions, with MacBride taking External Affairs and Noël Browne, a young, ambitious doctor who had just been elected for the first time, taking the important Health portfolio.

On his election as Taoiseach, Costello gave a modest, if less than inspiring, address to the assembled deputies:

21 January
The British writer George Orwell dies after a three-year battle against tuberculosis.

26 January
India becomes a republic formally, three years after gaining independence from Great Britain.

27 April
In South Africa, the Group Areas Act formally segregates the races and introduces legal apartheid.

13 May
The first race in the inaugural Formula One World Championship is held at Silverstone in England.

25 June
The Korean War begins with the crossing of the 38th parallel into South Korea by North Korean troops.

16 July
In Brazil, Uruguay beats the host nation 2–1 to win the 1950 World Cup in soccer.

12 August
In his Encyclical Humani Generis, Pope Pius XII declares that evolution does not contradict Catholic teachings.

2 November
Celebrated playwright George Bernard Shaw dies at his home in England at the age of ninety-four.

22 November
Shirley Temple announces her retirement from the film industry at the age of twenty-one.

25 December
Scottish nationalists take the Stone of Scone from Westminster Abbey in London.

This position was not sought by me nor wished for by me in any way. I would like to make it clear to this House and to the country that I lent neither my name nor my personality to any political manoeuvre. I consented to this nomination at the request of a number of Parties who felt that the interests of the country required that there should be an inter-Party Government and that the Prime Minister of that Government should occupy a position in political life detached from the controversial bitternesses of the past. It was in response to the urgent desires of all those Parties that I laid aside my own personal interests in order that this should come about.

(*18 February 1948*)

Despite his low-key start, Costello proved an effective chairman at cabinet meetings and utilised his friendship with both Norton and MacBride to ensure that the, at times, disparate coalition stayed the course until it was brought down in the wake of the crisis surrounding the Mother and Child Scheme in 1951.

Costello was also capable of dramatic action, and it was his decision, announced not in the Dáil but during a trip to Canada, that resulted in the State cutting its ties with the Commonwealth and declaring itself a republic.

Although he radically altered the State's relationship with Great Britain, de Valera never took the step of formally establishing Ireland as a republic. Indeed, when he became Taoiseach in 1932, de Valera was at pains to point out that it was the one constitutional step he wouldn't take:

The moment that the people are ready to stand for an independent Republic, we will be quite ready to lead them. We believed, in the last election, that … the people were not prepared, at the time, to take the full step that we would wish them to take; and in order to do our best to unite the country and to put into effect the economic policy which we stand for just as definitely as we stand for the political policy with which we are associated, in order to get on with that work we gave the assurance that, pending a further appeal to the people, we did not propose, in the field of international relations, to go beyond the points that were definitely asked for in our mandate.

(*27 April 1932*)

Notwithstanding the republican rhetoric of Fianna Fáil in the following years, and the substantial mandates de Valera received in 1938 and 1944, in particular, the State remained linked, however tenuously, to the British crown. Even though de Valera had removed the limited functions that the British monarchy had in relation to internal Irish affairs during the 1936 abdication crisis at the same time, through the External Relations Act, he maintained a titular role for the monarchy in external affairs, specifically in relation to the appointment of ambassadors – a role that was the one obstacle to declaring a republic.

De Valera held out the prospect of a legislative initiative in the future to repeal the External Relations Act and establish a republic, however, he stayed his hand over the coming years, hoping that by maintaining a link with the British monarchy it would assist in resolving the issue of partition at a later stage in the Dáil, he explained:

> I had a reason for hesitating about its removal. I use the word "hesitate" because, as I have said, I was contemplating the question of bringing its repeal before the Government. Naturally before I could take that step I would have to be quite satisfied in my own mind that what I was proposing to do was in the national interest. I hesitated particularly about taking that step because one of the purposes which that Act was intended to serve was to form, if possible, a bridge by which the separated counties might come to union with the rest of Ireland.
>
> *(24 November 1948)*

Few would have expected that, on taking office, a Fine Gael Taoiseach would be the person to finally cut all ties with the monarchy and declare Ireland a republic.

Fine Gael was traditionally the party most well disposed to maintaining relations with the British crown and the Commonwealth, and the move came as a surprise to the nation, particularly as Costello in August 1948, when asked in the Dáil to indicate the steps necessary to establish a republic, responded that the matter was 'purely one of nomenclature which I am not prepared to discuss.'

Even the staunchly republican element in Costello's government, Clann na Poblachta, seemed to accept that the establishment of a republic would not be on the agenda during this administration, with Seán MacBride admitting on the day he entered government:

> We cannot, however, claim that in this election we secured a mandate from the people that would enable us to repeal, or seek to repeal the External Relations Act and such other measures as are inconsistent with our status as an independent

1951

20 January
Avalanches in the Alps cause the deaths of 240 people. For a time, 45,000 are buried in Switzerland, Austria and Italy.

8 June
Jack Doyle, the 'Gorgeous Gael', defeats Tony Galento of America at a boxing match in Tolka Park.

1 July
Judy Garland performs the opening concert of a tour of the UK and Ireland in Dublin.

8 July
Parisians celebrate 2,000th anniversary of the founding of Paris.

18 July
The Abbey Theatre is damaged by fire hours after a performance of Casey's *The Plough and the Stars*. It will take fifteen years to restore the building.

1952

republic. These, therefore, have to remain in abeyance for the time being.

(18 February 1948)

Following his Canadian announcement, Costello introduced the Republic of Ireland Bill into the Dáil in November 1948, and, while at pains to point out that the measure should in no way been seen as a hostile act towards Britain, he said:

It is a Bill which, when enacted, will have consequences which will mark it as a measure ending an epoch and beginning what I hope will be a new and brighter epoch for the people of this country. This Bill will end, and end forever, in a simple, clear and unequivocal way this country's long and tragic association with the institution of the British Crown and will make it manifest beyond equivocation or subtlety that the national and international status of this country is that of an independent republic.

(24 November 1948)

The declaration of a republic entrenched views in the North, and Sir Basil Brooke, Prime Minister of Northern Ireland, used the opportunity to hold an election in February 1949, which increased the Unionist domination of the Stormont parliament. In Westminster, the government passed the Ireland Act 1949 – a measure that guaranteed the status of Northern Ireland as part of the United Kingdom.

While the establishment of a republic was popular, the inter-party government, especially the Labour and Clann na Poblachta elements, had sought a mandate from the electorate to deliver specific social-policy commitments. Labour made its intentions clear from the outset, securing the Social Welfare portfolio for Norton and the Local Government brief, which drove the State's housing programme, for O'Connell.

However, it was in the area of health, and specifically through the reforming zeal of Clann na Poblachta minister Noël Browne, that the inter-party government left its most indelible mark.

Browne became Minister for Health on his first day in Dáil Éireann, aged just thirty-two. A doctor, Browne was passionately committed to reform, a passion that would eventually contribute to the break-up of the government.

In the 1940s, tuberculosis (TB) – a fatal infectious disease which had in previous times been known as consumption – was rife in Ireland. In 1943, more than 4,300 people died of the disease, a rate twice that of England. Browne himself was painfully aware of the consequences of the disease: he had contracted TB while a

"**This Bill** will end, and end **forever**, in a **simple**, clear and **unequivocal** way this country's long and **tragic association** with the institution of **the British Crown** and will make it **manifest** beyond equivocation or subtlety that the **national** and **international** status of this country is that of an **independent republic**."

John A. Costello, 24 November 1948

student in Britain, and his parents and three sisters had fallen victim to the disease.

The previous government had begun efforts to tackle TB by passing legislation to establish dedicated TB hospitals. Even then, the level of knowledge as to the cause of the disease was confused and William Norton described the fear and shame which many people associated with TB:

> There is the most abysmal ignorance and superstition in the Irish people about tuberculosis. One would think that tuberculosis was like leprosy or worse. What we have to get over, what we have to combat in this country, is that type of superstition which imagines that the whole family name, honour and reputation and the sanctity of the entire home are lost simply because some member of the family is stricken with tuberculosis.
>
> (*31 January 1945*)

We know now that the main causes for the spread of TB are poor housing, over-crowding, poor sanitation and malnutrition – aspects of life that were all too common in Ireland in the 1940s and 1950s.

The prevalence of the disease had not been helped by the policy of the previous Fianna Fáil government, which, in an effort to control spending, cut the public-housing budget significantly. In 1938, Fianna Fáil could claim credit for the construction of more than 6,000 houses; by 1947, this figure had dropped to just 744. At the same time, in Dublin alone, the incoming government estimated that 20,000 working-class houses were needed. Labour Minister for Local Government, T. J. Murphy – and, following his death, his successor Michael Keyes – did much to reverse the trend, and over 7,000 local-authority houses were completed in 1951.

The previous government's investment in facilities bore no relation to the seriousness of the TB problem. Browne reported to the Dáil in July 1948 that in the fifteen years between 1932 and 1947, only 780 additional beds were made available for TB patients. Fianna Fáil's 1945 legislation was not accompanied by a corresponding political will to ensure the speedy delivery of the much-needed beds, an attitude that would characterise many of the Dáil's legislative efforts, particularly in the health area, for decades to come. As Fine Gael's Tom O'Higgins was to remark in 1954:

> There appears to be a mentality in this country … that you complete a necessary job of work by passing an Act to have it done. I want to assure

Deputies that you are only starting when you do that and you have to make sure that what is on our Statute Book is not merely so much window dressing in a shop front with nothing behind it.

(8 July 1954)

One thing the new Minister for Health did not lack was political will, and Noël Browne managed to practically double the number of beds available to treat TB, with more than 6,500 available throughout the State by 1951. Browne's crusade had an immediate effect, with the number of deaths from TB falling to 2,651 in 1949.

However, Browne's other significant initiative during the lifetime of the government – the Mother and Child Scheme – did not meet with the same success. Just before leaving office in 1948, de Valera's government passed a Health Act that provided for free maternity care for women and health care for children. The Catholic Church was opposed to this provision, believing that the State had no function in what should properly be a family matter. There the matter rested until Browne decided to revive the scheme in 1950.

Introducing his first estimate as Minister for Health in July 1948, Browne gave stark statistics that revealed Ireland's chronic infant-mortality problem. Referring to statistics for 1947, he stated:

> During the year the number of deaths of children under one year registered was 4,597 as against 4,390 in 1946 and 4,739 in 1945.
>
> Infant mortality has averaged the regrettably high figure of 71.2 per 1,000 live births for the ten years from 1937 to 1946. The figure for 1947 was 67. For 1947 the rate was 53 in Northern Ireland, 41 in England and Wales and 56 in Scotland.

(6 July 1948)

At seventy-one per 1,000 live births, Ireland's infant-mortality rate in 1947 was higher than that which prevails in countries such as Sudan and Eritrea today.

Browne believed that this appalling situation would not be improved without a comprehensive system of maternity care and education for mothers and in early 1951, he had decided to implement, in full, the Mother and Child Scheme, providing comprehensive, state-funded maternity care to mothers and health care for their children up to the age of sixteen, at an estimated annual cost of £2 million. Importantly, the provision would be universal, and no means test would apply.

1953

19 January
In America, 68 per cent of all television sets tune in to *I Love Lucy* to watch Lucy give birth.

31 January
A car ferry sinks in the Irish Sea in one of the worst gales of the winter, claiming the lives of up to 130 passengers and crew.

28 February
James D. Watson and Francis Crick announce that they have discovered the structure of the DNA molecule.

5 March
Joseph Stalin dies after suffering a stroke at the age of seventy-four. He has led the Soviet Union for thirty-one years.

Noël Browne.

The Catholic Church, and many medical professionals, would have no truck with Browne's expansive plan for state-provided care.

Following the rejection by the Catholic hierarchy, the cabinet abandoned the scheme, with Browne being the only dissenting voice. Browne refused to resign and, on 10 April, was forced to do so by his party leader Seán MacBride, creating a division that would prove fatal to the fortunes of Clann na Poblachta.

There is little doubt that Browne's handling of the Mother and Child Scheme partly caused its failure. While determined and driven, Browne could also be truculent, intransigent and dismissive of other opinions. Following his resignation, Browne's former cabinet colleagues lost no time in disowning him, attributing responsibility for the crisis to his personal traits, with Taoiseach John A. Costello claiming:

I had formed in my own mind … the firm conviction that Deputy Dr. Browne was not competent or capable to fulfil the duties of the Department of Health. He was incapable of negotiation; he was obstinate at times and vacillating at other times. He was quite incapable of knowing what his decision would be to-day or, if he made a decision to-day, it would remain until to-morrow.

(12 April 1951)

However, while Browne's attitude to the opponents of the scheme did little to assuage their fears, the fundamental reason for the crisis was not due to his personality, but rather to an important principle: the ability of the State to formulate and implement a health policy at variance with the teaching of the Catholic Church. The reluctance of the inter-party government to engage in such a clash was outlined by Browne's own party leader Seán MacBride in the debate following Browne's resignation:

> At all times, care should be taken to avoid the creation of a situation which might give the impression that there is a lack of harmony or a lack of co-operation between the Churches and the State. It is, therefore, always a very serious matter that a situation should arise in which the impression is created that a conflict exists between the Government and the Church. From another point of view, too, I think it is also regrettable that a position should ever arise in which the action of the Government, or the action of one of its Ministers, should become the subject of review or of criticism by the Hierarchy. From the point of view of the civil government of the country, it is never desirable that such a situation should arise.
>
> *(12 April 1951)*

Browne, for his part, was unrepentant and remained adamant that he had been betrayed by his cabinet colleagues:

> I regret that for the want of courage on their part they should have allowed the scheme to progress so very far—that they should have failed to keep me informed of the true position in regard to their own attitude and the attitude of others. I have, consequently, been allowed by their silence to commit myself to the country to implement a scheme which certain members of the Government at least did not want, on their own admission, to see implemented and which they were in fact aware could not be implemented …

27 July
The governments of the US, China, North Korea and South Korea sign an armistice agreement to end the Korean War.

29 August
Is it announced that Kilmainham Gaol is to be preserved as a national monument.

21 September
The Irish ploughing team leaves Dublin for the World Ploughing Championships in Canada.

1954

12 January
Finland and Germany officially end their state of war.

14 January
Marilyn Monroe marries baseball star Joe Di Maggio.

19 January
The government
announces plans to
build a new airport
at Ballygarvan, four
miles south of
Cork City.

As Minister for Health I was enabled to make some progress in improving the health services of the nation … I lay down my seal of office content that you – members of this House – and the people who are our masters here, shall judge whether I have striven to honour the trust placed on me.

(*12 April 1951*)

25 March
In America, RCA
manufactures the
first 12-inch colour
television set at a
price of $1,000.

Throughout its lifetime, the inter-party government faced enormous challenges but, as with so much of Irish politics, matters of a far more local nature also marked the government out for controversy and, indeed, ridicule.

Clann na Talmhan's Michael Donnellan, a government parliamentary secretary in 1948, told the Dáil of the words of advice given to him about constituency work when first entering the Dáil by long-standing Fianna Fáil TD Mark Killilea Snr. Although Killilea would later deny it, Donnellan related the following story:

20 April
Michael Manning, a
twenty-five-year-old
carter is hanged in
Mountjoy for the
murder of Catherine
Cooper. He is the
last person to be
executed in Ireland.

When I was only three months in Dáil Éireann Deputy Killilea said to me: "You are an awfully foolish man to be running down to the Custom House or over to the Board of Works about roads and drainage. Do what I have done. It has kept me in Dáil Éireann for 18 years. Do not do anything for them but keep promising them. They will always keep after you. If you do anything for them they will turn away from you."

(*6 July 1948*)

22 April
Senator Joseph
McCarthy begins the
hearing investigating
communism in the
US army.

One government minister who disagreed with Killilea's advice and had no hesitation doing favours for his constituents and supporters was James Everett, leader of National Labour. Everett was a TD for Wicklow and Minister for Post and Telegraphs in the inter-party government, a position that, in addition to its national responsibilities, allowed him to distribute a degree of patronage to his Wicklow constituents.

In 1950, a bizarre incident, which became known as 'The Battle of Baltinglass', sullied the reputation of Everett and the government he served in and had such a public impact that it became a byword for the localism and jobbery associated with Irish politics.

The controversy related to the appointment in 1950 of Michael Farrell, a local supporter of Everett's, to a sub-postmaster position in the Wicklow village of Baltinglass, ahead of a woman called Helen Cooke whose family had operated the post office for nearly a century and who, herself, had filled the role in a temporary position for over a decade. The appointment divided the sleepy village, with many

25 April
Biochemists Francis
Crick and James
Watson announce
their discovery of the
double-helix struc-
ture of deoxyribonu-
cleic acid (DNA) in
the journal *Nature*.

residents boycotting Farrell's business and going so far as to obstruct gardaí sent from Dublin to attend to the crisis.

Everett brazenly stood over his decision, and it was only in 1951, when Farrell decided to resign, that the controversy was resolved, although the long-term damage it did to the reputation of the government continued.

Reeling from the Battle of Baltinglass debacle and the controversy created by the Mother and Child Scheme, the government was dealt a fatal blow by the withdrawal of support by two Clann na Talmhan deputies in May over the very mundane issue of the price of milk. With its parliamentary majority now in ruins, Costello was forced to seek the dissolution of the Thirteenth Dáil and to call a general election for 30 May 1951.

The election produced another hung Dáil, with neither Fianna Fáil nor the inter-party alternative securing an overall majority. Fianna Fáil increased its vote but only managed to add one seat to its total because of the strong transfer patterns

> **"At all times**, care should be taken to **avoid** the creation of **a situation** which might give **the impression** that there is a lack of **harmony** or a lack of co-operation between the **Churches and the State."**

Seán MacBride, 12 April 1951

between the outgoing government parties. Fine Gael managed to turn around its electoral performance, gaining more than a quarter of the popular vote and increasing its Dáil strength to forty seats. The Labour Party fought the campaign on a united platform, having managing to patch over the rift between the two wings of the party, but it returned with sixteen seats, a net loss of three. Clann na Talmhan's decline continued, returning just six TDs.

However, the biggest loser in the 1951 election was Clann na Poblachta. Dr

5 May
CIÉ signs a £4.75 million contract to replace its steam trains with diesel locomotives.

6 May
British athlete Roger Bannister is the first person to run a mile in under four minutes.

17 May
The US Supreme Court reverses an 1896 ruling that education should be 'separate but equal', ruling that racial segregation in schools is unconstitutional.

17 May
Processions and marches take place all over Ireland to mark the Marian Year.

27 June
The first nuclear power station is opened in Obninsk, near Moscow.

Noël Browne, having left the party following the Mother and Child Scheme, fought the election as an Independent and was easily returned by his Dublin South-East constituency. His former colleagues, however, had a disastrous election, losing eight seats and returning just two TDs: Seán MacBride and John Tully.

Fianna Fáil, the largest party after the election, was only six seats short of a majority and de Valera managed to return to government with the support of four Independent TDs, including Noël Browne, who would join Fianna Fáil during the lifetime of the government.

De Valera's administration, which would last until 1954, was a lacklustre, conservative affair. Seven of the cabinet positions were occupied by ministers who had served in de Valera's first government which had been elected twenty years earlier, and de Valera himself was sixty-nine years old, taking office again. The overriding concern of the government was to implement a conservative fiscal policy and to reduce the substantial deficit which the previous administration had maintained. De Valera set the tone for the administration in his budget speech of April 1952:

1 August
The Yangtze River
floods in China,
killing 40,000 people
and forcing 10 million
others to leave
their homes.

I have often heard talk about imagination … I have heard it said that the people want a Government with imagination. Imagination is an excellent thing if it is governed by reason and prudence, but imagination can lead to rank growth. As I pointed out on a previous occasion, we find quite a number of people with imagination in the bankruptcy courts. We find quite a number of people with excellent imagination in the mental homes and we find quite a number of people with imagination even in our jails …

(24 April 1952)

6 September
Twenty-eight people
are killed when a
Dutch KLM plane
crashes into the
Shannon Estuary.

Commending the budget, which was one of the harshest in the history of the State, de Valera urged the population to look to the government's lead and to adopt the same conservative mentality:

6 September
Cork's Christy Ring
wins his eighth All-
Ireland medal in
front of a crowd of
85,000 people when
Cork beat Wexford
in Croke Park.

Our people must be prepared to make certain sacrifices also in the future. These sacrifices can be summed up in not having extravagant notions, in not attempting things that are clearly beyond our means, but in adapting our means to the end and the end to our means. If we do that and are prepared to work and be frugal, to be industrious and thrifty, then we can look forward to a healthy development … I ask people who are inclined to think of the

"Our people must be prepared to make certain sacrifices ..."

Eamon de Valera, 24 April 1952

16 October
A marble plaque is
unveiled at Westland
Row in Dublin to mark
the centenary of Oscar
Wilde's birth.

3 November
The modernist painter
Henri Matisse dies in
Nice, France, at the
age of eighty-four.

1955

7 January
Marian Anderson
becomes the first
African-American to
perform at the
Metropolitan Opera
in New York.

13 January
The Hill of Allen in
County Kildare, the
seat of the Leinster
kings and legendary
home of Fionn Mac
Cumhaill, is blown
up by Roadstone.

31 January
RCA demonstrates
the first music
synthesizer.

hardship it imposes to agree with us that there was no way out in the circumstances if we wanted to do our duty and present an honest Budget.

(*24 April 1952*)

The restriction on government spending, and the lack of economic investment, resulted in rising unemployment, with nearly 70,000 people on average unemployed throughout 1953, compared with 54,000 just three years earlier, a rise that led to the establishment of the Dublin Unemployed Association. However, rather than engaging in political agitation to work towards better jobs and conditions at home, thousands continued to follow the path of previous generations and emigrate to find work. In 1953, emigrants' remittances were estimated to contribute £11 million to the Irish economy, practically the same as the entire social welfare budget.

Despite this enormous financial contribution, Irish emigrants couldn't rely on support from their government, with Frank Aiken, the Minister for External Affairs, rejecting appeals from, among others, members of the Catholic hierarchy in Britain, to assist the growing disapora, particularly those living in poverty.

In 1953, to head off an opposition initiative, de Valera tabled a motion of confidence in the government. During the debate, Noël Browne, following a ferocious attack on Fine Gael and reaffirming his support for the government, acknowledged that Fianna Fáil had lost one of its most precious qualities: the ability to attract the empathy of the ordinary man and woman in the street:

> I think that the Fianna Fáil Government's record in the past would belie the suggestion that they are disinterested in hardship or in imposing unnecessary hardship on our people … but they have got into the position of feeling that the ordinary man-in-the-street or the ordinary woman understands their reading of the situation, their reading of balance sheets, Exchequer returns and statistics. The fact is that the people do not; the people are not clear as to where the Government is going, in what direction it is going or what it intends to do.

(*1 July 1953*)

Browne's continued support for his new-found colleagues in Fianna Fáil provoked a bitter response from Fine Gael in particular, with Thomas F. O'Higgins noting:

> A situation has now been reached wherein a man who for three years occupied

the position of Minister in the inter-Party Government comes in here stabbing in the back those with whom he worked as colleagues and he does that for the worst possible motive: he does it because he is fearful that if this vote goes against him and his new pets he will have to face the people. Political expediency has destroyed principle …

(1 July 1953)

Less than ten months later, on 23 April 1954, facing the prospect of another opposition motion of no confidence and fearing the loss of Independent support, de Valera dissolved the Fourteenth Dáil.

The final business in the Dáil that day cast some light on a scandal that every government ignored since the foundation of the State.

Peadar Cowan, having left Clann na Poblachta, sat as an Independent TD for the Dublin North-East constituency, where the Artane Industrial School was situated. Cowan related to the Dáil a shocking incident of physical abuse visited on a fourteen-year-old boy in the school. In the middle of a beating, the boy bolted, and, as Cowan explained:

> … he ran from the place in which he was being punished, lifted a sweeping brush, which was apparently standing in a corner, and held it up as a protection. At this stage, the second Brother arrived and seeing the brush in the boy's hands, snatched it from him, struck him on the head injuring him, struck him on the back injuring him, struck him on the arm and broke his arm. That happened on the 14th and the boy was taken to hospital on the 16th … The mother of the boy, although she lives not too distant from the school, was not informed of the injury the boy had received, but she heard about it during the week-end.

(23 April 1954)

Cowan concluded his speech calling for closer supervision of the standards in industrial schools, where the children were supposedly under the care of the Department of Education.

The industrial and reformatory school system had been in existence since the nineteenth century. Reformatory schools generally housed children convicted of a criminal offence, often of a very petty nature, while children were sent to industrial schools for a variety of reasons, including non-attendance at national school, begging,

---

20 March
In America, *Blackboard Jungle* opens in cinemas. It features the song 'Rock Around the Clock' by Bill Haley and his Comets and propels rock and roll into the spotlight. Teenagers jump from their seats to dance to the song.

15 April
Ray Kroc opens a McDonald's. Although it is the company's ninth restaurant since it was founded in 1940, Kroc revolutionises the company and oversees its world-wide expansion.

18 April
Albert Einstein, the greatest physicist, dies in New Jersey at the age of seventy-six.

14 May
The Warsaw Pact is signed by seven European communist nations including the Soviet Union, creating a military alliance in opposition to NATO.

14 June
Seventy-seven
people are killed
and dozens of others
are injured when a
racing car spins off
the track and into
the crowd at the
Le Mans race.

17 July
Disneyland, created
by Walt Disney, opens
in Anaheim, California.

27 August
The first edition of the
*Guinness Book of
Records* is published.

28 August
Fourteen-year-old
African-American
Emmett Till is abducted
and later murdered by
two white men in
Mississippi, after he
allegedly flirts with a
white woman.

30 September
Actor James Dean
dies at the age of
twenty-four in an car
accident in California,
having starred in only
three films.

Dublin Unemployed Association.

destitution or because of neglect on the part of their parents or guardians.

By 1929, there were nearly 6,000 children detained in industrial schools, with another 112 in reformatories, and, in a debate that year, Fianna Fáil TD, and future Minister for Education, Thomas Derrig accurately described the nature of these institutions:

> Since the industrial schools were founded in 1868 – that is a long time ago – there has been no improvement in the conditions or regulations governing these establishments. At that time the idea was to take homeless waifs and strays and provide for them some place, not exactly a workhouse, but like a workhouse, which even still, despite our boasted civilisation and desire to help those who cannot help themselves, bears the stigma of the workhouse.
>
> (*17 April 1929*)

These schools, together with Magdalen Laundries, were a symptom of the persistent neglect by the government to care for some of the most vulnerable citizens in Irish society. The system was run by religious orders, and the State repeatedly proved itself unwilling to guarantee the safety of children living within these institutions, despite the fact that because of their committal the children were, in theory at least, under the care of the Department of Education.

As has become shockingly clear in more recent times, children in reformatory and industrial schools were often subjected to the most horrific physical and sexual abuse. However, in the 1950s, Dáil Éireann maintained the official silence, with the annual budget for reformatory and industrial schools generally going through without debate. Despite Cowan's graphic portrayal of the abuse suffered by just one young boy, the ministerial response confirmed that the ignorance and denial that had informed the thinking of successive governments would continue, with Education Minister Seán Moylan saying:

> I would be as much concerned as the Deputy is if I thought it was anything other than a very isolated incident and in one sense what might be called an accident … I cannot conceive any deliberate ill-treatment of boys by a community motivated by the ideals of its founder. I cannot conceive any sadism emanating from men who were trained to a life of sacrifice and of austerity. They are also trained to have great devotion to a very high purpose …
>
> The point is that accidents will happen in the best regulated families and in this family there are about 800 boys … These boys are difficult to control at times. Maybe it is essential now and again that children should be punished … This is an isolated incident. I wish to express my sympathy to the parents of the child and I can assure them that nothing of the like will happen again.
>
> (23 April 1954)

Following the dissolution of the Fourteenth Dáil, the country went to the polls on 14 May 1954. Fianna Fáil's harsh economic policies cost the party dearly as it lost three seats, including that of Noël Browne, and, with them, any prospect of returning to office. Fine Gael, on the other hand, was the big winner, maintaining its momentum from the previous election, achieving over 30 per cent of the vote for the first time since 1938 and gaining ten seats into the bargain.

Of the smaller parties, Labour performed best, adding two seats and returning with eighteen TDs. Clann na Talmhan lost another seat, leaving it with five TDs, while Clann na Poblachta gained a seat, although with just three TDs in Dáil Éireann the future of the party looked bleak.

19 October
A crowd of 22,000 watch the Yugoslavian soccer team defeat Ireland 4–1 in Dublin, despite a call from Archbishop Charles McQuaid to boycott the game in protest at the imprisonment of Archbishop Stepinac by the Yugoslav government.

1 December
Rosa Parks refuses to give up her seat to a white man on a city bus in Montgomery, Alabama.

12 December
The Cork Opera House, in which the people of Cork have been entertained for a hundred years, is destroyed by fire.

14 December
Ireland is admitted into the United Nations.

1956

The Fifteenth Dáil met on 2 June, and, as he had done on each occasion since 1922, Richard Mulcahy rose to propose the nomination of a Fine Gael Taoiseach, to lead an inter-party government, with Labour and Clann na Talmhan. Clann na Poblachta supported Costello's nomination but didn't join the coalition.

Jack McQuillan, elected as a Clann na Poblachta deputy in 1948, had resigned from the party along with Noël Browne following the crisis over the Mother and Child Scheme and now sat as an Independent TD for Roscommon. During the debate on the nomination of Taoiseach, McQuillan pointed out an uncomfortable fact for the two largest parties: the only reason for their separate existence was the Civil War but in both social and economic terms the parties sang off the same hymn sheet:

> My personal views do not carry much weight in this House, but my personal views, for what they are worth, are that I would like to see in this State, in the autumn of their lives, Deputy de Valera, Deputy Mulcahy, Deputy MacEoin and Deputy Aiken—all those men on both sides of the House in Fianna Fáil and Fine Gael—on one side of the House and members of one Party, because there is no fundamental difference between them except a difference based on the bitterness of the civil war. All of them did marvellous things for the people of this country prior to 1922. But the political set-up in Ireland to-day is based on bitterness, and anything that is based on bitterness cannot hope to succeed.
>
> (*2 June 1954*)

Fine Gael held nine of the fourteen cabinet seats in the new government, Labour four posts – with Norton as Tánaiste and Minister for Industry and Commerce – and Clann na Talmhan occupied just one cabinet seat, with its leader Joseph Blowick serving again as Minister for Lands.

With a solid majority, the government was expected to stay the course for five years, but a worsening economic position and the renewed outbreak of IRA violence destabilised the government and caused it to collapse after only two and a half years.

Economic policy under the inter-party government remained inward-looking and focused on the domestic market rather than on export opportunities. It would take a radical shift in thinking, spearheaded by Lemass in the 1960s, to move beyond this vision of Irish industry that had its roots in the protectionism of the 1930s.

Irish consumers proved reluctant to support fully the type of economic

11 February
British spies Guy Burgess and Donald Maclean resurface in the Soviet Union after being missing for five years.

19 April
Prince Ranier of Monaco marries Grace Kelly, the Hollywood actress.

21 May
President Seán T. O'Kelly opens the first Cork Film Festival.

24 May
The Eurovision Song Contest is held for the first time. The contest, between fourteen countries is held in Switzerland, which also produces the winner. Austria, Denmark and the UK were all disqualified from the event for submitting their song entries after the closing deadline.

nationalism which had persisted for decades, with Minister for Industry and Commerce William Norton lamenting:

> There are people still tattooed with the idea that if a thing is foreign – if it is British, American or German – it must be good. They probably make a case against the Irish manufacture and say that if it is Irish it is no good because we still have not got the art of making such goods … unfortunately we still have the mentality which believes that if the same goods are bought outside the country they must be good.
>
> It is not just my task to kill that idea. It is the task of the Opposition, of ever man and woman who believe in Ireland, to kill that false economic philosophy. Whatever our difficulties are, we must get together in killing that notion … it is because of that problem that this Government will be compelled to take steps that may have to be stern steps, disagreeable steps, but whether they are stern or disagreeable they must be taken if we are to protect our whole economy.
>
> *(7 March 1956)*

However, Norton must have baulked at the 'stern steps' that Minister for Finance, Gerard Sweetman introduced in his budget in May 1956, which were as tough as anything introduced by the previous Fianna Fáil administration.

Faced with the prospect of a £5 million deficit, the Fine Gael Minister for Finance curtailed government spending and imposed tax hikes on tobacco, petrol and betting shops. Sweetman's plans for an even tougher budget in 1957 created serious division in the cabinet, even among the Fine Gael ministers. To add to the coalition's woes, the government's reaction to the IRA border campaign, which began in December 1956, alienated Clann na Poblachta, whose support was critical to its survival.

MacBride withdrew his support, and, facing the prospect of losing a confidence motion when the Dáil reconvened after the Christmas recess, Costello dissolved the Dáil. Another election was set for 5 March 1957.

11 August
The hard disk drive (5MB) is invented by an IBM team led by Reynold B. Johnson.

21 August
The GAA postpones the All-Ireland hurling and football finals because of an outbreak of polio.

13 September
Ronnie Delany wins Olympic gold for Ireland in the 1,500 metres in Melbourne.

26 October
The Russian Red Army invades Hungary after an attempted revolution in the country against the Soviet regime.

21 November
Our Lady's Hospital for Sick Children is opened in Crumlin, Dublin.

Selling Ireland, 1963. Seán Lemass
makes the cover of *Time.*

1957-1973

Let Lemass Lead On

'The historical task of this generation,
as I see it, is to consolidate the
economic foundations of our political
independence. These foundations are not
by any means firm enough to be
certain of their permanency.
The task of consolidating and extending
them cannot be postponed.'

1957-1973

PRIME MINISTER
SEÁN LEMASS

The real purpose of this ...
is to rivet the Fianna ...
ty on these benches ... the ... of Taoi...
was a c... na oe
the Taoiseach ...
and appears nothing better than an
insurance investment by people who believe –

The 1957 general election was held against a background

of chronic emigration, high unemployment and renewed IRA violence.

Turnout, at 70 per cent, was the lowest since 1944, and even those who did vote could hardly be blamed for casting a cold eye over the political system. The three previous governments had all failed to complete a full term in office, and, despite extensive election promises, no party had managed to present a coherent, realistic approach to the enormous social and economic challenges facing the country. Indeed, the very fact that in 1957 the main party leaders were old men – de Valera being seventy-four and Costello sixty-six – seemed to sum up the torpor that had gripped political life.

The census results of the previous year had only served to deepen the sense of national crisis. Forty years after the 1916 Rising, the population of the country was at its lowest level since the foundation of the State, with over 200,000 citizens having emigrated in the previous five years. They did so in the main to find work, to escape poverty and, perhaps, to find some excitement away from the culturally stagnant Republic where, for instance, over 6,000 books had been banned by mid-1956 and the film censorship regime, introduced in the 1920s, still held sway.

The collapse of the previous government, together with memories of the demise of the first inter-party administration, raised doubts about the ability of a Fine Gael-led alternative to form a viable government that would give the country a stable administration. Fianna Fáil exploited these concerns for all they were worth during the election, and the strategy worked: the 1957 election saw them return with seventy-eight seats, delivering the party its first overall majority since 1944. A young accountant, Charles Haughey, was one of the new Fianna Fáil TDs elected in the landslide.

Fine Gael and Labour both paid the price for their involvement in an unpopular government, losing ten and seven seats respectively, and both Costello and Norton would stand down from the leadership of their parties before the next election.

Results were no better for the smaller parties. Clann na Talmhan returned with just three TDs, and Clann na Poblachta lost the seat held by party leader Seán MacBride, returning just one TD to Dáil Éireann.

The 1957 election also saw the return of Noël Browne to Dáil Éireann as an Independent TD, though the following year he would form the National Progressive Democrats with his fellow Independent TD, and former Clann na Poblachta colleague, Jack McQuillan.

13 January
The Wham-O Company produces the first Frisbee.

16 February
In Britain, the 'Toddlers' Truce', a controversial television closedown between 6.00 p.m. and 7.00 p.m. is abolished.

25 March
Treaty of Rome is signed, establishing the European Economic Community (EEC), or Common Market

28 March
Artist Jack B. Yeats, brother of the poet William Butler, dies in Dublin.

5 September
Jack Kerouac's novel *On the Road*, based on the novelist's friendship with Neal Cassidy, is published. It becomes one of the best known works of the Beat Generation.

25 September
After prolonged resistance by local leaders, nine African-American students enter Central High School in Little Rock, Arkansas, under the protection of the National Guard.

29 September
The New York Giants play their last game at the Polo Grounds, losing to the Pittsburgh Pirates 9–1, before moving to San Francisco for the next season.

2 October
In Britain, David Lean's film *The Bridge on the River Kwai* opens in London.

4 October
The Soviet Union launches *Sputnik 1* into orbit.

3 November
The dog Laika becomes the first living creature to travel in space, on board *Sputnik 2*.

The renewed campaign of violence by the IRA also impacted on the election result. The campaign, which had begun in December 1956, was the first significant military action the IRA had carried out since the 1940s and involved armed assaults launched from the southern side of the border on targets in the North.

This futile border campaign would last for three years and claim nearly twenty lives. However, in its early stages, it garnered a degree of sympathy from those of a republican outlook, particularly following dramatic events such as the killing of IRA men Seán South and Fergal O'Hanlon in an abortive raid on Brookeborough Barracks in Fermanagh.

Sinn Féin contested the 1957 election, and four candidates were elected. However, as in the 1920s, Sinn Féin TDs ran on an absentionist ticket and refused to take their seats in Dáil Éireann. All four seats were lost at the next election in 1961.

Given Fianna Fáil's overall majority, de Valera was comfortably re-elected as Taoiseach, for what would prove to be the final time. While the cabinet still included many of those from the Civil War generation, one significant change saw Dr Jim Ryan becoming Minister for Finance, with de Valera's previous favourite for the office, the more conservative Seán MacEntee moved to Health.

MacEntee's tenure in Finance had been marked by his insistence on the need to balance budgets and restrict spending. His conservative approach to spending remained with him in Health, and he informed the Dáil during the debate on the health budget in 1958 that:

No one is likely to question that, consistent with the provision of an adequate and efficient service, the cost to public funds of the health services must be kept to a minimum. Our difficulty in effecting this, however, is not lessened by those who demand expanding facilities, coupled with more generous subventions to individuals, but refuse to consider how these are to be paid for … Nevertheless it is difficult to give a completely satisfactory answer to the question as to whether value is being received for the money spent. It is difficult because, in the nature of things, it is impossible to measure the amelioration of sickness and ill-health, the value of human lives prolonged, and the consequent relief and happiness experienced by individuals and their families in terms of pounds, shillings and pence.

(*22 April 1958*)

MacEntee's departure from Finance enabled Lemass and Ryan to fashion a new approach to industrial development, with the main economic departments beginning to focus on growth and expansion.

As in previous decades, de Valera's attitude to the IRA was, if anything, even more draconian than the previous Fine Gael-led government. At the outbreak of the border campaign, Cosgrave used the Offences Against the State Act to charge and imprison known IRA and Sinn Féin activists. The week after Fianna Fáil returned to office, Jack McQuillan TD, who was sympathetic to the republican's cause, if not their methods, demanded that these prisoners be released:

> … we have these young men in prison to-day. It is on behalf of these young men that I make a plea to the Minister in this new Government to release them. I am convinced … that these young men were nurtured on the heroic tales of the men who died in 1916. These young men have studied Irish history as they know it …
>
> The type of history lesson that all those young men were taught was that it was necessary to fight Britain with her own weapons, that blood must be spilled if anything was ever to be taken from Britain. Their belief—and that is where their teaching and where the example of the past comes to light— is the very same belief as was held by members of the Front Bench of Fianna Fáil and Fine Gael 35 or 40 years ago …
>
> (*26 March 1957*)

In response, the new Minister for Justice Oscar Traynor refused to countenance any such suggestion, seeing the prisoners not as misguided idealists but as a threat to the security of the State:

> I am wondering if the Deputy considers that that illegal organisation has a right to operate in this State where we have a Constitution which these people refuse to recognise, a Parliament which they refuse to recognise and an Army which they refuse to recognise. There can be only one Army in the State and that shall be the Army which has been established by this Parliament … Does the Deputy want this Government or any other Government to sit down and do nothing? … It gives me no pleasure … to have to deal with matters of this kind, but when we are confronted with them, they must be met and they must be dealt with.
>
> (*26 March 1957*)

4 January
Sir Edmund Hillary arrives at the South Pole. He is the first explorer to do so since Captain Scott in 1912.

4 January
Sputnki 1 falls to earth after orbit.

15 January
The floor of Carmody's Hotel in Ennis collapses causing the death of eight people and injuring dozens of others.

6 February
Seven Manchester United footballers are among twenty-one dead after an air crash in Munich.

17 February
Pope Pius XII declares St Clare the patron saint of television.

25 February
British philosopher
Bertrand Russell
founds the Campaign
for Nuclear
Disarmament.

24 March
The US army
inducts Elvis Presley,
transforming the King
of Rock and Roll into
US private number
53310761.

12 May
Ardmore Studios
opens in Wicklow.

18 May
America's F-104
Starfighter sets a
world speed record
of 1,404.19 mph.

8 September
Transatlantic jet
travel begins when
a PanAm Boeing 707
lands at Shannon
airport.

12 September
American Jack St
Clair Kilby invents first
integrated circuit –
the microchip – which
will revolutionise
computing.

The IRA's campaign continued, and, on 5 July, the day after the Dáil broke for the summer recess, de Valera's government introduced internment without trial for anyone suspected of involvement with subversive organisations.

Part of the reason that the IRA's border campaign attracted some popular sympathy in the late 1950s was public concern at the manner in which the Catholic minority was being treated by the sectarian Unionist government, opposition to which would ultimately lead to the formation of the Civil Rights movement in the late 1960s. During 1957, however, a scandal involving a mixed marriage in the quiet Wexford village of Fethard-on-Sea showed that sectarian instincts were not the exclusive preserve of those north of the border.

Sheila Kelly, a Protestant, and Seán Cloney, a Catholic, grew up as neighbours in the Wexford village and began a relationship despite the disapproval of the local Catholic clergy. The couple left for England, where they married and started a family before returning to Fethard-on-Sea in the 1950s. At the time, the Catholic Church insisted that any children of a mixed marriage had to be raised as Catholics. Sheila Kelly resisted this and, in April 1957, disappeared with her two children. Cloney was eventually reunited with his wife in Scotland.

Local Catholics in Fethard-on-Sea were outraged at the disappearance of the two children and wrongly blamed the local Protestant community for kidnapping them and denying them a Catholic upbringing. In May, Catholics, led by local priests, began a boycott of Protestant businesses in the town and shunned their Protestant neighbours.

In July, Noël Browne raised the issue in the Dáil, referring to the grave and growing disquiet throughout the country at the situation. De Valera, in a reply given to the Dáil by his parliamentary secretary, gave no succour to those engaged in the boycott, stating:

> I cannot say that I know every fact, but if, as Head of the Government, I must speak, I can only say, from what has appeared in public, that I regard this boycott as ill-conceived, ill considered and futile for the achievement of the purpose for which it seems to have been intended; that I regard it as unjust and cruel to confound the innocent with the guilty; that I repudiate any suggestion that this boycott is typical of the attitude or conduct of our people; that I am convinced that 90 per cent. of them look on this matter as I do; and that I beg of all who have regard for the fair name, good repute and well-being of our nation to use their influence to bring this deplorable affair to a speedy end.
>
> *(4 July 1957)*

De Valera's hopes for a speedy end to the scandal were not realised; the boycott continued for more than year; and the ill-will left by the affair would last a generation.

Despite incidents such as the Fethard-on-Sea boycott, political debate in the late 1950s was dominated by concern about the dire economic condition in the country. In October 1958, the Labour Party tabled a motion of no confidence in the government over the continuing high rates of unemployment and emigration, for which, it seemed, no party had the solution. During the debate, Brendan Corish referred to the frustration in the country at the failure of the political system to deal with the most pressing issues facing the people:

> As far as one can see, the only interests the Government seem to have or have had in the past three months are television, proportional representation and the Irish language. … We could talk for days, weeks and years about what the inter-Party Government did and what Fianna Fáil did, or what Fianna Fáil promised in 1932, but it would be no consolation to the odd 50,000 people who are unemployed or to the thousands of others who have to emigrate year after year. Reference to the past and to the arguments advanced by your opponents in the past is the type of thing which, more than anything else, makes the people cynical and causes them to say that Dáil Éireann is only a talking shop and that none of the Parties intend doing anything.
>
> *(29 October 1958)*

Ironically, Corish made his comments at a time when developments were in train that would transform the morbid Irish economy. T.K. Whitaker became the youngest Secretary General of the Department of Finance at the age of thirty-nine, and he availed of the arrival of Ryan in Finance, to radically alter economic policy.

Whitaker formed a committee in the Department of Finance to devise a new approach to the economy, and in November 1958, just a month after the Labour Party motion decrying the economic condition of the country was debated in the Dáil, the proposals of Whitaker and his colleagues emerged as government policy in a document entitled 'The Programme for Economic Expansion'.

The new economic programme advocated the end of protectionism, the facilitation of foreign capital, expansion of the exporting capacity of the economy and significant capital expenditure. More importantly, perhaps, the document formed a coherent plan; it provided a blueprint for economic development; and it sought to dispel the mood of despondency and despair that had settled over economic debate.

6 October
Ballymoss, trained by Vincent O'Brien, is the first Irish-trained horse to win the l'Arc de Triomphe in Paris.

28 October
Pope John XXIII succeeds Pope Pius XII as the 261st pope.

1959

1 January
Fidel Castro ousts the dictator Fulgencio Batista to become leader of Cuba.

1 February
A referendum in Switzerland rejects female suffrage.

3 February
Buddy Holly, along with Ritchie Valens and the Big Bopper, die in a plane crash near Clear Lake, Iowa.

8 February
Charles de Gaulle, the first elected president of the newly formed Fifth Republic of France, takes office.

It was an approach that Tánaiste and Minister for Industry and Commerce Seán Lemass strongly encouraged. Lemass had already introduced legislation that actively encouraged foreign investment and sought to dismantle some of the protectionism that stifled economic development, a system that Lemass had played a major role in establishing in the 1930s. However, by 1959, Lemass had a different vision for the Irish economy:

> Our pre-war industrial development was based on home market requirements and protection, and it served the purposes of that time … There is need now to raise our targets and, I believe, also to change our methods. We know that change always produces problems and difficulties, and it is certain that we will experience both, but the problems are not insoluble. The difficulties can in time be solved …
>
> It would be a very poor prospect indeed for this country if we had to look forward only to manufacturing industry limited to the home market demand, preserving old-fashioned techniques and traditional restrictive practices behind an ever-mounting tariff wall. Indeed, that milestone in our development is already far behind us.
>
> *(3 June 1959)*

9 March
The original Barbie doll makes her debut in American shops.

31 March
The spiritual leader of Tibet, the Dalai Lama, crosses the border into India after an epic fifteen-day journey on foot over the Himalayan mountains.

The economic transformation heralded by the new policy direction was remarkable. By the mid-1960s, employment and emigration had fallen significantly, exports had more than doubled, and foreign firms were beginning to establish production facilities in Ireland.

The Dáil never saw the need to formally discuss the issue, and so one of the most important shifts in economic thinking in the country was adopted and implemented without any significant input from parliament.

31 May
The last tram to run on the Hill of Howth tramway service makes its final journey.

One of the reasons why the Dáil gave scant attention to the new economic policy was de Valera's determination to change the electoral system and replace proportional representation with a first-past-the-post system. Ironically, it was de Valera who had ensured that the PR system was given constitutional status, and so it could only be changed by referendum.

The legislation to facilitate the referendum on PR was introduced in Dáil Éireann in November 1958, and it would not pass until May of the following year after substantial resistance, including the defeat of the legislation in the Seanad.

11 June
The Hovercraft invented by Christopher Cockerell is officially launched in Southampton.

When de Valera introduced the proposal on 12 November, both Costello and

Norton took the unusual step of opposing the first reading of the Bill – a move that created consternation on the government benches – and this first loud and unruly debate on the proposal would characterise the referendum campaign to come.

Costello was direct in his criticism of the move and, echoing the widespread disillusionment with politics at the time, stated:

> The proposals are ill-timed also because of the prevailing conditions of apathy, disillusionment and cynicism, and a torpid political electorate. In fact they are designed to exploit that apathy … The proposals are unjustifiable because in effect they aim at depriving reasonable minorities in the country of fair representation. They are intended to put the political power of the people into the hands of the major political Party sponsoring them. The aim of the proposals is the glorification of the power of that Party.
>
> (*12 November 1958*)

De Valera later rejected this claim. In his main speech on the issue, he explained that the overriding reason for seeking the change was his frustration at the multiplicity of parties that the PR system sustained. De Valera felt that politics should ideally be a direct contest between two groups: a government and an opposition. The first-past-the-post system facilitated this type of two-party politics while, according to de Valera, PR sustained multiple parties and resulted in unstable governments and fractured oppositions:

> As I have said, the main feature of the straight vote is that it is an integrating influence, whereas the other is a disintegrating influence. We have reason enough, goodness knows, for forming groups and Parties without, so to speak, being encouraged by our fundamental system to do so.
>
> (*26 November 1958*)

For Norton, the move to abolish PR was little more than an attempt by de Valera to ensure Fianna Fáil control of the corridors of power after his departure:

> … the Taoiseach said that everybody he met in 1948 … was bursting to have P.R. abolished. That is the kind of mushy, disreputable muck that is being used to justify the abolition of P.R. to this House and to the credulous people outside …

10 July
The first ban gardaí recruits are sworn in during a ceremony in Dublin.

2 October
In America, the classic anthology series *The Twilight Zone* premieres on CBS.

2 November
In Britain, the first section of the M1 motorway opens between Watford and Rugby.

1 December
A camera mounted on the nose of a missile takes the first colour picture of earth from space.

1960

21 March
More than fifty Africans die and 162 are injured as police open fire on a crowd of 15,000 in the South African township of Sharpeville.

The real purpose of this Bill is to rivet the Fianna Fáil Party on these benches when the Taoiseach is no longer an active member of the Party. Nobody on these benches can perform like the Taoiseach. Nobody can throw the somersaults which the Taoiseach can throw with such consummate skill. Nobody can give the people a phrase and then interpret it in ten different ways. Therefore, while the old warrior is here with all his skill and cunning and all the craft of the trapeze artist, that must be exploited to the full, so that before he leaves the Party, and this House, he will at least have made sure that the boys are firmly riveted in power, firmly riveted in this House.

(*26 November 1958*)

A presidential election was due in 1959, as by then the incumbent, Seán T. O'Kelly, would have completed the maximum two terms allowed under the Constitution. Fine Gael had already decided to run War of Independence hero and former Minister General Seán MacEoin, who was beaten for the post by O'Kelly in the 1945 presidential election. To the surprise of many of his political opponents, de Valera announced in January 1959 that he intended to contest the presidential election.

The government finally managed to pass the legislation, giving the green light to the referendum on 13 May, and, in his final comment in Dáil Éireann on the issue, de Valera expressed his belief that, given the political instability of the previous decade, the electorate would be attracted by the prospect of continuity that his proposal promised:

> I do not know what way they will decide it … but I believe the people will think about the welfare of the country, and about its future, and decide that stability is much more important than having this so-called representation of groups or Parties. The thing that has to be represented is the nation. We want to have a truly representative Parliament and we want to have a stable Government because that is the ultimate centre of power, of energy—the driving centre.

(*13 May 1959*)

Much to the annoyance of the opposition, the referendum and the presidential election were held on the same day, 17 June 1959.

In the race for the presidency, de Valera managed to comfortably defeat Seán MacEoin. His proposal to abolish PR, however, did not meet with the same

"The **real purpose** of this **this Bill** is to rivet the **Fianna Fáil Party** on these benches when **the Taoiseach** is no longer an **active member** of **the Party.**"

William Norton, 26 November 1958

9 November
John F. Kennedy wins the US presidential election and becomes the country's youngest president.

27 December
The French move a step closer to developing a compact nuclear bomb after a third test in the Sahara desert.

1961

1 January
In Britain, the farthing, used since the thirteenth century, ceases to be legal tender.

9 February
The Beatles perform in the Cavern Club in Liverpool for the first time.

12 April
Soviet cosmonaut Yuri Gagarin, aboard *Vostok 1*, is the first man to travel in space; he makes one orbit of earth during his 108-minute flight.

approval. In a remarkable display of independence, thousands of voters entered the polling booth backed de Valera's bid for the presidency and, with the next stroke of the pencil, rejected his proposal for electoral reform. The defeat of the referendum took the gloss off de Valera's emphatic victory, but, perhaps more importantly, the low turnout, with more than one in three voters staying away from the polls, revealed the dismay which many voters felt at the failure of the political system to address economic and social problems, as Noël Browne would later remark:

> Most responsible Deputies will have been terribly shocked, not by the failure to elect Deputy Mac Eoin and the election of the Deputy de Valera but by the mass voters' strike in this terribly important election. The significance of the abstention of one-third of the electorate, under the circumstances, when both major Parties attempted to bring them all out by every possible means open to them, and the refusal of an electorate, which has been noted over the years for its intense interest in political matters, to come to the polls in such large numbers is, to my mind … one of the most frightening, shocking and damning condemnations of our activities here over the past several months.
>
> (*23 June 1959*)

De Valera's departure from party politics marks a watershed in Irish political development. De Valera was seventy-six years of age when he handed over the reins of power to Seán Lemass, who was sixteen years his junior. Lemass had already shifted Fianna Fáil's economic outlook away from the narrow, nationalist-inspired policies of the past, and this process would accelerate in a very dramatic fashion when he became Taoiseach on 23 June 1959.

Lemass managed to redefine Fianna Fáil's vision of Ireland, which up until then had been focused on issues close to de Valera's heart, such as the revival of the Irish language, the ending of partition and contentment with a spiritually rich, if materially poor, standard of living. Lemass consigned that vision of Ireland to the history books and insisted that economic growth was now the primary national goal:

> The historical task of this generation, as I see it, is to consolidate the economic foundations of our political independence. These foundations are not by any means firm enough to be certain of their permanency. The task of consolidating and extending them cannot be postponed. It has got to be done now or in the years immediately ahead of us. This, I believe, is the crucial period in our

attempt to build up an Irish State which will be capable of maintaining permanent independence. If we fail, everything else goes with it and all the hopes of the past will have been falsified. But if we succeed, then every other national problem, including particularly the problem of Partition, will become a great deal easier of solution. We are not thinking of failure but of emphasising again and again our conviction that everything depends on the effort made now.

(3 June 1959)

In the same speech, Lemass also alluded to the difficulties that many of the hitherto-protected Irish industries would face:

It is essential now that we should develop a new outlook generally. I was at a meeting recently and there I heard a young man saying that any person who got the opportunity of running an Irish industry which failed should be regarded, not as an object of sympathy, but as a public enemy. I think that is the right approach. As it is, every Deputy knows that if some factory closes down because of incompetent management or because of reckless wastage of resources it becomes a matter of political agitation with demands to the Government to use public funds or further tariffs to buttress it up. It is better that badly run industries should fail. To the extent that there is dead-wood in our industrial forest it is far better to clear it out and make room for new growth.

(3 June 1959)

Lemass' elevation to the position of Taoiseach was overshadowed by the defeat of the referendum on PR, with most opposition deputies using the opportunity to rub salt into Fianna Fáil's wounds following the result. In the debate on Lemass' nomination, however, one deputy, Clann na Talmhan's Michael Donnellan, expressed the unease of some rural voters at Lemass' vision of Ireland and in doing so managed to display the latent anti-Semitism that occasionally reared its ugly head from a small minority of deputies in Dáil Éireann:

No matter what any Deputy says, I regard the Deputy who has been proposed for the position of Taoiseach as the decentest man in Dáil Éireann. Nevertheless, I shall vote against him. I will tell you why … Deputy Lemass has only a city outlook, a city mentality. Rural Ireland he does not know of … His outlook

17 April
US-backed Cuban exiles land at the Bay of Pigs in Cuba to overthrow Premier Fidel Castro's government. The mission is thwarted and the invaders killed or captured.

6 May
In Britain, Tottenham Hotspur becomes the first team in the twentieth century to win the soccer league and cup double.

17 June
Russian dancer Rudolf Nureyev breaks free from security guards at Paris airport and asks for asylum in France.

23 June
The Antarctic Treaty (signed in 1959) comes into effect. It pledges the twelve signatory nations to non-political, scientific investigation of the continent of Antartica and bars any military activity.

2 July
Writer Ernest
Hemingway commits
suicide in Ketchum,
Idaho, at the age
of sixty-one.

is for the industrialists. Many of them are sham industrialists. May I put it straight? In many instances the people's money was wasted in order to bring them in here. A lot of them are the damn Jews that should never be allowed in this country.

(23 June 1959)

13 August
The East German
government surrounds
West Berlin with
temporary fortifica-
tions during the night,
stopping the flight of
East Germans to the
West. The barrier is
soon replaced by the
concrete Berlin Wall.

The departure of de Valera was quickly followed by the resignation of Mulcahy from the leadership of Fine Gael, a move that also saw Costello depart from his role as parliamentary leader of the party. James Dillon defeated Liam Cosgrave in the ensuing election and became leader of Fine Gael. Change was also afoot in the Labour ranks, with Norton, suffering from ill-health, relinquishing the leadership and handing over to Wexford deputy Brendan Corish in 1960.

Labour's electoral experience after participation in the two inter-party governments in the post-war years had been bruising. For the next decade, Corish would spurn Fine Gael advances to form an anti-Fianna Fáil pre-election pact, and Labour contested elections as an independent party opposed to forming a government with either of the two conservative parties and instead concentrating its efforts on developing the party with the ambitious, if somewhat naive, goal of delivering a Labour-led government.

18 September
The body of UN
Secretary General
Dag Hammarskjold is
identified among the
wreckage of a plane
which crashed last
night outside the
Northern Rhodesian
town of Ndola.

By 1961, the government's economic strategy was beginning to bear fruit, with Lemass informing the Dáil in February that the rate of unemployment in 1960 was the lowest ever recorded and that growth in the economy that year was in the order of 4 per cent, higher than that envisaged in the Programme for Economic Expansion.

In spite of these impressive statistics and the genuine economic improvement that they indicated, life in Ireland, especially for the poor and vulnerable, was still harsh. One opposition motion, proposed in November 1960 by Fine Gael's Declan Costello, son of John A. Costello, cast light on just one ongoing scandal that Irish society tolerated: the treatment of children with a mental disability:

The object of this motion is to draw attention to a national scandal, to awaken a dormant consciousness in our society to a great social evil and to urge the Government to take action to alleviate a gross injustice in our midst … For too long have the plight and condition of mentally handicapped children and of their parents been neglected and their tragic situation been avoided. For too long have apathy and indifference contributed to official inactivity … There are approximately in this country 2,000 beds available for mentally

31 December
Telefís Éireann,
Ireland's first television
service, broadcasts
live from Áras an
Uachtaráin.

handicapped children. It has been reliably estimated that 7,000 more are needed. There are approximately 500 to 600 places in special schools for mentally handicapped children. It has been reliably estimated that 5,000 are needed … There is in this whole country one child guidance clinic. There was up to recently only one qualified educational psychologist.

(9 November 1960)

Regardless of Costello's warnings, children with mental and physical disabilities would be treated as second-class citizens for decades to come, even during the boom times of the Celtic Tiger.

Developments in European politics would provide Lemass with the pretext to call an election seven months earlier than was needed. In 1961, Britain applied to join the recently formed European Economic Community (EEC). Ireland, given its trade links with Britain, immediately followed suit, and Lemass sought a renewed electoral mandate, claiming that a new government with a full Dáil term ahead of it was necessary to conduct the negotiations to join the EEC. As it happened, Britain's application ran into the sand, derailing Lemass' goal of membership in the process, and Ireland would not join the EEC for more than a decade.

In his speech announcing the dissolution of the Sixteenth Dáil, Lemass spoke in characteristically optimistic tones while warning that continuity, particularly Fianna Fáil continuity in government, was vital:

> Emphasis is now on change and innovation in every sphere of national activity. Plans and policies which were developed in the past, and which were often defended vigorously and enthusiastically in the past, are now ceasing to be appropriate. The world to which these plans and policies were relevant no longer exists. This is a time for new ideas …
>
> The country is like an aeroplane at the take-off stage. It has become airborne, but I would emphasise that that is the stage of maximum risk when any failure of power can lead to a crash. It will be a long time yet before we can throttle back in level flight. We know we have not yet achieved the certainty of continuation of economic effort—and certainty in that respect is what we require.
>
> *(2 August 1961)*

While Lemass may have believed that the country was in take-off mode, Fianna Fáil certainly wasn't. Facing the electorate for the first time without de Valera at the

17 January
Chubby Checker tops the chart with 'The Twist'.

4 February
The Sunday Times becomes the first newspaper to print a colour supplement.

10 February
Gary Powers, the American pilot shot down by the Soviet Union in 1960, is released in exchange for a Soviet spy captured by the US.

3 July
After a bitter war, Algeria is granted independence from France.

10 July
AT&T's Telstar, the world's first commercial communications satellite, is launched into orbit and is activated the following day.

"...This is
a time for
new ideas..."

Seán Lemass, 2 August 1961

helm, the party fared badly, losing eight seats and its overall majority. Fine Gael, under new leader James Dillon, gained seven seats, and Labour also performed well, returning with fifteen TDs, an increase of four. Both Browne and McQuillan were returned under the National Progressive Democrat banner and would join the Labour Party during the lifetime of the newly elected Dáil.

Fianna Fáil was returned to office with the support of Independents, and, despite the instability that many predicted following the inconclusive election result, the government would serve a full term.

Aside from the election of Lemass as Taoiseach, the debate when the Seventeenth Dáil reconvened was notable for the independent stance taken by the Labour Party under Corish. Labour refused to support Dillon's nomination for Taoiseach, calling instead for Fianna Fáil and Fine Gael to form a government. Cork TD Dan Desmond put the issue bluntly:

> For too long too many people outside have thought it should be the role of the Labour Party, a small political Party, to act as a tail-end of one of the larger Parties … We of the Labour Party believe that while the distance to be travelled may take a little while yet, Fianna Fáil and Fine Gael will eventually have to come together. There is nothing between them except the old sores that we hope are nearly now healed. When that time comes, inside this Chamber and outside it, people will realise that the Labour Party … will be the only alternative to the existing system.
>
> *(11 October 1961)*

James Dillon, for one, was not impressed with the new-found independent streak in the Labour Party and its calls for a realignment of Irish politics on a left–right basis. He lampooned the contention that there was an ideological basis for politics in Ireland:

> There are few, if any, Deputies in this House who accept the materialist philosophy of left wing, if not, Marxian socialism. If there are some, they are as reluctant to proclaim their faith as they are vocal in deriding their fellow Deputies for lack of faith to proclaim. I invite those whited sepulchres to come out into the open and tell us their true beliefs so that some day we can finally determine whether politics in Ireland are founded on the ideological differences of Continental Europe or whether, sharing common fundamental

19 July
The final edition of *The Evening Mail,* Dublin's oldest newspaper, goes on sale. It was founded in 1823.

5 August
Movie star Marilyn Monroe is found dead of a barbiturate overdose at her home in Los Angeles, California.

11 September
The Beatles record their first songs – 'Love Me Do' and 'P.S., I Love You' – for the music label EMI.

28 October
US President John F. Kennedy welcomes Russia's announcement that it will dismantle its missiles based in Cuba.

1963

30 January
French president Charles de Gaulle vetoes the UK's entry into the EEC.

beliefs, we can here in Ireland, as they do in the 50 sovereign States of the United States of America, argue out our differences in the presence of our own people who do understand the issues … Come now then—the reds, the pinks, the pale pinks, and those who are no more than blushing for their own secret convictions. Let them come out in the open.

(11 October 1961)

Lemass couldn't resist a passing comment on the division in the opposition ranks:

I must say that I was somewhat puzzled by the main theme of Deputy Dillon's remarks when he turned and seemed to be addressing the benches occupied by the Labour Party, to denounce Reds and Pinks and apparently able to see a Marxist under every bench over there … I must say I thought, listening to the Deputy, that he had come to accept the reality of the fact that the old coalition link-up between Fine Gael and Labour was gone for good and that he was, in fact, telling the Labour Party that their grapes were sour.

(11 October 1961)

Lemass used his re-election as Taoiseach to bring new talent into the government ranks, and a new generation of TDs – such as Charles Haughey, Neil Blaney and Paddy Hillery – played prominent roles in future Fianna Fáil cabinets in the 1960s. As well as continuing economic reform, the government introduced reforming legislation, which included the abolition of the death penalty for most cases of murder, putting the legal-aid system on a statutory footing and establishing the National Building Agency.

While unemployment remained high, there was a general feeling of prosperity, in some sections of society at least. By March 1962, there were more than 8,000 people on the waiting list for a telephone, and in the previous month the increased number of cars on the roads had prompted a Dáil question about rush-hour traffic congestion in Dublin. Emigration had dropped significantly, and the increased numbers of young people staying in Ireland to make a living provided an enthusiastic audience for the growing showband circuit; even The Beatles saw fit to play in Dublin. Those who stayed away from ballrooms could watch RTÉ television of an evening, which had begun broadcasting on New Year's Eve 1961.

This new feeling of confidence gained a significant boost with the announcement that President John F. Kennedy would visit Ireland in June 1963. His visit included

Kennedy mobbed, 2 June 1963. President John F. Kennedy is almost lost among a crowd of well-wishers during his visit to Ireland.

a speech to the joint Houses of the Oireachtas, the first time the Dáil and Seanad came together in such a fashion.

The speech dealt chiefly with the long association between America and Ireland and Ireland's growing participation in international affairs. Ireland had joined the United Nations (UN) in 1955, after initially being blocked by the Soviet Union, and Irish soldiers first served abroad as peacekeepers in the Congo in 1960, an expedition that would exact a high price, including the death of ten soldiers in an ambush at Niemba within months of arriving. However, Kennedy also referred to the progress of recent years:

> And it is the present and the future of Ireland that today hold so much promise to my nation as well as to yours, and, indeed, to all mankind, for the Ireland of 1963, one of the youngest of nations, and the oldest of civilisations, has

28 August
More than 200,000 people participate in the March on Washington, demanding full civil rights for African-Americans. The day culminates in Martin Luther King's 'I Have a Dream' speech.

26 September
The New York Review of Books is published for the first time.

7 November
The Beatles cause havoc in Dublin as fans gather in Middle Abbey and O'Connell streets ahead of the band's concert.

18 November
The first push-button telephone goes into service.

22 November
President John F. Kennedy is assassinated in Dallas, Texas. He was the first Catholic and the youngest man to hold the office, being the first American president born in the twentieth century.

23 November
In Britain, the first episode of *Dr Who* is broadcast.

12 December
Kenya gains independence.

discovered that the achievement of nationhood is not an end, but a beginning. In the years since independence, you have undergone a new and peaceful revolution, an economic and industrial revolution, transforming the face of this land, while still holding to the old spiritual and cultural values. You have modernised your economy, harnessed your rivers, diversified your industry, liberalised your trade, electrified your farms, accelerated your rate of growth, and improved the living standard of your people.

(28 June 1963)

The economic transformation of the Lemass years also heralded an unprecedented level of industrial disputes, as workers sought to gain improved pay and conditions in the new economic dispensation. An ESB strike in 1961 forced the government to recall the Dáil to pass emergency legislation protecting electricity supplies, an essential service which most of the country now enjoyed thanks to the rural electrification programme, and a Coras Iompar Éireann (CIÉ) strike in 1963 saw army lorries deployed in Dublin to ferry citizens to and fro. The government's emphasis on industrial growth and expansion also led to widespread farmer protests, driven by a belief that rural Ireland was being left behind in the brave new world of modernisation.

In the face of industrial unrest, Lemass harnessed the new unity in the trade union movement, which had seen the Irish Congress of Trade Unions formed in 1959, and concluded a national wage agreement between employers and labour, a development that foreshadowed the social partnership model successfully employed in later years.

However, despite the new national agreement, industrial unrest continued. A dispute in the building industry was the last straw for Paddy Smith, the Minister for Agriculture and a founding member of Fianna Fáil. He resigned from office in protest at what he saw as the fraudulent activity of the trade union movement in seeking pay rises outside the scope of the national agreement. Smith's resignation represented a wider unease among sections of the party with Lemass' urban focus.

On becoming Taoiseach, Lemass indicated a significant change in policy towards Northern Ireland. Fianna Fáil's traditional attitude to partition, and the language in which it was couched, may have appealed to nationalist sentiment but it offered no practical grounds for progress. A speech on the issue by de Valera, delivered more than a decade before Lemass took over the reins of power, is reflective of the thinking of much of the Fianna Fáil party at the time:

They must know that the occupation of the Six Counties by Britain is a flagrant violation of the fundamental national rights and sovereignty of the Irish people; they must know that they have no more right to occupy these six counties of our country than a foreign Power would have to occupy some area of England in which there happened to be a political minority opposed to the will of the majority … So long as a minority in any country is used, as our minority is used, to serve the interests of an external power, all attempts to find a just solution of the world's problems, or to find a secure basis for world peace, are doomed to failure.

(30 January 1946)

De Valera nuanced his approach in later years, and, in an address to the Oxford Union, Lemass addressed this central theme of Irish politics and outlined his belief that mutual cooperation with the North on social and economic issues was the only practical course of action available. He repeated his views during a subsequent Dáil debate:

It is true that this nation of ours is divided at present by deep-rooted prejudices, misunderstandings, fears and hostilities. These divisions were used as a pretext for Partition in the first instance and are used as a justification for maintaining it now.

It seems to me that the aim of national policy must always be to endeavour to remove those divisions, to eliminate, if we can, those barriers of fear, prejudice and misunderstanding which are keeping our people divided.

We want to end the partition of our country, not merely because we wish to see the whole of the national territory brought under the jurisdiction of an Irish Parliament but primarily because we wish to bring about the re-unification of our people and to eliminate the misunderstanding, hates and fears which have kept them asunder, so that the re-united nation would be better able to promote the economic, cultural and social welfare of the whole Irish community.

In order to bring about that situation I believe that we should seek to promote all possible contacts between the people in the two areas, social, cultural and economic contacts.

(10 November 1960)

Lemass' hopes of fostering a closer relationship with Northern Ireland received a boost in 1963 when Terence O'Neill replaced Lord Brookeborough as Prime Minister.

11 January
US Surgeon General states that smoking may be dangerous to human health.

18 March
A driving test is to be introduced for Irish drivers to replace the practice of people buying a licence over the counter at garda stations.

21 March
Brendan Behan, the Dublin house painter, poet and writer, who died at the age of forty-one, is buried in Dublin. His is one of the largest funeral processions the city has seen in forty years.

13 April
Sidney Poitier becomes the first black actor to win an Academy Award, for his performance in *Lilies of the Field*.

18 May
In Britain, scores of youths are given prison sentences following violent clashes between gangs of Mods and Rockers.

27 May
Jawaharlal Nehru, the founder of modern India and its current prime minister, dies suddenly at the age of seventy-four.

12 June
The leader of the anti-apartheid struggle in South Africa, Nelson Mandela, is given a life sentence for sabotage.

15 June
The last French troops leave Algeria.

2 July
The Civil Rights Bill – one of the most important piece of legislation in American history – is signed into law by President Johnson.

In a historic move, Lemass travelled to Belfast in January 1965 to meet O'Neill, a move that represents the first significant thaw between the North and South.

A by-election defeat for Fianna Fáil in March 1965, where Labour's Eileen Desmond won the vacancy caused by the death of her husband Dan Desmond, gave Lemass the opportunity to call an election, confident that his government's policy on the economy and Northern Ireland would provide an overall majority.

Fianna Fáil fought the election under the slogan of 'Let Lemass Lead On', and it did lead Fianna Fáil to an overall majority – proof, if it was needed, that Lemass had successfully filled de Valera's shoes in terms of electoral appeal. For the second election in a row, Labour fought on an independent platform and, benefiting from the industrial unrest of the previous years, managed to increase its share of the popular vote to 15 per cent and return twenty-one TDs, its best result since 1943.

Fine Gael entered the election seeking support for its new 'Towards a Just Society' programme, a left-of-centre policy initiative driven mainly by Declan Costello that saw the party advocate a free medical service, increased spending on social services, an expansion of public housing and education reform. It was a dramatic step, too dramatic indeed for some of the party grandees, with Dillon and Sweetman, in particular, having grave reservations about the 'Just Society' initiative. However, despite Fine Gael's radical policy agenda, which was only announced during the election campaign, the Labour Party maintained its anti-coalition stance, neutering Fine Gael's appeal and seeing the party return to Dáil Éireann with forty-seven TDs, the same level of strength it had gained at the previous poll.

The biggest losers in the 1965 election were Independents and smaller parties. Clann na Talmhan disappeared from the political map, and Clann na Poblachta again returned just one TD. The relatively strong performance of all three major parties also saw the number of Independents dramatically reduced, and only two Independent candidates won seats.

The 1965 election confirmed that, on the eve of the fiftieth anniversary of the 1916 Rising, a new generation had firmly taken hold of Irish politics. Lemass' new cabinet contained only two members directly involved in the foundation of Fianna Fáil: Lemass himself and Frank Aiken. Following his failure to return Fine Gael to power at the election, James Dillon resigned from the leadership of Fine Gael and was replaced by Liam Cosgrave.

If change was afoot regarding a new generation of TDs, the male stranglehold on Dáil Éireann remained as tight as ever. Just five women were elected in 1965, all with strong family connections to politics, four of them being widows of former deputies. At just 3.5 per cent, women's representation in Dáil Éireann was lamentably low, and, remarkably, the situation would deteriorate at the next election in 1969 when, despite thirty-seven new TDs entering the Dáil, only three women were returned. Whatever other social changes were occurring in Ireland in the 1960s, Dáil Éireann remained very much a boys' club.

Given Lemass' victory at the polls, the opposition hardly raised a whimper when the Eighteenth Dáil met, and a new Fianna Fáil government was installed. A deteriorating economic situation resulted in continuing industrial and agricultural unrest, and two of the rising stars of the government, Brian Lenihan and Charles Haughey, resorted to draconian measures to restore order. A union-recognition dispute involving telephonists saw the Offences Against the State Act being used to remove the picket, with the Justice Minister Brian Lenihan claiming he was defending the State against Communist infiltration, as four of those arrested were members of the small, left wing group the Civil Liberties League.

Whatever credibility Lenihan's claims of Communist infiltration in a dispute in working-class Dublin may have had, Haughey certainly couldn't lay the blame at Lenin's door the following year when, during a demonstration over milk prices by the Irish Creamery and Milk Suppliers Association, 176 protesters were arrested under the same Act outside Leinster House. The strong-arm tactics deployed against the farmers were quickly dropped, however, partly due to the imminent presidential election in 1966 where de Valera's re-election attempt, managed by Haughey, was in danger of being derailed by a vigorous campaign by Fine Gael's Tom O'Higgins, son of Thomas F. O'Higgins and a nephew of Kevin O'Higgins. Eventually, de Valera scraped home by 10,000 votes, but the campaign revealed a noticeable shift in public opinion from the previous year's general election.

1966 also saw a dramatic outpouring of national spirit for the fiftieth anniversary of 1916. A huge Easter parade took place in Dublin, commemorative medals were struck, and RTÉ broadcast a highly idealised film about the Rising written by Hugh Leonard.

Militant republicans, largely inactive since the Border Campaign, also emerged to present their fiftieth-anniversary gift to the people: blowing up Nelson's Column in O'Connell Street in the heart of the capital in March 1966. The republicans' blow for freedom caught the mood of the times, ensuring the Number 1 slot in the charts for a song entitled 'Up Went Nelson'. The Irish army, charged with removing the stump of the column, met with less success than the republican effort,

12 July
A massive manhunt is underway across Britain after one of the gang involved in the Great Train Robbery, Charlie Wilson, breaks out of a high-security prison in Birmingham.

27 July
The number of US troops in Vietnam increases to 21,000.

15 September
The Sun newspaper is published for the first time, replacing the *Daily Herald*.

18 September
Sean O'Casey dies of a heart attack at his home in England.

1965

7 January
The comedian Jimmy O'Dea dies aged sixty-five.

24 January
Winston Churchill, wartime leader of Britain, dies in London aged ninety.

6 February
Sir Stanley Matthews plays his final First Division game for Stoke City, at the record age of fifty years and five days.

15 February
Canada adopts the red maple leaf flag as its new national flag, replacing the Royal Union flag, also known as the Union Jack.

21 February
Black activist and leader Malcolm X is fatally shot at the Audubon Ballroom in Harlem, New York.

3 March
The Sound of Music, starring Julie Andrews and Christopher Plummer, premieres in American cinemas.

however, causing extensive damage in O'Connell Street that left the government with a £30,000 bill for damages.

Following the fiftieth-anniversary celebration, Seán Lemass, aged sixty-seven, retired as Taoiseach. Charles Haughey and George Colley sought the leadership of Fianna Fáil and were later joined in the race by Donegal TD Neil Blaney. Lemass tried to avoid the divisions in the party that such a contest would cause and Jack Lynch, the Minister for Finance and Cork hurling legend, reluctantly stood as a compromise candidate. Haughey and Blaney withdrew from the contest; and, while Colley pushed the issue to a vote, Lynch won the contest and was elected Taoiseach on 10 November 1966.

The battle over Lemass' succession revealed the fault lines between the ambitious cabinet ministers that emerged in the 1960s. Colley and Haughey had come to despise each other, and both dreamed of becoming leader of Fianna Fáil and Taoiseach, with Colley having the backing of the traditionalist wing of the party, led by Frank Aiken, while Haughey's support revolved around the newer generation of ministers, such as Lenihan and Donagh O'Malley.

This group of ministers – the so-called 'men in mohair suits' – were intelligent, ambitious, brash and closely associated with the new business class, which had established itself in the 1960s. Even at this stage, Haughey's links to business had begun to raise suspicions which would only grow in the following years when, as the new Minister for Finance, he would play a prominent role in Taca, a Fianna Fáil fundraising organisation bankrolled in the main by the building sector.

In May 1967, at a Fianna Fáil meeting, Colley attacked those in the party with low standards in high places, a veiled attack on Haughey and his financial friends, as Fine Gael's Gerry L'Estrange would later point out:

> We know that Deputy Colley spoke about low standards in high places and many of us believe he was speaking about those closely associated with the Fianna Fáil Party, who largely subscribe to the Fianna Fáil Party. Members of Taca subscribe £100 to sit down to dinner and sign bankers' orders for £100 a year and to many of those Deputy Colley was referring.
>
> *(13 March 1968)*

The debate on the nomination of Lynch's government continued for three days, with opposition deputies lining up to launch political and personal attacks on the government and the manner of Lynch's elevation to the office of Taoiseach, which

Removing the stump, 9 March 1966. The Irish army remove the remainder of Nelson's Column in the centre of O'Connell Street after it was partially demolished by an IRA explosion.

21 March
Martin Luther King leads 3,200 civil rights activists on the third march from Selma, Alabama, to the state capital, Montgomery.

1 August
Cigarette advertising is banned on British television.

11 November
Rhodesia, the African country later known as Zimbabwe, declares its independence from Britain.

1966

14 February
The Australian dollar is introduced as legal tender.

1 March
Arkle winds the Leopardstown Stakes for the third year in a row.

was seen as a last-minute play to postpone the inevitable clash between Haughey and Colley. Recently retired Fine Gael leader James Dillon launched a particularly stinging attack on those around Haughey:

> Then the battle will begin. But do not imagine for a moment that it is not going on now. There is not an hour, or a day, or a week, until they break his heart, that the clash of knives will not be heard in the corridors of Fianna Fáil and that the affairs of the nation will not be made a secondary consideration … I make no apology for the fact that in certain regards I am proud that it was in our house that Davis wrote the words "And righteous men must make our land a nation once again". I ask our people to remember those words and then to look at O'Malley, Haughey, Lenihan and Blaney and ask themselves the question: was it men like these that Davis was thinking of when he wrote

these lines? Were theirs the standards which he considered the hallmark of righteous men?

(*11 November 1966*)

Lynch concluded the marathon debate in typical low-key style, saying:

> Certain remarks were made about me during the course of this debate. I shall not defend myself. I may have been reluctant to let my name go forward for nomination as Taoiseach. I had my personal reasons but these are now irrelevant. I have put them aside. I can assure the Deputies opposite that I shall not be a reluctant Taoiseach. On the contrary, I shall be a vigorous and progressive one.

(*16 November 1966*)

While Lynch's leadership could hardly be described as vigorous, his government did undertake a number of progressive measures, with Justice Minister Brian Lenihan relaxing the censorship laws in 1967 and Donagh O'Malley making strides to fulfil his promise of free second-level education until his untimely death in March 1968.

Substantial education reform, including an expansion of the vocational education sector and the laying of the foundations of the comprehensive-school system, had been undertaken by Paddy Hillery, who was Minister for Education from 1959 to 1965. A key Organisation for Economic Co-operation and Development (OECD) report on education in Ireland, produced in 1965, was critical of the lack of investment and long-term planning, an issue Donagh O'Malley would grasp on becoming Minister for Education.

Much to the surprise of his cabinet colleagues and the nation, on 10 September 1966, O'Malley announced his intention to introduce three years of free second-level education for every child. Two months later, speaking on the Education estimates, O'Malley countered criticism that his scheme was unworkable and unaffordable. While a mercurial figure, given to the grand gesture, O'Malley was undoubtedly one of the brightest of his generation, and, while far from complete, his plan to introduce free second-level education was on a firm footing;

> In relation to my proposal, it must be borne in mind also that as Minister for Education and acting as a member of a responsible Government, I cannot place any Utopian scheme before the House. It is very easy to promise the

sun, moon and stars when there is little prospect of your being called upon to implement such promises. When in September last I announced that I would introduce a scheme of free education the members of the principal Opposition Party told all and sundry that I was making a promise that would never be fulfilled. They asked where was the money going to come from. Suddenly it dawned on them that here was something that was going to be implemented and implemented in a responsible way. They then rushed out their policy for education and the scene changed over night. The country which was bankrupt in their eyes a few weeks ago is now so opulent that the buoyancy in revenue can be expected to be such as to pay for an education plan running into many millions without any resort to additional taxation.

(*30 November 1966*)

The vision behind O'Malley's move was perhaps most succinctly summed up by his party colleague, Roscommon TD Dr Hugh Gibbons:

He has been criticised because the details have not been fully worked out, but, to my mind, that is not a wise criticism, nor do I think it is a criticism any Minister should have to answer coming in here on a question such as this. Had he waited until all the details were worked out, we would be waiting a further 30, 40 or, perhaps, 50 years.

(*30 November 1966*)

Not all the government's initiatives were as successful as O'Malley's, however, and another attempt to scrap PR and replace it with the first-past-the-post electoral system failed in 1968, with 60 per cent of the electorate rejecting the proposal.

At the same time, the Dáil was debating an issue that would haunt Irish politics long after attempts to change the electoral system had faded from memory: planning, specifically allegations of planning corruption.

The growing closeness between senior Fianna Fáil figures and business people, particularly those with property interests, had raised serious questions about the planning process. The formalisation of the link through Fianna Fáil's Taca organisation drew condemnation from many, including Labour leader Brendan Corish:

I suppose 1967 could be marked as the year of the establishment of Taca. This was the most cynical, materialistic manoeuvre of the past decade or two. I

30 July
England win soccer's World Cup for the first time since the tournament began in 1930 when they beat Germany 4–2.

13 August
China announces a Cultural Revolution, with plans for a 'new leap forward' after the first meeting in four years of the Communist Party's Central Committee.

8 September
In America, the first episode of *Star Trek* is aired.

21 October
Tragedy hits the Welsh village of Aberfan as a coal slag tip engulfs a school killing 144 people and injuring many more.

25 October
Spain closes its Gibraltar border to non-pedestrian traffic.

2 February
B & I starts a
container service
between New Ross,
County Wexford and
Newport in Wales.

4 March
The first North Sea
gas is pumped ashore
at Easington in the East
Riding of Yorkshire.

12 May
The British
government gives the
go-ahead to proposals
to convert Stansted
into London's third
international airport.

25 May
Celtic become the first
British team to win the
European Cup,
beating favourites
Internazionale
Milan 2–1.

9 October
Marxist revolutionary
Ernesto 'Che' Guevara
is killed during a
battle between army
troops and guerillas
in the Bolivian jungle.

shall not dwell on the matter too deeply … the establishment of Taca was a cynical, materialistic manoeuvre and appears nothing better than an insurance investment by people who believe — whether or not they get it — that there will be some benefit from supporting the Fianna Fáil Party and the Government by handing in big subscriptions.

(13 December 1967)

In January 1968, Fine Gael introduced a Planning Appeals Bill. The reason for the proposed legislation was bluntly put by Fine Gael's Fintan Coogan:

It is right to take out of the hands of the Minister power that has been abused in such a way that Party hacks … and all the lickspittles they have can get through. We are now in the position that the pawgreasers and the Taca men are running one section of our country … It is about time this graft—I will not withdraw one word of it—was stopped. This Bill will go a long way to drive out that sort of thing.

(20 February 1968)

Minister for Local Government Kevin Boland gave a more benign view of the Taca organisation:

These people have come together voluntarily to support our Party. They know that we regard the entrepreneur purely as a means to an end. We appreciate that the initiative of private enterprise helps to develop the economy. We have no interest in the entrepreneur as such … People who knew that, for one reason or another, they could not give to our Party service of the high quality that … voluntary members of the organisation throughout the country do, decided to try to help in a small way … by a certain amount of fund raising which is a comparatively small supplement to our main source of finance — the national collection.

(28 February 1968)

The Taca organisation would be wound up by the end of the decade, but the concerns about planning corruption and business contributions to public figures would continue to cast a shadow over Irish politics, only to be finally investigated and exposed by tribunals of inquiry established in the late 1990s.

One of those at the centre of the tribunals in later years was enjoying considerable good fortune by the end of the 1960s. Finance Minister Charles Haughey already owned a number of racehorses, had purchased an offshore island and was about to move into a Gandon mansion, Abbeville, in north County Dublin, the former summer home of Britain's lord lieutenants in Ireland.

Haughey introduced a blatant election budget in May 1969, including generous social welfare and children's allowance increases, to prepare the ground for the

> **"... the establishment of Taca was a cynical, materialistic manoeuvre and appears nothing better than an insurance investment by people who believe — whether or not they get it — that there will be some benefit from supporting the Fianna Fáil Party and the Government by handing in big subscriptions."**
>
> *Brendan Corish, 13 December 1967*

forthcoming election campaign. One of Haughey's great interests, the arts, received a major boost when he used the budget to introduce a tax-free regime for creative work, a move that many have lauded for the encouragement it gave artists over the following decades.

On 21 May 1969, Lynch dissolved the Dáil, and the election was held on 18 June. Fianna Fáil, buoyed up by the reaction to its populist budget, held itself out as the only party able to provide stable government. Jack Lynch, its popular, soft spoken, pipe-smoking leader, was also centre stage of the campaign.

Fianna Fáil and Fine Gael had one campaign strategy in common: strong attacks on the Labour Party. Corish had shifted his party dramatically to the left, and the party that even a few years earlier had seemed embarrassed at the mention of the word 'socialism', now espoused a very definite, radical left-wing programme. The

3 December
South African surgeon Christiaan Barnard performs the first heart transplant operation. The patient, Louis Washkansky, survives for eighteen days.

1968

17 March
The poet Patrick Kavanagh is remembered in Dublin as a commemoration seat by the canal on Baggot Street is unveiled in his honour.

24 March
The Aer Lingus plane, the *St Phelim*, crashes off the Tuskar Rock killing all sixty-three passengers and crew.

28 March
In London, Ringo Starr announces that there will be no more public appearances by The Beatles.

shift to the left was combined with rapid expansion. Membership increased significantly, and leading intellectuals, such as Justin Keating, Conor Cruise O'Brien and David Thornley, joined and stood for Labour at the general election. Corish now proclaimed that the 'seventies will be socialist', and Labour ran a total of ninety-nine candidates, its largest ever, in the June 1969 election, seeking a mandate for a Labour government.

Labour's new-found socialist voice did not sit well with all in the party, including many of the more conservative TDs in rural constituencies, who were less impressed with the left-wing agenda. Indeed, one TD, James Tully, informed the Dáil of what he thought of the earnest, left-wing radicals then active in Irish universities:

> In my opinion, they are a group of little brats. If their parents had the good sense, when they found out that they were masquerading in this city from some of the universities to bring them home to do some work, instead of allowing them to fool others as gullible as themselves, it would be better for all concerned.
>
> (*12 February 1969*)

Fianna Fáil employed the 'red scare' tactic against Labour during the election, with Conor Cruise O'Brien, for instance, being labelled Conor 'Cuba' O'Brien after he suggested establishing diplomatic relations with Castro's regime. Ironically, the same type of propaganda had been employed against Fianna Fáil in 1932. Fine Gael, spurned by Labour since Corish assumed the leadership and hence without a real prospect of power, didn't hesitate to embarrass its former coalition colleagues either.

The election result was a major disappointment for Labour. While it increased its national vote to 17 per cent, it dropped three seats and returned to the Nineteenth Dáil with eighteen TDs.

Fine Gael's national vote remained steady, and the party managed to increase its seats to fifty.

Fianna Fáil emerged triumphant. Their two additional seats, bringing their total to seventy-four, ensured Lynch an overall majority, with new TDs Ray MacSharry and Ber Cowen, father of future Taoiseach Brian Cowen, among those returned.

The 1969 election is also notable for the continuing dominance of the three main parties. Throughout the 1960s, the number of Independents and TDs from smaller parties had dropped steadily, decreasing from eleven TDs in 1961 to three TDs in 1965. The 1969 election returned only one TD from outside the ranks of the major parties, Joseph Sheridan, who was elected as an Independent for

Longford–Westmeath. This election also saw James Dillon, Seán Lemass and John A. Costello bowing out of public life.

Lynch was re-elected Taoiseach, but, again, the bitterness between Fine Gael and Labour was probably the most remarkable feature when the Nineteenth Dáil reconvened after the election. Labour lambasted both Fine Gael and Fianna Fáil for their conduct during the campaign and reasserted its independent stance, with Dublin TD Frank Cluskey stating:

> We, in the Labour Party, fought the recent general election with the express intention of forming a Labour Government. There was, unfortunately, a most scurrilous and scandalous campaign waged by both Fianna Fáil and Fine Gael during the course of the election and this calculated campaign of scurrility and scandal resulted in the Labour Party's policy being completely distorted … We are also confident that the only policy that can cure the many ills besetting the people of this nation is true socialism, the socialism contained in our policy document … when next a Labour spokesman rises in this assembly to propose the Leader of the Labour Party for the position of Taoiseach, it will not be, as may be commented by some, an isolated political gesture; it will be because the people, realising the content of our policy and appreciating its gross misrepresentation by others, will give the necessary support to ensure the election of a Labour Taoiseach in the twentieth Dáil.
>
> *(2 July 1969)*

While those on the Labour benches, publicly anyway, continued to plan for the great socialist leap forward, Fine Gael made its views on Labour's decade of independence clear, with former presidential candidate Tom O'Higgins declaring:

> I fail to understand what has been taking place for the past 20 minutes. We have heard the Leader of the Labour Party whinging about misrepresentation and whinging about smears. We have witnessed him being interrupted by the Fianna Fáil Party but the plain fact is that he is the greatest friend Fianna Fáil have in this Dáil, and so are the horny-handed sons of toil who sit behind him …
>
> The plain fact is that the people of Ireland, the voters of this country, reacted against the Labour Party's refusal to play a realistic role in Irish politics. That is why there are fewer of them in this Dáil today, and that is why there

14 January
'It's time to make way for a younger man.' Football legend Sir Matt Busby announces he will step down as manager of Manchester United.

4 March
In Britain, the Kray twins, Ronald and Reginald, face life sentences after being found guilty of murder at the Central Criminal Court.

20 May
US and South Vietnamese troops capture Hamburger Hill after one of the bloodiest battles of the Vietnam War.

7 July
Former Rolling Stones guitarist, Brian Jones, drowned after taking a cocktail of drink and drugs, an inquest is told.

US *Apollo 11*
astronauts Neil
Armstrong and Edwin
'Buzz' Aldrin land on
the moon. Armstrong
becomes the first
person to step on the
moon's surface.

will be fewer of them in the Twentieth Dáil. Political Parties and political
personalities, prima donnas or otherwise, have a responsible role in Irish politics,
and that is, to aim towards the achievement in Government of the rectification
and the remedying of the ills they criticise and talk about. The Irish people
have no use for those who carry perpetual chips on their shoulders and have
no intention of ever doing anything about them.

(2 July 1969)

31 July
Ireland loses its
halfpenny coin as the
country looks towards
decimalisation.

The Dáil sat for July and then took its summer break, reconvening on 22 October.
In the mean time, events that summer in Northern Ireland changed the political
landscape on both sides of the border.

Since the foundation of the Northern Ireland Civil Rights Association
(NICRA) in 1968, the government in Stormont – under the leadership of Terence
O'Neill – had come under sustained pressure to reform the discriminatory and
sectarian policies of the northern state, especially in relation to housing and voting
rights. NICRA organised marches and demonstrations, some of which ended in
confrontations with the RUC. Unionist opinion viewed these civil rights campaigners
as a dangerous, republican-inspired conspiracy that would threaten their dominance,
and O'Neill's Unionist Party split between those seeking compromise and those
who proposed a hardline attitude.

15 August
On the opening day
of the Woodstock
Arts and Music
Fair in upstate
New York, promoters
overwhelmed by
the hundreds of
thousands in
attendance, decide to
waive admission fees.

In July and August 1969, the powder-keg situation exploded with violent
clashes in Derry and Belfast between the RUC and civil rights demonstrators,
nationalists and more radical left-wing elements, all of which was extensively covered
on television. It culminated in a pogrom in the Clonard area of Belfast during
August, where Catholic families were burned out of their homes in streets bordering
the Protestant Shankill Road. The British government deployed the army in an
attempt to restore order, and the violence, murder and mayhem that became known
as 'The Troubles' began in earnest.

5 October
In Britain, *Monty
Python's Flying Circus*
airs for the first time.

The sense of crisis engendered by the events of August 1969 cannot be overstated.
Lynch made a televised speech on RTÉ in which he said that the Republic would
not stand idly by; army field hospitals were established along the border; accommodation in army camps was provided for families fleeing the outbreak of violence in Belfast
and Derry; and attempts were made to send a UN peacekeeping force to the North.

24 October
Samuel Beckett is the
winner of the Nobel
Prize for Literature.

The political fallout from the continuing violence was such that Lynch felt
compelled to inform the Dáil on its return from the summer recess that an armed
invasion of the North wasn't something he contemplated:

I feel it my duty to repeat again what I said on a number of occasions recently, namely, that the Government in this part of Ireland have no intention of mounting an armed invasion of the Six Counties. We could give a number of reasons for this attitude but the most cogent, in our conviction, is that the use of force would not advance our long-term aim of a united Ireland. Nor will the Government connive at unofficial armed activity here directed at targets across the Border.

(*22 October 1969*)

The government's initiatives in relation to Northern Ireland included the establishment of a fund for the relief of distress. The ultimate use of this fund would create an unprecedented political controversy: the Arms Crisis.

Charles Haughey was given authority to dispense the fund, and, along with Neil Blaney and two other ministers, he was appointed to a cabinet sub-committee to liaise with nationalists in the North. Lynch made the fateful decision not to sit on the committee, and his absence allowed Haughey and Blaney to launch their own northern initiative, an initiative that involved the delivery of arms, in direct contravention of Lynch's stated policy.

Over the coming months, mainly through the offices of an army intelligence officer, northern nationalists – including some senior republicans who would later emerge as prominent figures in the Provisional IRA – informed Haughey and Blaney that arms were needed north of the border to defend Catholic communities.

Blaney's and Haughey's efforts to send weapons to Northern Ireland gathered pace, and a consignment of weapons, which was ultimately destined for the North, was due to arrive at Dublin airport in April. Haughey, as Minister for Finance, was to arrange customs clearance for the delivery, and he rang Peter Berry, the Secretary of the Department of Justice, to ensure that the gardaí wouldn't interfere with the consignment. Berry, who was growing increasingly alarmed at intelligence reports about ministerial contact with subversives, informed the Minister for Finance that Garda Special Branch was aware of the attempt to import arms and would seize the weapons. According to Berry, Haughey then replied, 'I had better have it called off.' The consignment never arrived.

Berry's political boss, the Minister for Justice, Michael Moran, who suffered from ill health which was exacerbated by a drinking problem, had been incapable of decisive action for some time. After consulting the President, Eamon de Valera, on what course of action he should take, Berry – now convinced that government

29 October
The first message is sent over ARPANET, the forerunner of the internet.

1970

10 January
As Ireland play South Africa at rugby, 6,000 people protest against the match outside Lansdowne Road in Dublin.

16 January
Colonel Muammar Gaddafi assumes the role of prime minister of Libya four months after leading a successful coup against the monarchy.

23 March
Dana returns to Ireland following her win at the Eurovision Song Contest with 'All Kinds of Everything'.

11 April
A statement from Paul McCartney that he is leaving The Beatles confirms the break up of the group.

22 April
Earth Day, an event
intended to increase
public awareness
of environmental
issues and promote
conservation of the
world's resources,
is celebrated for the
first time.

4 May
Four students are
killed at Kent State
University in Ohio
when the National
Guard opens fire
during protests
against America's
involvement in the
Vietnam War.

18 September
Rock guitarist Jimi
Hendrix dies of
drug-related causes
at the age of twenty-
seven in London.

1971

2 January
Sixty-six football
supporters are killed
following a clash
between Celtic and
Rangers at the Ibrox
Park stadium in
Glasgow.

ministers were involved in an illegal attempt to import arms – went directly to see Lynch to inform him of the involvement of two senior ministers, Haughey and Blaney, in the gun-running affair.

However, in the mean time, Haughey had been hospitalised following a horse-riding accident, although the rumour mill suggested a much more salacious reason, possibly involving an irate husband, for the Finance Minister's incapacitation, and Lynch delayed meeting the two ministers to seek their resignations.

Initial contacts between Lynch and the two ministers proved inconclusive, with Lynch saying that both men had asked for more time to consider his request for their resignations. Michael Moran, who was by now receiving hospital treatment, tendered his resignation on 5 May, following a request from Lynch.

By this stage, the Fine Gael leader Liam Cosgrave had become aware of the attempted arms importation, most likely from sources within the Gardaí, and he met with Lynch on the evening of 6 May, when he informed him of the information at his disposal. Lynch would prevaricate no longer.

Following the meeting, the Taoiseach confronted both Haughey and Blaney and demanded their resignations. They refused. Lynch then sacked them both, and, as a result, Kevin Boland resigned in protest at Lynch's actions. Boland's parliamentary secretary in the Department of Local Government, Paudge Brennan also resigned.

In a matter of forty-eight hours, nearly one-third of Lynch's cabinet had resigned or was sacked, and the nation became aware of the attempted gun-running plot. The dramatic events created a genuine sense of crisis. When the Dáil sat the following morning, business was suspended until 10 p.m. to allow for a crisis meeting of the Fianna Fáil parliamentary party. Lynch managed to reassert his control at this crucial meeting and returned to the Dáil that evening to nominate the new ministers, including Des O'Malley, who would replace Haughey, Blaney, Boland and Moran. During the debate, Lynch outlined the tumultuous events of the previous weeks, and Liam Cosgrave gave vent to the deep concern the affair had caused:

> The House will now be aware from the statement the Taoiseach has made and from the brief recital of the information I have given that this is a situation without parallel in this country, that not merely involved here is the security of this State but that those who were drawing public money to serve the nation were, in fact, attempting to undermine it, and that there was a failure to deal with this situation by the Taoiseach …
>
> The situation that has now developed is such that the very security of this

Arms Crisis, 1970. Having been acquitted some of those – including Captain James Kelly, businessman Albert Luykz and republican John Kelly – leave court.

25 January
In Uganda, Idi Amin becomes president following a coup.

27 March
Charles Manson and three members of his hippy cult are sentenced to death in Los Angeles.

11 April
The GAA's ban on its members playing or attending soccer, rugby or cricket matches ends when Rule 27 is formally deleted.

12 May
The Rolling Stones singer Mick Jagger marries his fiancee Bianca Perez Morena de Macias after a row with the media nearly halts proceedings.

3 July
American rock singer Jim Morrison, leader of the Doors, dies in Paris of a drug overdose.

State is being threatened. The lives of the people not only in the greatest part of Ireland for which freedom was won at such great price have been put in peril. But, even worse than that, the people, particularly the minority about whom we are so concerned in the Six Counties, have their lives and their welfare put in jeopardy. That is a situation without parallel in the history of this country.

(*7 May 1970*)

On the Labour benches, Michael O'Leary echoed the sense of crisis:

Even at this late stage in the day one must admit to a feeling of total bewilderment at the succession of events since early morning. We might have read of such happenings in some far eastern country or some banana republic of South America … to find that we have such a situation here, whatever our policies in this assembly may be, is bewildering, to put it mildly.

(*7 May 1970*)

9 September
Inmates at the state prison in Attica, New York, take thirty guards hostage in a revolt over prison conditions. Forty-three prisoners and guards die in the revolt.

15 November
Intel launches the world's first microprocessor.

1972

11 January
Writer and lyricist Pádraic Colum, whose best known lyrics include 'She Moved through the Fair', dies in America aged ninety.

26 February
Pelé appears at Dalymount Park when his team, Santos, plays at the ground.

2 April
Raidió na Gaeltachta goes on air.

Kevin Boland, in explaining his reasons for resigning from government, displayed the hardline nationalist approach that led a minority in Fianna Fáil to have sympathy with Haughey and Blaney and, indeed, for more sinister forces organising in the North:

> The British are illegally in our country … While a policy ruling out force is appropriate and almost unanimously accepted as far as I know for this 26 County State there is no doubt that the people in the Six Counties are, in fact, in the same position as the people in the whole country were in before 1916, and they are entitled to make their own decisions … it would be presumptuous for us to attempt from the snugness of this 26 County State to dictate to our fellow countrymen who are suffering under British imperialism, because that is what they are suffering under.

(7 May 1970)

Lynch's credibility was severely damaged at the outset of the Arms Crisis, widely criticised for his negligence and his procrastination. After the scandal broke, however, he displayed a firmer hand, and the views expressed by Boland were to have no place in Fianna Fáil under his leadership.

Boland and Blaney would, eventually, leave the party and set up rival groupings. Boland founded Aontacht Éireann which collapsed in 1973 after failing to return a single TD at the 1973 election. Blaney's Independent Fianna Fáil organisation, which was largely confined to his own Donegal constituency, would be more durable, however, and last for nearly forty years, ending only when his successor and nephew, Niall Blaney, rejoined Fianna Fáil in 2006.

The Arm Crisis continued to have reverberations for Lynch's government, with both Blaney and Haughey, along with others, facing criminal charges in the aftermath of the initial crisis. The charges against Blaney were dropped, but those against Haughey proceeded.

Haughey was acquitted in October, and his trial saw a direct conflict of evidence between himself and Jim Gibbons, the Minister for Defence, with the judge drawing attention to the fact that one of the men had perjured himself as the evidence that both men had given could not be correct.

Haughey's acquittal saw the issue again take centre stage in the Dáil, with Fine Gael tabling a motion of no confidence in Gibbons on 9 November 1971. The government saw off the challenge, with Haughey voting for the government, a clear indication that, unlike Blaney and Boland, he saw his political future firmly within

Fianna Fáil, though few at that stage could see a route back to high office for the Dublin deputy.

The tumultuous events of the Arms Crisis and the worsening violence in Northern Ireland dominated political events during the early 1970s. In April 1970, Garda Richard Fallon was killed by the republican group Saor Éire during an armed robbery in Dublin and the activities of republican paramilitaries, particularly the Provisional IRA provoked a strong response from Lynch's government. Non-jury trials in the Special Criminal Court were reintroduced by Justice Minister Des O'Malley in March 1972 and Minister for Post and Telegraphs, Gerry Collins sacked the RTÉ Authority after it broadcast details of an interview with IRA Chief-of-Staff, Seán Mac Stíofán, later that year.

1972 would prove to be the bloodiest of the Troubles. The British government introduced internment without trial the previous year, and, on 30 January 1972, British paratroopers shot dead thirteen civilians in Derry on Bloody Sunday; the British Embassy in Dublin was burned during subsequent protests.

Attempts by the IRA and the British government to negotiate a resolution collapsed, and the IRA continued its violent onslaught, including the coordinated explosion of more than twenty no-warning car bombs in Belfast on Friday, 21 July, that claimed eleven lives and injured hundreds. Bloody Friday now joined Bloody Sunday in the litany of horror. To add to the terror, loyalist paramilitaries began a campaign of assassination against Catholics. In all, 467 people died in 1972.

It was against this background that O'Malley introduced the Offences Against the State Amendment Bill in November 1972. The legislation increased the powers of the gardaí to secure a conviction against a person for membership of an illegal organisation, with O'Malley explaining at the time:

> The problem is that we have people who are self-confessed leaders and members of unlawful organisations but who, under the existing rules of evidence, cannot, save in exceptional circumstances, be convicted … The duty of the Government in this situation is clear and beyond question. If the existing law is inadequate to enable the community to protect itself against those who are dedicated to the overthrow of the democratic institutions of the State, including this Parliament, then the Government must seek to have the law amended in such a way as to make it adequate …
>
> Nobody should be under any illusion about the true nature of the problem with which this Bill is designed to deal. The men of violence at whom the

17 June
Five men are arrested in a burglary of Democratic Party offices in the Watergate building in Washington DC. The cover-up of White House involvement will lead to President Richard Nixon's resignation in 1974.

29 July
Gilbert O'Sullivan's ballad 'Alone Again (Naturally)' reaches Number One in the US Billboard Hot 100 chart. In total, the song spends six weeks in the top slot.

7 August
The Ugandan leader Idi Amin sets a deadline for the expulsion of most of the country's Asians.

12 August
The last American ground combat troops are withdrawn from Vietnam.

4 September
At the Olympic Games in Munich, American swimmer Mark Spitz wins his seventh gold medal as part of the US 400-metre relay team.

Bill is aimed are the enemies of society. These people like to represent themselves in glowing terms as the heroes and martyrs of a holy war waged in the name of what they call patriotism. The reality is very different, very ugly and very sordid. The gospel of these people is a gospel of hatred and malice, and their only language is the language of physical force.

(*29 November 1972*)

5 September
Palestinian terrorists take eleven members of the Israeli Olympic delegation hostage and later kill them in a firefight with German police.

The proposal raised serious civil liberties concerns and was opposed vehemently by the Labour Party. Opinions in Fine Gael were divided, with party leader Liam Cosgrave in the minority that favoured supporting the government's proposal. At the time, Cosgrave was an increasingly isolated leader, with senior Fine Gael figures privately questioning his ability to lead the party into government. The embattled Cosgrave lost the argument over the proposed legislation, and Fine Gael Justice spokesperson Paddy Cooney tabled an amendment rejecting the bill on the grounds that it 'contains matter which is unnecessary and excessive and which is repugnant to the basic principles of justice and liberty and the long-established fundamental rights of citizens'.

3 October
The USSR performs its first nuclear test.

A bitter debate ensued, with Fianna Fáil accusing the Labour Party of being sympathetic to the IRA, Fine Gael accusing Fianna Fáil of helping to establish the IRA, and Labour attacking the civil rights credentials of both parties.

Given the combined strength of Fine Gael, Labour and the votes of those who had left Fianna Fáil following the Arms Crisis, the legislation was heading for defeat, and suspicions that Lynch would call a general election in response abounded. However, the first civilian deaths from explosions on the streets of Dublin, which occurred during the debate, had a dramatic effect on Fine Gael's stance.

22 December
The Chilean Air Force finds fourteen survivors two months after their plane crashed in the Andes. Their story is later told in the book and film, *Alive*.

Fine Gael's Tom O'Higgins rose to speak on 1 December 1972, maintaining his party's opposition to the legislation:

> We have a responsibility which we cannot renege on, a responsibility to examine carefully each proposed piece of legislation and if we think it goes too far, if we think it is excessive, if we think it is unjust, if we think it is wrong, we have a responsibility to point that out, to seek amendment, to oppose, no matter what the consequences may be. I believe this is such an occasion.

(*1 December 1972*)

1973

1 January
Ireland, the UK and Denmark all join the European Community.

As O'Higgins continued his speech, word reached Dáil Éireann that two bombs had exploded at Liberty Hall and Sackville Place in Dublin. Two people were killed

The lost generation, 12 April 1972. Children hijack vehicles to celebrate the shooting of a British soldier by a IRA sniper in West Belfast.

11 January
The first graduates from the Open University are awarded their degrees after two years studying from home.

16 January
During excavations in Wine Tavern Street, Dublin, archaeologists unearth major finds that give further insight into how the city was during pre-Norman times.

23 January
President Nixon delivers a nationwide address to the American people announcing that terms for a ceasefire in Vietnam have been agreed.

24 January
The renowned Clare piper Willie Clancy dies.

26 March
Women are allowed on to the trading floor of the London Stock Exchange for the first time in the institution's 200 year history.

in the explosions. Shortly before 10 p.m., within thirty minutes of O'Higgins declaring his objection to the government proposal, Fine Gael's Paddy Cooney entered the Dáil chamber:

> Tragic events have overtaken Parliament and conscious, and indeed anxious, about the fact that our amendment, if supported by those Members of the House known as the dissidents and now revealed as fellow-travellers of the IRA . . . might have the effect of plunging the country into the turmoil of a political crisis when, above all, in view of recent events stability is required, we have decided to put nation before party and accordingly we withdraw our amendment, but in no way conceding that a Bill of such a repressive nature as this Bill should be of more than temporary duration and subject to mature consideration later.
>
> (*1 December 1972*)

The Dáil remained in session until four in the morning and passed all stages of the legislation. The explosions had not only ensured the passage of the new law, they also secured Cosgrave's leadership of Fine Gael as his critics within the party retreated.

27 March
Marlon Brando
refuses his Oscar
for *The Godfather*
in protest of
Hollywood's
treatment of
Native Americans.

7 April
Archbishop John
Charles McQuaid dies
in Dublin at the age of
seventy-eight. During
his thirty-two-year
tenure as archbishop,
he had a dominant
and influential role in
the country.

8 April
Spanish painter
and sculptor Pablo
Picasso dies at his
villa in France at the
age of ninety-one.

19 June
*The Rocky Horror
Show*, the stage
musical later
developed into the
cult-classic film
*The Rocky Horror
Picture Show*,
opens in London.

The growing campaign for reform from the women's movement also found expression, and opposition, during the lifetime of the Nineteenth Dáil. The Irish Women's Liberation Movement had been founded in 1970, and, in that year, Lynch's government established the first Commission on the Status of Women.

Another key goal of the women's movement, a liberalisation of the ban on contraception, met with stiffer resistance. In February 1972, Dr Noël Browne, supported by Labour TD Dr John O'Connell, tried to introduce a bill to amend the law. It mirrored a similar initiative launched the previous year by some members of the Seanad, including Mary Robinson and John Horgan. The government blocked the printing and distribution of Browne's bill and effectively stifled discussion.

The campaign for reform continued and secured a legal breakthrough in December 1973. Mary McGee, a mother of four whose health would be at serious risk if she conceived again, won a case in the Supreme Court that asserted her right to import contraceptives, one of a number of landmark judgments in the area of personal rights that the court would make during the 1970s.

Over the coming years, the Dáil's response to the *McGee* judgement would reveal the bitter divide between liberal and conservative views on issues of personal morality, divisions that went right to the heart of government.

One of the outstanding achievements of Lynch's government was the successful conclusion of negotiations for Ireland's entry into the European Economic Community (EEC). The combined strength of Fianna Fáil, Fine Gael and many leaders in the business and farming community ensured the passage of the referendum by an overwhelming majority, with more than 80 per cent of voters supporting membership in a referendum held in May 1972. When the Dáil debated a motion approving membership of the EEC, Taoiseach Jack Lynch, in a rare demonstration of rhetorical flourish, declared:

It is a salutary exercise to reflect on the kind of Europe – even the kind of world – we would have today if the European statesmen in the seats of power at the beginning of this century had been endowed with the same vision, the same dedication to peace and the same sense of Community as were Schuman, Spaak, Adenauer and de Gaspari. It is conceivable that Europe and the world would have been spared two devastating wars, that we would not have had the division of Europe into two blocs and that we would be nearer to a solution of the problems of the developing world.

It is easy for us, with the benefit of hindsight, to pass judgment on the shortcomings of previous generations of political leaders. Let us not, however, forget that we in turn will be judged by posterity. Today we stand at a most important crossroads in our history. The road we take will determine not only the future of our country for generations to come, but also the contribution we make to the creation of a Europe that will measure up to the high ideals of the founders of the Community. I am confident that the decision we take will reflect our people's faith in their capacity to help fashion for themselves and for future generations of Irish men and women a better Ireland in a better Europe.

(21 March 1972)

Ireland's membership of the EEC was to have a profound effect, not least with the significant cash transfers in terms of structural funding and agricultural supports that flowed in the coming decades. However, in the early years of membership, the effects on social and employment policy were probably the most profound. European-inspired legislation on issues such as equal pay, non-discrimination of women in employment, and safety and health in industry was enacted.

Two other constitutional changes – one to reduce the voting age from twenty-one to eighteen and another to remove the special recognition of the Catholic Church afforded by the 1937 Constitution – were passed in December 1972.

The reduction of the voting age meant that more than 100,000 young voters would be given a voice at the polls when the new electoral register came into force in April 1973. However, that was not to be. Moves to establish an alternative Fine Gael–Labour coalition had stalled, and Lynch, seeking to take advantage of the disarray in opposition ranks, dissolved the Dáil during the Christmas recess and called a general election for 28 February, effectively disenfranchising voters under the age of twenty-one.

The calling of the election brought the turbulent Nineteenth Dáil to an end. No one in advance of the 1969 election could have foreseen the unprecedented events that convulsed the parliament, and the nation, during its term.

27 July
The government lifts restrictions on colour transmissions by RTÉ.

11 September
Chile's socialist president Salvador Allende dies during a military coup led by General Augusto Pinochet and supported by the US.

20 September
In a $100,000 tennis match at the Houston Astrodome, billed as the Battle of the Sexes, Billie Jean King defeats Bobby Riggs in straight sets, 6–4, 6–3, 6–3.

31 October
Three Provisional IRA prisoners escape from Mountjoy after a hijacked helicopter lands in the prison yard.

'The crimes perpetrated by the men of violence have brought discredit to the name of Irishmen throughout the world and death and damage to our own people...'

Dublin marches, 1979. Tens of thousands march in protest at PAYE tax rates.

the Irish Government cannot continue spending over £1.40p for every £1 received.

1973-1982

On the Road to
God Knows Where

*'We really are a strange people, that
five or six ageing men are willing
to sit in this Parliament and solemnly
discuss urine dipsticks in order to
decide whether we are going to legislate
along the fine tightrope of morality that
the people expect of us.'*

"The crimes perpetrated by men of violence
have brought disgrace on the name of Irishmen
throughout the world... I would appeal to our
own people... Let the message go out clearly
bring forth
from here today... fruit

1973-1982

In sporting terms, 1973 would be remembered as a year when barren spells marked only by defeat were brought to an end. Limerick ended a thirty-three-year drought and won their first All-Ireland hurling title since 1940, and September also saw Cork footballers hold aloft the Sam Maguire cup for the first time since 1945.

In politics, too, change was on the cards, and it began with the re-emergence of the prospect of a Fine Gael–Labour coalition.

Labour, following its disappointment at the polls in 1969 was open to an election pact with Fine Gael. Talks between the two parties floundered, but Lynch's decision to call a snap election brought a new sense of urgency to the project, and the prospect of power ensured that a deal was quickly hammered out. At the outset of the campaign, both parties issued a fourteen-point agreed programme and presented the voters with a united front under the 'National Coalition' banner – the more exciting 'People's Coalition' title having been ruled out on the grounds that it sounded too socialistic to some in Fine Gael.

Fianna Fáil produced little new to attract voters, relying instead on the personality of Lynch and returning to its old theme of the instability of coalition governments. However, given the turmoil witnessed within Fianna Fáil over the previous three years, the argument carried little weight with voters. Divisions in Fianna Fáil also led directly to the retirement from parliament in bitter circumstances of Frank Aiken, a towering presence in Irish politics since the 1920s.

Aiken disliked Haughey. He was appalled at his ambition, his extravagance and his arrogance, traits that Aiken believed had no place in the party he helped to establish in 1927. After the Arms Trial, Aiken wanted Haughey out of the party but took no direct action to bring it about. As the 1973 election approached, the old Civil War warrior made his opinion clear to Jack Lynch – if Haughey stood for Fianna Fáil, he would not contest the election in protest and would make public his reasons for doing so. Haughey remained on the Fianna Fáil ticket, and so Aiken stood down after fifty years in Dáil Éireann. He was convinced not to publicly reveal the reason for his retirement in the interests of party unity, but the affair revealed the potential for division that the continued presence of Haughey caused within the ranks of Fianna Fáil.

When the votes were counted, Fianna Fáil's national vote increased slightly from 1969, but the strong transfer patterns between Labour and Fine Gael saw it lose six vital seats, bringing to an end its sixteen-year grip on power. Fine Gael

1974

4 January
President Nixon refuses to hand over tapes to the Watergate Committee.

5 February
The nineteen-year-old daughter of the millionaire American publisher, Randolph Hearst, is kidnapped from her home in California.

13 February
Nobel-winning writer Aleksandr Sozhenitsyn is expelled from the Soviet Union. He will remain in exile until 27 May 1994.

24 April
Stephen King's first novel *Carrie* is released.

12 July
The manager of Liverpool football club, Bill Shankly, announces his retirement.

20 July
Thousands of
Turkish troops invade
northern Cyprus after
last-minute talks in
Athens, fail to reach
a solution.

19 August
President Richard
Nixon, facing
impeachment by
Congress for his
role in Watergate,
resigns at noon. Vice
President Gerald Ford
is sworn in to
succeed him.

23 September
Ceefax is started by
the BBC as a public
information system.

1975

7 January
Six fishermen
drown when their
ship, the *Evelyn
Marie*, sinks off the
Donegal coast.

increased its seat tally to fifty-four, recording 35 per cent of the popular vote, and Labour, even though its national vote dropped by more than three points on the 1969 election, returned with nineteen TDs, an increase of one.

The election of Liam Cosgrave as Taoiseach saw none of the bitterness that had characterised many of the previous debates of this nature. This was largely due to Lynch's decency in defeat. The new government took office, with Fine Gael occupying ten cabinet seats, including Finance, Foreign Affairs, Education, Justice and Defence. Labour had five seats at cabinet, with Corish appointed Tánaiste and Minister for Health and Social Welfare.

Northern Ireland and the economy dominated the agenda of the new government. Negotiations between the Ulster Unionist Party, the Social Democratic and Labour Party (SDLP), the Alliance Party of Northern Ireland and the two governments resulted in the Sunningdale Agreement in December 1973, which proposed a power-sharing government in Northern Ireland, with an input for the Republic through a new Council of Ireland. The brief hope of stability and peace offered by the agreement was short-lived, however, and the new arrangement collapsed the following spring, under pressure from militant Unionists.

The economic situation deteriorated rapidly just months after the coalition took office. An international economic crisis, precipitated by a disruption to oil supplies, saw the price of fuel increase fourfold and created huge inflationary pressures and queues at petrol stations across the country. Controlling rising prices had been one of the coalition's fourteen commitments outlined before the election, but spiralling inflation, which reached 25 per cent in 1975, did much to undermine confidence in the government's ability to live up to its promise. On 6 February 1974, Finance Minister Richie Ryan acknowledged as much in the Dáil:

> Nobody is more disappointed than the Members of this Government that their hoped for control of prices has not been more effective but the Government's record must be looked at in the light of the fact that this country, in common with every other country in the world, is now lying in the path of a hurricane of inflation the like of which the world has not experienced in the last quarter century.
>
> (*6 February 1974*)

The economic setback created by the Oil Crisis would continue to bedevil the government, with Fianna Fáil exploiting every opportunity to highlight divisions within the government on economic policy. As the government attempted to tackle the crisis, its botched efforts to introduce reform in another area compounded the difficulties the coalition faced.

Following the *McGee* judgment in the Supreme Court, the government introduced legislation to regulate the sale of contraceptives to married couples only. The proposal made it unlawful for single people to buy contraceptives, a move necessary to secure support for the measure among conservative members of both the Fine Gael and Labour parliamentary parties.

As the issue was adjudged to be one of personal conscience, the government granted a free vote to Fine Gael and Labour TDs, a move that allowed those with moral objections to vote against the legislation without fear of sanction. Fianna Fáil allowed no such latitude and demanded that all its TDs oppose the reform.

The debate on the legislation was contentious and bitter. In the main, Fianna Fáil highlighted the technical flaws in the proposal, but some deputies did give vent to their fervent moral opposition to any moves to legalise contraception, with Galway Deputy Michael Kitt, the father of three future TDs, stating:

> Éamonn de Valera, speaking as Taoiseach of this country, on St. Patrick's Day, 1943, to the people of Ireland at home and abroad said: "The Ireland which we have dreamed of would be the home of a people who valued material wealth only as the basis of a right living, of a people who were satisfied with frugal comfort and devoted their leisure to things of the spirit; a land whose countryside would be bright with cosy homesteads, whose fields and villages … would be joyous with the sound of industry, with the romping of sturdy children, the contest of athletic youths, the laughter of comely maidens whose firesides would be forums for the wisdom of old age … It would, in a word, be the home of a people living the life that God desires men should live …"
>
> Contraception and all that comes in its way is not going to have our people living the life that God desires that men should live. I abhor this legislation. What is morally wrong cannot be made legally right and I hope, and pray, that this House will throw it out.

> *(11 July 1974)*

However, opposition to the bill was not confined to Fianna Fáil, with Fine Gael's Oliver J. Flanagan stating his opposition to the legislation in characteristically forthright terms:

> I deplore this Bill. It is morally wrong. As I said, the cure will be worse than

10 January
Second World War Japanese soldier Private Teruo Nakamura surrenders on the Indonesian island of Morota.

15 January
International Women's Year is launched. It includes an annual celebration of International Women's Day on 8 March.

11 February
The British Conservative Party chooses Margaret Thatcher as its new leader. She is the first woman to lead a political party in Britain.

10 March
In Japan, the bullet train, the shinkansen, opens between Fukuoka and Osaka.

4 April
Bill Gates founds Microsoft in New Mexico.

30 April
The Vietnam War
ends when Duong
Van Minh, president
of South Vietnam,
surrenders
unconditionally to
North Vietnamese
communist forces.

the disease. If contraceptives are made readily available, people who would never have thought of using them may be tempted into doing so. This Bill is a violation of the laws of God and His Church … An evil tree cannot bring forth good fruit. That is as true to-day as it was when it was first spoken 2,000 years ago. This is an evil Bill and it cannot bring forth good results.

(11 July 1974)

"An evil tree cannot bring forth good fruit."

Oliver J. Flanagan, 11 July 1974

5 July
American tennis
player Arthur Ashe
becomes the first
black man to win the
Wimbledon singles
championship.

31 July
Jimmy Hoffa, the
former president of
the Teamsters Union,
is reported missing.
Although his body
has never been found,
he is believed to have
been kidnapped and
murdered.

Labour's, Barry Desmond, a strong proponent of reform, highlighted a particular trait of Irish parliamentary politics that impacted on the debate in the Dáil. Speaking immediately after his colleague Eileen Desmond had drawn attention to the support for the measure among women, the Dún Laoghaire TD remarked:

One of the difficulties in discussing this particular measure is the fact that Dáil Éireann, as currently constituted, is an almost totally male dominated Assembly … It is ironic that we have had only one woman Member contributing to the debate … We have a male dominated Assembly deciding whether or not 41,000 women currently 'on the pill' are acting criminally or otherwise. It is a unique experience for our Parliament to find itself in that kind of analytical situation. There are all the elements of a rather sick debate because of the peculiar structure of the House.

(11 July 1974)

29 October
General Franco's
dictatorship is
effectively ends with
the announcement
that heir designate
Prince Carlos
will take over as
provisional head
of state.

The Dáil voted on the proposal on 16 July, and, in a move that shocked the political system, the Taoiseach and the Minister for Education Dick Burke joined Fianna Fáil deputies in the 'no lobby' and voted against their own government's legislation contributing to the defeat of the proposal.

The Taoiseach's action was unprecedented, and Cosgrave kept his intentions to himself right up until he cast his vote, a fact that added to the strains within government following the incident; however, in the following days, the coalition hung together, winning a vote before the Dáil broke for the summer recess, although emotions ran high following the Taoiseach's action, with David Thornley stating:

> The mood of the country is that the National Coalition have achieved things in the realm of social welfare, health and housing which justify their retention in office. I remain, because I can count, an ardent coalitionist. Whatever personal ill-feeling may exist between me and the Taoiseach because of what happened on July 11th – and a considerable amount, at least as far as I am concerned, does exist – my vote tomorrow night can be in no doubt. I nevertheless feel that it is a sorry state for this nation that we should be brought into a situation where we should be confronted by two alternative leaders one of whom treats (a) an area of intense private morality and conscience, (b) the Supreme Court and (c) the Constitution, with contempt – I refer to Deputy Lynch – and on the other side a Taoiseach who fails to give leadership to people who expected it. If I may compete with Deputy Flanagan in my knowledge of the Bible may I say, as the Good Book says: "All we, like sheep, were led astray."
>
> (*25 July 1974*)

Division over reform of the family-planning regime wasn't the only political crisis to grip the coalition government. In 1973, Eamon de Valera completed his second term as president and left Áras an Uachtaráin, aged ninety. In the subsequent election, Fianna Fáil's Erskine Childers, a former Tánaiste, beat Fine Gael's Tom O'Higgins, who had come close to defeating de Valera for the post in 1966. The election demonstrated the well-established dynastic trait in Irish politics – Childers' father was one of the first to be executed by the Free State Government during the Civil War, and O'Higgins was the nephew of Kevin O'Higgins, a member of the government that had approved Childers' execution.

The new president brought an energy to the office that had been lacking during de Valera's tenure. However, in November 1974, he suffered a fatal heart attack. Cosgrave and Lynch negotiated an agreed candidate to replace Childers and avoid an election, which resulted in former Attorney General and judge of the European Court of Justice, Cearbhall Ó Dálaigh becoming president.

3 November
Queen Elizabeth II formally opens the operation of the UK's first oil pipeline at a £500,000 ceremony in Scotland.

19 December
The Altair 8800, a do-it-yourself computer kit, goes on sale for $397.

1976

12 January
Novelist Agatha Christie dies in England aged seventy-six.

21 January
The first Concordes simultaneously take off from London and Paris.

16 March
British prime minister Harold Wilson resigns. He is succeeded by James Callaghan.

Violence in Northern Ireland continued following the collapse of the Sunningdale Agreement. While never experiencing the terror that played out daily on the streets of Northern Ireland, the coalition government was confronted with the spectre of violence at regular intervals. March 1974 saw the murder of Fine Gael Senator Billy Fox, and loyalist bombings in Dublin and Monaghan two months later resulted in the deaths of thirty-three people. In July 1976, the IRA murdered the British Ambassador to Ireland, Christopher Ewart-Biggs.

In the wake of the killing of Ewart-Biggs, Cosgrave, a Taoiseach who always placed a high priority on law-and-order issues, recalled the Dáil and declared a State of Emergency. In doing so, Cosgrave had to abolish the State of Emergency which, incredibly, had remained in place since the outbreak of the Second World War. Introducing the measure at the end of August, Cosgrave stated:

> The first duty of a democratic government is to protect the lives of their citizens and to allow them to live and go about their legitimate business in peace. We have seen in Northern Ireland how violence, if it gets out of control, can destroy personal and community life. There has been an overspill of that violence into this part of the country, an overspill with the most serious consequences and with even greater implications … The crimes perpetrated by the men of violence have brought discredit to the name of Irishmen throughout the world and death and damage to our own people … Let the message go out clearly from here today that the Irish people, through their elected representatives, their democratic Government and their security forces are pledged to break and rid our country once and for all of this conspiracy of hate and evil.
>
> (*31 August 1976*)

Despite concerns among many in the Labour Party, the government won the vote on the State of Emergency and immediately moved to introduce the Emergency Powers Bill, which brought about seven-day detention for those suspected of terrorist offences. This was opposed by Fianna Fáil, with many deputies, supported by some on the government side, referring to widespread allegations of mistreatment of suspects in garda custody. The bill passed, despite Labour's David Thornley voting against it, but that was by no means the end of the affair.

Under the 1937 Constitution, the president can refuse to sign into law a piece of legislation if he or she has concerns about its constitutionality, and can request the Supreme Court to decide on the matter. President Ó Dálaigh referred the

"The **crimes** perpetrated by the **men of violence** have brought discredit to the name of **Irishmen** throughout the world and **death** and **damage** to our own people ... Let the **message** go out clearly **from here today** that **the Irish people** ... are pledged to break and **rid our country** once and for all of this **conspiracy** of hate and evil."

Liam Cosgrave, 31 August 1976

The Troubles come to Dublin, 17 May 1974. A wrecked car on Talbot Street, Dublin. The explosions in Dublin and Monaghan killed thirty-three people and injured nearly 300 others.

17 June
Violence spreads through South African township of Soweto in clashes between police and demonstrators.

2 July
North Vietnam and South Vietnaam unite to form the Communist country, the Socialist Republic of Vietnam.

Emergency Powers Bill to the Supreme Court on 24 September. The president's actions caused deep concern within the government, with the Defence Minister, Paddy Donegan, using the opportunity of a visit to Columb Barracks in Mullingar on 18 October to call Ó Dálaigh a 'thundering disgrace'.

Donegan's insult caused a storm of protest. The Taoiseach and Donegan apologised for any offence, and the Minister for Defence offered his resignation to Cosgrave, who refused to accept it. On 21 October, the Dáil debated a Fianna Fáil motion demanding Donegan's resignation, with Lynch claiming that the incident had the capacity to erode confidence in the institutions of the State.

The government rejected all attempts to give the incident the type of constitutional importance that Lynch tried to ascribe to it and it comfortably won the Dáil vote, but the crisis didn't end there.

The president resigned the following day, and, a week later, on 28 October, the Dáil debated a motion of confidence in the government. Again, the government won the vote but Cosgrave concluded the debate on what would prove an ominous note:

> As regards this debate, everybody recognises that there was generated a temporary state of mass hysteria … this is an era in which the first headline on the media takes over and it goes on as long as it can go. Sometimes it dies suddenly… In the course of almost every speech made here today their comments were prefaced or interspersed with references to the economy, realising that there was no real substance in this debate, no real belief or conviction among the Opposition that there was any serious problem so far as the State is concerned.
>
> *(28 October 1976)*

Cosgrave's assessment that the economy was the main weak point for the government was correct. The Oil Crisis and the worldwide recession that followed hit the Irish economy hard. In March 1973, when the government entered office, unemployment stood at 73,000. By December 1976 unemployment approached 112,000, an increase of more than 50 per cent.

Richie Ryan's budget strategy attempted to control rising inflation and restrict government spending, which had risen to over 50 per cent of gross national product (GNP) by 1976. His budget that year also saw the introduction of a tax amnesty in an attempt to bring evaders into the tax net, a tactic that would be used again in later years. However, Ryan's increases on the 'old reliables' – beer, cigarettes, spirits and petrol – did little to raise the government's popularity, and he was labelled 'Richie Ruin' by RTÉ's hit satirical TV show *Hall's Pictorial Weekly*.

Despite the economic gloom, the government succeeded in bringing forward a number of key reforms. In addition to the legislation on social and employment policy required by Ireland's membership of the EEC – much of which was steered through the Dáil enthusiastically by Minister for Labour Michael O'Leary – other significant legislative changes were introduced.

These included social-welfare payments for unmarried mothers, deserted wives and prisoners' wives. Progressive law-reform measures also saw the passage of the Family Home Protection Act which gave protection to spouses fearful of a family home being sold from under them and the Law Reform Commission was established on a statutory basis.

However, as the coalition faced into an election, with increased unemployment, and high inflation, there was concern that a swing against the government would

4 July
Americans celebrate the 200th anniversary of the Declaration of Independence.

5 July
In a dramatic raid, Israeli commandos fly to Uganda to save 100 hostages held by pro-Palestinian hijackers at Entebbe airport.

5 August
In London, Big Ben suffers internal damage and stops running for nine months.

2 September
The US *Viking 2* spacecraft lands on the surface of Mars, where it analyses the soil and climate and sends back some of the first close-up photographs of the planet.

9 September
Mao Tse Tung, China's communist leader dies in Beijing aged eighty-two.

25 September
Larry Mullen Jr forms the Larry Mullen Band, which later changes its name to U2.

27 September
Dublin wins the All-Ireland football final for the first time in forty-two years when they beat Kerry 3–8 to 0–10.

1977

6 January
The music publisher EMI ends its contract with The Sex Pistols, the notorious punk rock group, after reports of abusive behaviour at Heathrow airport.

17 January
Gary Gilmore is the first person to be executed by firing squad after the state of Utah lifts its ban on capital punishment.

26 February
The first flight of the Space Shuttle takes place.

see it removed from office. Some solace was had from the fact that the election would take place under new constituency boundaries, which had been revised by Minister for Local Government, Labour's James Tully, in 1974. The constituency changes, which became known as the 'Tullymander' – a play on the practice of gerrymandering whereby constituency boundaries were manipulated to achieve unfair electoral results – were beneficial to the coalition. Fianna Fáil fought the proposals tooth and nail, with Bobby Molloy claiming:

> The Government who introduced this Bill should be thoroughly ashamed of themselves. It is the most shameful piece of gerrymandering that has been carried out in any part of the country at any time … This shameless political manipulation clearly indicates that the exercise is a political one for the purpose of gaining political advantage in whatever way the Minister thinks he can best gain it.
>
> *(15 November 1973)*

Tully and his cabinet colleagues weathered the storm of criticism from Fianna Fáil and Richie Ryan also tried to boost the coalition's fortunes by introducing a populist budget on 26 January 1977. Opinions within government on the date of the election were divided. Some cabinet members favoured a June contest to gain the electoral benefit from the budget while others argued to delay until the autumn when signs of an improving economy would be apparent.

Fine Gael held its national conference at the end of May 1977, and, three days later, Cosgrave, quietly confident of a victory for the coalition parties, settled the question and called a general election. It proved to be a disastrous decision.

Remarkably, the coalition parties only commissioned an opinion poll after the decision to go to the country had been taken. The results, delivered nine days into the campaign confounded Cosgrave's assessment of the political temperature of the nation. The combined strength of Fine Gael and Labour was just 35 per cent, and Fianna Fáil was storming ahead, recording 59 per cent in the poll. Details of the poll were kept confidential, and, right up to polling day, the majority of the media predicted a return of the coalition. However, the die was cast.

In the summer of 1977, the Bay City Rollers hit the American charts with 'You Make Me Believe in Magic'. It could well have served as the Fianna Fáil anthem in the election. Lynch's party fought the campaign on a giveaway manifesto that promised a heady mix of lower taxes, increased spending and good times for all. The manifesto proposed the abolition of rates and motor tax, grants for first-time house buyers and unprecedented job creation.

During the campaign, which was orchestrated by its young General Secretary Séamus Brennan, Fianna Fáil vigorously promoted the genial, popular image of GAA hero Jack Lynch, compared with the more reserved approach of the outgoing Taoiseach Liam Cosgrave. The personalised nature of the Fianna Fáil campaign – with the country being urged to 'Let's Back Jack' – showed that US-Presidential-style campaigning had truly arrived in Ireland and that Fianna Fáil was more adept at seizing the opportunities presented by this significant change.

The election resulted in a landslide for Fianna Fáil, giving Lynch a comfortable overall majority. Fianna Fáil achieved over 50 per cent of the popular vote, returning with eighty-four seats. For Fine Gael, the result was disastrous. It achieved 30.5 per cent of the popular vote and held just forty-three seats, its worse result since 1957. Labour also lost support, and the party returned to Dáil Éireann with sixteen TDs.

The election saw the return to office of Charles Haughey, who had been reappointed to the Fianna Fáil frontbench two years earlier after a spell on the backbenches following the Arms Trial. He put his time in the political wilderness to good use by cultivating the Fianna Fáil grass roots, attending meetings of the organisation across the length and breadth of the country. This far-from-glamorous toil would pay huge dividends to Haughey during his later career as leader when his loyal followers within the organisation mobilised to support their embattled leader.

Fianna Fáil's victory led to the resignations of Liam Cosgrave and Brendan Corish from the leadership of Fine Gael and Labour; they were replaced by Garret FitzGerald and Frank Cluskey. On the day he was elected Taoiseach, Lynch told the Dáil:

> The Government's priorities have been fully set out in our manifesto which we published the day after the dissolution of the 20th Dáil. We got a strong endorsement from the people to implement our policies. The fact that we have an unprecedented majority will certainly not make us complacent. We intend to undertake our task with urgency and determination.
>
> The Irish electorate, as always, have proved themselves to be most discerning and discriminating. They have rejected the Coalition Government. The same Irish electorate will be equally discriminating at the next general election if this Government do not create the real economic progress and the improved quality of life our people are entitled to expect.
>
> (5 July 1977)

27 March
At least 570 people die when two jumbo jets collide on a runway in the popular holiday destination of Tenerife.

1 April
Optical fibre is first used to carry live telephone traffic.

2 April
Red Rum gallops into racing history by winning the Grand National for a record third time.

25 May
Liverpool win the European Cup for the first time with a 3–1 win over Borussia Mönchengladbach.

25 May
Star Wars premieres in America to become the highest grossing film at that time.

Jack Lynch, 1978. Lynch led Fianna Fáil to a landslide victory in 1977 but would be replaced as Taoiseach by Charles Haughey by the end of the decade.

Given Lynch's success in 1977, few would have imagined that before the next election was called he would have been deposed as leader. However, in the next two and a half years, the sliding popularity of Fianna Fáil, coupled with the ambition of Charles Haughey, would see the man who had led Fianna Fáil to a historic overall majority resign from the leadership of the party.

When forming his government, Lynch introduced legislation to establish a new political post in Irish politics, that of junior minister. These positions had previously been referred to as parliamentary secretaries, and seven had been appointed by the previous coalition. In 1977, ten junior ministers were appointed, including Máire Geoghegan Quinn, the first woman to hold a government post since the foundation of the Free State.

The growth in government jobs was greeted with scepticism on the opposition benches, with Fine Gael's John Bruton contending:

> It is fairly clear that this will involve the creation of more Ministers with more State cars, more State offices provided at considerable expense. The question ought to be asked whether we have enough Ministers and Parliamentary

Secretaries already and if we really need the creation of more jobs for members of Fianna Fáil.

I submit that there is strong evidence to suggest, so far as the existence of Ministers and Parliamentary Secretaries is concerned, that we are already not under-governed but over-governed...

One is entitled to ask if we need the new Ministries which the Government proposes to set up when ... other countries, with infinitely more complex societies than ours, are able to get along with a far smaller number of Ministers.

(19 October 1977)

Despite Bruton's arguments, the number of junior ministerial posts continued to grow in following years, even when Bruton occupied the post of Taoiseach. Thirty years after the introduction of the postition by Jack Lynch, twenty junior ministers were appointed when Bertie Ahern returned to power after the 2007 election.

The new government set about the task of implementing its election promises, and the Fianna Fáil manifesto was transformed into national policy. The government was helped by a general improvement in the economic situation. In 1978, economic growth was a healthy 7 per cent, with approximately 30,000 jobs being created, and inflation had fallen back to under 8 per cent. Against the benign economic backdrop, Minister for Finance George Colley increased government borrowing to finance the tax cuts and spending increases promised by Fianna Fáil during the election.

The 1977 Fianna Fáil manifesto also included a commitment to legislate for the consequences of the *McGee* judgment, an initiative which the coalition government had proved incapable of achieving. The task to introduce the very limited liberalisation of family planning law fell to Health Minister Charles Haughey.

Haughey's proposal, which he famously described in Dáil Éireann as 'an Irish solution to an Irish problem', restricted the availability of contraceptives to married couples, who were required to present a doctor's prescription to pharmacists to purchase condoms.

The legislation took six months to steer through Dáil Éireann, where the same clash between liberal and conservative viewpoints witnessed in the debate on the same issue in 1974 raged. The fact that Lynch, no fan of Haughey, had landed him with this challenge was not lost on the opposition, with Labour's John Horgan, who was strongly critical of the conservative nature of the legislation, noting just before the final vote in Dáil Éireann:

12 September
South African student leader Steven Biko dies whilst in police custody. His death sparks international protests.

16 September
Pop star Marc Bolan is killed in a car crash in southwest London.

1 October
Pelé plays his final professional football game as a member of the New York Cosmos.

14 October
Bing Crosby dies of a heart attack at the age of seventy-four.

28 October
In Britain, *Never Mind the Bollocks Here's the Sex Pistols* is released.

15 December
Women are employed by An Post for the first time to help with the Christmas postal rush.

This is a sorry piece of legislation and one which reflects little or no credit on the Government which introduced it and pushed it through the House … or on the Minister who has piloted it through … One is almost tempted to think that if anybody had wanted to devise a Bill which would have done the political reputation of the Minister concerned more damage they could not have possibly chosen a better one than the one we are disposing of this evening.

(26 June 1979)

1978

Despite the unease at the legislation among many in Fianna Fáil, Haughey stuck with his task, declaring during the same debate that:

In devising this legislation I have sought to tread the middle ground. I am faced with the necessity to make artificial contraceptives available to married persons or for family planning purposes. On the other hand, I do not and cannot accept the situation where artificial contraceptives would be made freely available to everybody without any limitation of any kind. The system put forward in the legislation is one which anyone who studies this situation will eventually come round to adopting. If we want to have artificial contraceptives made available to married persons or for family planning purposes and if we do not want to have artificial contraceptives flooding the country without hindrance, there must be some system of control.

(26 June 1979)

The bill passed Dáil Éireann later that evening, despite the fact that more than twenty Fianna Fáil TDs absented themselves from the vote. The legislation, however conservative, would in time enhance Haughey's reputation as a reformer. However, for one member of Dáil Éireann at least, the wisdom of such detailed, lengthy debates on the issue was questionable, with Fine Gael TD John Kelly remarking:

We really are a strange people, that five or six ageing men are willing to sit in this Parliament and solemnly discuss urine dipsticks in order to decide whether we are going to legislate along the fine tightrope of morality that the people expect of us. When did we ever apply that exquisite care to deciding other moral issues, to the justification of violence in any part of this country or outside it. When did we devote this exquisite finicking care to deciding issues of morality such as dishonesty towards the State, such as failing to make correct income tax returns or claiming social benefits to which we are not entitled? These are moral issues also. My own view is that they are more important than what we are talking about.

In a way I am ashamed to be part of this debate except for the purpose of pointing that out … I think it fantastic, and something that one would find only in a country inhabited by leprechauns whom life had spared from most of the major decisions the rest of the world has to face, that a handful of ageing men could sit around here talking about moral decisions that would be right or wrong depending on whether something was right or wrong with a urine dipstick.

(29 March 1979)

In addition to the new family-planning legislation, Haughey as Health Minister significantly increased health spending, introduced the first measures to restrict advertising and sponsorship by the tobacco industry and advanced negotiations on a new hospital consultants' contract that would finally be agreed in 1979, when Haughey was Taoiseach. The contract gave consultants state-salaried posts while facilitating their private practices within the public hospital system. Nearly thirty years later, it would take more than four years of negotiations to replace the contract put in place under Haughey's watch.

The government also introduced new laws enhancing consumers' rights, and, in 1979, passed legislation that paved the way for a referendum to extend voting rights for university seats in the Seanad to graduates of colleges other than Dublin University (Trinity College) and the National University of Ireland. The proposal was overwhelming endorsed by over 90 per cent of voters. The approved change has yet to be introduced thirty years later.

The general positive economic conditions in 1978 were dealt a severe blow towards the end of the year as the world economy reeled from another oil crisis. Over the next twelve months, the price of crude oil would increase by 80 per cent, and the consequences for Ireland were severe.

In his budget in February 1979, Finance Minister George Colley envisaged steady economic growth at 6.5 per cent. In fact, growth halved during the year. Colley also set a target of 5 per cent for inflation for the year, whereas inflation increased to 13 per cent by year-end. As the economic situation deteriorated, the government resorted to substantial borrowing. At the beginning of 1979, Colley estimated a

9 May
Aldo Moro is murdered.

12 May
The US Department of Commerce declares that hurricanes will no longer be named exclusively after women.

17 May
The coffin containing the body of Charlie Chaplin – missing since his grave was pillaged nearly two months ago – is found.

25 July
Louise Joy Brown, the world's first 'test-tube' baby, is born in England. She is the product of in vitro fertilisation, in which her mother's egg were fertilised outside her body.

15 September
American boxer Muhammad Ali becomes the first man to win the world heavyweight title three times when he defeats Leon Spinks.

1979

borrowing requirement of £779 million in reality, the government ended up borrowing more than £1 billion.

Colley's 1979 budget also included a provision to tax farming profits. Since joining the EEC, Irish farm incomes, bolstered by the Common Agricultural Policy (CAP), had increased significantly, but the sector paid very little tax, contributing just £38 million in 1978 compared to the £526 million brought in by income taxes, an issue that caused palpable anger among PAYE workers.

Colley attempted to lance growing urban anger at the inequitable tax system by imposing a 2 per cent tax on farm profits in his budget. However, Colley had totally misjudged the feeling of Irish farmers. The previous twelve months had seen an effective reduction in support from Brussels, and farmers were in no mood to accept an additional tax burden.

In the following weeks, farmers took to the streets in protest against the tax, and the proposal was effectively dropped in a deal struck with farming leaders at the end of February. This provoked even larger protests by PAYE workers and trade unions the following month, culminating in a massive march by an estimated 150,000 people in Dublin on 20 March 1979.

Against this background, the government faced its first electoral test at the European Parliament elections in June. The result was an unprecedented slump in Fianna Fáil support, and it gained just 34 per cent of the vote and won only five of the fifteen seats. The electoral defeat increased criticism of Lynch's leadership within the parliamentary party with many of the TDs newly elected in 1977 fearing for their political futures.

Barry Desmond of the Labour Party was clear where the government's problems emanated from, and some in Fianna Fáil privately agreed with him when he stated in the Dáil:

> Real political leadership is called for to cope with the recession as we enter it and to explain with conviction to the people the very unpopular decisions we must now all face as a direct consequence of successive Fianna Fáil policies since the notorious 1977 manifesto … we need real political leadership and not a philosophy of a manifesto which merely pandered to every known human electoral soft option and which was designed by Fianna Fáil for a return to power at any cost … Is it any wonder, then, that some of the Fianna Fáil backbenchers had almost to be restrained from burning a copy of the said manifesto during their day-long European and local elections wake on Wednesday last? …

Marching for reform, 23 January 1980. PAYE workers march in protest at the high rate of personal tax.

8 January
The oil terminal on Whiddy Island is engulfed in flames when the French tanker the *Betelgeuse* explodes off the Cork coast killing the fifty-two man crew.

16 January
The Shah of Iran flees the country following months of increasingly violent protests against his regime.

1 February
Ruhollah Khomeini returns to Iran following the overthrow of the Shah, claiming the shah and his American allies were 'robbing us of our brains'.

2 February
Sex Pistols' bassist Sid Vicious dies of a heroin overdose in New York.

9 February
Football club Nottingham Forest clinches Britain's first £1 million transfer deal.

Those of us who ... predicted that the political chickens would come home to roost with a vengeance were treated at the time by the then Deputy Colley, to use a Cork expression, as a crowd of uninformed cábógs ... Those of us who were aghast that the limited and scarce financial resources of the State should be frittered away in the way being proposed by Fianna Fáil were treated as defeatist Jeremiahs peddling perpetual doom.

(*18 July 1979*)

The Dáil rose for the summer recess the same day, and, before it reconvened in October, the actions of the IRA would again cast a shadow over the course of politics.

1979 was another bloody year in Northern Ireland. In April alone, ten British soldiers, RUC officers and prison officers were killed by the IRA. Despite the jailing of the 'Shankill Butchers' gang that year, loyalist attacks against innocent Catholics continued. The Irish National Liberation Army (INLA) killed British MP Airey Neave, a close confidant of Margaret Thatcher, in a House of Commons car bombing in March, and the IRA brought its campaign of violence to the continent that month, assassinating Richard Sykes, the British ambassador to the Netherlands, in The Hague.

The Republic was not immune to bloodshed, with Eamon Ryan a thirty-two-year-old civil servant killed while protecting his young son during an IRA robbery in Tramore, County Waterford on 7 August.

Then, on 27 August, the IRA struck at the heart of the British establishment. Lord Mountbatten, a cousin of the Queen and former Viceroy of India, was killed when a bomb exploded on his boat during a fishing trip near his family estate at Mullaghmore in County Sligo. Three other people, including Mountbatten's grandson and a fifteen-year-old local boy, Paul Maxwell, were also killed in the explosion. Hours later, the IRA murdered eighteen British soldiers in a double bomb attack at Warrenpoint in County Down.

Following the 27 August attacks, Lynch met with the recently elected British Prime Minister Margaret Thatcher, and new cross-border security arrangements were agreed, including permission for British army helicopters to cross the border when pursuing possible terrorist suspects. For many in Fianna Fáil, this concession was a step too far, and Síle de Valera TD, granddaughter of Eamon, launched a barely concealed attack on Lynch's policy in a speech delivered at the annual commemoration for Liam Lynch, a republican hero of the Civil War, in September.

The visit of Pope John Paul II at the end of September proved a welcome

---

18 February
It snows in the Sahara Desert for thirty minutes.

5 March
Christy Ring, the greatest hurler of his generation is buried in his native Cloyne, County Cork.

28 March
A nuclear disaster at the Three Mile Island plant in America increases public concerns about the safety of nuclear power.

11 April
Idi Amin is overthrown as president of Uganda. During his brutal regime, an estimated 300,000 civilians were killed.

3 May
Margaret Thatcher leads the Conservative Party to victory in Britain's general election and becomes the nation's first female prime minister.

respite for Lynch, who, at this stage, was already considering resigning in the New Year. Dissention in the Fianna Fáil parliamentary party continued, and those who wanted rid of Lynch could scent victory.

The Dáil resumed after the summer recess on 17 October, and two by-elections, both on Lynch's home patch in Cork, were set in train. The by-elections were held on 7 November, and Fianna Fáil failed to win either, further undermining the Taoiseach's authority. Colley was Lynch's favourite to succeed him, and the Minister for Finance convinced Lynch to resign earlier than expected so that his rival, Charles Haughey, would be caught off guard. On 5 December 1979, Jack Lynch announced his resignation as Taoiseach.

Just as Colley had misjudged the mood of farmers earlier that year, this time he misjudged the intentions of the Fianna Fáil parliamentary party, which, following a brief campaign, elected Haughey as leader by forty-four votes to thirty-eight. Colley had the support of nearly every cabinet member and assumed victory on that basis. However, Haughey's careful cultivation of the Fianna Fáil grass roots over the previous decade ensured huge support among backbench TDs and delivered him the victory. Haughey's ascension to the leadership would divide the party for years to come.

On 11 December, the Dáil met to elect Haughey as the new Taoiseach. Doubts about his probity and standards had existed since his early days as a minister and his role in undermining Lynch only served to confirm the grave doubts, which Garret FitzGerald alluded to when responding to Haughey's nomination:

> In a way that has no precedent I am conscious of speaking for a large part of the Irish people, regardless of party, and I am very conscious of the difficulty of responding adequately and sensitively to this unique situation. I must speak not only for the Opposition but for many in Fianna Fáil who may not be free to say what they believe or to express their deep fears for the future of this country under the proposed leadership, people who are not free to reveal what they know and what led them to oppose this man with a commitment far beyond the normal …
>
> Deputy Haughey presents himself here, seeking to be invested in office … but he comes with a flawed pedigree. His motives can be judged ultimately only by God but we cannot ignore the fact that he differs from his predecessors in that these motives have been and are widely impugned, most notably but by no means exclusively, by people within his own party, people close to him

1 June
Rhodesia formally ends nearly nintey years of white minority rule.

3 July
The US begins covert support for anti-Soviet forces in Afghanistan.

14 July
In Crossmaglen, County Armagh, GAA supporters parade silently in protest against the British army's commandeering of part of the local football pitch.

17 July
The left-wing Sandinistas take control of Nicaragua after forty-six years of dictatorial rule by the Somoza family.

20 July
Severiano Ballesteros of Spain wins the Open at Lytham St Anne's. He is only the second golfer from continental Europe to win in Britain.

"... but he comes with a flawed pedigree ..."

Garret FitzGerald, 11 December 1979

who have observed his actions for many years and who have made their human, interim judgment on him. They and others, both in and out of public life, have attributed to him an overweening ambition which they do not see as a simple emanation of a desire to serve but rather as a wish to dominate, even to own the State.

(11 December 1979)

Labour leader Frank Cluskey spoke in equally trenchant terms about the prospect of Haughey's arrival in the Taoiseach's office:

The people about whom I spoke, the speculators, the dealers in land, the peddlars of human misery, who I believe form Deputy Haughey's main political constituency, will take great heart from his apparent election as Taoiseach in this House today. As far as this party are concerned, we also have reason to take great heart from it because it is now in clear terms, unobscured by the personal qualities of Deputy Jack Lynch, what that party really stand for and what is their real political constituency, what price ordinary people in this country have to pay for the pandering and the catering to that small, vicious group of men of no conscience.

I make this appeal, and I do not speak as Leader of the Labour Party; I do not even speak as a member of the Labour Party; I speak as an Irish man to fellow Irish men and women: in the name of Ireland, in the name of Irish society, in the name of the Irish nation … think very hard indeed before walking through those lobbies today … and voting for Charles J. Haughey as Taoiseach, a man whom you know more than I is totally unfit for that position.

(11 December 1979)

The attacks on the character of an incoming Taoiseach were without precedent, but Haughey remained impervious to the assaults, safe in the knowledge that the office he had pursued with such naked ambition, was now within his grasp.

On the same day that Haughey was elected Taoiseach, his friend and fundraiser Des Traynor opened a bank account in Guinness & Mahon in Dublin. At the time, Haughey had built up debts of over £1 million with AIB. With the prospect of Haughey becoming Taoiseach, the bank agreed to settle the debt for £750,000. Over the next two months, five lodgements, totalling some £785,000 were lodged to the Guinness & Mahon account to pay off the debt. Property developer Patrick

9 August
In Britain, the first nudist beach is established at Brighton.

14 August
Dozens of yachts are lost and at least three people killed after a freak storm blows during the Fastnet yacht race.

29 September
Pope John Paul II arrives in Ireland at the start of his three-day visit.

14 October
Over 100,000 supporters march on Washington DC, in the first US national gay rights march.

3 November
Sixty-three Americans are taken hostage at the US embassy in Iran.

24 December
The Soviet Union invades Afghanistan.

13 February
The automated
Pass machine is
introduced by the
Bank of Ireland.

20 February
The Boomtown
Rats are refused
permission to play
a concert at
Leopardstwon
Racecourse by the
Circuit Court.

4 March
Robert Mugabe is
elected prime minister
of Zimbabwe.

7 March
The Derrynaflan
Chalice, found in
a field in Tipperary,
goes on display
at the National
Museum in Dublin.

25 March
The State's first
bus lane comes into
operation in Dublin.

Gallagher gave £300,000, but, despite extensive investigations thirty years later by the Moriarty Tribunal, the identities of the donors behind the other lodgements have never been uncovered. Haughey continued to receive huge sums from business figures over the next two decades, none of which were declared for tax. Following revelations at the Moriarty Tribunal, the taxman eventually caught up with Haughey, and, in 2003, it concluded a settlement of more than €6 million with the former Taoiseach.

Haughey's cabinet saw his loyal supporters rewarded, but to ensure government stability, he had to include a number of those who had bitterly opposed his leadership bid, including his arch rival George Colley, who was removed from Finance and became Minister for Tourism and Transport, a significant demotion. Another Haughey opponent, Des O'Malley, was appointed Minister for Industry and Commerce.

The cabinet was remarkable for another development: Máire Geoghegan Quinn, was elevated to cabinet, becoming the first female cabinet minister since Countess Markievicz was appointed Minister for Labour by the First Dáil in 1919.

When Haughey's government got down to work, it was faced with the growing crisis in the public finances. In the New Year, Haughey made a television broadcast informing viewers that, as a nation, we were living beyond our means, which, given what we now know of his own lavish lifestyle, was particularly ironic.

Haughey's broadcast prepared the ground for the budget delivered on 27 February 1980 by new Finance Minister Michael O'Kennedy, the only cabinet minister to support Haughey in the leadership election.

The budget saw a new PAYE allowance introduced, and the tax bands were increased so that fewer workers paid the higher rate of tax. Welfare payments were increased to try to keep pace with inflation, which would reach 18 per cent by year-end. A 20-pence increase in a gallon of petrol, 10 pence on cigarettes and 6 pence on the pint took any populist sheen off the budget.

In response to concern about public finances, O'Kennedy announced strict limits on public spending to meet a borrowing target of £896 million. In the event, there was no discipline in the public finances, and the government resorted to borrowing £1,217 million in 1980, 35 per cent more than O'Kennedy had estimated.

O'Kennedy also predicted a budget deficit of £353 million for the year. The actual deficit was 58 per cent higher. The goal of 'bringing our finances into balance', which O'Kennedy announced in the budget, was in tatters. The economy continued to decline – the month before Haughey became leader, 84,680 were on the live register, a year later, that figure had increased to 114,970.

Gene Fitzgerald replaced Michael O'Kennedy in Finance when O'Kennedy was appointed to the European Commission in December 1980. Fitzgerald's promotion was largely based on Haughey's need to bolster the party in Cork following Lynch's resignation rather than Fitzgerald's financial acumen. Despite the perilous economic state, Fitzgerald managed an upbeat, if totally unrealistic, note when presenting his first budget in January 1981:

> While international economic prospects this year are uncertain, there are grounds for optimism. The worst phase of the recession has passed and a gradual upturn should soon be under way.
>
> *(28 January 1981)*

Unsurprisingly, the Finance Minister's optimism proved unfounded. At year-end, the budget deficit of £802 million was 62 per cent higher than projected. Borrowing continued to spiral out of control, and Fitzgerald's borrowing target of £1,296 million proved meaningless. The government was forced to raise £1,722 million in 1981 to stay afloat, 215 per cent higher than 1977 when Lynch returned Fianna Fáil to office.

Despite the growing sense of crisis, Fianna Fáil, and the Minister for Finance in particular, refused to face reality. Responding to a Labour Party motion on the government's handling of the economy, Gene Fitzgerald stated:

> I am glad to say that all the unemployment indicators are contrary to the unsupported and irresponsible allegations made by … the prophets of gloom in Opposition now who were such prophets of gloom in Government in 1976 and 1977. The live register figures to date indicate a considerable slowing down on the rate of unemployment increase … An early decline in unemployment, rather than an increase … is a realistic prospect when account is taken of the current job creation programme.
>
> *(19 May 1981)*

Within a month of Fitzgerald's statement, unemployment had increased to 123,000.

February 1981 had brought terrible tragedy when a fire in the Stardust ballroom in Artane, in the heart of Haughey's Dublin North Central constituency, claimed the lives of forty-eight young people and injured over a hundred.

The Stardust tragedy resulted in the cancellation of the Fianna Fáil Árd Fheis

18 April
The southern African nation of Rhodesia is formally renamed Zimbabwe after it is granted black majority rule.

19 April
Johnny Logan wins the Eurovision Song Contest with 'What's Another Year'.

26 April
In Iran, terrorists begin to disperse the American hostages.

29 April
British-born director Alfred Hitchcock, best known for psychological suspense films, dies at the age of eighty.

5 May
The siege of the Iranian embassy in London comes to a dramatic end after a raid by SAS commandos, which is screened live on television.

due that weekend. Many believed that Haughey had planned to use the occasion to launch his first general election campaign as leader of Fianna Fáil. In the event, the moment passed, and Haughey waited until May to seek the dissolution of the Twenty-First Dáil. It proved a costly delay. Those short few months between February and May 1981 had seen a dramatic development in the prisons in Northern Ireland, a development that would ultimately deprive Haughey of the overall majority he sought.

The general election on 11 June was held against the background of the H-Block hunger strikes. In March 1981, republican prisoners in the Maze Prison outside Belfast, also known as the H-Blocks due to the design of the prison buildings, began a hunger strike in protest at the denial of political status. Bobby Sands was the first hunger striker to die, on 5 May, and his death provoked riots and protests both north and south of the border. Three more hunger strikers died before the election, generating significant sympathy for the protest and, to a lesser extent, for the wider republican movement.

The H-Block Campaign stood nine candidates in the general election and achieved 10 per cent of the vote, largely at the expense of Fianna Fáil, a factor that would frustrate Haughey's plans for an overall majority. Two H-Block candidates, Paddy Agnew and Kieran Doherty, were elected. Doherty was on hunger strike in the Maze Prison at the time he was elected and died two months later. The hunger strike eventually ended in October, after ten men had died.

The number of seats contested in the 1981 election increased to 166, up from the 148 seats available in 1977. Despite the increase in seats, Fianna Fáil returned seven fewer TDs and attained just 45 per cent of the vote, down 5 per cent on its 1977 result.

Fine Gael, which had revamped its organisation under new leader Garret FitzGerald, had a spectacular result, gaining 36.5 per cent of the popular vote and delivering the party an additional twenty-two seats. The Labour Party lost 1 per cent of its share of the national vote and two TDs, including party leader Frank Cluskey in Dublin South Central. Michael O'Leary became Labour leader in the wake of Cluskey's defeat. Jim Kemmy, who led the small Democratic Socialist Party, which eventually merged with the Labour Party in 1990, also won a seat in 1981. The election saw the entry to Dáil Éireann of the first TD for Sinn Féin the Workers' Party (SFWP), with Joe Sherlock winning a seat for the party in Cork East. The party, which later dropped 'Sinn Féin' from its title, had emerged from the split in the republican movement in the late 1960s, with those who favoured a Marxist

Death of Bobby Sands, 1981. Hunger strike marchers attack garda lines barring their approach to the British embassy on Merrion Road, Dublin.

20 August
Austrian Reinhold Messner becomes the first solo climber to reach the summit of Mount Everest.

7 September
Joe Connolly lifts the McCarthy Cup as Galway win the All-Ireland hurling final for the first time in forty-seven years.

22 September
Iraq bombs several Iranian air and military supply bases, including Tehran's international airport, at the start of what appears to be all-out war.

27 October
Over 2,000 people take part in the first RTÉ Radio 2 Dublin marathon.

4 November
Former film star and Republican challenger Ronald Reagan defeats Jimmy Carter in the US presidential election.

political approach led by IRA Chief-of-Staff Cathal Goulding forming the SFWP, while those Sinn Féin members who advocated a purely military approach formed the Provisional IRA.

Goulding's supporters, in what became known as the Official IRA, ceased paramilitary attacks in Northern Ireland in 1972, but a military infrastructure remained in place, contributing to a further split in the movement in 1992 when those committed to a purely parliamentary approach, led by Proinsias De Rossa, formed Democratic Left.

With twenty-two new Dáil seats, the most change by far occurred within the Fine Gael parliamentary party with, for instance, Gay Mitchell, Ivan Yates and Ted Nealon winning seats for the first time. Significantly, the party saw a number of new women candidates, including Nuala Fennell, Mary Flaherty, Nora Owen and Madeline Taylor-Quinn win seats. Garret FitzGerald's liberal approach to social issues had attracted many women to the party, but not all female TDs shared his philosophy, with 1981 also seeing Alice Glenn, who would prove an implacable opponent of FitzGerald's liberalising instincts, win a seat in Dublin Central. In total, eleven women were elected to the Twenty-Second Dáil, 6.5 per cent of the total number of TDs.

The 1981 general election heralded an era of unprecedented political instability. In the seventeen months between June 1981 and November 1982, voters would go to the polls three times to elect a government. The strain on political parties, sitting TDs and ambitious candidates was immense. In all, there would be five general elections during the 1980s.

The election produced a hung Dáil, with Fianna Fáil six seats short of a majority and the Fine Gael–Labour alternative three seats short. Garret FitzGerald was elected Taoiseach by the Dáil on 30 June 1980 with the support of Jim Kemmy. Even with Kemmy's support, the government didn't have an overall majority, and it would last just seven months.

Immediately on becoming Taoiseach, FitzGerald discovered that the budget framework announced by Gene Fitzgerald the previous January bore no relation to what was really happening to the national finances. He spoke in the Dáil later that day, and, while barracked from the opposition benches, he didn't mince his words:

> In the couple of hours since I was appointed Taoiseach … I have learned something of the scale of the damage done. I have to say I am shocked to find the position is even worse than our most pessimistic … [interruptions] … This Government have an enormous task ahead of them … The scale of the mess is beyond anything that had to be faced previously.
>
> *(30 June 1981)*

1981

Given the state of the public finances, the new Finance Minister John Bruton introduced an emergency budget on 21 July. ESB and CIÉ charges were increased; a freeze on public-service jobs was imposed; the 10 per cent VAT rate was increased to 15 per cent; and additional tax was imposed on beer, cigarettes and petrol.

Bruton's July budget may have temporarily plugged the hole in the nation's finances, but it did little to turn around the economic crisis that was affecting every community in Ireland. Job losses continued, and, within a year, unemployment would rise to 150,000. High inflation, which reached 20 per cent in 1981, and rising unemployment led to the return of mass emigration, which during the 1980s reached levels not seen for thirty years.

Bruton introduced a full budget on 27 January 1982. For the first time, the announcement of the budget and the response of the opposition was broadcast live on radio. Little did listeners know of the drama that would unfold. Introducing his budget, Bruton stated:

In the last six months the Government have campaigned to bring realism back into economic debate in Ireland. Only by starting from reality can we make our economy efficient and competitive. If the Government are realistic about their own finances, this will inject realism into the economy as a whole … the Irish Government cannot continue spending over £1.40p for every £1 received.

Budget deficits are demoralising. They encourage the myth that one can spend what one has not earned, and that it is right to ask the taxpayers of the future to pay the price of present weakness and extravagance. It is our duty to ensure that there is a secure and prosperous future for the children of this country. They will have neither prosperity nor security if we continue to spend their birthright.

(27 January 1982)

The proposals introduced by the Finance Minister certainly didn't contain any extravagance. In addition to continuing the stringent budgetary policy announced the previous July, Bruton imposed an 18 per cent VAT rate on clothing and footwear – and he rejected any exemption for children's clothes and shoes. This was too much for Jim Kemmy, who withdrew his support, voted against the government

" ... the Irish Government cannot continue spending over £1.40p for every £1 received. "

John Bruton, 27 January 1982

on a motion related to an increase in excise duty on beer and caused its collapse. FitzGerald went to the president that night to request a dissolution of the Dáil.

Given the Dáil arithmetic, Haughey believed he could form an alternative government without an election. As FitzGerald travelled to Arás an Uachtaráin, Haughey and senior members of his front bench, including Brian Lenihan, attempted to ring the president, Paddy Hillery, beseeching him to refuse a dissolution of the Dáil. The Constitution gives few powers to the president, but one important

7 January
Announcements are made for a major redevelopment of a twenty-six acre site at Custom House Quay in Dublin.

20 January
The fifty-two American hostages, who have been held at the US embassy in Tehran for more than fourteen months, arrive in West Germany on their way home to the US.

14 February
Fire spreads through the Stardust disco in Artane, killing forty-nine people.

16 February
At the Belfast Motor Show, the de Lorean sports car is unveiled to much acclaim.

29 March
Thousands of people jog through the normally quiet Sunday streets of England's capital to try and cross the finish line of the first ever London marathon.

30 March
President Ronald Reagan is shot and wounded when a lone gunman opens fire on him in Washington.

24 April
IBM introduces its first personal computer, the IBM PC. Its enormous success soon leads competitors to clone the machine.

11 May
Jamaican-born reggae singer Bob Marley dies of cancer.

13 May
Pope John Paul II is shot in St Peter's Square. He recovers after weeks in the hospital.

3 June
Shergar wins the Derby by ten lengths.

22 June
John McEnroe is censured for his behaviour at Wimbledon.

power is the dissolution of the Dáil at his or her 'absolute discretion'. President Hillery refused to accept the phone calls, but the events of that night would eventually destroy Brian Lenihan's chance of becoming president in 1990.

The general election, the second in eight months, was held on 18 February. The result was another hung Dáil. Fianna Fáil improved on its previous performance gaining eighty-one seats, two short of a majority. Fine Gael lost two seats, and Labour returned with fifteen TDs, the same as the previous June. The small swing to Fianna Fáil ensured that Haughey was on the verge of power. The Workers' Party increased its representation, returning three TDs. In Dublin Central, Tony Gregory, a young teacher involved in community activism, won a seat as an Independent.

On the cusp of power, Haughey secured Gregory's vote by agreeing to a massive social-investment programme in inner-city Dublin, one of the most deprived areas of the State, where the recent emergence of heroin had heaped further misery on the community.

When the Dáil met to elect a Taoiseach on 9 March 1982, Haughey, to the surprise of many, also received the support of the avowedly left-wing Workers' Party deputies, who supported the election of a Fianna Fáil government, first, to provide the country with an administration and, second, to ensure that John Bruton, whose cutbacks and general economic approach they abhorred, didn't return to Finance. Haughey was elected by a margin of seven votes, with the Workers' Party TDs having to scramble into the Dáil chamber through the press gallery for the vital vote because of the hordes of Fianna Fáil supporters present that day who inadvertently blocked access to the Dáil chamber.

After appointing his government, Haughey gave an uplifting address:

The return of the Fianna Fáil Government to office today is an historic occasion since it marks the 50th anniversary of the election of the first Fianna Fáil Government in 1932 … We believe that the entry of this Government into office will bring the political uncertainty of recent times to an end, and initiate a period of the kind of political and parliamentary stability required for effective Government.

We face major economic difficulties but this Government do not intend to spend valuable time decrying our situation, nor do we propose to engage in the negative politics of berating our predecessors. Our people now want a positive outlook, a new start and an end to political uncertainty and economic gloom … We will move away from the abnormal and depressing atmosphere which has recently prevailed. We will create the opportunities that our young people need and the comfort and security that our older people have earned.

(9 March 1982)

On his election, Haughey received a tribute from an unlikely source, Fine Gael's Oliver J. Flanagan, who, by 1982, was the longest-serving member of the House:

> May I wish the Taoiseach good health, strength and an abundance of wisdom so that he will carry out well the duties assigned to him today. To many of us the Taoiseach appears to possess unusual qualities. These unusual qualities that he possesses are such that we cannot close our eyes to them, and here I want to say that as he has survived successfully the events of the seventies and the leadership problems in his party he has also survived the campaign of disgraceful vilification by the media … I, too, was a victim of vilification by the media after the Locke's Tribunal in 1948 … it is only right when a new Government take office that it should be made very clear here that it is this Parliament and the Government who run the country, not a group of journalists or penpushers.

(9 March 1982)

Despite Haughey's buoyant air on becoming Taoiseach, all was not well in Fianna Fáil. Before the Dáil met, he had to head off a potential leadership challenge from his opponents including Des O'Malley, George Colley and Martin O'Donoghue. It was the first of many heaves that he would have to face during his tenure as leader of Fianna Fáil.

Within two weeks of his appointment as Finance Minister, Ray MacSharry delivered his budget. While MacSharry maintained the general budgetary framework outlined by Bruton only two months earlier, he introduced some changes, including the scrapping of VAT on clothes and shoes.

Again, the budgetary framework proved illusionary. At the end of 1982, the budget deficit was £988 million, far from the £679 million planned for by the Minister for Finance, and, to fund this overrun, borrowing approached £2 billion, 16 per cent ahead of the target set.

However, MacSharry's arrival in Finance marked a different approach to the national finances. In July, as it became clear there was no chance of adhering to the budget framework, MacSharry postponed public-service pay increases and cut back

29 July
Britain's Prince Charles marries Lady Diana Spencer in an internationally televised ceremony in St Paul's Cathedral in London.

1 August
Music Television (MTV) debuts on the air with the video of the Buggles' 'Video Killed the Radio Star'.

7 September
Christy Brown, the author and poet, dies at the age of forty-nine. His most famous work, his autobiography *My Left Foot,* was made into an Academy-award-winning film starring Daniel Day Lewis.

6 October
Egyptian president Anwar al-Sadat is assassinated by Muslim extremists.

12 November
The Church of England Synod votes to admit women to holy orders.

spending. His influence was also to be seen in the government's most significant policy initiative, the production of a national economic plan, entitled 'The Way Forward', which included a commitment to eliminate the budget deficit by 1986. Haughey believed 'The Way Forward' had the potential to transform the economy in much the same way that Lemass' economic plan had done:

> The launching of the first Programme of Economic Expansion 24 years ago set out to convince our people that they had the strength and capacity to lift themselves out of the economic and social depression of that time. They had to be convinced — and they were — that, as Seán Lemass said, a rising tide lifted all boats. The launching of that programme marked the beginning of a new and unprecedented era of Irish economic and social development. This National Economic Plan will, I am convinced, do the same.
>
> Success is largely an attitude of mind. When the will to succeed cannot be thwarted success comes well within reach. I ask every section of our people to give us their support in this great task which we have now undertaken. For them and for our nation the rewards which success will bring are great indeed and well worth striving for.
>
> *(27 October 1982)*

However, Haughey's 1982 government would not be remembered for its long-term economic vision. While Haughey tried to portray the image of a united government, the reality was totally different. The division within Fianna Fáil over his leadership grew increasingly bitter as the year went on. The government survived a no-confidence motion in July but, in October, Des O'Malley and Martin O'Donoghue resigned from the government when Haughey demanded that all cabinet ministers profess their loyalty to him.

Newspapers reported the details of the civil war taking place within Fianna Fáil, and, in an attempt to find the source of the leaks to the press, Minister for Justice Seán Doherty arranged for the tapping of the telephones of journalists Bruce Arnold and Geraldine Kennedy. Doherty's claims that the Taoiseach knew of the telephone tapping would eventually led to Haughey's political demise nearly a decade later.

The paranoia in government engendered by Haughey didn't stop at journalists, with Finance Minister Ray MacSharry securing garda bugging equipment to record conversations he had with Martin O'Donoghue, during which O'Donoghue informed him that if TDs were backing Haughey because they were financially

1 February
Corporal punishment is banned in schools in the Republic.

5 February
Pioneering budget airliner Laker Airways collapses owing £270 million to banks and other creditors.

22 February
After a stunning one-man display by Ollie Campbell, Ireland win rugby's Triple Crown for the first time in thirty-three years.

12 March
Ireland's first crematorium is officially opened at Glasnevin Cemetery in Dublin. Cremations will cost £30 less than a traditional burial.

2 April
Argentina invades the Falkland Islands, a British dependency. Britain responds by sending in its armed forces to retake the islands.

"**Success** is largely an attitude of mind. When **the will** to **succeed cannot** be thwarted **success** comes well within reach."

Charles Haughey, 27 October 1982

5 June
The first Rubik's
Cube world
championship is
held in Budapest,
Hungary.

13 September
Lindy Chamberlain
who claims her nine-
week-old daughter
was killed by a dingo,
appears in court in
Australia charged
with her murder.

14 September
Princess Grace of
Monaco, formerly
American film actor
Grace Kelly, dies of
injuries she received
in a car accident.

16 September
Maeve Binchy's first
novel, *Light a Penny
Candle*, is published.

16 September
Kerry are denied a
fifth consecutive
All-Ireland football
win in a thrilling
match when Offaly
win 1–15 to 0–17.

compromised then finance would be available to sort the matter. The whiff of scandal around the government persisted, with concerns raised about Justice Minister Seán Doherty's interference in operational garda matters. Worse was to come.

During the summer, the brutal murder of a nurse, Bridie Gargan, in the Phoenix Park and a farmer, Donal Dunne, in County Offaly shocked the country. A massive manhunt led, incredibly, to the house of the Attorney General, Patrick Connolly, where the suspected murderer Malcolm Macarthur was found. Connolly returned from holidays in the USA and resigned. In response to the events, Haughey stated at a press conference 'It was a bizarre happening, an unprecedented situation, a grotesque situation, an almost unbelievable mischance.' Former TD and implacable Haughey opponent Conor Cruise O'Brien did his own editing of Haughey's statement and coined the phrase GUBU (grotesque, unbelievable, bizarre and unprecedented). The term entered into common usage and was used as shorthand to describe the government and the increasing number of scandals and rumours associated with it. Macarthur pleaded guilty to the murder of Bridie Gargan and received a life sentence. Controversially, he was never prosecuted for Donal Dunne's murder.

Despite the lavish launch of 'The Way Forward', Haughey's government was in crisis. Following the resignation of O'Malley and O'Donoghue, another heave against Haughey's leadership was launched by Charlie McCreevy, and Haughey survived a vote of confidence at a Fianna Fáil parliamentary party meeting in October by fifty-six votes to twenty-two. Ugly scenes followed the announcement of the vote, and Haughey's old adversary from the Arms Trial Jim Gibbons was assaulted by some of the Haughey supporters who had arrived in Leinster House to await the vote. The instigator of the heave, Charlie McCreevy, had to leave Leinster House protected by gardaí as the shouts of 'blueshirt' and 'bastard' from Haughey supporters rang in his ears.

Nearly twenty years later, Des O'Malley informed Dáil Éireann of the atmosphere of fear that gripped Fianna Fáil at the time:

> Life in Fianna Fáil under Haughey was not exactly pleasant. If you disagreed with the leader's views you could be intimidated, threatened, even assaulted within the precincts of this House by his more thuggish supporters. Haughey sought to establish a close identification between the party and his own personality. At times even the nation, the party and himself became confused with one another in his own mind. His leadership was based on a type of

unquestioning personal loyalty – demeaning to those who offered it, shallow to him who received it. Debate and discussion were discouraged, dissenting views were silenced, we were into the era of *"uno duce, una voce."* Charles Haughey created a new climate within Fianna Fáil, one very different from that which prevailed under his predecessors – Lynch, Lemass and de Valera. He created a climate of fear, a climate of greed, a climate of secrecy and conspiracy.

(10 February 1999)

Seeking to exploit the open revolt in Fianna Fáil, a motion of no confidence was tabled by the opposition in November. The Workers' Party withdrew its support for Haughey's government; Tony Gregory abstained in the vote of confidence, and, despite desperate attempts by Haughey's supporters to keep the government in office, it lost by two votes. President Paddy Hillery dissolved the Dáil, and the second general election campaign of 1982 began.

Fianna Fáil wasn't the only party riven by internal dissent in 1982. The Labour Party was divided over the issue of coalition. Those on the left of the party, led by Michael D. Higgins, vehemently opposed coalition and argued that the party shouldn't prop up any government led by either of the two conservative parties. Leader Michael O'Leary and coalition proponents believed that the party had to be in government if it was to deliver for its constituency and protect welfare, health and housing from the cutbacks to which both Fine Gael and Fianna Fáil were committed.

The issue came to a head at the party's conference in Galway at the end of October. After a heated debate, the conference decided that the decision to enter coalition could only be taken by a special delegate conference after the election. Frustrated at this defeat, O'Leary stunned the party by resigning his leadership within days of the vote. He joined Fine Gael shortly after and won a seat for the party in the general election in November 1982.

Labour was shocked at O'Leary's decision, and, in a quickly convened leadership contest, Dick Spring, a thirty-two-year-old TD for Kerry, who had been in Dáil Éireann for less than eighteen months, was elected leader on 1 November. On 4 November, Haughey's government collapsed, and Spring was faced with his first general election as leader after only days in the job.

1 October
Sony launches the first consumer CD player (model CDP-101).

8 October
In Poland, the Solidarity trade union movement is banned.

11 October
The *Mary Rose*, flagship of King Henry VIII, is raised after 437 years at the bottom of the Solent.

18 November
Actor and theatre producer Hilton Edwards dies aged seventy-eight. In 1928, he had co-founded the Gate Theatre with Micheál Mac Liammóir.

1 December
Dublin's Grafton Street officially opens as a pedestrianised street.

'I have always sought to act solely and exclusively in the best interests of the Irish people.

Three Taoisigh, 1983. Charles Haughey, Albert Reynolds and Bertie Ahern.

'It is a debate about the way in which a once great party has been brought to its knees by grasping acquisitiveness of its leade

1982-1992

Debt, Divorce, Dessie and Dick

"We have been exposed, in the eyes of the international financial community, as an economy willing to tolerate cowboys. More than that, if we spot a cowboy the Government immediately supply him with six shooter and a Stetson ..."

Intransigence is always easier than acting with courage. States ... authors ... history, ... politicans are its prisoners.

1982-1992

'Thatcher Wants Garret. Do You?' This was just one of the slogans adorning Fianna Fáil leaflets in the November 1982 election. Fianna Fáil entered the campaign in considerable disarray – the battle over Haughey's leadership had badly damaged the party in the eyes of the public, and the July spending cuts announced by MacSharry were beginning to bite. In an attempt to shore up the core Fianna Fáil vote, Haughey concentrated on Northern Ireland policy during the latter stages of a bitter campaign striking a traditional nationalist chord that played well with the grass roots.

The election was held on 24 November, and Fianna Fáil lost six seats, significantly fewer than many feared at the outset of the campaign. Fine Gael's resurgence under FitzGerald continued, and the party increased its share of the national vote and achieved seventy seats, its best ever electoral performance. Labour survived the election, marginally increasing its support from the previous February and returned to Dáil Éireann with one extra TD, bringing its total to sixteen. Workers' Party leader Tomás Mac Giolla won a seat for the first time, but the party was punished for its support of Fianna Fáil, returning just two TDs to Dáil Éireann.

Garret FitzGerald and Dick Spring began negotiations to form a government, with the two men hammering out a deal in the calm environs of a convent on Eglinton Road in Dublin. Notwithstanding the significant opposition to coalition within the Labour Party, the deal was approved by its special delegate conference, and the Twenty-Fourth Dáil met on 14 December to elect Garret FitzGerald to the position of Taoiseach.

Finance Minister Alan Dukes introduced the coalition's first budget on 9 February. It included substantial hikes in VAT, income tax and a new property tax. Despite Dukes' harsh measures, his stated aim, shared by many within Fine Gael, of eliminating the budget deficit by 1987 would come to naught.

The economy continued to deteriorate. When Dukes delivered his first budget, 190,000 were registered as unemployed, and this had increased to 237,000 three years later. Against this background, and with Labour determined to protect spending, the budget deficit increased over the lifetime of the government.

Fianna Fáil's attempts to exploit the coalition divisions were overshadowed by its continuing internal leadership woes. In January 1983, the new Minister for Justice, Michael Noonan, revealed the tapping of Bruce Arnold's and Geraldine Kennedy's telephones by the previous administration. The controversy sparked a renewed attempt to oust Haughey from the leadership of Fianna Fáil, but he survived by a margin of just seven votes.

6 January
An Air Corps helicopter flies supplies to Inisbofin Island which has been isolated for a month because of bad weather.

17 January
Britain's new breakfast news programme on the BBC is broadcast for the first time.

22 January
Björn Borg retires from tennis having won five consecutive Wimbledon championships.

9 February
Shergar is kidnapped from Ballymany Stud in County Kildare. Although a ransom is demanded, the horse is never seen again.

In early 1983, the issue of abortion moved centre stage in Dáil Éireann. In advance of the 1982 November election, Fianna Fáil had published the wording of a proposed constitutional referendum on abortion to satisfy the demands of the Pro-Life Amendment Campaign (PLAC). Abortion was, and still is, illegal in Ireland, and the pattern of Irish women travelling to England for a termination of pregnancy was well established, with more than 3,500 travelling in 1981. PLAC was a powerful, well-orchestrated lobby group, largely composed of conservative Catholics, and it used the political volatility of the early 1980s to further its demand for a referendum to enshrine a ban on abortion in the constitution. Following Fianna Fáil's move, Garret FitzGerald – fearful of the impact the group could exert during the election – gave a commitment to PLAC to introduce the same amendment if returned to office.

The legislation to provide for the referendum was introduced in February 1983. However, FitzGerald had serious concerns about the proposed wording to which he had committed his party but his efforts to belatedly amend the wording failed.

Fianna Fáil enthusiastically supported the referendum and lambasted FitzGerald for trying to renege on the original wording. Many TDs, such as Michael Woods, used the opportunity to boast of their anti-abortion credentials:

> We should be quite clear that this Bill is of great historic significance not only in Ireland but beyond our shores. Its introduction at a time when man's inhumanity to his fellow man and his lack of respect for life has reached a new level of degradation is a challenge to the international communities with whom we have relations. Just as we as a small nation campaigned for nuclear disarmament to avoid a nuclear holocaust so too should we be the ones to cry stop to the holocaust of pre-born children which we see around us in today's world and take the necessary action through our constitutional safeguards to ensure that what happened in other countries cannot, without the consent of the majority, be introduced here.
>
> (*9 February 1983*)

A minority of TDs had grave reservations about the way the proposed constitutional amendment had been foisted on the Oireachtas by PLAC, with Fine Gael's John Kelly stating:

> I find abortion a revolting and horrible thing. It is easy to be revolted by the sins of others, particularly when one is in the nature of things in no danger

Still in power, 1983. Charles Haughey leaving the Dáil after defeating a vote – by forty votes to thirty-three – calling for his resignation as leader of Fianna Fáil.

of being tempted oneself. It is easy and cheap, and I do not want credit from anybody for saying that I find abortion revolting … Before I go any further, having made that as clear as I possibly can make it, I want to protest against the way this issue has been politicised … I regard the way in which a delicate moral issue has been politicised as disgusting. I regard it as disgusting that the Leaders of the two biggest parties should have felt compelled … in the heat of an approaching election to give undertakings about a matter so serious as amending our Constitution … It is a dreadful reflection on the degeneracy of the way in which politics is now conducted that, with all the other things we might have done with the Constitution, we now find ourselves debating this Bill today for no other reason than that a well-meaning – and I concede that 100 per cent – concerned and anguished lobby came forward within the visible octave of an election in 1981, and again in 1982, and extracted from party leaders what ultimately amounted to a commitment on an ultimatum to which there was a date attached, if you do not mind.

(9 February 1983)

26 September
Australia II is the first non-American winner of the America's Cup yacht race.

25 October
Thirty-eight Republican prisoners escape from the Maze Prison outside Belfast.

1984

18 January
Fords plant in Cork closes with the loss of 1,000 jobs.

24 January
The first Apple Macintosh goes on sale.

28 January
The *Late Late Show* appeals for donations to raise £100,000 to finance a liver transplant in America for Colin McStay.

30 January
Luke Kelly of the Dubliners dies aged forty-three.

The majority of Labour TDs opposed the amendment, and, as part of the coalition deal, the party was not required to support the government's proposal. Frank Cluskey warned of the division that a referendum campaign on abortion would cause:

> Even at this late stage I appeal to Members on all sides not to let any amendment on this issue go through this House … It will be the most divisive thing that we have seen in this country since the thirties. This House is not at the people's demand or insistence, except for a small fanatical group, to inflict this amendment on Irish society. I appeal to Deputies on all sides not to do that. We will all regret it.
>
> (*27 April 1983*)

Despite Cluskey's appeal, the decision to hold the referendum was passed by eighty-five votes to eleven, with most Fine Gael members abstaining because FitzGerald's attempts to amend the wording of the referendum had been defeated. The campaign that followed was as divisive as Cluskey predicted, but the referendum was passed 67 per cent to 33 per cent.

The clash between conservative and liberal Ireland was played out again the following year when Health Minister Barry Desmond moved to liberalise the sale of contraceptives. Desmond's proposal increased the number of outlets legally entitled to sell contraceptives and made them available to anyone over the age of eighteen. Fianna Fáil and some conservative members of Fine Gael opposed the measure, with Fianna Fáil's Health spokesperson Rory O'Hanlon outlining his opposition to the move when he spoke, ironically, on Valentine's Day, 1985:

> I should like to place on record that I would oppose any move to allow contraceptives to be freely available to single people. I do not think it would be morally right, I do not think it would be right in the broader Christian sense.
>
> The Minister gave us absolutely no reason this morning to change our opinion about this Bill. It is a bad Bill and it is not in the interests of the Irish people. There is not a great demand for it … We also believe that it will lead to the indiscriminate distribution of contraceptives.
>
> (*14 February 1985*)

The Workers' Party supported the government's proposal, with Dublin North West TD Proinsias De Rossa identifying the measure as a critical test of the State's capacity to legislate in an area where the Catholic Church, in particular, had strong and vocal views:

> Perhaps one of the crucial points is that we have been challenged by the bishops to obey. If we knuckle under to that demand we do so at the expense of the sovereignty of this House. Put very simply, why should we bother standing for election, having the expense of this apparatus of democracy if all we need are a couple of dozen men sitting in Maynooth, who have the benefit of all understanding, all wisdom, who can decide what is right or wrong, what the common good is and declare "This must be done and you must vote for it"? We are wasting our time … It is a denial of democracy and should be seen and recognised as such. The dangers inherent in it should be recognised by every Deputy.
>
> *(19 February 1985)*

The legislation was passed by eighty-two votes to seventy-nine. One TD who wasn't in the division lobbies for the vote was Fianna Fáil's Des O'Malley. O'Malley, an arch critic of Haughey, had opposed the attempt to introduce legislation on the issue in 1974, claiming at the time that it was the parliament's task to deter 'fornication and promiscuity'. A decade later, however, O'Malley's view had changed, and he informed the Dáil that he wouldn't oppose the government's proposal:

> The politics of this would be very easy. The politics would be, to be one of the lads, the safest way in Ireland. But I do not believe that the interests of this State, or our Constitution and of this Republic, would be served by putting politics before conscience in regard to this. There is a choice of a kind that can only be answered by saying that I stand by the Republic and accordingly I will not oppose this Bill.
>
> *(20 February 1985)*

This latest display of dissension from the party line now gave Haughey the opportunity to be rid of his rival once and for all. At a Fianna Fáil parliamentary party meeting a week after the vote, O'Malley was charged with conduct unbecoming a party member, which resulted in his expulsion from Fianna Fáil.

Internal dissent wasn't unique to Fianna Fáil during the lifetime of the Twenty-Fourth Dáil. In late 1983, a major row erupted in cabinet over a £125 million rescue

8 May
Twelve weeks before the opening ceremony of the Los Angeles Olympic Games, the USSR announces it will not attend.

22 May
US President Ronald Reagan visits his ancestral home of Ballyporeen in County Tipperary.

22 June
Virgin Atlantic Airways makes its inaugural flight.

9 July
Violence erupts as fans gathered for the Bob Dylan concert at Slane.

9 July
In Britain, lightening sets fire to the fourteenth-century York Minster.

23 July
A new train service, the Dart, begins. It connects Howth and Bray.

30 August
The space shuttle
Discovery takes off
on its maiden flight.

16 October
Dr Leonard L. Bailey
performs the first
transplant of a
baboon heart into a
human at Loma Linda
University Medical
Center in California.

4 November
Nine people, includ-
ing four journalists,
are killed when their
plane crashes in
Sussex, England.
They had been
travelling from
Dublin to Paris for
the annual Beaujolais
wine race.

25 November
Thirty-six of Britain
and Ireland's top
musicians gather in a
Notting Hill studio to
form Band Aid and
record the song
'Do they Know it's
Christmas?'. All
money from the
record, which is
released four days
later, is donated to
famine relief
in Ethiopia.

package that Industry and Energy Minister John Bruton proposed for the troubled private company Dublin Gas. The initiative was opposed by Labour, with Frank Cluskey the most vocal opponent in cabinet, insisting that the company should be nationalised rather than propped up with government funds. Bruton won the argument, and Cluskey resigned from government and returned to the backbenches. In a reshuffle, Ruairi Quinn was promoted to cabinet as Minister for Labour.

Problematic as the resignation of Frank Cluskey was, a failed reshuffle in early 1986 proved even more embarrassing for the government. In advance of an election, FitzGerald wanted to refresh his cabinet team, and among the proposed changes was the transfer of Labour's Barry Desmond out of Health. Desmond had tenaciously defended the budgets for health and social welfare, creating significant tensions in government, and his forthright approach on policy issues had also made him enemies within the medical profession and the media, especially with his plans to limit

> **"It occurs to me that any woman voting for divorce is like a turkey voting for Christmas."**
>
> *Alice Glenn, 14 May 1986*

tobacco advertising. Although the reshuffle had been agreed between the Taoiseach and Tánaiste in advance, Barry Desmond refused to budge, threatening to resign rather than vacate the Department of Health.

The situation descended into farce with FitzGerald unable to announce his reshuffle to the Dáil as planned on the morning of 13 February. Later that day, the new line-up, which saw John Bruton replace Alan Dukes in Finance, was announced, and Barry Desmond remained on as Health Minister, though he lost the social-welfare brief. In the wake of the debacle, Fianna Fáil tabled a motion of no confidence, and Haughey used the opportunity to attack Garret FitzGerald:

The Irish people have been presented with an incredible spectacle … They have seen a situation unfold during the course of which the head of the

Government has been shown to be unsound in his judgment, treacherous in his relationships, vacillating in his decisions, incompetent in the management of his party and his Government. The outcome of his burlesque performance has been to leave the country with a Government shaken to their foundations, uneasy and unhappy in their membership and obviously incapable of acting as a collective authority as they are directed by the Constitution to do.

(20 February 1986)

The botched reshuffle wasn't the only setback for the government that year. Marital breakdown was a reality for thousands of people, but the 1937 Constitution specifically prohibited divorce. The Fine Gael–Labour Programme for Government included a commitment to introduce a divorce referendum and the government brought its proposal before Dáil Éireann in May.

Fianna Fáil officially adopted a neutral stance to the proposal, with a handful of TDs, including David Andrews and Charlie McCreevy, indicating their support for the measure; however, in practice, Fianna Fáil opposed the introduction of divorce. Fine Gael TD Alice Glenn broke ranks with her party, famously declaring in the Dáil that:

> Let me say that I pray that God will save Ireland, its families and its Constitution, which has stood us in good stead. To use present day parlance, there is hardly a nation out there now suffering from that culture that would not give an arm and a leg to have the protection we enjoy and which I hope we will not be foolish enough to throw away at the behest of the individualist liberals …
>
> The Constitution is to protect the family but a woman cast aside is not a family. She becomes a non-person. She loses all protection under the Constitution. The wife and the children are diminished. But the opposite happens to the male. He will have formed an alliance with somebody in the workforce who is bringing in plenty of money. That is all he is interested in. This is what has happened everywhere else and it will happen here. It occurs to me that any woman voting for divorce is like a turkey voting for Christmas.

(14 May 1986)

Glenn's party colleague Monica Barnes, an enthusiastic supporter of the proposal and a forthright campaigner for women's rights, expressed her frustration at some

3 December
A dense cloud of lethal gas escapes from a chemical factory in the central Indian city of Bhopal, killing thousands of people.

1985

17 January
In Britain, British Telecom announces that it will phase out the distinctive red telephone box.

4 February
Twenty countries (but not the US) sign a UN treaty outlawing torture.

11 March
Mikhail Gorbachev is named first secretary of the Soviet Communist Party.

13 March
Dawn Run delights the crowds at Cheltenham when the horse, ridden by jockey John Jo O'Neill, wins the Gold Cup.

23 March
The *Asgard II*, the
State's sailing
training ship, leaves
Cork for its inaugural
transatlantic
crossing.

28 March
The modernist
painter Marc Chagall
dies in France aged
ninety-seven.

23 April
Coca-Cola
changes its formula
to become 'New
Coke'. However, the
new drink is not well
received and the
company reverts to
its original recipe
within three months.

11 May
At least fifty-two
people die and many
are missing after fire
engulfs Bradford City
football stadium.

29 May
Thirty-nine Juventus
fans are crushed
during rioting at the
European Cup Final
between Liverpool
and Juventus in
Brussels.

contributions during the debate and predicted huge support from women in particular for the proposal:

> I and other women had to listen to a chorus of men in this House talking about how we would victimise women through this legislation. I thought I was living in some other planet. My God, when I think of the women deserted bringing up their children or single mothers bringing up their children and realise the lack of protection they got from the State, I wonder what such women think about this House, what perception they must have of the kind of speeches that have been spewed out in this House in the past three days. No wonder we would be considered irrelevant, no wonder women do not consider themselves part of the planet we inhabit … Once the women of this country realise the unprotected situation they are in, they will be queuing up to vote.
>
> (*16 May 1986*)

The legislation passed, and another divisive campaign, reminiscent of the 1983 abortion referendum, ensued. In April, just before the Dáil debated the proposal an *Irish Times*/MRBI poll revealed 57 per cent of voters were backing the constitutional change, with 36 per cent opposed. Support for the proposal ebbed away during the campaign as those in favour of the referendum lost control of the agenda and a vigorous, well-funded No campaign raised doubts about a range of issues, including succession rights and the status of the second family. The referendum was held on 26 June and over 60 per cent of voters rejected the proposal. Nine years later, the question would be put to the people again.

While the coalition's attempts to reform the constitution were rejected by the voters, the government did manage to introduce significant legislative initiatives. Landlord and tenant law was reformed, the Combat Poverty Agency was placed on a statutory basis, and work to establish the Garda Complaints Board and to abolish the concept of illegitimacy was advanced. The most significant achievement of the government was a breakthrough in Anglo-Irish relations. In November 1985, the Anglo-Irish Agreement was signed in Belfast, and, for the first time, London accepted an input from Dublin into Northern Ireland matters, albeit on an advisory basis. The agreement also enshrined the principle of consent and contained a blueprint for a devolved assembly. Speaking during the Dáil debate on the agreement, Taoiseach Garret FitzGerald addressed Unionist concerns and gave expression to his hopes about where the agreement would one day lead:

Counting the vote, 1986. Jim Tunney of Fianna Fáil watches as votes in the divorce referendum are counted.

8 June
Barry McGuigan, wins the World Featherweight title in London.

10 July
The Greenpeace flagship *Rainbow Warrior* is blown up in Auckland harbour by the French secret service.

13 July
The Live Aid concert for the starving in Africa, the world's biggest rock festival held in London and Philadelphia, raises £30 million.

22 July
Two women in Ballinspittle, County Cork, claim to have seen a 'moving' statue and the shrine becomes a focus of worship for thousands.

4 September
The first pictures of the wreck of the *Titanic* are released seventy-three years after the liner sank with the loss of 1,500 lives.

Towards that end I wish myself, turning towards those 900,000 Unionists, to assert quite plainly and without equivocation that if they read what this agreement contains, and in particular if they read Article 1 of this agreement, they will see that, while as Nationalists we retain our aspiration to Irish unity achieved by free consent and agreement, we repudiate formally, and do so now in an international agreement, any question of seeking the unity of this island otherwise than with the consent of a majority in Northern Ireland … I want this message to get through. I want it to penetrate the haze of emotion and the miasma of fear into which some political leaders in Northern Ireland have sought to plunge the Unionist population …

The Government, together with the British Government, have sought painstakingly, employing every resource of knowledge and imagination that they possess, to find the optimal way forward between the dangers that beset us on either side: the danger of Nationalist alienation overflowing into such widespread tolerance of or support for the IRA as to risk an escalation of violence by the terrorists of that persuasion; and the alternative risk of so destabilising the Unionist population as to create the danger of an escalation of violence by the other terrorists in the Loyalist camp. I believe we have, together, come as near as is humanly possible to achieving the right balance at this time. And I commend to the House the results of our work, which has been designed with honesty and dedication for one purpose alone: to bring peace and stability to Northern Ireland, and to preserve peace throughout these islands.

(19 November 1985)

The agreement provoked considerable resistance among the Unionist parties in Northern Ireland. In the south, Haughey refused to support the agreement with one of the party's rising stars, Dublin Central TD Bertie Ahern, stating:

> The saddest aspect of this agreement is that the very best it can hold out before the people of Northern Ireland is a devolved Government of some sort at some future date, with a gradual withering away of Irish governmental function as the Unionists come to their senses. So the hope of the future is the failure of the past. Devolved government had its day and was swept aside by the dominant factor that has been constant in the North: the Unionist veto and the British guarantee … the Taoiseach stated that both he and Maggie Thatcher went to the negotiations with different title deeds. Maybe so. But Deputy Garret FitzGerald meekly handed over the title deeds to our national sovereignty, while Maggie Thatcher was extremely happy to return to London with the Government's undertaking to underwrite the political future of a state that has totally failed.

(20 November 1985)

For one Fianna Fáil TD, opposition to the Anglo-Irish Agreement was the final straw. Mary Harney, a close associate of Des O'Malley, broke with the party and voted for the agreement. She was expelled from the party within a matter of days, and, within a month, she, along with Des O'Malley and a former Fine Gael activist Michael McDowell, launched the Progressive Democrats.

Despite Fianna Fáil's opposition, the majority of the electorate backed the agreement – an *Irish Times*/MRBI poll in November 1985 showed support for the agreement in the Republic at 59 per cent; in February 1986, this rose to 69 per cent.

The agreement represented the first significant political development in Northern Ireland for a decade and helped develop a dynamic between London and Dublin that would bear fruit in future decades.

The breakthrough in Anglo-Irish relations aside, the strains over budgetary policy

19 September
An earthquake measuring 8.1 on the Richter Scale strikes Mexico City, killing more than 9,000 people, injuring 30,000 and leaving 95,000 homeless.

2 October
The AIDS crisis gains widespread public attention following the death of American actor Rock Hudson, the first celebrity to publicly announce that he has AIDS.

18 October
In America, the Nintendo Entertainment System is released.

between Fine Gael and Labour, would ultimately result in the coalition's collapse. The emergence of the Progressive Democrats strengthened the hand of those in Fine Gael, such as John Bruton, who wanted to adopt a stronger line on control of the national finances. The Progressive Democrats had garnered significant support since its launch in December 1985, and its economic policy agenda – focusing on controlling spending, cutting borrowing and reducing taxes – stuck a chord with many voters, particularly middle-class voters who formed the bedrock of Fine Gael support.

In the autumn of 1986, wary of the threat the Progressive Democrats posed to its urban support base and facing a worsening economic situation, Finance Minister John Bruton proposed significant spending cutbacks – cutbacks which Labour wouldn't accept.

Whereas, previously, Taoiseach Garret FitzGerald had successfully mediated a solution between the competing interests in his cabinet, often overruling his own Fine Gael ministers, this time the Finance Minister had his full backing. Speaking during a no-confidence motion tabled by Fianna Fáil in December 1986, FitzGerald made his view on the economic situation clear:

> Moreover, as they enter their fifth year, this Government will not flinch from taking the necessary further decisions to control Government spending even though a combination of unforeseeable circumstances has made necessary tougher decisions in this area than any Government have had to take since the war years. We will not run away from these problems. We will not take refuge in a flight to the country in advance of the presentation of our budgetary proposals … I do not believe that a majority of Deputies will want to make themselves responsible for such a débacle by defeating a budget along these lines. The consequences of doing so, of precipitating an election, by rejecting these constraints would be gravely damaging for those who precipitated such an event. Those who did that would be stigmatising themselves as cowards, who would not deserve and would not receive from the people a mandate to govern this country.
>
> (*19 December 1986*)

The coalition survived the no-confidence motion by just one vote, but it proved to be the final act of that Dáil. Spring and his party colleagues refused to stand over the cutbacks proposed by Bruton, and, in January, with the coalition partners unable to agree a budget, Labour ministers resigned from government and FitzGerald called an election for 17 February 1987.

24 October
The inaugural flight to Rome leaves the newly opened Knock airport in County Mayo.

1986

4 January
Phil Lynott, the lead singer with Thin Lizzy, dies from heart failure and pneumonia at the age of thirty-six.

20 January
The British and French governments announce plans to construct the Channel Tunnel.

24 January
Halley's Comet is seen from earth for the first time since 1910. It won't be visible from earth again till 2061.

28 January
In Florida, the space shuttle *Challenger* explodes seventy-three seconds after liftoff.

19 February
In a pothole protest in County Kerry, people gather to protest against the state of the roads in the Kingdom.

20 February
The Soviets open a new phase in space exploration with the launch of the world's biggest space station, *Mir*.

28 February
Swedish Prime Minister Olof Palme is shot dead on his way home from the cinema.

26 April
The world's worst nuclear disaster occurs at the Chernobyl plant in the Ukraine. Hundreds of thousands are exposed to dangerous levels of radioactive debris.

Des O'Malley, 1986. Founding the Progressive Democrats – the party would secure fourteen seats in its first general election outing in 1987.

The nation's economic woes formed an important backdrop to the 1987 election campaign. While the Fine Gael–Labour coalition had significant success in reducing inflation, which had fallen from 12.5 per cent in 1983 to under 5 per cent by 1986, recession still gripped the economy. At the time the coalition collapsed, unemployment stood at 254,000 and economic growth was negligible.

Opinion polls throughout 1986 revealed high levels of disaffection with the government – an *Irish Times*/MRBI poll in October revealed that 75 per cent of the electorate were dissatisfied with the government – and both Fine Gael and Labour paid the price for the government's unpopularity. Fine Gael returned with just fifty-one seats, down from the record seventy seats it achieved in November 1982. Labour fared no better, achieving its lowest national vote in living memory and returning just twelve TDs to Dáil Éireann, with party leader Dick Spring hanging on to his seat in Kerry North by just four votes.

Despite no significant increase in its national vote, Fianna Fáil managed to win eighty-one seats. The story of the election, however, was the Progressive Democrats. Fighting its first national election, the party secured fourteen seats and overtook Labour as the third largest party.

The Twenty-Fifth Dáil met on 10 March, and whether Fianna Fáil could muster the votes to return to power remained in doubt until the eleventh hour, with many

TDs fearing another general election would be necessary. Ultimately, Dublin Central TD Tony Gregory abstained on the vote for Taoiseach, a decision that proved crucial, and Haughey was elected on the casting vote of the Ceann Comhairle, after the Dáil divided 82-82 on his nomination.

Within weeks of taking office, Finance Minister Ray MacSharry presented his first budget to Dáil Éireann. While Fianna Fáil had made political capital during the election campaign by attacking the previous government's proposed cuts – including a famous billboard that declared 'Health cuts hurt the old, the sick and the handicapped' – MacSharry presented a harsher budget than that advocated by the previous government. Outlining the situation to the Dáil, he stated:

> We simply cannot afford our present level of public services. For as long as public expenditure and, in consequence, taxation and borrowings remain at their present levels, productive activity in the economy will be stifled and we will not achieve the recovery in output and employment that this Government are determined to bring about …
>
> The message I have to deliver is unpalatable but it is critical to the revival of our economic prospects. We cannot be content to announce our intention to curtail spending while at the same time deferring action. We have to act now. Some schemes must be terminated, others must be reduced in scope and all public services must become more cost-effective. I am only too well aware of the number of lobbies for increased spending and how vigorously they will contest any curtailment of State services. But the national interest must take precedence over sectoral concerns.
>
> *(31 March 1987)*

MacSharry's budget included an embargo on public-sector recruitment, cutbacks in health and education spending, the introduction of hospital charges and a range of other cost-cutting measures. Fine Gael and the Progressive Democrats had both proposed a similar approach to economic policy during the election and were left with no option but to acknowledge Fianna Fáil's conversion to fiscal rectitude, although, as Fine Gael's Michael Noonan pointed out, the hairshirt policy was one Fianna Fáil condemned rather than condoned during the campaign:

> This is grand larceny of our policy as put before the electorate. The road to Áras an Uachtaráin will now take precedence over the road to Damascus.

17 April
John McCarthy is abducted on his way to the airport and three bodies, believed to be of British hostages, are also found. McCarthy is released on 8 August 1991.

26 May
The European Community adopts the European flag.

12 June
Two giant pandas on loan from China, arrive at Dublin Zoo for a three-month visit.

6 August
Ireland's first American Football National Championship game – Shamrock Bowl 1 – is played between the Craigavon Cowboys and the Dublin Celts. The Cowboys win 6–0.

25 August
Hurricane Charlie hits Ireland causes millions of pounds worth of damage.

Only one conversion took place on the road to Damascus. We had 15 on the road to Áras an Uachtaráin. If the Government were subject to the Trades Description Act they would be in the dock tonight for putting before the Irish people a product totally different from what they were contracted to deliver.

(*31 March 1987*)

26 February
The Church of England's General Synod votes by a huge majority in favour of the ordination of women priests.

Fine Gael's support for the budget was consolidated later that year when its new leader Alan Dukes, who won the leadership after Garret FitzGerald stood down following the February election, announced in a speech to the Tallaght Chamber of Commerce that Fine Gael would not attempt to bring down Haughey's minority government as long as it remained committed to conservative budgetary policies. Thus was born the 'Tallaght Strategy'.

6 March
Forty-nine people are confirmed dead and dozens are missing as a car ferry, the *Herald of Free Enterprise*, capsizes just outside the Belgian port of Zeebrugge.

The growing consensus in Dáil Éireann regarding the government's economic approach was given a further boost in October 1987 when the first national agreement between the social partners, 'The Programme for National Recovery' was agreed. The agreement saw the trade unions deliver industrial peace in return for modest wage increases and a commitment to lower taxes on the PAYE sector. Social partnership would become an integral part of social and economic planning in the future years.

Unlike previous ministers, MacSharry was determined that the strict budget limits he set would be adhered to, regardless of the political fallout. This unswerving approach had a dramatic effect on the national finances. At the end of 1986, government borrowing at £2,145 million accounted for 13 per cent of GNP. Within three years, borrowing was reduced to £479 million or 2.4 per cent of GNP, the lowest level in decades.

23 March
Over 1 million tickets are sold for the first draw of the new National Lottery.

However, this remarkable turnaround in the national finances was not without significant social cost. Within eighteen months of MacSharry delivering his budget, nearly 3,000 hospital beds had been lost. Cutbacks in local-authority housing building resulted in just 900 homes being built in 1989, compared with more than 3,000 two years earlier. According to Labour's Michael D. Higgins, the government's economic and fiscal policies were creating divisions in Irish society that would remain for years to come:

19 April
In America, *The Simpsons* cartoon is aired for the first time as part of *The Tracy Ullman Show*.

The financial logic … will go a great way towards establishing further in the public mind an acceptability of the fact that there are now two Irelands and that there are clearly opening up for the next several decades two levels of citizenship. It is of some distress to me, and to those who support my political views, that there is such high public acceptability for that ... Thus it is that in April 1988 we are discussing a Finance Bill that will continue the immoral immunity given to wealth and speculation in the Irish economy with all its social effects.

Let it be said: there is a consensus in this country, a consensus now in favour of individualism, greed, the financial institutions, cowardly politics, people with no conception whatsoever of what it means to live in a republic. In fact, the message of all speeches — and I have listened to every one of them — we have heard in favour of the provisions of this Finance Bill is that any attempt at egalitarianism is abandoned. We are unique in another respect — a Republic without a concept of equality ... There is one for you ... I repeat we are creating two tiers of citizenship in relation to access to health, education and social provision.

(21 April 1988)

In addition to strict control of government spending, Fianna Fáil's plan also included specific job-creation projects. In his 1987 budget, MacSharry announced plans to create an International Financial Services Centre in Dublin. The scheme, which was met with scepticism in many quarters when it was announced, would emerge as a tangible sign of Ireland's economic growth. Another Fianna Fáil pet project, the expansion of Ireland's beef industry, announced in June 1988, would meet with less success, and the controversy surrounding the beef sector would create significant political problems in the coming years.

Notwithstanding Haughey's initial opposition to the Anglo-Irish Agreement, the new government continued to work within the agreement's parameters, despite Unionist opposition to the deal and continuing IRA violence.

The extent to which the IRA was preparing for a long war was clear to all when 150 tons of arms and explosives supplied by Colonel Muammar Gaddafi's regime in Libya were discovered by French authorities on board the *Eskund* in November 1987. The horror which such a cargo could inflict was made all too evident that month when the IRA detonated a bomb during a Remembrance Day Service in Enniskillen, killing eleven people and seriously injuring sixty-three. Behind the scenes, the SDLP's John Hume and Sinn Féin's Gerry Adams would soon initiate a dialogue, and Haughey would open a line of communication to Sinn Féin through his special adviser Martin Mansergh, but the results of these crucial developments would not be apparent until the following decade.

4 June
After winning 107 straight times in the 400-metre hurdles, Edwin Moses loses his first race in nearly ten years when Danny Harris outruns him in Madrid.

11 June
Margaret Thatcher becomes the first prime minister elected to three consecutive terms as prime minister of the United Kingdom in the twentieth century.

20 June
New Zealand win the inaugural Rugby World Cup with a 29–9 victory over France.

1 July
The Single European Act is passed by the European Union.

11 July
The world population reaches 5 billion, the number of people on the planet has doubled since 1950.

Despite the cooperation offered by Fine Gael, Haughey remained frustrated by the minority status of his government. On issues not central to the economy, Fine Gael pursued the government and, together with other opposition parties, forced changes to government policy. The tight Dáil arithmetic often resulted in government defeats on opposition motions – the government lost five Dáil votes in its first two years in office – and, indeed, Fine Gael's Alan Shatter used the opportunity to ensure that his legislation, which established a legal framework for separated people, passed into law, the first time since 1958 that opposition legislation made it to the statute book.

In April 1989, Labour's Brendan Howlin tabled a motion calling on the government to establish a £400,000 fund for haemophiliacs who had contracted HIV through infected blood products supplied by the State. Contributing to the debate, Garret FitzGerald urged the government to accept its responsibility, advice which was ignored then and in future years, when a Fine Gael-led government was dealing with women who had contracted Hepatitis C through infected blood products:

> The issue in the debate on this motion is the moral responsibility of the Government … We are not talking about blame, nobody is adducing blame; we are talking about responsibility which is quite a different issue. Is the Minister disputing liability? Is he going to drag this issue through the courts so that these people, many of whom would be dead by the time the issue was settled, would have to face that ordeal without getting any compensation or any assistance with their problems while they are still alive?
>
> *(26 April 1989)*

The government attempt to defeat Howlin's motion failed. For Haughey, it was the final straw. Bolstered by positive opinion-poll ratings – 49 per cent of voters expressed satisfaction with the government in an *Irish Times*/MRBI poll in January, and, most importantly, Haughey's own satisfaction rating in the poll was 67 per cent – he made plans to hold a snap election. Haughey was confident that Fianna Fáil's record of economic probity would resonate with the electorate and deliver him the overall majority he so dearly sought. The Dáil sat for another month, and, on 25 May, Haughey sought its dissolution, launching the fifth general election of the decade.

When the campaign began, Fianna Fáil support began to decline. Health cutbacks in particular significantly undermined the party's traditional working-class support, and voters blamed Haughey for calling an unnecessary election. The party lost four seats and returned to Dáil Éireann six seats short of a majority.

Fine Gael and the Progressive Democrats had fought the election on a joint platform. While Fine Gael performed well, returning fifty-five TDs, the Progressive Democrats had a disastrous election. To some extent, the writing had been on the wall for the party for the previous twelve months as opinion polls showed the Progressive Democrats were unable to retain the voters who had flocked to the party in 1987. In the end, the party lost half its national vote and returned to the Dáil with just six TDs, eight fewer than it had won just two years earlier.

Both Labour and the Workers' Party attracted voters disillusioned by the cuts in social spending, particularly in the health area. Labour gained 9.5 per cent of the national vote and achieved a total of fifteen seats, regaining its place as the third largest party in the State into the bargain. The Workers' Party, contesting its first election with Proinsias De Rossa at the helm, made significant gains in Dublin, returning to Dáil Éireann with seven seats. De Rossa also topped the poll in the European elections in Dublin. The 1989 election saw the election of the first Green TD, with the shock victory of Roger Garland in Dublin South.

The election result produced another hung Dáil with no party or group able to command a majority. Labour and the Workers' Party stuck by their pledge not to form a government with either of the two conservative parties.

Alan Dukes, facing internal opposition within Fine Gael to his Tallaght Strategy, which many viewed as lumbering the party with responsibility but not power, proposed a grand coalition of Fianna Fáil and Fine Gael, each with an equal share of seats at cabinet and with each party holding the post of Taoiseach on a rotating basis. The suggestion was dismissed out of hand by Fianna Fáil. Indeed, Fianna Fáil was opposed to any option that involved coalition, let alone on the incredible terms offered by Dukes. For the first time in the history of the State, the Dáil was unable to elect a Taoiseach and a government when it reconvened on 29 June.

The Dáil met on 3 July, and, with Fianna Fáil's opposition to coalition proving a major stumbling block, there was no sign of a government being formed. During the short Dáil debate that day, Haughey made his preference clear: a minority Fianna Fáil government. However, for Des O'Malley, the prospect of supporting Fianna Fáil from the opposition benches was a non-runner. If a government was to be formed, Fianna Fáil would have to drop its historic opposition to coalition:

15 October
Southern Britain begins a massive clear-up operation after the worst night of storms in living memory.

19 October
The UK stock market bottoms out after shares on Wall Street plummet following a wave of panic selling.

5 November
In London, the television presenter Eamonn Andrews dies from heart failure aged sixty-four.

11 November
Irises, a painting by Vincent Van Gogh is sold for £27 million – a world record for a work of art.

18 November
Twenty-seven people die when fire sweeps through King's Cross station in central London.

1988

1 January
Dubliners begin celebrations to mark the city's millennium.

19 January
Writer Christopher Nolan, who cannot move or speak because of an accident at birth, wins the Whitbread Book of the Year prize.

15 March
NASA reports the accelerated breakdown of the ozone layer.

15 May
Soviet troops begin to withdraw from Afghanistan.

20 August
The eight-year Iran–Iraq war ends. An estimated 1 million people were killed during the conflict.

That Fianna Fáil have had a tradition of not offering or participating in coalitions is true, but they also had a tradition for nearly 50 years of obtaining working majorities. I am now calling on Deputy Haughey and the entire Fianna Fáil Party to overcome history, to look to their claim to be the "party of reality" to rise above rivalry and to join in giving this country a Government based on partnership...

Intransigence is always easier than acting with courage. Statesmen are the authors of history, mere politicians are its prisoners.

(3 July 1989)

O'Malley's argument won out. Not only would 1989 see Fianna Fáil form a coalition for the first time in the party's history, but it would do a deal with the Progressive Democrats, a party whose roots could be traced back to the outright warfare between O'Malley and Haughey.

It would take two more sittings of the Dáil, as well as intensive negotiations between Fianna Fáil and the Progressive Democrats, before a coalition government could be formed on 12 July. The deal saw the Progressive Democrats take two seats at cabinet, with Des O'Malley becoming Minister for Industry and Commerce and Bobby Molloy taking the Energy portfolio. Among the Fianna Fáil appointees Ray Burke was made Minister for Justice but retained his responsibilities for Communications, an unusual move that John Bruton remarked upon:

I also think it is highly unhealthy that in this reallocation of responsibilities the portfolio of Communications seems to have become the personal property of Deputy Raphael Burke. That Deputy has been moved twice from one Department to another and on each occasion he has brought Communications with him, as if it somehow or other belonged to him ... as if he alone, of all the members of the Government, had the ability to cope with the problems in that area.

It seems quite unusual, not to say suspect, that the Government believed that no other Member was capable of carrying this portfolio. I really wonder what is the secret agenda that Deputy Burke and he alone is capable of fulfilling in that area ...

(12 July 1989)

Bruton's suspicions were to prove well founded. Over a decade later, the Flood Tribunal found that, in 1989, Ray Burke had received a payment of £35,000 in cash from Oliver Barry, a businessman behind the new national radio station, Century

Radio. In all, it was a busy fund-raising year for Ray Burke, and, among the donations received to support the democratic process, the vast majority of which were lodged to his own personal bank accounts, was £30,000 from builders JMSE and £30,000 from the Fitzwilton Group.

Not to be outdone, the newly elected Taoiseach Charles Haughey continued to maintain his opulent lifestyle through undeclared donations from businessmen routed through a network of offshore accounts. On the day of the 1989 general election, developer Mark Kavanagh gave Haughey £100,000. Only £25,000 found its way to Fianna Fáil; the rest was kept for Haughey's benefit. At this time, Haughey was also in receipt of substantial funds from Dunnes Stores magnate, Ben Dunne. In August 1997, the McCracken Tribunal estimated that Dunne gifted Haughey at least £1.3 million over a number of years.

> ## "Intransigence is always easier than acting with courage. Statesmen are the authors of history, mere politicians are its prisoners."
>
> *Des O'Malley, 3 July 1989*

Haughey also ensured that taxpayers' money contributed to his upkeep by using funds from the party leader's allowance to bankroll his spending habits. The allowance was paid to political parties by the State to assist with staffing, research and other political work. Haughey used the account to take care of day-to-day personal expenses, including expensive dinners and an equally expensive taste in Parisian shirts.

Haughey saw nothing wrong with the State contributing to the cost of his personal lifestyle, though others dependent on a more formal system of social welfare at time were forced to make do on State support of a much lower order – in 1989, the old-age pension stood at just £58.50 a week, and unemployment benefit was the princely sum of £45 per week.

12 June
Ray Houghton sparks celebrations around the country when he heads home against England in a famous 1–0 victory in Euro '88.

6 July
An out-of-control fire on a North Sea oil rig is feared to have claimed the lives of most of those on board.

12 July
It is announced that Dalymount Park which has been the home of Bohemians Football Club for eighty-seven years, is to be sold.

28 August
In Germany, seventy-five people are killed and 346 are injured at an air show at the Ramstein Air Base. Three jets from the Italian air demonstration team collide and one aircraft is sent crashing into the crowd of spectators.

While extravagance may have been a hallmark of the personal finances of senior cabinet ministers, no such latitude was applied to the national finances. Finance Minister Albert Reynolds, who had replaced MacSharry after his appointment as EU Commissioner, retained a tight hold on the purse strings with the aim of continued reductions in the budget deficit and borrowing. While the 1990 budget did see some modest improvements in social spending, such as the doubling of the carers' allowance and the expansion of the social employment scheme, the overall thrust of the budget or economic policy didn't change.

Haughey's government introduced a range of measures to enhance the protection of children, including a Children's Act and a new Child Care Act. Despite the fine intentions behind these measures, they were not sufficient to alleviate the problems faced by our child-welfare systems, which continued to function on a crisis basis due mainly to a lack of funding. The government also established the Marine Institute on a statutory basis, and the Health and Safety Authority began work to enforce a new workplace health and safety regime ushered in by Minister for Labour, Bertie Ahern. The transformation of the Temple Bar area of Dublin was also initiated by the government at this time, and Junior Minister Mary Harney banned the burning of smokey coal in Dublin to deal with the worsening smog problem.

However, Reynolds' boast during his budget speech that we could face the new decade with confidence did not extend to all sectors of the economy, especially the troubled beef sector, and events over 3,000 miles away were to create an unprecedented crisis. On 2 August 1990, Iraqi dictator Saddam Hussein invaded Kuwait. The action immediately provoked international trade sanctions and would ultimately result in the First Gulf War.

The trade embargo and Iraq's refusal to honour debts threatened to cripple the Irish beef sector, especially the dominant Goodman Group, which exported significant amounts of beef to the country. This extensive trade was backed by government-guaranteed export credit insurance, the lion's share of which had been granted to the Goodman Group since Fianna Fáil's return to power in 1987. The Iraq crisis was compounded by the closure of other markets for Irish beef in the Middle East because of concerns about BSE.

As Goodman's creditors circled, the government was forced to recall the Dáil in August and pass emergency legislation to protect the company from the banks. Ironically, one of Goodman's most dogged critics, Des O'Malley, who was now Minister for Industry and Commerce, sponsored the legislation which was passed in a day, but the debate enabled critics of the Goodman Group in Dáil Éireann to air their concerns about the business and the alleged favouritism shown to it by Fianna Fáil, with Dick Spring declaring:

> The relatively innocuous legislation that we are asked to deal with is, in a way, a smokescreen. Hidden behind that smokescreen are some of the most serious questions we could possibly ask. Perhaps the most fundamental one is this: how much has our concept of democracy already been undermined by the exercise of secret power, by the pulling of strings in book-lined offices and in gracious drawing-rooms, and by the willingness of a democratically elected Government to acquiesce in the greed and ambition of individuals?
>
> The Irish beef industry, one of the cornerstones of Irish agriculture and the largest exporting industry in the country, has been brought to the brink of destruction by adventurism, greed and the determination of one man to concentrate material and political power in his own hands, and by the venality of politicians…
>
> We have been exposed, in the eyes of the international financial community, as an economy willing to tolerate cowboys. More than that, if we spot a cowboy the Government immediately supply him with a six shooter and a Stetson …
>
> *(28 August 1990)*

The Goodman Group wasn't the only issue exercising Dick Spring's mind in 1990. A presidential election was due that year, and the Labour Party had persuaded Mary Robinson to contest it. Robinson, a noted civil-rights lawyer and campaigner, was a former senator and Labour member who resigned from the party over the Anglo-Irish Agreement, believing it had been foisted on the Unionist community without consultation. Although she contested the election as an Independent candidate, her campaign was strongly backed by Labour and also attracted the support of others from the left or liberal element of Irish society.

Fianna Fáil nominated Brian Lenihan, a loyal supporter of the Taoiseach and a politician who had earned the respect of many outside the ranks of the party. Wrong-footed by Labour's success in getting Mary Robinson to stand, Fine Gael put forward Austin Currie, a former leading member of the SDLP in Northern Ireland who had won a seat for Fine Gael in the 1989 election. However, Currie's late entry into the race, Robinson's vigorous campaign and Spring's growing stature as the most tenacious opponent of Haughey resulted in the election becoming a

7 January
In Japan, Emperor Hirohito dies, ending the sixty-two-year Showa period. His son, Akihito, becomes emperor the following day, beginning the Heisei period.

18 January
The Communist Party of Poland votes to legalise Solidarity.

23 January
Salvador Dali, leader of the surrealist movement in painting, dies in Spain aged eighty-four.

2 February
The satellite television service, Sky Television, is launched in Europe.

14 February
Iranian Muslim leader Ayatollah Khomeini issues a death threat against British author Salman Rushdie and his publishers over the book *Satanic Verses*.

two-horse race between Robinson and Lenihan. As the contest entered its final stage, the ghost of governments past caught up with Brian Lenihan.

On the evening of 27 January 1982, the Fine Gael–Labour coalition collapsed, and several senior members of Fianna Fáil had rang Áras an Uachtaráin in an attempt to speak to President Hillery to urge him not to dissolve the Dáil, a move which would have given Haughey time to try and form an alternative government. The fact that senior members of Fianna Fáil had attempted to contact the president that night was well established. Indeed, on 3 July 1989, during the long negotiations to form the Fianna Fáil–Progressive Democrat coalition, the issue had been raised in the Dáil and was not challenged or denied by Haughey. However, during a debate on RTÉ's *Questions & Answers* programme in October 1990, Lenihan flatly denied any involvement in attempts to contact and influence the president. Garret FitzGerald was also on the programme and challenged Lenihan's contention. FitzGerald, of course, had been in Áras an Uachtaráin tendering his resignation as Taoiseach on the night the phone calls were made.

The following day, *The Irish Times* entered the fray and claimed it had evidence that Lenihan had lied about his involvement. The newspaper held a press conference where a taped interview, which Lenihan had given some time earlier to a politics student and in which he clearly admitted attempting to contact the president, was produced. Despite this evidence, Lenihan still stuck solidly to his denial and defended his position in an RTÉ news interview, claiming that the information he gave to the student was incorrect and that on 'mature recollection' he never contacted the president that night.

As the controversy continued, the Progressive Democrats played their hand and demanded that Lenihan resign from his post as Tánaiste and Minister for Defence. Lenihan resisted attempts by Haughey to secure his resignation, and the impasse threatened the survival of the government. Eventually, Haughey submitted to the Progressive Democrat ultimatum and sacked Lenihan.

Haughey's failure to stand by his old colleague in face of Progressive Democrat threats outraged many in Fianna Fáil, including Albert Reynolds, who was the only cabinet minister to stick by Lenihan. This growing displeasure with the capitulation to the Progressive Democrats would later contribute to another attempt to oust Haughey a year later. But, for now, the Taoiseach made no secret of his displeasure at having to sack Lenihan, telling the Dáil:

> Brian Lenihan is a good man; he has more humanity in his little finger than Alan Dukes and Garret FitzGerald put together. He has had a political

career of distinction, and given unstinting service to the people in every one of the seven ministries he has served in …

Can the parties here not give the people of this country a break? For a long and painful period of years our people had to endure economic stagnation and a sense of national failure. The country was brought to the verge of bankruptcy. Now that at last the people are seeing and enjoying success, … do you really intend to bring all this progress to an end? If you do, it will be a sad day for Ireland and the future prospects for her people.

(31 October 1990)

However, Dick Spring used the opportunity to launch his fiercest attack on Haughey and his desire for power:

This debate is not about Brian Lenihan, when it is all boiled down. This debate, essentially is about the evil spirit that controls one political party in this Republic, and it is about the way in which that spirit has begun to corrupt the entire political system in our country. This is a debate about greed for office, about disregard for truth and about contempt for political standards. It is a debate about the way in which a once great party has been brought to its knees by the grasping acquisitiveness of its leader. It is ultimately a debate about the cancer that is eating away at our body politic — and the virus which has caused that cancer, An Taoiseach, Charles J. Haughey.

In the 1989 General Election, I said that Fianna Fáil was a party that had become stultified in the grip of one man. As I have watched the events of the last week unfold, in common with thousands of other mystified and outraged citizens of the country, the conviction has been borne in on me more and more that Fianna Fáil is incapable of recovering its former stature for as long as that man is in a position to exert a stranglehold on the party. I have watched the elected Taoiseach of our country tell lies to the Dáil, and brazenly accuse others of lying when he knew the accusations were false; I have watched the Tánaiste try to turn himself into an Irish version of Richard Nixon, staring straight into television cameras and telling lies to the entire nation without so much as a blink.

(31 October 1990)

Lenihan did benefit from a wave of sympathy following his sacking, but a crass interview by Fianna Fail's Pádraig Flynn in the final days of the campaign, where

25 May
Mikhail Gorbachev is elected Executive President of the Soviet Union.

4 June
Months of student-led pro-democracy demonstrations in Beijing's Tiananmen Square end after the Chinese army crushes the protests.

14 July
The French celebrate the 200th anniversary of the storming of the Bastille, symbol of the French Revolution.

20 July
The military regime of Burma puts Aung San Suu Kyi, the leader of the opposition movement to restore democracy in the country, under house arrest.

9 August
The *Limerick Leader* celebrates its 100th anniversary.

he launched a highly personal attack on Mary Robinson, halted his momentum, and Robinson was elected President of Ireland on 7 November 1990. The humiliation of coming third in the election was too much for Fine Gael, and, after a successful heave against Alan Dukes, John Bruton became leader.

The new year brought little relief to Haughey's increasingly battered government, with the emergence of a series of business scandals Suspicions of the existence of a wealthy 'golden circle' of high flyers, many with connections to Fianna Fáil, gained ground as it emerged that UCD paid £8 million for the former teaching-training college in Carysfort, Blackrock, which had been bought for £6.5 million just six months earlier by truck importer Pino Harris. Property was also at the cen-

> **" It is a debate about the way in which a once great party has been brought to its knees by the grasping acquisitiveness of its leader. "**
>
> *Dick Spring, 31 October 1990*

tre of a scandal, where a site purchased by private investment vehicle UPH for £4 million was later bought by the State-owned phone company Telecom Éireann for more than £9 million.

1991 also saw the emergence of more serious allegations against the Irish beef industry and the Goodman Group in particular. *World in Action* broadcast a damning report on abuses, tax evasion and alleged corruption within the sector. O'Malley threatened to pull out of government unless a tribunal of inquiry was established into the allegations, and, faced with the prospect of an election, Haughey caved in.

Workers' Party TD Pat Rabbitte had been at the forefront of those calling for an investigation into the beef sector, and when the Dáil established the tribunal on 24 May 1991, he concentrated his fire on the Goodman Group:

While legitimate and honourable State companies were being stripped and crippled by the Fianna Fáil Administration and we were hearing the usual railings about the unhealthy cartel status enjoyed by State companies, Fianna Fáil were furiously setting up a new State company in the Goodman organisation. It was essentially a State company — but a very Fianna Fáil State company. All the stops were pulled out. When Fianna Fáil decide to do something like this it is indeed a sleek operation to behold…

Above all, the tribunal must seek to establish the charge that Goodman was effectively bigger than the law; that his operations and scams were immune from prosecution. Is it because this very Fianna Fáil State company have the inside political track, that our international reputation for quality was put at risk in grotty re-packaging and re-stamping operations in Goodman plants, in operations heavily subsidised by the Irish taxpayer.

(24 May 1991)

Haughey, irritated by Rabbitte's dogged questioning on the matter, wouldn't take his allegations lying down:

Deputy Rabbitte was the most vociferous in demanding this tribunal of inquiry. I do not know that he really wants it at all. From his point of view he has probably done his work now. Again here today he trotted out the same accusations one after the other … Does it not reveal that he has a simple, straightforward, political motive in everything he says and does over there?

It is not in the interests of the beef processing industry or of ascertaining truth, it is simply to keep up his campaign of denigrating this Government and this party in every way he can … Deputy Rabbitte keeps on this incessant, monotonous attack, allegation after allegation, against Fianna Fáil because we are the bulwark of democracy in this country … That is why he has to listen to toadies and informers and sneak into pubs and come in here making all sorts of allegations, but, as I said in my opening remarks, the moment of truth is now.

(24 May 1991)

Haughey was wide of the mark in his assertion that the moment of truth was at hand. It would take another three years for the Beef Tribunal to report, and evidence at

17 October
A powerful earthquake rocks San Francisco killing nine people and injuring hundreds.

9 November
German citizens begin to demolish the Berlin Wall, which has separated East Germany from West Germany since 1961.

16 November
South African President F.W. de Klerk announces the scrapping of the Separate Amenities Act.

22 December
Berlin's most famous landmark, the Brandenburg Gate, opens for the first time in nearly thirty years.

22 December
Samuel Beckett dies aged eighty-three at his home in Paris.

1990

the tribunal would eventually bring down the government of the man who now plotted Haughey's demise – his cabinet colleague Albert Reynolds.

1991 also saw a significant downturn in the economy and the steady, if modest, reduction in unemployment witnessed since 1987 was reversed, with the numbers signing on increased to nearly 270,000 by the end of the year. Emigration continued to be the only viable option for many young people, with thousands applying for the new US visa scheme secured by US Congressman Bruce Morrison.

Local elections in June 1991 were disappointing for Fianna Fáil, and many in the party, led by senior ministers Albert Reynolds and Pádraig Flynn, still resented the involvement and influence of the Progressive Democrats, which gave the government a distinct right-wing feel and alienated much of Fianna Fáil's traditional electoral base.

In particular, the frequent contributions of Michael McDowell irritated many in Fianna Fáil. McDowell, a founding member of the Progressive Democrats, became chairman of the party after he failed to be re-elected in 1989. Seen by many as the intellectual driving force behind the Progressive Democrats, he was not slow to criticise the government, a stance that infuriated members of Fianna Fáil. At times, McDowell's comments descended into outright abuse: he once famously described a Fianna Fáil backbench initiative to examine the constitutional impact of the Maastricht Treaty as akin to a bunch of chimpanzees, screwdrivers in hand, gathered around the back of an open TV set. Independent Fianna Fáil TD Neil Blaney spoke for many of his former party when he attacked McDowell's role:

> Regarding the Progressive Democrats, I will not mention any names because I believe it is not fair to mention names of people outside the House … In this case that person will have had his say and no doubt will be afforded by the media generally more say than anybody over there or here. I refer to the ayatollah who is not in this House but who controls the Progressive Democrats. It is an extraordinary situation. A man who is not a Deputy is calling the shots as to what the Government will do with the coalition and whether they will survive. It is bloody ludicrous. The little ayatollah should be told where he gets off.
>
> (*16 October 1991*)

The growing turmoil in Fianna Fáil, and ongoing revelations regarding business standards, led to an opposition motion of no confidence in the government when the renewed Programme for Government was agreed. Haughey used the opportunity to round on those who had challenged his personal integrity as scandal after scandal raised serious questions about his conduct of government during 1991:

> I have now been under personal character attack for 12 years, from the very day I first became Taoiseach. I have endured these personal attacks in the knowledge that I had nothing to fear or conceal. In all those 12 years, my detractors have failed to substantiate one single accusation against me, but this has not deterred them. These attacks on me personally have had the basic objective also of damaging the Fianna Fáil Party. But they have failed in their principal aim, to deter me from applying myself to the best of my ability to the better welfare of my fellow citizens, which should be the aim of everyone in political life.
>
> In this Government and in Fianna Fáil we have no concern, we hold no brief, for that comparatively small group of persons in our society who behave dishonourably, who break the rules, who abuse the trust and confidence placed in them by the rest of us. Any illegalities, malpractice or unprofessional behaviour will be uncovered and disclosed, and all appropriate action will be taken. Nobody will be protected from the consequences of their actions...
>
> *(16 October 1991)*

In response, and sensing the growing crisis in the government, newly elected Fine Gael leader John Bruton deliver a scathing critique of both parties in government and identified the lack of accountability to parliament as part of the reason for public unease, a theme that would be repeated in Beef Tribunal Report three years later.

> But let me turn to more fundamental issues. The recent spate of scandals arose precisely because we do not have a proper system of accountable parliamentary democracy in Dáil Éireann. If the Dáil had proper powers of scrutiny, and if the Government and State bodies had felt themselves to be genuinely accountable to the House on an ongoing basis in the past four years, then none of those scandals would ever have happened. It is because the Dáil has not been reformed, because the Dáil does not have the means to call Ministers and State bodies to account before decisions are taken that there has been this depressing and damaging succession of scandals. The source of the problem lies ultimately in the unreformed nature of this House.
>
> *(16 October 1991)*

11 February
Nelson Mandela is freed from prison after serving twenty-seven years. He was sentenced to life imprisonment in 1964 for sabotage, treason and violent conspiracy.

1 March
The Royal New Zealand Navy discontinues its daily rum ration.

11 March
The Westlink toll bridge on the M50 is officially opened.

15 April
The enigmatic Swedish film actress Greta Garbo dies in New York.

24 April
West and East Germany agree to merge their currency and economies in July.

17 May
The World Health
Organisation removes
homosexuality from
its list of diseases.

25 June
In Italia '90, Ireland's
soccer team defeat
Romania in a
dramatic penalty
shootout. Packie
Bonner and David
O'Leary are the
heroes of the hour.

2 August
Shortly after
midnight, 150,000
Iraqi troops invade
neighbouring
Kuwait, capturing
the capital city
by dawn.

24 August
The Irish hostage,
Brian Keenan, is
released in Beirut
after more than four
years in captivity.

2 October
The German
Democratic Republic
(East Germany)
ceases to exist at
midnight, and East
and West Germany
are formally reunited.

The government survived the motion of confidence, and Reynolds stayed his hand as Haughey made moves to reassure the parliamentary party that he was preparing to step down from the leadership. But further revelations — this time related to dealings at the former State-owned sugar company Greencore — resulted in a direct challenge to Haughey's leadership at a Fianna Fáil parliamentary party meeting at the beginning of November. Both Reynolds and Flynn threw down the gauntlet and backed the challenge to Haughey's authority. Both men were sacked from cabinet immediately.

In advance of the meeting, tensions ran high. Reynolds later spoke of his suspicions that his home in Longford was under surveillance, rumours circulated that the phones of some of those opposed to Haughey were tapped and Gerry Collins, the Minister for Foreign Affairs, made an emotional appeal on RTÉ calling on Reynolds not to 'burst the party'.

The fateful meeting began at 11.30 a.m. on 9 November and continued until 2 a.m. Haughey insisted on an open roll-call vote rather than a secret ballot, and, in the face of this pressure, many TDs who had indicated their support for the challenge had a dramatic and late change of heart. Haughey won the vote by fifty-five votes to twenty-two, and, for the moment, his leadership seemed secured.

In the subsequent cabinet reshuffle to fill the positions left vacant by the sacking of Reynolds and Flynn, Haughey attempted to freshen up his cabinet team by appointing two backbenchers, Noel Davern and Jim McDaid. McDaid, a popular doctor from Donegal, had been elected for the first time in 1989, and his nomination as Minister for Defence raised many an eyebrow in Leinster House.

On 13 November, Haughey began the formal Dáil debate on the two new cabinet appointments. Fianna Fáil settled in for the traditional opposition assault on the government, but worse was in store.

Fine Gael and the Workers' Party were in possession of press cuttings that showed McDaid on the steps of the Four Courts in Dublin celebrating the release from jail of a Donegal man after an attempt to extradite him to Northern Ireland was rejected by the Supreme Court. The Donegal man, a constituent of McDaid's, was James Pius Clarke. In 1979, Clarke had been convicted for the attempted murder in 1977 of an off-duty RUC man and sentenced to eighteen years' imprisonment. He escaped in a mass breakout of thirty-eight IRA prisoners from the Maze Prison in 1983. Clarke remained at large until he was arrested by gardaí in the Republic and extradition proceedings began.

The fact that the proposed Minister for Defence had appeared beside a convicted IRA man was seized upon by Fine Gael and the Workers' Party deputies with both

Waiting in line at the US embassy, 1987. For many in the 1980s, emigration remained the best option of finding work.

12 November
Tim Berners-Lee publishes a formal proposal for the World Wide Web a day before the first World Wide Web page is written.

22 November
Margaret Thatcher is to stand down as prime minister after her cabinet refuses to back her in a second round of leadership elections.

23 November
Childrens' author Roald Dahl dies from a rare blood disease at the age of seventy-four.

25 November
Lech Walesa wins Poland's first popular election.

1 December
Workers from the English and French sides of the Channel Tunnel meet, establishing the first ground connection between Britain and mainland Europe since the last Ice Age.

parties claiming McDaid was unfit for office and in the tense atmosphere the term 'Provo fellow-traveller' was thrown around more than once.

The opposition attacks raised the heckles of Fianna Fáil TDs, who saw in McDaid's actions nothing more sinister than a local TD supporting a constituent. The Progressive Democrats, unaware of McDaid's role in the Clarke case up until then, took a more serious view of the implications of the appointment. After the allegations were laid in the Dáil, McDaid went to see both Progressive Democrat ministers, Des O'Malley and Bobby Molloy, and, following that conversation, McDaid decided to withdraw his nomination.

For many in Fianna Fáil, the affair was yet another occasion whereby its junior coalition partner had forced the party into an embarrassing climbdown, with many in Fianna Fáil bemoaning the failure of the leadership to stand its ground against the Progressive Democrats. However, speaking in the debate after McDaid's nomination was withdrawn, backbencher Brian Cowen saved his ire for the tactics employed by Fine Gael and the Workers' Party:

The political attack came from a poisonous coalition of Ceausescu's political children in The Workers' Party and Franco's mongrel foxes in the Fine Gael Party. Anyone who has to listen to their political litany of character assassination based on assertion and innuendo can only have been appalled … That action was all the more prudent when the highest court in the land decided to refuse to extradite Mr. Clarke. It should be a matter of pride that a Deputy would act in the way in which Deputy McDaid did. Deputy Noonan, despite his protestations about the IRA, aped their most notable and foul method of political and character assassination shamelessly and with some degree of enthusiasm, even in front of the man's wife and children. Last night in this Chamber we witnessed the ugly sound of tramping feet echoing the darkest days in the history of the State.

(*14 November 1991*)

Ironically, just as allegations from the past had done for Jim McDaid, the ghost of old controversies would bring to an end the political career of Taoiseach Charles J. Haughey within a few short months.

Seán Doherty had been Minister for Justice during the 1982 GUBU government and had taken responsibility for the tapping of journalists' phones during the period. Since his fall from grace, Doherty's political career had floundered, and Haughey felt no obligation to rehabilitate the Roscommon TD.

Doherty lost his Dáil seat in 1989 and was now Cathaoirleach of Seanad Éireann. He decided to use RTÉ's quirky light-entertainment programme *Nighthawks* to drop a bombshell: Doherty claimed that Haughey had known all along that journalists' telephones had been tapped in 1982 – a claim Haughey had always vociferously denied. When broadcast in January 1992, the *Nighthawks* programme created a sensation, and Doherty waited six days before he held a press conference in Dublin in which he provided more detail about his claims.

The following day, Des O'Malley and Bobby Molloy refused to attend a cabinet meeting, and the Progressive Democrats left Fianna Fáil in no doubt that the revelation would see either the end of Haughey or the end of the government and a general election – an election that few in Fianna Fáil wanted to face with Haughey at the helm. Haughey faced the inevitable and informed a Fianna Fáil parliamentary party meeting on 30 January that he intended to bring his thirteen-year leadership of Fianna Fáil to an end. When the Dáil reconvened on 11 February after the Christmas recess, Haughey rose to give his final speech in

Dáil Éireann as Taoiseach, citing Shakespeare in his valedictory address to the packed house:

> Over 35 years in Dáil Éireann I have developed a deep affection for this House and its traditions…Dáil Éireann is the democratic forum of this nation, to establish which our forefathers made many sacrifices, and of which they would be proud. I would urge all Deputies to continue to stand up for and enhance the standing of the Dáil and the status of its Members and to foster a sense of pride in all our democratic institutions …
>
> Above all, I thank the people of Ireland for the support they have given me over such a long period of years and indeed for the great deal of affection they have shown me from time to time. As I leave office, I bid them a fond farewell and wish them every success and happiness.
>
> The work of Government and of the Dáil must always be directed to the progress of the nation, and I hope I have been able to provide some leadership to that end in my time. I have always sought to act solely and exclusively in the best interests of the Irish people. Let me quote Othello:
>
> "I have done the state some service; they know't
> No more of that."
>
> (11 February 1992)

In contrast to Haughey, Albert Reynolds, his successor as Taoiseach, was more associated in the public mind with country singer Jim Reeves than Shakespeare, although his first act as Taoiseach bore some resemblance to the final act of *Hamlet*, as Reynolds sacked eight Fianna Fáil cabinet members, an unprecedented cull.

His cabinet included new faces, such as former Fianna Fáil maverick Charlie McCreevy in Social Welfare, David Andrews in Foreign Affairs and backbencher Brian Cowen, aged just thirty-two, was appointed Minister for Labour.

In his brief address to the Dáil, Reynolds identified employment creation, Northern Ireland, protection of the environment and European integration as his main priorities.

When the Dáil next met, on Thursday, 13 February, Proinsias De Rossa requested the suspension of business to deal with an issue not even contemplated by Reynolds just two days earlier: abortion – in particular, the State's attempt to prevent a fourteen-year-old rape victim travelling to Britain for a termination.

The particular tragic sequence of events which became known as the *X* case began when the parents of a fourteen-year-old girl, who became pregnant as the

21 May
Rajiv Gandhi, former prime minister of India, is assassinated during election campaigns. His mother, Prime Minister Indira Gandhi, was assassinated in 1984.

20 July
The 'tall ships' leave Cork for the next stage of the Tall Ships Race.

25 August
Eddie Jordan, having become the first Irish-owned construction team in a Formula One Championship, gives Michael Schumacher his racing debut.

6 September
Leningrad is, once again, to be known as St Petersburg. The change to Leningrad was made in 1924.

24 September
Theodor Seuss Geisel, writer of children's books under the pseudonym Dr Seuss, dies in California, at the age of eighty-seven.

"I have always sought to act solely and exclusively in the best interests of the Irish people. Let me quote Othello: 'I have done the state some service; they know't; No more of that.'"

Charles Haughey, 11 February 1992

result of a rape, decided to terminate her pregnancy in Britain in accordance with her wishes. The parents asked the gardaí if forensic evidence from the foetus would be beneficial in a prosecution against the rapist. The gardaí sought clarification from the Director of Public Prosecutions who subsequently informed the Attorney General, Harry Whelehan.

It appears the Attorney General believed that the constitutional amendment on abortion passed in 1983 required the State to stop any abortion taking place, even if that meant preventing a citizen travelling outside the State. Whelehan sought a High Court injunction to prevent the fourteen-year-old girl from travelling, and, when the High Court application came to light, it created widespread public outrage. For many opposed to the original 1983 anti-abortion amendment, Whelehan's interpretation of the law confirmed their worse fears about that flawed constitutional amendment.

The injunction was granted to the Attorney General on 17 February, and the girl's parents appealed the decision to the Supreme Court. The day after the High Court judgment, a shell-shocked Dáil dealt with the matter by way of statements from the party leaders. In his contribution, Reynolds was at pains to defend the actions of the Attorney General:

> I would, in fact, like at this point to answer further those who have suggested that the Attorney General, having been informed of the proposal to bring the girl to England for a termination of pregnancy, should have turned a blind eye to the requirements of the highest law in the land, the Constitution. I reject that suggestion.
>
> I do not believe that the people of this country want — or deserve — a situation of nods and winks in the application of the law. If the principal law officer of the State were to engage in such conduct in the present case, how could he ever again be trusted to observe the Constitution or the law in any future situation where there might be an obvious temptation, from whatever motive — or where there might appear to be a temptation — for him to take the easy way out and ignore the Constitution and the law?
>
> *(18 February 1992)*

While Reynolds' point about the Attorney General's duty to uphold the Constitution was accurate, the situation that now faced the legislature in the face of the High Court judgement was stark, as Dick Spring outlined:

5 November
The body of the millionaire newspaper publisher Robert Maxwell is found in the sea off the coast of Tenerife.

24 November
Freddie Mercury dies aged forty-five, just one day after he publicly announced he was HIV positive.

25 December
Mikhail Gorbachev resigns as Soviet president, and Communist Russia ceases to exist.

1992

7 February
Ministers from the twelve countries in the European Community (EC) take another step towards political and economic union in the Treaty of Maastricht. Officially, the EC is now the European Union (EU) and a definite timetable and framework for economic and monetary union is laid down.

In making that decision, the court have left behind a clear definition. That definition is sufficiently clear for us to be able to predict that in the future, the courts will grant injunctions in similar circumstances against any woman, except a woman who is in imminent physical danger of her life. It will not matter if the woman is a child, or if she has been the victim of an evil and depraved act like incest, or if she is mentally handicapped. All that will matter is that the moment she becomes pregnant, under the terms of our Constitution she is carrying something that is more precious than she is.

Secondly, it also seems clear that injunctions will be available to anyone wishing to prevent an abortion, including any evil and depraved man who wishes to force his victim to carry a child conceived through violence.

(18 February 1992)

The short debate concluded after the four party leaders – Reynolds, Bruton, Spring and De Rossa – had spoken, with Fine Gael's Monica Barnes loudly protesting the fact that no female member of the Dáil was afforded the opportunity to contribute.

Eventually, the Supreme Court overturned the High Court judgment and ruled that the fourteen-year-old girl was entitled to an abortion as she was suicidal and so her life prevailed over the right to life of the foetus. While it resolved the immediate dilemma for the family at the centre of the case and the Oireachtas, the decision infuriated anti-abortion campaigners.

Eventually, the government proposed another 'Irish solution to an Irish problem', and two constitutional amendments, one guaranteeing the right to travel and one guaranteeing the right to information were passed in November 1992. The amendments ensured that women wishing to travel to Britain for an abortion could do so without fear of State interference. However, a third referendum designed to row back the Supreme Court judgment which legalised abortion if the life of the mother was at risk, including if that risk was through suicide, failed.

The economy continued to go through rough times in 1992, with unemployment topping 300,000 by the end of the year. The government was forced to increase borrowing and to make additional cutbacks, including the 'dirty dozen' social-welfare cuts introduced by Charlie McCreevy, which were instituted before a currency crisis in the autumn saw the government spend a small fortune in a futile attempt to prevent the devaluation of the punt. Not surprisingly, the government's popularity remained low, and tensions between the coalition partners increased during the year, reaching crisis point after Des O'Malley's evidence at the Beef Tribunal.

"All that will matter is that the moment she becomes pregnant, under the terms of our Constitution she is carrying something that is more precious than she is."

Dick Spring, 18 February 1992

28 April
In Madrid, the artist Francis Bacon dies of a heart attack at the age of eighty-two. He leaves his estate to his partner, John Edwards, who donates the contents of Bacon's studio to the Hugh Lane gallery in Dublin.

7 May
Bishop Eamon Casey of Galway resigns following revelations that he is the father of a teenage boy.

9 May
In Sweden, Linda Martin wins the Eurovision Song Contest with 'Why Me?', a song written by Johnny Logan.

31 May
Christy O'Connor Jr wins the British Masters golf tournament.

15 June
The first Berlin Air Show for sixty years takes place.

The decision to grant export credit insurance to the Goodman Group in relation to its business in Iraq was made in 1987 by Albert Reynolds and was the focus of inquiries by the Beef Tribunal. When Des O'Malley gave his evidence to the tribunal in July 1992, he was strongly critical of Reynolds' actions, describing them as 'reckless and foolish'.

Reynolds was furious at O'Malley's evidence, and the strained relations between the coalition partners deteriorated further. During his own appearance before the tribunal in October, Reynolds described O'Malley's remarks as 'ridiculous, irresponsible and dishonest' – he had basically accused his coalition partner of perjury. The government imploded.

The Progressive Democrats pulled out of government, and the subsequent Dáil debate revealed the extent to which the relationship between the government parties had deteriorated. O'Malley laid the blame for the collapse of the government squarely at Reynolds' door:

> I have never been overly sensitive to criticism, of which I have received at least my fair share. The same goes for abuse. Unlike others, I have not sought to protect my reputation by litigation with the news media. I have broad shoulders and can easily bear disparagement from my competitors. But I cannot properly or honourably acquiesce in a premeditated and repeated charge that I knowingly and dishonestly deceived a tribunal on oath when that charge — which is acknowledged by independent observers as a charge of criminal behaviour — came from the leader of the Government of which I was a member and to which I owe my loyalty.
>
> (*5 November 1992*)

Reynolds refused to accept responsibility for precipitating the crisis, despite his evidence at the Beef Tribunal. In defending his actions, Reynolds revealed the deep antipathy he had always held towards the coalition and the Progressive Democrats' role in it, with Michael McDowell featuring once again:

> The problems we had to contend with came in the main from people outside this House, who expected and demanded an influence in the name of the Progressive Democrats wholly disproportionate to the size of their democratic mandate … We had the experience of the Government being held to ransom and threatened with a premature election on many occasions, if we did not

fall into line with the minority party's demands, while their leaders in the Dáil remained silent …

I would strongly suggest that what has been wrong all along has been the attitude of the Progressive Democrats Coalition, and their belief that they had the right to dictate terms to the Government. Now that they have found this impossible, they have decided to tear up the Joint Programme for Government in a clear breach of contract and to go to the country in a huff.

(5 November 1992)

Fine Gael's John Bruton was in no doubt as to where responsibility for the collapse lay, driving home the message that Fianna Fáil in general, and Reynolds in particular, were incapable of maintaining a coalition.

We seem to have a Taoiseach who sees himself in the role of the biggest bully in the schoolyard. He has made contempt for his Government partner a defining characteristic and his highest objective, and has been satisfied with nothing less than the humiliation of his partner in Government at every opportunity. While espousing so-called "open" government, he seems to specialise in the insincere word, the sweet and sugared double-talk which hides hostile motives.

The general election was held on 25 November, and, although many voters agreed with Bruton's analysis of why the government fell, it didn't garner increased support for Fine Gael. Since Fianna Fáil's return to government in 1987, Dick Spring had emerged as the leading figure on the opposition benches, and opinion polls reflected this new status. The internal strife within Labour over coalition had been put to one side, and the Robinson victory in the 1990 presidential election coupled with a good showing in the local elections in 1991 left Labour well placed going into the general election. The Labour manifesto tapped into concerns about employment, health and ethics in government, and it held out the prospect of change. It proved to be a winner. During the campaign, Spring's high personal ratings, which stood at 71 per cent on the eve of the election, transferred into support for the party, which doubled its vote to 19 per cent and won a record thirty-three seats.

22 June
Two skeletons excavated at Yekaterinburg in Russia are identified as Czar Nicholas II and his wife Alexandra.

25 July
The Olympic Games opens in Barcelona with all countries present for the first time in modern history.

31 October
Pope John Paul II lifts the edict of the inquisition against Galileo that had lasted nearly 400 years.

3 November
Bill Clinton defeats incumbent president George Bush and businessman Ross Perot in the US presidential election.

This is a Government profoundly committed to change. We should lead on change, not be afraid of it. It is better to manage change successfully than to fear it …

An aghaidh leis an obair.

An uneasy partnership, January 1993.
Dick Spring and Albert Reynolds
agree to form a coalition after the
1992 general election.

Many political leaders set themselves in life certain priorities and goals but for whatever reasons were not around long enough to achieve them …

1992-2002

Peace, Prosperity
and Perdition

'You win some, you lose some but throughout my life in politics and business I have been delighted to be a risk taker. If you are not a risk taker you will not achieve anything.'

'What is being offered and an attack on decency. What we are offering is another of the amnesties, elevating to an unprecedented status the role of the fixer, the stroke puller, the cute hoor, the dodger.'

1992-2002

and an attack on

Nuala O'Faoláin covered the election count in Albert Reynolds' Longford-Roscommon constituency for *The Irish Times*. It was a hardship posting with not a chair to be found in the cold, dreary count centre as anxious tallymen stubbed their cigarettes out on the sawdust-covered floor.

Reynolds stayed away from the count centre until 10 p.m., preferring to contemplate the unfolding electoral disaster at home, a fact that only prolonged O'Faoláin's discomfort. Responding to questions about the Taoiseach's whereabouts, one Reynolds supporter was anxious to ascribe a higher purpose to Reynolds non-appearance – he was, it was claimed, attending to the ongoing currency crisis, fighting off a renewed assault on the Irish punt. The excuse further undermined confidence in the embattled currency on the international markets, but this element of farce seemed to sum up Fianna Fáil's 1992 campaign.

The election was a low point in Reynolds' career. He had a poor campaign, with opinion polls delivering increasingly bleak news. Despite Reynolds' attempts to dismiss the obvious collapse in Fianna Fáil support, the pollsters proved correct, with the party recording its worst election result in its history, gaining just 39 per cent of the national vote, losing nine seats and returning only sixty-eight TDs.

The election was little better for Fine Gael. Squeezed by the Labour surge and a relatively strong performance by the Progressive Democrats, the party gained just 24 per cent of the vote, its lowest since 1948, and returned forty-five TDs to Dáil Éireann – twenty-five seats fewer than Garret FitzGerald had secured for the party just ten years earlier.

The Progressive Democrats surprised many and, by concentrating resources on key constituencies, managed to win an additional four seats, including Michael McDowell in Dublin South East, bringing its Dáil strength to ten.

For Democratic Left, formed just eight months earlier, the election couldn't have come at a worse time. Despite losing two seats, the party managed to establish its own identity and took solace from the fact that its former colleagues in the Workers' Party failed to win a seat. The first Green TD, Roger Garland, lost his seat in Dublin South, however, the victory of Trevor Sargent in Dublin North ensured there would be at least one Green voice in the new parliament.

The 1992 election also saw the highest number of women – twenty – elected to Dáil Éireann since the foundation of the State, comprising 12 per cent of the Dáil and three more women would be elected at by-elections during the lifetime of the Dáil.

1 January
In the 'Velvet Divorce', Czechoslovakia is dissolved into the Czech Republic and Slovakia.

1 January
Trade borders in Europe are abolished creating the European single market.

14 February
Police confirm a body found on a railway embankment in Merseyside is that of missing two-year-old James Bulger.

26 February
A terrorist bomb explosion kills five people and badly damages the World Trade Center in New York.

10 March
The GAA is
granted planning
permission for the
redevelopment Croke
Park which will cost
£110 million and
take fifteen years.

19 April
At least seventy
people are feared
dead in a fire at
the besieged
headquarters of
the Branch Davidian
sect near Waco
in Texas.

30 April
In Germany,
tennis player
Monica Seles is
stabbed in the back
by an obsessed fan of
her rival Steffi Graf.

Labour's remarkable performance ensured that Spring would be the kingmaker in the Twenty-Seventh Dáil. Following the election, negotiations on the formation of a government began, though it would take more than a month before a coalition between Fianna Fáil and Labour was eventually approved by the Dáil.

Fine Gael's refusal to contemplate any Democratic Left involvement in government, and Labour's similar attitude towards the Progressive Democrats, quickly scuppered any prospect of a coalition involving Bruton and Spring, a prospect not helped by the poor personal relationship between the two men that had its roots in the 1982–1987 coalition.

By December, it was clear that a Fianna Fáil–Labour deal, incorporating much of Labour's agenda, was on the cards. The process was assisted by Reynolds' coup in securing £8 billion in European structural funding at the Edinburgh Summit that month.

As negotiations between Fianna Fáil and Labour continued, the Dáil met on 5 January, and Fine Gael leader John Bruton, now facing into another period of opposition, delivered a scathing attack on the Labour leader for contemplating coalition with Fianna Fáil:

I do not think I could improve on Deputy Spring's own words in describing Fianna Fáil's position on issues of integrity and standards. On 5 November 1992, exactly two months ago, he said, in reference to Fianna Fáil, that:

"I believe one political party in this House has gone so far down the road of blindness to standards, and of blindness to the people they are supposed to represent, that it is impossible to see how anyone could support them in the future without seeing them first undergo the most radical transformation."

Yes, this is the very party, Fianna Fáil, that exactly two months later Deputy Spring seems to want to put back into Government for another four years even though it is already six years in office and in that six years has left behind it a trail of scandals unparalleled in recent Irish history …

Yes, Deputy Spring did receive a mandate; he received a mandate for change. Now he proposes to give us that change by putting back in office the same Taoiseach, the same Ministers, the same political party against whom he spoke with such precious and high flown rhetoric here in this House on 5 November last and for the previous five years.

(5 January 1993)

In response, Spring was in no mind to accept criticism for attempting to put together a coalition deal.

> The Labour Party does not need lectures from the leader of the Fine Gael Party; I find them offensive … I will confine myself to saying that there is absolutely nothing in the mandate the leader of the Fine Gael Party received from the Irish people which gives him the right or the moral authority to lecture anyone else about their duty in this House … I hope that if and when an agreement is finally reached … it will be given a fair chance. If it is I have no doubt that those who worry about the possibility of change in Ireland receding will have their minds put at rest.
>
> (*5 January 1993*)

The Fianna Fáil–Labour deal was eventually agreed, and, on 12 January, Reynolds was elected Taoiseach and Spring became Tánaiste and Minister for Foreign Affairs. Labour secured five other seats at cabinet, with Minister for Education, Niamh Bhreathnach, becoming only the fifth newly elected TD to be appointed straight to cabinet, following in the footsteps of Noël Browne, Kevin Boland, Martin O'Donoghue and Alan Dukes.

One significant figure was missing from the Fianna Fáil cabinet team: conveniently, Reynolds' former ally Pádraig Flynn, a *bête noire* for many in the Labour Party, especially following his attack on Mary Robinson during the 1990 presidential election, had been dispatched to Brussels earlier that month as Ireland's EU Commissioner.

The Programme for Government reflected much of Labour's policy agenda. However, despite the success the party achieved in policy terms, the fact that Labour had returned Fianna Fáil to power would rankle with some in the months to come.

At the outset of the government's term of office, the unprecedented coalition between Fianna Fáil and Labour, which provided the government with the largest parliamentary majority in the history of the State, held out the prospect of a new departure in Irish politics. In commending the cabinet to the Dáil in January 1993, Albert Reynolds detailed the new direction the government would take while recalling the past connections between the two parties:

> The close relationship between Fianna Fáil and Labour in the early days of Irish democracy and their many common roots going back to 1916 or before

24 June
English mathematician Andrew Wiles wins worldwide fame after presenting his solution for Fermat's Last Theorem, a problem that has been unsolved for more than 300 years.

17 August
In London, the general public is allowed inside Buckingham Palace for the first time.

9 September
The Palestine Liberation Organisation agrees to recognise Israel's right to exist, and Israel agrees to recognise the PLO as the representative of the Palestinian people.

26 October
Roddy Doyle is the first Irish writer to win the Booker Prize for his novel *Paddy Clarke Ha Ha Ha*.

1994

have not been forgotten. The radical social policies of the 1930s in relation to public housing and the introduction of unemployment assistance were carried through with Labour support … In 1932 the first leader of the Labour Party, Tom Johnson, predicted about Labour and Fianna Fáil: "We shall have to coalesce some day".

This is a Government profoundly committed to change. We should lead on change, not be afraid of it. It is better to manage change successfully than to fear it … Ar aghaidh leis an obair.'

(12 January 1993)

One issue that Reynolds didn't deal with in detail that day was Northern Ireland. During the negotiations for government, Reynolds informed Spring that behind-the-scenes talks had the capacity to lead to a significant breakthrough. In 1992, though, few could have imagined then the progress that would be made over the next eighteen months.

Of more immediate concern to the new government was the economic situation. In January 1993, unemployment stood at over 300,000, and there was little good news on the horizon with the closure of the technology firm Digital in Galway and the loss of over 2,000 jobs. Against the gloomy background, the 1993 budget included revenue-generating measures, such as the imposition of a 1 per cent employment levy and increased taxes on cigarettes and tobacco.

Another revenue-raising scheme launched in 1993 would have more damaging political repercussions. In 1988, Finance Minister Ray MacSharry had introduced a tax amnesty enabling defaulters to own up to evasion. It was estimated that the measure would raise £30 million. In the end, approximately £500 million flowed into government coffers. In 1993, the government decided another amnesty was in order and, this time, tax cheats were offered even better terms, paying just 15 per cent on money mostly hoarded in offshore accounts with those who came clean also being guaranteed confidentiality.

The Minister for Finance Bertie Ahern, along with senior Revenue and Finance officials, opposed the amnesty, mainly on the grounds that it was grossly unfair to compliant taxpayers, but Reynolds insisted on its adoption. Labour didn't threaten the stability of the government over the issue and was content to ensure that a large amount of the proceeds would go towards reducing health board debt.

However, the government's opponents, particularly in the Progressive Democrats and Democratic Left, condemned the amnesty, with the Progressive Democrats' Pat Cox declaring:

> It says to every compliant taxpayer, you are a sucker if you pay your bill, if you play by the rules, if you believe in decency in terms of how any ordinary, proper, well-managed society ought to run its overall affairs. What is being offered is a con job and an attack on decency. What we are doing in this mother of all amnesties is elevating to an unprecedented status the role of the fixer, the stroke puller, the cute hoor, the dodger.

> *(30 June 1993)*

The amnesty raised approximately £200 million in revenue. However, the generous terms it offered infuriated many, particularly in the PAYE sector, and the affair did serious damage to Labour's claims about restoring standards in Irish life.

Labour enjoyed a short political honeymoon and an MRBI poll for *The Irish Times* in March revealed a 35 per cent slump in Spring's satisfaction rating and a drop in Labour support to just 13 per cent. However, the poll revealed that the widespread media criticism of Spring for entering coalition with Fianna Fáil wasn't shared by the electorate, with 68 per cent of Labour supporters agreeing with the decision to go into government. Labour's poor poll rating was related to more bread-and-butter issues, such as rising unemployment and the health levy introduced in the recent budget.

Despite the poll results, Labour buckled down to delivering on the programme for government, and a Family Planning Bill, which finally managed to provide widespread access to contraceptives, was introduced by Health Minister Brendan Howlin within months.

1993 also saw the government introduce legislation to decriminalise homosexual acts, another key Labour demand in the negotiations for government. This important development for the gay community followed the successful conclusion of a lengthy campaign by Senator David Norris, who, in 1988, won a landmark victory in the European courts which found that Ireland's criminal law against homosexual acts was a breach of human rights. Legislation to give effect to the *Norris* judgment was introduced by Minister for Justice Máire Geoghegan Quinn and, while many in Fianna Fáil were less than enthusiastic about the proposal, the most vocal opponent of the change was Louth Fine Gael TD Brendan McGahon:

12 February
Edvard Munch's painting *The Scream* is stolen in Oslo. It is recovered on 7 May.

7 April
Civil war erupts in Rwanda a day after an airplane carrying the nation's president, Juvénal Habyarimana, is shot down.

8 April
Kurt Cobain, the lead singer of grunge rock band Nirvana, is found dead in his Seattle home.

8 April
Michelangelo's fresco *Universal Judgement* in the Sistine Chapel, is reopened to public after ten years of restoration.

22 April
Former president Richard Nixon dies of a stroke at the age of eighty-one.

66 What is being offered is a **con job** and an attack on decency. **What** we are doing in this **mother** of all **amnesties** is elevating to an unprecedented status the role of **the fixer**, the **stroke puller**, the **cute 'hoor**, the dodger. **99**

Pat Cox, 30 June 1993

Homosexuality is a departure from normality and while homosexuals deserve our compassion they do not deserve our tolerance. That is how the man in the street thinks. I know of no homosexual who has been discriminated against. Such people have a persecution complex because they know they are different from the masses or normal society.

(23 June 1993)

McGahon's comments were in a minority though, and the legislation passed through the Dáil without the controversy that had marked so many other debates in previous years regarding private morality. Máire Geoghegan Quinn concluded her contribution to the debate in very human terms:

… the person who had the most influence on my thinking in this regard was the mother of a young homosexual man who indicated that when her 19 year old son told her he was homosexual her reaction was to tell him he would grow out of it … after a painful 18 months she realised that this was something with which she had to live.

She had to ask herself a very serious question, one which any parent should ask. In particular those who have doubts or difficulties with this legislation should ask what they would say to a son of 17 or 18 years of age — whom they had loved since birth — if he told them he was homosexual. They would need to show him love, understanding and tolerance. I hope this House will do that in regard to this Bill.

(23 June 1993)

The reforming zeal of the new government was also focused on the Dáil itself. For some years, many members felt that the work of Dáil Éireann was becoming irrelevant in the eyes of the public. The arcane procedures for debate contributed to the reduced standing of parliament in a world increasingly attuned to the instantaneous news coverage driven by the broadcast media.

Dáil procedures had remained largely unchanged since the foundation of the State, and the decision in 1990 to allow for the televising of Dáil proceedings increased the impetus for Dáil reform. Ironically, the televising of the Dáil also contributed to the demise of real debate in Dáil Éireann. The advent of television increased the number of TDs who relied on prepared scripts, just one of the points that Fine Gael leader John Bruton addressed during a debate on government spending in 1992:

30 April
Ireland wins the Eurovision Song Contest for the third year running with 'Rock 'n' Roll Kids' by Charlie McGettigan and Paul Harrington. However, it is the interval performance of *Riverdance* that becomes the talking point of the show.

1 May
The world-class Brazilian racing driver Ayrton Senna dies in a crash at the San Marino Grand Prix in Italy.

2 May
South African president F.W. de Klerk concedes defeat and Nelson Mandela claims victory in the country's first multiracial presidential election.

6 May
The Channel Tunnel linking England to France officially opens. It is hailed as one of the century's greatest feats of civil engineering.

This debate … will be the biggest waste of parliamentary time this year — a total and complete waste of time … Not a single word said on either side of the House will alter a single comma or full stop in the Minister's Budget Statement. It is all fixed and agreed. This debate simply gives Members an opportunity to let off steam. That is no way to treat people, each one of whom is directly elected and has a serious parliamentary responsibility … We have an entirely empty Press Gallery. The reason is that I supplied my prepared script in advance to the journalists … They see no need to come here to listen to what I am saying. That is a complete farce … We have a completely word processed debate. We might as well not meet in this House because everything is already written somewhere else.

(30 January 1992)

Bruton was a passionate advocate of Dáil reform and made a number of thoughtful contributions on the subject, but he also had a keen eye for some of the more absurd practices that had evolved in parliament, taking the opportunity in February 1993, for instance, to provide his colleagues with an up-to-date list of the terms of abuse prohibited in parliament:

It is worth noting that there are a number of things one is not allowed to say in the House about Members. For instance you may not accuse them of slander, chicanery, dishonesty, being a black marketeer, a criminal or a gangster; have cheated or swindled, or being bribed. One cannot accuse them of being an acrobat or an acrobat in a circus; of barking or grunting; of being a brat or acting the brat; of being a chancer, a clown, a clown in a circus, a comedian, a Communist, a cornerboy, a cur, a Fascist, a gurrier, a guttersnipe; an informer, a stool pigeon or Pontius Pilate; a stooge, a trick-of-the-loop, a twister, a yahoo or of yapping.

(19 February 1993)

The new government took steps to reform Dáil Éireann and, in February 1993, government Chief Whip Noel Dempsey presented a package of reforms to the House which included the expansion of the committee system, the relaxation of certain rules of debate and the introduction of electronic voting in the Dáil chamber. However, the initiative met with limited success – the proposal to introduce electronic voting in the Dáil chamber took nine years to implement – and the issue of Dáil reform would resurface time and again over the coming years.

Change was also afoot in Northern Ireland during 1993 as efforts intensified to produce a diplomatic breakthrough that would result in an end to twenty-five years of violence. Talks between John Hume and Gerry Adams had resulted in both Dublin and London working on the text of a declaration that would represent a new departure in Anglo-Irish relations. The active involvement of recently elected US president Bill Clinton in the process added a vital element to the initiative.

Eventually, intense negotiations between Reynolds and British Prime Minister John Major led to the Downing Street Declaration on 15 December 1993. The declaration confirmed that Britain had no selfish strategic or economic interest in Northern Ireland and that the political future was to be decided by the people on the island of Ireland, North and South, although any change in the status of Northern Ireland required the consent of the majority of its citizens.

The declaration was to prove a vital building block in the emerging peace process. When Reynolds returned to Dáil Éireann after the declaration was announced he received a standing ovation from TDs on all sides before he summed up his hopes:

> The Declaration is a charter for peace in Ireland. It sets out to demonstrate to every shade of opinion in Northern Ireland that their political aims and ideals can be far more effectively pursued by purely democratic methods …
>
> In the final analysis this Joint Declaration is particularly addressed to the people and organisations on both sides who can most directly deliver peace. While none of us can ever condone the deeds committed over the past 25 years, I believe it is right to acknowledge what I believe are serious and courageous efforts that have been made for some time by some in the Republican leadership to find a path to peace out of the impasse …
>
> Let us not set rigid new preconditions. Let us remember that it is better to end violence than to preach against it. There has never been, and there never will be, a better opportunity for peace.
>
> (*17 December 1993*)

The opportunity for peace presented by the declaration wasn't immediately grasped by all and 1994 saw continuing violence, including IRA mortar-bomb attacks on Heathrow airport and the Ulster Volunteer Force (UVF) murder of six Catholic men watching a football match in a bar in Loughlinisland, County Down.

5 August
In Cuba, the first protests since 1959 against Fidel Castro's government take place.

22 September
The first episode of the sitcom *Friends* is aired on NBC. It continues for ten years and becomes one of the most popular series on television.

13 November
Voters in Sweden decide to join the EU in a referendum.

13 December
In Britain, fifty-three-year-old Fred West is charged with murdering twelve people (including two of his daughters) whose bodies were found at his house in Cromwell Street, Gloucester. His wife Rose is charged with ten murders, though it is believed they have killed up to thirty people.

Throughout the year, diplomatic activity to secure movement from the IRA continued and finally, on 31 August 1994, the IRA declared a ceasefire. Speaking in the Dáil, Reynolds spoke with confidence about what the future could hold:

> Let us all make the most of this new historic opportunity, the opportunity literally of a lifetime. Let 1 September 1994 go into the annals as one of the most important dates in Irish history. Let us all inside and outside this House share the determination that from here on we will go forward and not back. There have been enough sacrifices. Let no more generations suffer in this way. Ireland has the capacity to be one of the finest countries in the world. From today, that is now a real possibility … Let us leave violence behind and take the gun, bullet and bomb out of Irish politics forever.

> (*31 August 1994*)

"The Declaration is a charter for peace in Ireland."

Albert Reynolds, 17 December 1993

Ironically, at a time when the government delivered a historic departure in Northern Ireland, relations between Fianna Fáil and Labour were deteriorating to such an extent that the future of the government was in doubt.

Throughout 1994, ministers had introduced a range of measures to deliver on the Programme for Government. Family-law reform, to pave the way for another divorce referendum, was passed; the Legal Aid Board was established on a statutory basis; and there was a gradual reduction in unemployment.

In June, Labour Minister of State Eithne Fitzgerald was finalising details of the Ethics in Public Office Bill that would require members of the Oireachtas to declare their financial interests and also established a commission to investigate complaints against abuse of public office.

Just weeks before the legislation was introduced to the Dáil, the government was rocked by the passport-for-investment scandal. Since 1988, governments had granted Irish passports to foreign nationals in return for substantial investment in Irish businesses. In June 1994, it emerged that the wife and son of wealthy Palestinian businessman Khalid Masri were granted passports in return for a £1 million investment in C&D Petfoods in Longford – a company founded by Albert Reynolds, although the Taoiseach had no day-to-day role in the company's affairs.

The fact that Reynolds' family business had benefited from the scheme created an outcry and allegations about the procedures followed in granting the passports were raised. The scandal created serious tensions within government and, in an attempt to get to the bottom of the affair, Dick Spring examined the files on the passport application held by the Department of Justice and subsequently declared that everything was above board. Spring's actions in defending the Masri passports affair were rounded on by the opposition – with the Progressive Democrats' Michael McDowell the most outspoken:

> The Ethics in Public Office Bill was put into the Programme for Government to serve as the Labour Party's political prophylactic; it is a legislative condom which it proposes to wear in its partnership period which will prevent it from picking up anything it should not pick up from its partners in Government and, at the same time, enables it to participate fully in Government without that contamination …
>
> People were sold Irish citizenship for a soft loan to a company of which the Taoiseach was the greatest beneficiary in circumstances in which dishonest and evasive explanations were given to the public. That amounts to a grave abuse of public office, but it seems to be acceptable to the ethical faculties of the Labour Party. If the Tánaiste and the Minister see nothing wrong with what happened, their consciences, judgments and ethical faculties must be questioned; they must be brain dead …
>
> *(23 June 1994)*

Within weeks of the Masri affair, the publication of the long-awaited Beef Tribunal Report would bring relations between the government partners to rock bottom. The report was delivered to Government Buildings at the end of July 1994. What

20 February
Dublin's Thom McGinty, better known as 'the Diceman', dies of Aids.

19 March
In Cork, boxer Stephen Collins beats reigning champion Chris Eubank to win the world super middleweight title at a fight.

20 March
In Tokyo, members of the Aum Shinrikyo religious cult release sarin gas on five railway trains, killing twelve people and injuring 5,510 others.

19 April
A truck bomb blows up outside the Alfred P. Murrah federal building in Oklahoma City, killing 168 people.

25 May
The *Irish Press* prints its last edition as it closes with debts of over £19 million.

occurred next bordered on farce, with Labour advisers unable to get a copy of the report and the Taoiseach refusing to take calls from his Tánaiste.

The cabinet had earlier agreed that the government would formulate a joint response to the report. Albert Reynolds, convinced the report had vindicated him, decided not to wait and issued his own statement. It was a decision that nearly sank the government.

The Dáil was recalled to discuss the Beef Tribunal Report on the day the IRA announced its ceasefire, so the debate was delayed. When the Dáil did discuss the report the following day, the breach between the government parties overshadowed the actual contents of the report, with Dick Spring making pointed reference to the damage inflicted on the coalition:

> … the initial handling of the beef tribunal report failed to reflect the "close co-operation and trust" on which the Programme for Government is founded and has to be founded. In that sense, it was completely unacceptable to me. It was also counter-productive.
>
> The Taoiseach is aware of my strong feelings in this matter … We have discussed the leaking of sections of the report candidly with one another. He knows that that action damaged trust. The Taoiseach knows that I am prepared to work to restore it, and I believe he is too.
>
> *(1 September 1994)*

As subsequent events would prove, trust was never restored between Reynolds and Spring, and the government would collapse within a matter of weeks.

No sooner had the dust settled on the Beef Tribunal affair than the coalition was at loggerheads again, this time over Reynolds' insistence that Attorney General Harry Whelehan should be appointed President of the High Court. Spring resisted the appointment, and the issue caused friction within the government, until Reynolds and Spring seemed to come to an agreement in early October that involved the appointment of Whelehan, with Labour securing a review of the entire process of judicial appointments.

Serious questions then arose about the failure of the Attorney General's office to deal with an extradition request from the RUC in relation to a priest called Brendan Smyth, who was subsequently convicted of appalling crimes against children by a Belfast court. Spring now renewed his objections to the appointment of Whelehan and demanded that it be postponed until a full explanation for the delay in dealing with the extradition case was provided. Reynolds ignored his Tánaiste's demand and went ahead with the appointment of Whelehan after Labour ministers walked out of cabinet. The government was on the rocks.

What occurred over the next four weeks was a bizarre, confused and enthralling period in Irish politics. Reynolds addressed the Dáil on Tuesday, 15 November, defending Whelehan's appointment but holding out an olive branch to the Labour Party at the same time. Part of Reynolds' defence of the handling of the *Smyth* case related to the fact that it was the only case of its kind in the Attorney General's office.

However, before Reynolds delivered that speech, the new Attorney General, Eoghan Fitzsimons, discovered a similar case, the *Duggan* case, where the extradition proceeded without undue delay. For some reason, that fact wasn't included in Reynolds' speech, and the coalition edged further towards collapse.

The following day, the Dáil was again gripped by the crisis. Reynolds, now fully briefed on the *Duggan* case, spoke in even more apologetic terms towards the Labour Party, admitting that the appointment of Whelehan was a mistake while urging the Labour Party to rejoin the government:

> Had the full information been made available to us our decision would have been different. I now accept that the reservations voiced by the Tánaiste are well founded and I regret the appointment of the former Attorney General as President of the High Court … I also regret my decision to proceed with the appointment against the expressed opposition of the Labour Party. I guarantee that this breach of trust, a trust on which the partnership Government was founded, will not be repeated.
>
> (*16 November 1994*)

Spring was willing to accept Reynolds' very public apology, until he discovered from the new Attorney General that knowledge of the existence of the *Duggan* case had been made available to Reynolds before he made his speech on Tuesday, 15 November. The suspicion that Reynolds had deliberately withheld that information during the speech was the final straw for Spring:

> The key issue, throughout this entire episode, has been accountability — the right of the public to secure adequate explanations and the responsibility of the holders of high office to take responsibility for their actions … it will be obvious to the House that neither I nor any of my colleagues can vote

17 October
French woman Jeanne Calment reaches the age of 120 years and 238 days, making her the oldest person ever recorded. She lives to be 122 years 164 days.

4 November
The Israeli Prime Minister, Yitzhak Rabin, is assassinated at a peace rally in Tel Aviv.

14 December
The Dayton Peace Agreement ending the Bosnia War is signed in Paris.

1996

29 January
French President Jacques Chirac says France will no longer test nuclear weapons after uproar over Pacific tests.

5 February
The FAI appoints Mick McCarthy as the new manager of the Irish soccer team.

Resignation and elevation, 17 November 1994. Albert Reynolds resigns and is succeeded by Bertie Ahern.

19 February
In Madrid, nearly 1 million people, including prime minister Felipe Gonzalez, participate in a silent march against recent terrorist attacks committed by ETA.

confidence in the Government at the conclusion of this debate. All my Labour colleagues in Cabinet and all Ministers of State who are members of the Labour Party will resign from their offices before the vote is taken. The House is entitled to nothing less from us.

(*16 November 1994*)

The following morning, Reynolds announced his resignation to Dáil Éireann. Unlike Haughey's departure, Shakespeare wasn't invoked, but Reynolds' simple resignation statement recorded his two primary achievements, and, in his final remarks as Taoiseach, he summed up better than anyone his approach to politics and life:

29 February
The siege of Sarajevo is officially over – four years to the day since Bosnian Muslims and Croats voted in a referendum to break away from Yugoslavia.

When I became Leader of Fianna Fáil and Taoiseach I set myself two political objectives — to achieve peace in Northern Ireland and on the whole island and to turn the economy around. I was fortunate in such a short space of time to achieve those two political objectives. Many political leaders set themselves in life certain priorities and goals but for whatever reasons were not around long enough to achieve them …

Now you will know why I have been single minded on many occasions in the pursuit of what I passionately believed in, often to my own detriment. In life, in business and politics, you cannot win them all. You win some, you lose some but throughout my life in politics and business I have been delighted to be a risk taker. If you are not a risk taker you will not achieve anything. The easiest way in life is not to be a risk taker. Yes, I was a risk taker in politics and business but I am quite happy that, having taken the risks, the successes far outweigh the failures.

(17 November 1994)

Finance Minister Bertie Ahern became leader of Fianna Fáil and caretaker Taoiseach. Moves were then put in place to rebuild the Fianna Fáil–Labour coalition with Ahern as Taoiseach. Just as the negotiations was falling into place, the Brendan Smyth affair again scuppered the deal, when it emerged that Ahern had also known about the *Duggan* case before Reynolds made his original speech on the issue on 15 November. Fianna Fáil–Labour negotiations broke down for a final time.

Events now took an entirely different course. Fine Gael and Democratic Left had co-operated on the opposition benches and now that the prospect of government arose, Fine Gael enthusiastically embraced Democratic Left as a coalition partner, and the two parties and Labour agreed a deal that would see John Bruton becoming Taoiseach.

Eventually, after weeks of unprecedented drama and turmoil, the Dáil met on 15 December to elect John Bruton as Taoiseach. In the negotiations, Labour had managed to secure the Finance portfolio for Ruairí Quinn. Democratic Left leader Proinsias De Rossa became Minister for Social Welfare, and his colleague Pat Rabbitte was made a junior minister with the right to attend cabinet meetings.

Among the Fine Gael ministers appointed were Nora Owen in Justice, Michael Lowry in Transport, Energy and Communications, and Michael Noonan in Health. It was the first time in the history of the State that a new government was elected without a general election. Accepting the nomination as Taoiseach, John Bruton set himself and his colleagues high standards:

I should reflect on the word "Taoiseach". In Gaelic Ireland, the Taoiseach was one who led by example rather than by exhortation, by character rather than coercion and who exercised such authority as he had as a service to the people. In the same way that I seek simplicity in the office of Taoiseach I seek simplicity

13 March
A lone gunman goes on a shooting spree at a school in Dunblane, Scotland, killing sixteen children and their teacher.

10 May
A sudden storm engulfs Mount Everest with several climbing teams high on the mountain, leaving eight dead.

23 June
The Nintendo 64 is released in Japan.

16 July
In Japan, an outbreak of E.coli food poisoning affects 9,500 people, mostly school children, and kills eleven.

24 July
Michelle Smith wins her third gold in swimming at the Athens Olympics.

in government and national policy. Good government is a public service and it should be kept simple. This is a Republic. Public office is a privilege that must be paid for in hard work and long hours. The Government must go about its work without excess or extravagance and as transparently as if it were working behind a pane of glass. The same holds for national policy.

(*15 December 1994*)

Bruton moved quickly to put his mark on the Peace Process, and one of his first acts as Taoiseach was to end the State of Emergency that Liam Cosgrave had instituted in September 1976.

The government inherited an improving economic situation. While unemployment remained high at 280,000, there was growth in the economy, and jobs were being created. Government finances were also on a sound footing with improvements such as borrowing being reduced to 2.2 per cent of GNP, down from 13 per cent just a decade earlier.

Ruairí Quinn, Labour's first Minister for Finance, delivered his budget in February 1995. While maintaining the financial discipline of previous administrations, it included a commitment to abolish third-level fees within two years, an £8 million package to reduce hospital waiting lists and social-welfare increases, particularly in the area of child benefit.

1995 saw the government put its proposals to remove the constitutional ban on divorce before the people. Having learned the lessons of the failed 1986 referendum, Minister for Equality and Law Reform Mervyn Taylor had piloted measures through the Dáil that removed many of the issues that had caused confusion during the previous campaign. The issue now to be decided was if separated people, of which there were at least 70,000 in the country at the time, would have the right to remarry.

Opponents of divorce, such as the 'No Divorce Campaign' led by former High Court judge Rory O'Hanlon claimed that its introduction would alter the status of every marriage, an idea Fianna Fáil's Charlie McCreevy dismissed:

When the anti-divorce campaign spread confusion, it does it with slogans that have little substance but carry a scary tune. It is like the minor key music which starts when the villain appears in a movie. It sets out to get a shiver going up the spine of the nation by telling the people that the minute divorce is on the Statute Book every marriage will become temporary and conditional.

That is such tripe … Nobody would even suggest that. Why would the introduction of law on remarriage make a happy marriage suddenly disintegrate? Nobody elects any of us to this House to create legislation built on fiction. It is fiction to suggest that divorce on the Statute Book will rock every good marriage in the country – that is pure fiction, comic book stuff.

(3 October 1995)

McCreevy's warning about the 'scary tune' of the anti-divorce campaign was to prove accurate. Right-wing, conservative Catholic groups waged a vigorous, if at times disgraceful, campaign against the amendment with one poster declaring, 'Hello Divorce, Bye Bye Daddy.' Support for the referendum declined as the No campaign gathered momentum – in September 1995, an *Irish Times*/MRBI poll showed a comfortable 31 per cent margin for the Yes side, which narrowed to just 3 per cent in the final poll on 21 November. The government also received a further setback when, just weeks before the vote, Green Party MEP Patricia McKenna

"Why would the introduction of law on remarriage make a happy marriage suddenly disintegrate?"

Charlie McCreevy, 3 October 1995

won a legal case that prevented the spending of public money to promote only one side of the argument. It effectively derailed the government campaign, and political parties had to hastily step into the breach and increase their efforts for a Yes vote.

The referendum was held on 24 November 1995 and passed by the narrowest of margins – 50.3 per cent to 49.7 per cent. Only 9,144 votes separated the Yes and No sides when the count was completed.

The division and bitterness generated by the divorce referendum was quickly replaced by a feeling of national pride when US president Bill Clinton visited Belfast and Dublin in December. The IRA ceasefire of August 1994 had been followed within weeks by a similar move by some loyalist paramilitaries and Clinton,

25 September
The last Magdalen Laundry closes.

27 September
The Taliban, an Islamic fundamentalist movement in Afghanistan, captures the country's capital, Kabul.

6 November
Bill Clinton is re-elected as President of America. He is the first Democrat to be re-elected since Franklin D. Roosevelt.

1997

9 January
The British lone yachtsman, Tony Bullimore, feared drowned after his boat capsized in the Southern Ocean five days ago, has been found safe and well.

27 January
It is revealed that the Nazis stole nearly 2,000 pieces of art from French museums.

6 February
In England, the
Court of Appeal
makes an historic
judgment in favour
of Diane Blood who
will be allowed to
be inseminated
with her dead
husband's sperm.

who remained deeply committed to the Peace Process throughout his presidency, addressed a joint sitting of the Dáil and Seanad on 1 December 1995 paying a warm tribute to those involved:

> They have taken great risks without hesitation. They have chosen a harder road than the comfortable path of pleasant present pieties. But what they have done is right and the children and grandchildren of this generation of Irish will reap the rewards.

> *(1 December 1995)*

13 February
The Birr telescope's
£1 million restoration
is complete, a
personal
achievement for
the seventh
Earl of Ross.

Despite Clinton's optimistic words, the impasse over the decommissioning of paramilitary weapons bedevilled peace efforts. Unionist politicians refused to engage in all-party talks as long as the IRA maintained its arsenal. Despite ongoing efforts to break the deadlock, no progress was achieved.

On Friday, 9 February 1996, the IRA exploded a massive bomb in Canary Wharf in London, bringing its ceasefire to an end. The return of violence was a crushing blow for all those who had worked tirelessly to bring about peace. Within days, the Dáil met in sombre mood to discuss the breakdown of the ceasefire, with John Bruton stressing the futility of violence:

13 February
The Dow Jones
Industrial Average
closes above 7,000
for the first time,
gaining 60.81 to
7,022.44. It will
reach 8,000 in July.

> I am satisfied that a viable basis exists, despite the terrible act on Friday, to restore peace to the people of these islands and this time to underpin it on a democratic basis, provided Sinn Féin uses its influence for peace, and the IRA clearly says that a total cessation is again in place.

> I ask the IRA to think again. A quarter of a century of violence did not progress any of your political aims. It divided Ireland more than ever before. There is no escaping the truth that bombs and bullets do not persuade people to change their minds. Violence is a bankrupt substitute for peaceful persuasion and patient negotiations.

> *(13 February 1996)*

22 February
Scientists in
Scotland announce
that they have
successfully cloned
an adult sheep
named Dolly, who
was born in
July 1996.

Continuing efforts to restore the ceasefire and kick start the talks process met with little success. IRA violence continued, and confrontation at the annual Orange Order parade in Drumcree only served to deepen the crisis. In June, Garda Jerry McCabe was killed by the IRA during an attempted robbery in Adare, County Limerick, setting back further any hopes of a breakthrough.

June also saw another brutal murder shock the political system when crime journalist Veronica Guerin was killed in cold blood on the Naas Road. Guerin had been to the forefront of exposing Ireland's criminal underworld, and her murder confirmed for many that criminal gangs were operating with impunity.

Since going into opposition in December 1994, Fianna Fáil, and Justice spokesman John O'Donoghue in particular, attacked the government continuously over the issue of crime. O'Donoghue had proposed a series of tough measures, including the seizure of criminal assets and a referendum to restrict access to bail. The government had resisted these measures, but the murder of Veronica Guerin led to a dramatic change in approach. Within days of Guerin's murder, the government allowed a debate on O'Donoghue's proposal to seize criminal assets where he maintained pressure on the government over its approach to gangland crime:

> The killing of Veronica Guerin was a calculated attack on the freedom of each and every person in this country. It was an act designed to silence not alone the late Veronica Guerin but everybody who might follow in her footsteps … The Bill is an example of democracy in action … I have stated on numerous occasions in the House that we would support legislation introduced by the Government when it was required, and that when the Government failed to introduce necessary legislation we would introduce it. The pity and sorrow is that every genuine effort made by my party in the House in the past 18 months has been thwarted, not in the interests of the public but for political expediency.

> *(2 July 1996)*

The government's belated efforts to prove it was tough on law and order were too little too late, and Fianna Fáil tapped into public unease with a popular zero-tolerance policy on crime. Coalition attempts to regain the initiative following Guerin's murder weren't helped when it emerged that because of a mix-up in the Department of Justice, a Special Criminal Court judge, Dominic Lynch, had been left hearing cases despite being officially discharged of his duties three months earlier. The debacle resulted in the release of sixteen high-security prisoners, though they were subsequently rearrested.

Despite the political damage inflicted on the government over the crime issue, the coalition succeeded in implementing the Programme for Government agreed between the three parties in 1994. The law on domestic violence was overhauled;

22 March
The comet Hale-Bopp makes its closest approach to earth. Two days later in San Diego, California, thirty-nine members of the Heaven's Gate UFO religious cult commit suicide. They believe their souls will be transported to a UFO that was hiding behind the comet.

24 March
The State's last manned lighthouse, the Bailey, is automated.

8 April
Frank McCourt wins the prestigious Pulitzer Prize for his novel *Angela's Ashes*.

13 April
Golfing sensation Tiger Woods wins the US Masters, the youngest player ever to do so at twenty-one years.

2 May
The British Labour Party wins the general election by a landslide, leaving the Conservative Party in tatters after eighteen years in power.

11 May
IBM computer Deep Blue beats chess champion Garry Kasparov in a six-game series. It is the first time a computer beats an international grand master in a multigame match.

30 June
Harry Potter and the Philosopher's Stone is published in Britain.

1 July
At the end of its ninety-nine-year lease on the territory, Britain returns Hong Kong to Chinese control.

The end of innocence, 26 June 1996. Veronica Guerin's murder causes outrage.

a Refugee Act updated the previous arcane arrangements; historic freedom-of-information legislation was introduced; and the funding of political parties was tackled, with new legislation capping donations and limiting election spending.

The government had less success, though, in trying to deal with the fallout from another scandal involving contaminated blood products supplied through the State-run Blood Transfusion Service Board (BTSB). Over 1,000 women had been exposed to the Hepatitis C virus through contaminated blood products. The scandal first emerged in 1994, and, by 1996, the government had established a non-statutory compensation scheme. For many of the women involved the compensation scheme was deeply flawed. If compensation was accepted, the right to any further legal action was waived, and, more importantly, the compensation scheme didn't involve an apology or admission of liability by the State.

Many of those unhappy with the compensation scheme pursued their cases through the courts. One of the women was Brigid McCole, a mother of twelve from Donegal. The State adopted a hardline approach to her case, hoping a vigorous defence would convince women to go the compensation route. As Mrs McCole's condition deteriorated, the BTSB finally wrote to her on 20 September 1996 admitting liability and making an offer of compensation, which Mrs McCole accepted. She died within a fortnight.

In a Dáil debate held days after Mrs McCole's funeral, Minister for Health Michael Noonan defended the State's strategy in the High Court case, and his ill-considered comments managed only to insult further the memory of Mrs McCole, her family and the other victims of the tragedy.

> On reflection, would not the solicitors for the plaintiff have served their client better if they had advised her to go to the compensation tribunal early this year? … She would not have had to face the enormous stress of court proceedings. Could her solicitors not, in selecting a test case from the hundreds of hepatitis C cases on their books, have selected a plaintiff in a better condition to sustain the stress of a High Court case? Was it in the interest of their client to attempt to run her case not only in the High Court, but also in the media and the Dáil simultaneously?
>
> (*16 February 1996*)

The opposition condemned Noonan for his remarks, for which he subsequently apologised. However, the government's handling of the scandal damaged its standing in the eyes of many.

At the end of the year, the government was rocked by another scandal. On 28 November, voters went to the polls to vote in a referendum on reform of the bail laws. The following morning, as the votes were counted, it was clear that the referendum had been overwhelmingly endorsed by the people, but a story by journalist Sam Smyth on the front page of the *Irish Independent* took the shine off the government's victory. Smyth revealed that government minister Michael Lowry had extensive building work on his home paid for by Dunnes Stores. Lowry owned a refrigeration business that supplied the supermarket chain, and it would later emerge that the building work was part of wider arrangement that saw Lowry receive undeclared payments from Dunnes through offshore accounts.

The story ended Lowry's cabinet career and speaking in the Dáil following his resignation, Fianna Fáil leader Bertie Ahern claimed the moral high ground:

> Politics and participation in public life is a career of public service. It is not an avenue of enrichment or lifestyle enhancement from private donors, even where they only want to help people perform in a particular manner. My party and my Front Bench are determined that financial scrupulousness will

15 July
Italian fashion designer Gianni Versace is shot dead on the steps of his Miami mansion.

31 August
Princess Diana of England dies along with her companion, Dodi Fayed, when their car crashes in Paris while evading photographers.

5 September
Mother Teresa, the Nobel Peace Prize winner who devoted her life to helping the sick and the poor, dies at the age of eighty-seven.

12 September
Scotland votes decisively for home rule in a referendum on how they want the country to be governed.

27 October
After a record drop in the Dow Jones index, Wall Street cuts off trading for the first time.

31 October
A Boston jury finds
Englishwoman
Louise Woodward,
nineteen, guilty of
second degree
murder for killing
Matthew Eappen
the baby in her care.

be strictly observed by all our elected members without fear or favour. Anyone who abuses their position or knowingly flouts the rules will go. The political fabric of our democracy is precious. The public are entitled to have an absolute guarantee of the financial probity and integrity of their elected representatives, their officials, and above all of Ministers. They need to know that they are under financial obligations to nobody, other than public lending institutions, except to the extent that they are publicly declared …

(*3 December 1996*)

11 December
The Kyoto Protocol
on climate change is
adopted by a United
Nations committee.

Ahern's stern words would come back to haunt him within days when further revelations exposed his political mentor Charles Haughey as another beneficiary of Ben Dunne's largesse.

An independent investigation of the revelations, conducted by Judge Buchanan, led the government to establish a tribunal of inquiry into the matter on 6 February 1997. The tribunal, chaired by Judge Brian McCracken, heard evidence in public regarding the payments to Lowry and Haughey – evidence that for the first time threw light on an offshore-banking system in the Cayman Islands – the Ansbacher accounts – where the many of the great and good of Irish society stashed money away from the tax authorities. The tribunal witnessed high drama after initial efforts by Haughey to frustrate its work collapsed, and he was forced to face the over-whelming evidence against him. In 2000, Haughey faced a criminal charge for obstructing the tribunal.

19 December
James Cameron's
Titanic premiers in
America. It goes on
to be the highest
grossing film of all
time and wins a
record eleven
Oscars.

When the Dáil debated the 'McCracken Tribunal Report' in September 1997, Democratic Left's Pat Rabbitte added a new epithet to the political career of Charles Haughey:

1998

The persona which Mr. Haughey affected, where Micheál Mac Liammóir meets the Great Gatsby, seemed to regard the huge private payments not merely as being permissible but as being the natural order of things. Just as the chieftains of ancient times lived off the fat of the land, our modern day warrior took it all as his due entitlement … This was the high point of the new political culture ushered in when the men in mohair suits took over from the men with no arses in their trousers.

(*10 September 1997*)

22 January
Dell announces the
creation of 3,000
jobs at its new
manufacturing plants
in Limerick and Bray.

As the political system recovered from the Dunnes Stores revelations, all parties geared up for a general election, which was expected in 1997. Since the Rainbow Coalition had come into office, economic growth had increased by 14 per cent, unemployment had fallen by 31,000, and more people were at work than at any time in the history of the Sate. In January 1997, Ruairi Quinn delivered his final budget before the election, and, whereas his predecessors had to grapple with deficits, he was the first minister to budget for a significant surplus. Concluding his speech on a positive note, Quinn stated:

> The celebration of success should not be confused with the contentment of complacency ... Seventy-five years ago this nation established a new fledgling State, leaving the strength and wealth of a powerful country to pursue a destiny and a vision of its own. We are today the inheritors of that vision ... The budget, when implemented in full, will bring us closer to achieving that vision.
>
> (*22 January 1997*)

Before calling the election, the Rainbow Coalition announced the reduction of corporate tax rates to 12.5 per cent, an important move that copper-fastened economic growth and, in particular, guaranteed the continued influx of foreign direct investment.

Despite the remarkable economic performance, the coalition faced the election with a degree of trepidation. Concern about crime and the scandals over the *McCole* case and the Judge Dominic Lynch affair had damaged the government's reputation, and these issues were pursued vigorously in opposition by Fianna Fáil and the Progressive Democrats.

The coalition government delayed setting a date for the election, just like its Fine Gael–Labour predecessor had twenty years earlier. Opinion was divided, with some ministers and advisers favouring an autumn poll. Others, fearful that the government would become a target for every sectional interest group if it went to the very end of its term favoured a summer election. In the end, the latter argument won out, and Taoiseach John Bruton dissolved the Dáil on 15 May 1997. The three Rainbow Coalition parties sought re-election on a joint programme entitled '21 Goals for the 21st Century'. The electoral strategy between Fianna Fáil and the Progressive Democrats was not as formalised, but it was clear to voters that there were two alternative governments on offer.

The stakes were high at the election: not only would the victors gain power but they would also be gifted an economy and an exchequer experiencing unprecedented expansion. For the first time in its history, Ireland could describe itself as wealthy,

26 January
In America, President Bill Clinton makes a television address, denying that he had 'sexual relations' with former White House intern Monica Lewinsky.

3 February
A Nato aircraft kills twenty people at an Italian ski resort when it severs their cable car line.

1 March
Comedian Dermot Morgan dies suddenly in London.

2 March
In Austria, ten-year-old Natascha Kampusch is abducted by Wolfgang Priklopil, who holds her captive until 23 August 2006.

7 March
In America, the Imperial Wizard of the Ku Klux Klan is fined for burning a cross in his garden.

Continuing the Rainbow, May 1997. The leaders of the Rainbow Coalition parties prepare for the start of the 1997 election campaign.

and the new government could contemplate the opportunities of plenty rather than the perils of penury.

Fianna Fáil's campaign, designed around the personality and energy of Ahern, was the most presidential since the foundation of the State. Ahern's whistle-stop tour of the country in glorious summer weather was breathlessly relayed to the nation by RTÉ's Charlie Bird and actor Sylvester Stallone was even drafted in to add some Hollywood glamour to the putative Taoiseach from Drumcondra. At the same time, the party hammered home its two key election messages on tax and crime.

John Bruton had grown in stature and gravitas during his term as Taoiseach, and this was reflected in the opinion polls. In an *Irish Times*/MRBI poll in April 1997, Bruton recorded a 63 per cent satisfaction rating, and the same poll put Fine Gael on 30 per cent as the election loomed. Once again, the experience of government gave Fine Gael and its leader a shot in the arm, and its campaign went well, with many judging Bruton the winner in the television debate with Ahern.

The performance of the Labour Party, however, was critical to the survival of the Rainbow government, and the outlook on this score looked bleak. Labour had delivered the vast majority of its policy agenda since entering government in

January 1993, but, as the saying goes 'eaten bread is soon forgotten', and the party had struggled in the polls, barely rising above the 10 per cent mark in the six months leading up to the election. The question for Labour, and its coalition partners, was how bad the damage would be.

Voters went to the ballot box to deliver their verdict on 6 June 1997 and the election was a success for Fianna Fáil. While at 39 per cent the party barely managed to increase its share of the vote compared to 1992, tight vote-management and a new-found ability to attract transfers resulted in a gain of nine seats, giving the party seventy-seven TDs. Fine Gael also had a good election, gaining 28 per cent of the national vote and returning fifty-four TDs to Dáil Éireann, also a gain of nine seats. It was clear that the election strategy that pitted Ahern against Bruton paid dividends for the two largest parties, and the smaller parties paid the price.

Labour, clearly out of favour with the electorate, lost nearly all the gains it had made in 1992. It saw its vote drop to 10 per cent, resulting in a loss of nearly half its Dáil strength, and it won just seventeen seats.

Likewise, the Progressive Democrats had a dismal performance, reduced to just four TDs. Among those who lost was Michael McDowell, beaten for the final seat in Dublin South East by the Green's John Gormley after a marathon recount.

Gormley's victory gave the Greens two seats in the new Dáil, while Democratic Left, who had won two by-elections in the previous Dáil, struggled to make an impact in the campaign and returned just four seats, the same as 1992. Sinn Féin's Caoimhghín Ó Caoláin won a seat in Cavan–Monaghan and, as the party had dropped its absentionist policy, became the first Sinn Féin TD to enter Dáil Éireann since de Valera led his supporters out of parliament in 1922.

The Twenty-Eighth Dáil met on 26 June 1997. A coalition deal between Fianna Fáil and the Progressive Democrats had been easily concluded, and Ahern used his negotiation skills to tie in the support of three Independent deputies in return for extensive deals on local constituency issues.

The new Taoiseach appointed Progressive Democrats leader Mary Harney as Tánaiste and Minister for Enterprise, Trade and Employment. Harney – who had become the first female leader of an Irish political party when she won the election to take over from Des O'Malley in October 1993 – became the first female Tánaiste in the history of the State.

The return of Fianna Fáil to power contributed to a breakthrough in the stalled Northern Ireland Peace Process. The election of Tony Blair in May 1997 created a new dynamic in Downing Street towards Northern Ireland and Ahern and Blair

10 July
In America, the diocese of Dallas agrees to pay $23.4 million to nine former altar boys who claimed they were sexually abused by former priest Rudolph Kos.

12 July
After two goals by midfielder Zinedine Zidane, host country France beats defending champions Brazil 3–0 to win the soccer World Cup.

12 July
The Tour de France starts in Dublin as the first two legs of the race are held in Ireland for the first time.

17 July
In St Petersburg, the remains of Czar Nicholas II and his family are buried in St Catherine Chapel, eighty years after they were killed.

7 August
Bomb explosions at
the US embassies in
Kenya and Tanzania
kill 244 people.
Osama bin Laden is
widely suspected of
ordering the attacks.

17 August
President of
the United States,
Bill Clinton,
admits having an
inappropriate
relationship with
former White
House intern
Monica Lewinsky.

7 September
In California,
Stanford University
PhD candidates Larry
Page and Sergey Brin
found Google, Inc.

20 September
TV3, Ireland's new
television station,
goes on air to provide
an alternative to RTÉ.

would go on to create a unique relationship that became central to the successful conclusion of all-party talks.

Ray Burke, the new Minister for Foreign Affairs, looked forward to the beginning of talks on a permanent political solution in Northern Ireland – but it was not to be. In advance of the election, rumours about payments to Burke began to surface. Before appointing him to cabinet, Ahern questioned Burke about the allegations and initiated his own enquiries. Assured by Burke's denials, Ahern went ahead with the appointment. It was to prove a serious misjudgement.

Questions of payments to politicians and allegations of political corruption would be a prominent feature of the Twenty-Eighth Dáil. Ironically, at a time when the political system was delivering immense achievements with regard to Northern Ireland and the economy, the standing of politics and politicians was dragged through the mire as light was shone on long-standing suspicions of financial chicanery, offshore accounts and planning abuses.

When the Dáil reconvened in September, it immediately turned its attention to the report of the McCracken Tribunal. McCracken's landmark report detailed the payments made to Michael Lowry and Charles Haughey by Ben Dunne and also revealed details of the offshore Ansbacher banking operation orchestrated by Haughey's long-time colleague Des Traynor. The Dáil established another tribunal, the Moriarty Tribunal, to investigate further the payments to Lowry and Haughey.

Speaking during the Dáil debate on McCracken's revelations, Taoiseach Bertie Ahern distanced himself from his former mentor Charlie Haughey:

Paying tax is not something just for the little people. No one, however eminent, is above the law. Tax evasion is a form of stealing from the public purse, which pays for schools, hospitals and many other social services …

It is unacceptable that people who have held high office and enjoyed a high degree of public trust should give evidence that is "unacceptable and untrue", or deliberately conceal vital information from this House or from a tribunal established by this House. There is no excuse for this. It is also unacceptable that in the case of Mr. Haughey full co-operation was withheld from the tribunal forcing it to undertake lengthy, painstaking and costly research to establish facts, which could have been established almost at once with his full co-operation.

(*10 September 1997*)

John Bruton, in his response to the tribunal report, alluded to the support that many of those within Fianna Fáil, including current cabinet ministers, had given to Haughey during his political career:

> Part of our response to the McCracken report must be to ensure it does not happen again … that a Taoiseach can never again live as a kept man, leading a fraudulent lifestyle, probably many million of pounds beyond his means, evading tax in off shore accounts in the Cayman Islands and treating the public like suckers.
>
> One can only wonder how an entire political organisation, strong and powerful like Fianna Fáil, that fought so many battles with outsiders, could be so cowed into fearful silence by its own leader … The ruthlessness with which he eliminated all his internal opponents within Fianna Fáil clearly had more than a political purpose.
>
> *(10 September 1997)*

The same day also saw Ray Burke and Michael Lowry make personal explanations to the Dáil. In Lowry's case, he was forced to apologise for the impression he had previously given that he did not have an offshore account. In marked contrast to Lowry, the Minister for Foreign Affairs Ray Burke was not in apologetic mood. Hitting out at the accusations made against him, he denied any wrongdoing, while accepting that he received £30,000 from building firm JMSE in 1989.

Following his statement, many believed that Burke had successfully dealt with the issue, but more was to follow. In early October, allegations that the JMSE payment in June 1989 was related to procurement of planning permission hit the headlines and pressure increased on Burke. On 7 October, Ahern announced to the Dáil that the Minister for Foreign Affairs had resigned from the government and from Dáil Éireann. Ahern paid tribute to his former colleague and condemned the media and opposition role in his departure:

> In the case of Ray Burke, I see a much more sinister development, the persistent hounding of an honourable man to resign his important position on the basis of innuendo and unproven allegations. Some who would class themselves as protectors of basic civil rights have harried and hounded this man without according him the basic right of due process which deems us innocent unless proven guilty. The according of due process is not just a basic right but the very

12 March
One of the twentieth century's finest musicians Yehudi Menuhin dies, at the age of eighty-two.

24 March
In the Alps, a fire in the Mont Blanc tunnel kills thirty-nine people and closes the tunnel for nearly three years.

30 March
A jury in Portland, Oregan, orders Phillip Morris to pay $81 million to the family of a man who died of lung cancer after smoking Marlboros for four decades.

20 April
At Columbine High School in Denver, two teenage students shoot and kill twenty-five of their classmates and injure at least fifteen others.

21 May
Gay Byrne hosts the
Late, Late Show for
a final time. He has
hosted the weekly
show for thirty-
seven years.

essence of common decency … There comes a time when even the strongest shoulder bows, the stoutest heart falters and the very best can resist no longer.

(7 October 1997)

Revelations regarding Ray Burke led to the establishment of a third tribunal – the Flood Tribunal – which focused on alleged corruption in the planning process in Dublin. Ahern's defence of his colleague was later undermined by further revelations involving significant payments to Burke. The Flood Tribunal passed a damning verdict on Burke's fundraising activities and, in January 2005, he was sentenced to six months' imprisonment for Revenue offences.

A presidential election in November 1997 saw Fianna Fáil's Mary McAleese elected to succeed Mary Robinson. Labour had backed anti-nuclear campaigner Adi Roche, and after a gruelling campaign, she was beaten into fourth place, behind Fine Gael's Mary Banotti and Independent candidate Dana Rosemary Scanlon. Following the defeat, Labour leader Dick Spring decided to call time on his fifteen-year leadership of the party, telling the House:

> I led our party to the best of my ability for the past 15 years. We have had our difficulties and exchanges, but I would like to believe many good friendships have been made … I think I am doing the right thing, to use John B. Keane's words, when you are from Kerry and as ignorant as us, you have to be fierce clever.
>
> *(6 November 1997)*

The following month, Finance Minister Charlie McCreevy delivered the first of the government's five budgets. 1997 was a remarkable one for the Irish economy: over 50,000 jobs were created, growth approached double figures, and the outlook was positive. No Minister for Finance had had more resources at his disposal in the history of the State.

McCreevy delivered on the coalition's tax-cutting pledge. Before the 1997 budget, income-tax rates had stood at 26 per cent and 48 per cent. By 2002, these had been cut to 20 per cent and 42 per cent. In his first budget, McCreevy also cut the rate of Capital Gains Tax from 40 per cent to 20 per cent. These tax cuts would cement McCreevy's reputation as a right-wing finance minister, but the resources available to him also saw the government boost social spending, with, for example, enhanced old-age pension payments, a policy that the coalition would continue to pursue.

Fine Gael's Michael Noonan could do little more than remind the Fianna Fáil

26 May
The first Welsh
assembly in 600
years opens in
Cardiff.

26 May
Manchester United
beat Bayern
Munich to win the
Champions League.

27 May
The International
Criminal Tribunal in
The Hague indicts
President Slobodan
Milosevic of Serbia
for crimes against
humanity in Kosovo.

16 July
Off the coast of
Martha's Vineyard
in America, a plane
piloted by John F.
Kennedy Jr crashes,
killing him, his wife
Carolyn Bessette
Kennedy and her
sister Lauren
Bessette.

benches from whom they had inherited the economic boom, while adding a note of caution:

> The applause from the Government benches reminds me of a scene from a Victorian novel where distant and impoverished relatives are informed they are the beneficiaries of a huge inheritance and applaud the solicitor who reads the will. However, Government backbenchers should remember that the novel usually continues with the dissolute and spendthrift relatives scattering their inheritance to the four winds in as short a time as possible through foolhardy and imprudent action.
>
> *(3 December 1997)*

With the restoration of the IRA ceasefire in July 1997, political negotiations had begun in earnest and reached a dramatic conclusion the following year when, on 10 April 1998, the Good Friday Agreement was signed after marathon talks in Belfast.

The Good Friday Agreement established a devolved power-sharing parliament in Northern Ireland and also required changes to the territorial claim contained in Articles 2 and 3 of the Irish Constitution. In proposing the referendum that would make these changes and endorse the Good Friday Agreement, Ahern, who had played a crucial role in the talks, stated:

> I am laying before the House a settlement for peace in Northern Ireland … Our immediate task is to have the agreement approved on both sides of the Border. This will represent a concurrent act of self-determination by the people of Ireland as a whole for the first time since 1918. Such a vote will remove any false vestige of democratic self-justification for further acts of violence from any quarter, republican or loyalist … The whole basis of the settlement is the recognition that we have to live together on this island and for that we need peace, stability and reconciliation. Neither tradition has the means to impose its will on the other.
>
> *(21 April 1998)*

The referendum was held, on both sides of the border, on 22 May. Voters in the Republic passed it by an overwhelming 94 per cent. In Northern Ireland, the agreement was accepted by 71 per cent to 29 per cent and elections to the new devolved assembly in Stormont followed in June 1998. Ongoing problems in relation

11 August
Up to 350 million people in Europe and Asia witness the last total solar eclipse of the century.

6 November
Australians reject a proposal to break ties with the British monarchy and become a republic.

31 December
President Boris Yeltsin resigns as president of Russia leaving prime minister Vladimir Putin in charge as acting president.

2000

1 January
As millennium celebrations take place around the world, the transition to Y2K passes without any major problems.

10 January
In the largest ever corporate merger, America Online agrees to be bought by Time Warner for $162 million.

26 January
In New York, Rage Against the Machine, the rap-metal band, play in Wall Street and cause the early closing of trading because of crowds.

12 February
The creator of the 'Peanuts' cartoon strip, Charles 'Sparky' Shultz, dies aged seventy-seven in California.

17 February
Microsoft release Windows 2000.

3 May
The Love Bug computer virus begins to spread around the world as an e-mail attachment, eventually infecting one in every five personal computers and resulting in nearly $10 billion in damages.

to decommissioning and the release of paramilitary prisoners delayed the actual establishment of the Northern Ireland Executive for an additional eighteen months – but, before then, a more sinister force would threaten the peace process.

Despite the historic breakthrough in April with the signing of the Good Friday Agreement, loyalist and republican violence continued in Northern Ireland. During the summer of 1998, dissident republicans attempted to continue the 'armed struggle' with sporadic gun and bomb attacks. On 15 August, a group styling itself the Real IRA brought its campaign of violence to the streets of Omagh, County Tyrone, and detonated a no-warning bomb that killed twenty-nine people.

The bombing created revulsion across the island of Ireland, and the Dáil was recalled from its summer recess to pass emergency security legislation in early September. Taoiseach Bertie Ahern condemned those responsible with sentiments that were echoed across the Dáil chamber:

> The attack on Omagh was not just an indiscriminate attack on democracy and the British-Irish Agreement. It was a reckless attack on a community, on a people … That is the evil done by the self styled "Real IRA" at Omagh – death, pain, suffering, grief and horror – that will unfortunately echo down through the years …
>
> Paradoxically, this evil act has brought forth an outpouring of goodness and solidarity, a community of emotions and convictions shared almost universally among people throughout this island. Amidst the grief and pain, we have seen sincere and significant statements and actions that give hope for the future and which must be further built upon … The British-Irish Agreement is about dialogue, trust, compromise, peace and democracy. The attack on Omagh was designed to undo all that by generating fear and hatred and more violence and by trying to force everything back into the melting pot. It has abjectly failed.
>
> (*2 September 1998*)

Northern Ireland aside, politics in the Dáil continued to be dominated by scandals, both old and new. The Ansbacher offshore scandal unearthed by the McCracken Tribunal revealed a layer of systemic tax evasion among many prominent figures in Irish society. Minister for Enterprise, Trade and Employment Mary Harney used existing company law to investigate the matter further, and new evidence regarding the scale of the fraud was revealed in the High Court in September 1999 as she sought additional powers to ratchet up the investigation. There was initial fury in the Dáil when the identities of 120 Ansbacher account holders were kept under wraps as the investigation proceeded. However, the list of names was eventually made public in the summer of 2002, and Socialist TD Joe Higgins presented the Dáil with a caricature of the aptly named 'Ansbacher man':

> Ansbacher man was brought into being in the 1970s. Like his creator, he had a complex, dual personality, one half of which was "Ansbacher man the shadow," a shadowy persona who inhabited a secret world of offshore islands, coded bank deposits, fiddled taxes and secret loans … Ansbacher man the shadow was as furtive as a thief. He was driven by greed and the inordinate desire for personal enrichment. He was a walking conspiracy to defraud the taxation system of tens of millions, if not hundreds of millions, of pounds.
>
> Meanwhile, his other half, "Ansbacher man the public persona," was generally basking in the warm glow of an approving establishment. Business colleagues, priests and political party leaders all deferred to him and his picture was in the business pages of *The Irish Times* every second day. He was on high powered committees which laid down industrial policy for this country for years and decades to come … In the 1980s he was forthright in calling on the unemployed and the crucified, compliant PAYE taxpayer alike to tighten their belts in the national interest …
>
> (*11 July 2002*)

By the end of 2006, the Revenue Commissioner had investigated 237 cases linked to the Ansbacher accounts and had recovered more than €66 million in taxes and penalties.

However, it wasn't just the upper echelons of Irish society that were doing all in their power to avoid paying tax. In 1986, the government imposed a tax on interest received from deposit accounts, unfortunately named DIRT (Deposit Interest Retention Tax). The tax didn't apply to accounts of non-residents, a fact that the banks and their customers were quick to grasp with a resulting exponential rise in the number of non-resident accounts held tax free in Irish banks. The vast majority of these non-resident accounts were bogus, with thousands of people living in towns and cities across Ireland signing a declaration to the effect that they resided abroad and then strolling home, safe in the knowledge that the interest on their accounts was now guaranteed tax-free status. The Revenue Commissioners

12 May
The Tate Modern Gallery opens in London.

22 July
Shelbourne FC's home Uefa Cup tie against Rangers is moved to Prenton Park in England because of fears of sectarian trouble. Despite taking a 3–0 lead, Shelbourne lose 3–5.

25 July
Concorde crashes minutes after take-off from Charles de Gaulle airport near Paris killing 113 people.

12 August
The Russian submarine K-141 *Kursk* sinks in the Barents Sea and despite attempts to raise the sub all 118 men on board die.

31 October
Boyband Westlife score their seventh UK number one and remain the only artist in UK chart history to have seven straight chart-toppers.

8 January
In America, Noah, a gaur, is born and is the first individual of an endangered species to be cloned.

20 January
George W. Bush is sworn in as the forty-third president of the United States.

19 February
A five-mile exclusion zone is placed around an abattoir in Essex after a suspected case of foot-and-mouth disease is detected.

22 March
Prime Minister Tony Blair agrees the mass slaughter of livestock on farms in England and Scotland in an effort to halt the spread of foot-and-mouth disease. In Ireland, after the first case of the disease is confirmed, hundreds of events and St Patrick Day parades are cancelled.

and the Central Bank struggled to deal with the burgeoning scandal, and, eventually, in late 1998, the scale of the fraud was exposed by *Magill* magazine.

The Dáil's Public Accounts Committee established an inquiry into the matter, that was chaired by Fine Gael TD Jim Mitchell. The hearings, which were televised live by TG4, grabbed the attention of the nation, and the committee's report confirmed the widespread use of bogus non-resident accounts, the connivance of the banking sector in the system and the failure of the State authorities to stop it, even when details of the fraud were well established. The report also demonstrated the ability of Dáil committees, operating in a non-partisan manner, to investigate serious allegations within a relatively short time frame.

The work of the DIRT Inquiry represented a breakthrough for parliamentary accountability and, by 2006, the Revenue Commissioner had recovered nearly €850 million through its subsequent investigations into bogus non-resident accounts.

Two other significant Dáil inquires were subsequently established. One examined the fatal shooting of a young man, John Carthy by members of the gardaí following a siege in Abbeylara, County Longford, in 2000 and another committee began hearings into cost overruns on a signalling system, called Mini-CTC, installed on part of the national rail network by CIÉ. However, the belief of many parliamentarians that a new era of parliamentary accountability was to hand was quickly dashed. A legal challenge to the authority of a Dáil committee to investigate the Abbeylara shooting was taken by members of the gardaí and the Supreme Court upheld the challenge, which severely restricted the power of the committee system to inquire into issues of public concern. Both the Abbeylara and the Mini-CTC inquiries collapsed in the wake of the Supreme Court judgment and, to date, no proposals to reassert the power of Oireachtas committees to conduct hearings and issue reports into similar controversial issues have been pursued.

While the business and banking sectors took centre stage in the Ansbacher and DIRT inquiries, the continuing questions of payments to politicians was never far away. It emerged that former minister and serving EU Commissioner Pádraig Flynn received £50,000, again in 1989, from property developer Tom Gilmartin. When the story broke, Gilmartin maintained that the money was intended as a donation to Fianna Fáil; however, the money was lodged to a personal account that Flynn held in London. In January 1999, Flynn appeared on RTÉ's *Late Late Show*, and, in a remarkable interview – during which he sought public sympathy for the tremendous strain of having to run homes in Mayo, Dublin and Brussels – he managed only to insult Gilmartin when attempting to dismiss questions about the donation.

There were calls for Flynn to answer why the Gilmartin donation ended up in his personal accounts and, in February 1999, under pressure from the Progressive Democrats, Fianna Fáil was forced to support a motion calling on the EU Commissioner to make a comprehensive statement. Pat Rabbitte – now a Labour TD following the merger of Labour and Democratic Left the previous month – attacked the typical bravado behind his fellow Mayo man's attitude to the issue:

> There is the matter of three pensions, three homes, three housekeepers, two cars, one cheque and no answers. The man who was so eager to answer all the questions from Gay Byrne thumbs his nose at the Taoiseach, the Tánaiste and the Government. The man who has talked himself and the Government into another fine mess has suddenly donned the mantle of a Trappist monk. For the man who has played so many parts, more parts than an Abbey actor, his latest reticence does not become him.
>
> (*10 February 1999*)

Flynn's daughter Beverley had followed him into politics and had won a seat in Mayo at the 1997 general election. Defending her father in typical family style, she condemned Fianna Fáil for conceding to Progressive Democrat pressure which had led to the Dáil motion:

> What we are seeing tonight is political expediency at its most cynical … If Pádraig Flynn is a victim of a travesty, he is not alone because his fellow casualties include integrity, fair play and basic justice …
>
> Fianna Fáil should not collude in its own destruction or in the continuing portrayal of our party as intrinsically, essentially and eternally flawed by seeming to reward others who claim to be our moral guardians. Every time we do it, we are buying today's survival at the cost of tomorrow's existence. We are eroding our faith in ourselves and we are betraying our supporters … That is why, until I see the votes counted, I will not bring myself to believe that the party I know would collaborate with the Opposition parties on this tacky motion …
>
> (*10 February 1999*)

When the votes were counted, the motion was passed, and Beverley Flynn later resigned from the Fianna Fáil parliamentary party. Her break with the party was

23 March
Russia sends its space station, *Mir*, into a controlled descent into the Pacific Ocean, ending the station's fifteen-year mission to test how long human beings can remain in space.

8 April
Tiger Woods becomes the first golfer in history to win four consecutive major tournaments, known as golf's grand slam, by winning the Masters tournament in Augusta.

1 June
The heir to the throne of Himalayan kingdom of Nepal massacres the royal family before turning the gun on himself.

2 June
In America, the world's first self-contained artificial heart is implanted in Robert Tools.

20 July
The twenty-seventh
G8 summit takes
place in Genoa,
Italy. The meeting
sparks massive
demonstrations by
anti-globalisation
groups. One
demonstrator, Carlo
Giuliani, is shot
dead by police and
several others are
badly injured during
police attacks.

9 September
In Estonia, sixty-
eight people die
after drinking bootleg
alcohol that
contained methanol.

11 September
Terrorists hijack
commercial planes in
the US and in suicide
missions crash them
into the two towers
of the World Trade
Center in New York
and into the Pentagon.
The passengers on
a fourth plane crash
it to the ground
before it reaches
its intended target.

7 October
Following the 9/11
attacks, America
invades Afghanistan.

complete following revelations of her role in selling an offshore investment scheme when she worked for National Irish Bank.

The coalition continued to implement its Programme for Government. Ireland's Celtic Tiger economy was in full roar. By the end of 2000, unemployment, which had stood at 10 per cent in 1997, had been reduced to 4 per cent, approximately 160,000 jobs had been created and economic growth approached 10 per cent each year. McCreevy continued his tax-cutting agenda and successfully reformed the tax system with the introduction of tax credits. McCreevy's other great reforming measure in the tax area, individualisation, which rewarded double-income families, met with less success and had to undergo significant change.

While the tax agenda of the coalition gave it a distinct right-of-centre image, the government did undertake a number of socially progressive measures. Mary Harney introducing minimum-wage legislation in 2000, old-age pensions increased nearly 50 per cent by 2002 and child benefit was also high on the government agenda with the 1997 payment rate of £30 per month for the first two children in a family increasing to £92 per month over the course of McCreevy's five budgets.

Despite the government's attempts to set the political agenda and focus in particular on Northern Ireland and the economy, the reverberations from the two tribunals sitting in Dublin Castle continued to distract the Dáil and the nation with revelations in 2000 in particular proving hugely damaging.

In April 2000, former government press-secretary-turned-lobbyist Frank Dunlop, under intense pressure from the Flood Tribunal, changed his evidence and admitted paying bribes to county councillors in return for support for rezoning motions. Dunlop's explosive evidence confirmed rumours that had circulated for years about planning in the greater Dublin region.

Not to be outdone, the Moriarty Tribunal had uncovered evidence about a £100,000 donation that property developer Mark Kavanagh gave to Charles Haughey in 1989 for the Fianna Fáil party. Only £25,000 found its way to the party and, in June 2000, hearings at the tribunal raised serious questions about the nature of information that Fianna Fáil had provided to the tribunal on the matter.

As the pressure over these revelations grew, the government managed to add to the controversy in May 2000 when Minister for Finance Charlie McCreevy appointed former Judge Hugh O'Flaherty to the European Investment Bank. O'Flaherty had resigned from the Supreme Court in 1999 following his intervention in what became known as the *Sheedy* case which involved the release from prison after only a year of a man sentenced to four years following his conviction for driving while drunk and causing the death of a young mother from Tallaght. Tensions over the affair nearly saw the Progressive Democrats pull out of government in 1999.

The decision to rehabilitate O'Flaherty and appoint him to the European Investment Bank caused public and political uproar. The government limped towards the summer recess with its popularity seriously damaged. The previous month, Mary Harney compounded the government difficulties by declaring in an interview that she believed Charles Haughey should be convicted at his forthcoming trial in relation to obstruction of the McCracken Tribunal. Harney's comments were later cited as one of the reasons why the trial was postponed indefinitely. Meanwhile, the Moriarty Tribunal was investigating the source of approximately £8.5 million that had flowed through Haughey's accounts over three decades.

Tapping into public unease at the O'Flaherty appointment, continuing revelations regarding corruption and ongoing problems in key public services, the opposition put down a motion of no confidence in the government before the Dáil broke for the summer. During the debate on the motion, Labour's Finance spokesperson Derek McDowell reflected on the words of his former party leader Dick Spring over a decade earlier:

> It is time for the Government to go because it is, by some distance, the most ideologically right-wing Government the country has had for some time, it has shamelessly used the fruits of economic growth to benefit the better off … the party which leads it is hopelessly tainted with the corruption of its recent past and the behaviour of Fianna Fáil threatens to destroy the faith of our people in the very institutions of our democracy …
>
> People are fed up with the politics of sleaze. The nation needs to move away from the politics of sleaze to the issues which affect the lives of our citizens: education, health, housing and the economy. Where this Government has a problem is that it is no longer possible for it to get us back to normal politics. It is dogged and tainted by the corruption of the recent past and damned by the fact that it tolerated it for so long … I remember ten years ago hearing Deputy Spring on the benches comment on Charles Haughey. He said that Haughey was a cancer in the Irish body politic. I remember thinking at the time the language used was over the top, but how right he was. The spread of that cancer has continued ever since. It threatens to consume our democracy. It has already infected this Government and make no mistake, it is terminal.
>
> (*30 June 2002*)

23 October
Apple launches the iPod.

17 November
The GAA vote to abolish Rule 21 which had banned members of the British army and PSNI from joining the association.

22 December
A flight from Paris to Miami is diverted to Boston after a passenger Richard Reid attempts to set his shoe, filled with explosives, on fire.

2002

1 January
Euro notes and coins are issued in France, Spain, Germany, Italy, Portugal, Greece, Finland, Luxembourg, Belgium, Austria, Ireland and the Netherlands.

"**People are fed up with the politics of sleaze.**"

Derek McDowell, 30 June 2002

In a stout defence of his government, Taoiseach Bertie Ahern listed the coalition's achievements, a record that, he maintained, overshadowed any allegations from the past emerging at the tribunals:

> Let us look at what has been achieved. We have ended the era of mass unemployment and emigration and are coming close to full employment for the first time in our history ... The most dramatic fall has been in long-term unemployment which now stands at only 1.7 per cent. This is because of the focus we have placed on helping the most disadvantaged to get jobs through new approaches to training, support and investment. Many of these policies were opposed or dismissed by the Opposition, but they have worked. There are almost 300,000 more jobs today than there were three years ago. At around 1.7 million, we have by far the highest number of people at work ever. Our young people have an unprecedented choice of mostly well paid career opportunities in Ireland while Irish people living abroad can choose to come home ... Politics should be about implementing policies that make a real difference to all our lives, not the sound bite culture of daily denunciations that do not indicate any policies.

> *(30 June 2000)*

The government won the motion of no confidence, but the array of controversies was taking its toll.

Charlie McCreevy's populist budget in December 2000 went some way to restoring the standing of the government. Income-tax rates were cut to 42 per cent and 20 per cent respectively, old-age pension payments broke the £100 per week mark for the first time, child-benefit payments rose sharply and the plan to provide all those over seventy with medical cards, regardless of income, was unveiled. In the following Finance Bill, as the country came to terms with the introduction of the euro, the Minister for Finance announced details of new Special Savings Incentive Accounts that would see the government contribute €1 for every €4 deposited by a saver. Concluding his budget speech, McCreevy stated:

> In the popular television series, "Yes Minister" ... the loyal civil servant, Sir Humphrey, often advised his political master as follows: "To be precise, many things may be done, but nothing must ever be done for the first time." It will scarcely surprise that I do not subscribe to this political maxim ... The measures

29 May
Before the start of
the soccer World
Cup in Japan and
Korea, Roy Keane
sensationally leaves
the Irish camp in
Saipan after a row
with manager
Mick McCarthy.

I have announced today will improve the quality of life of all our people. They will lead to a fairer society, with opportunity for all. They will raise living standards for all, and encourage and reward effort and enterprise.

(6 December 2000)

While the opposition bitterly contested McCreevy's claim that the budget would led to a fairer society, it certainly did put a fairer wind behind the government, with an MRBI poll in *The Irish Times* in January 2001 revealing that 70 per cent of the electorate thought the budget was good for the country. After a horrid twelve months, government satisfaction increased by 15 per cent.

30 May
In Listowel, County
Kerry, John B.
Keane, the play-
wright and novelist
dies from prostate
cancer aged
seventy-three.

The poll was bad news for Fine Gael, with the party barely achieving 20 per cent. Bruton's opponents in Fine Gael, including Michael Noonan and Jim Mitchell, moved to challenge him and, on 1 February 2001, Bruton lost a motion of confidence at a parliamentary party meeting. Michael Noonan won the contest to replace him and became leader just fourteen months before the next general election.

As the new Fine Gael leader contemplated the electoral challenge before him, another electoral outing was on the mind of the government. The Nice Treaty provided for the enlargement of the European Union, admitting ten new countries, including many members of the former Soviet Eastern Bloc. The referendum on the Nice Treaty was held in June 2001, and the lacklustre campaign by the government and most political parties in favour of the treaty revealed a high degree of complacency. It was a fatal error.

21 August
In Britain, forensic
experts confirm that
bodies found days
earlier are those of
Holly Wells and
Jessica Chapman.
Ian Huntley and
Maxine Carr are
later charged in
relation to
their deaths.

In the end, the referendum on the Nice Treaty was defeated 54 per cent to 46 per cent, with only two Dáil constituencies, Dublin South and Dún Laoghaire, voting in favour of ratification. That said, apathy appeared to be the biggest winner as just 35 per cent of the electorate cast their vote. It later emerged that cabinet minister Éamon Ó Cuív voted against the treaty.

The start of 2002 saw political parties adopt a campaign footing for the election expected in the summer, yet developments at the Flood Tribunal would ensure that the spectre of political corruption would again convulse Dáil Éireann in the most dramatic of ways.

7 October
In California, the
discovery of the
dwarf planet
Quaoar is
announced.

Former Fianna Fáil TD Liam Lawlor had engaged in a long-running battle with the Flood Tribunal over the disclosure of documents. His failure to co-operate with the tribunal had resulted in him being jailed on two occasions by the High Court for contempt. In February 2002, he was jailed for the third time, and the Dáil unanimously agreed a motion calling on him to resign. The motion was debated on

7 February 2002 and the errant TD won the right to attend the Dáil to contribute. In a remarkable scene, Lawlor was taken by prison van from Mountjoy to Leinster House to take part in the proceedings and then returned to prison. Speaking during the debate, Labour leader Ruairi Quinn appealed to Lawlor to go:

> In the march to freedom for this nation, there were many people who said we could never govern our own affairs. The great colonialist myth was that we were not up to it, could not handle it and were ungovernable. This nation has to demonstrate that we have the strength of character, the generosity of spirit and the humanity to govern our own affairs … I appeal to Deputy Lawlor … to respect the traditions of this State and venerate the memory of the people who came before us, namely to acquiesce without protest to our request that he voluntarily resign from this House and, by so doing, reinforce the foundations of this Republic.
>
> *(7 February 2002)*

Despite the unprecedented nature of the cross-party call for Lawlor to resign, he was unrepentant and defended his actions to the hilt:

> I apologise that it has happened but when a person thinks he is slightly more than half right, he must stand up for what he believes and address that matter with whatever tools are available … In doing so, I hope that when people come to judge this phase that I will account for every penny I got and no one in the witness box will be able to make the slightest suggestion of corruption against Liam Lawlor.
>
> *(7 February 2002)*

The coalition was to attempt one significant policy initiative in the months before the general election. To the surprise of many, the government announced its intentions to hold a referendum to row back on the 1992 Supreme Court judgment in the *X* case and remove the risk of suicide as grounds for an abortion. A similar move had been defeated in November 1992, but the government was confident that its proposal would pass. It was wrong. The referendum was held on 6 March 2002 and the proposal was narrowly defeated with the margin of victory just 10,000 votes.

Seven weeks later, at the very end of a day's business in Dáil Éireann, Taoiseach Bertie Ahern announced to a virtually empty chamber that he would ask the president to dissolve the Dáil. The election was set for 17 May.

11 October
Geraldine Kennedy is appointed the first female editor of *The Irish Times*.

12 October
Reports from the Indonesian holiday island of Bali say more than fifty people have been killed in two explosions.

25 October
In London, Richard Harris dies of Hodgkin's Disease at the age of seventy-two.

8 November
In a growing crisis, the UN Security Council unanimously approves Resolution 1441, forcing Saddam Hussein to disarm or face 'serious consequences'.

9 December
United Airlines files for bancruptcy.

'We do not need more than 58 separate health agencies. It has become a jumble and it has led to below-par results for patients and below-par value for money for taxpayers'

Election success, 6 June 2002
Bertie Ahern leaves the Dáil after being elected Taoiseach for a second time.

'Opportunity has replaced despondency, peace has replaced bloodshed and we have a new

2002-2008

The End of an Era?

'He said: 'I am one of the few
socialists left in Irish politics.'
Immediately, Tomás Ó Criomhthain came
to mind, as he lamented the last of
the Blasket Islanders: 'Ní bheidh
a leithéidí arís ann'. I then thought:
'Good, Taoiseach. There are two of us in
it and we will go down together.'

'Opportunity has re[placed] despondency, peace has r[eplaced] bloodshed in [...] The Irish [...] The have never ceased to believe that better times would come.'

2002-2008

Despite the question marks over senior members of the party, Fianna Fáil was in a strong position going into the 2002 election campaign. Recent economic performance had resulted in higher standards of living for most of the population and Ahern's handling of the Northern Ireland peace process was praised by all sides. Against this, opinion polls regularly revealed that the health service, crime and education were the most important issues facing the country, facts that Fianna Fáil's election slogan 'A Lot Done, More to Do' explicitly acknowledged.

An outgoing government hadn't been re-elected to office since the 1960s, but the Fianna Fáil–Progressive Democrats coalition attempt to break the trend was assisted by the poor performance of Fine Gael, the leading opposition party.

Michael Noonan's heave against John Bruton the previous year was triggered by Fine Gael's poor ratings in opinion polls. Noonan proved unable to turn the situation around, and the Fine Gael slide continued. In an *Irish Times*/MRBI poll published in January 2002, Fine Gael was at 21 per cent, seven percentage points lower than its 1997 general election performance. Significantly, Noonan's personal ratings were also worse than Bruton's.

Fine Gael's attempts to bolster its support appeared increasingly desperate. It proposed that investors who had lost money in the eircom flotation should be compensated by the government. Likewise, it was in favour of State payouts to taxi drivers who had lost out when the industry was deregulated. These moves undermined the credibility of the party, and it faced into the election with trepidation.

Labour under Ruairi Quinn shunned any pre-election pact with Fine Gael and campaigned on an independent platform seeking a mandate for the implementation of its policy priorities on health, crime and social welfare.

The campaign itself became largely dominated by economics, with Fianna Fáil using every opportunity to undermine confidence in the ability of the opposition, and Fine Gael in particular, to manage the economy. Fianna Fáil wasn't reluctant in proposing grandiose election gestures either, promising to abolish hospital waiting lists within two years, a promise that was quickly abandoned after the election.

Fine Gael recorded its worst result since the 1940s, with just 22.5 per cent of the national vote and the loss of twenty-three seats. Michael Noonan resigned from the leadership as the results unfolded and was replaced by Mayo TD Enda Kenny.

While Fine Gael stared into the abyss, Fianna Fáil basked in triumph. The party increased its vote to 41.5 per cent and won eighty-one seats, just short of an

2003

21 January
The Millennium Spire on Dublin's O'Connell Street is finally complete after months of construction.

1 February
The space shuttle *Columbia* breaks apart and burns while re-entering earth's atmosphere, killing all seven crew members.

14 February
Dolly the sheep, the first mammal cloned from adult cells, is put to death because of premature ageing.

16 February
100,000 people in Dublin and 30,000 in Belfast march in protest against the imminent invasion of Iraq by US and British troops. Worldwide, 10 million people protest in over 600 cities.

26 February
In Vietnam, an American business-man is admitted to the Vietnam France Hospital in Hanoi with the first identified case of SARS. WHO doctor Carlo Urbani reports the unusual highly contagious disease to the organisation. Both businessman and doctor die of the disease within months.

13 March
The journal *Nature* reports that 350,000-year-old upright-walking human footprints have been found in Italy.

20 March
The US launches a war against the regime of Iraq's authoritarian leader Saddam Hussein by staging a massive bombardment of Baghdad, the Iraqi capital. It is the start of the 'shock and awe' campaign of rapid dominance.

overall majority. It was a remarkable achievement for Ahern, who, again, had been central to Fianna Fáil's election strategy. He had come within a whisker of securing an overall majority, a scenario long dismissed as unfeasible by most commentators.

Labour had a disappointing result. Quinn had campaigned well but, as election day loomed, opinion polls indicated that the party wouldn't be necessary as far as government formation was concerned. Pushed to the margins as the campaign approached its final days, the party returned twenty TDs, the same result as in 1997 when the seats gained from the merger with Democratic Left are taken into account. Among the Labour TDs not to return to Dáil Éireann was former leader Dick Spring who narrowly lost his seat to Sinn Féin's Martin Ferris in Kerry North.

Labour's standstill result, together with Fine Gael's meltdown and the return to power of Fianna Fáil led some to question Labour's electoral strategy, which had already been criticised by Pat Rabbitte. Ruairi Quinn resigned in the weeks following the result and Rabbitte won the election to succeed him.

Unlike Labour, the Progressive Democrats had managed to remain relevant to the formation of the next government throughout the election campaign, thanks in no small measure to Michael McDowell. After losing his seat in 1997, McDowell distanced himself from the Progressive Democrats but gradually returned to the fold after being appointed Attorney General in 1999. In the final stages of the campaign, with polls showing Fianna Fáil heading towards an overall majority, McDowell drove the Progressive Democrats' final campaign message, summed up in the catchy poster slogan 'Single Party Government – No Thanks'. The tactic proved effective and contributed to the party doubling its number of TDs to eight, despite a drop in its national vote share.

The election also resulted in significant gains for the Green Party, Sinn Féin and Independents, partly due to the general disillusionment with traditional party structures engendered by sleaze and corruption allegations. The Greens trebled their strength in Dáil Éireann, returning six TDs, and Sinn Féin gained four extra seats, giving it five TDs in the new Dáil. The appeal of Independents was enhanced by the generous deals that the TDs who supported the previous government had received for their constituencies, and thirteen Independents were returned at the election, the highest number since 1951. The Socialist Party retained the seat that Joe Higgins had won for the party in 1997.

The Dáil met on 6 June, when Bertie Ahern was comfortably elected Taoiseach with the support of the Progressive Democrats, who had concluded another coalition agreement with Fianna Fáil.

The Dáil sat for another month, but the gruelling election campaign resulted in a low-key start for the Twenty-Ninth Dáil, which even managed to find time for statements on Ireland's performance in the World Cup, where deputies diplomatically avoided reference to the departure of Roy Keane from the training camp on Saipan, ignoring the fact that this was the issue consuming the country.

Despite the post-election lull during June, Labour TD Róisín Shortall raised the circumstances of a compensation deal that the former Minister for Education Michael Woods had concluded with the religious orders. The scale of abuse endured by children in industrial and reformatory

Election 2002. The Progressive Democrats campaign stopped Fianna Fáil in its bid for a single-party government.

schools had first been revealed in an RTÉ documentary *States of Fear*, broadcast in April 1999. The powerful programme not only recounted appalling abuse inflicted by some members of religious orders who ran the institutions but also exposed the failure of the State over decades to take responsibility for the children sent there.

Following the broadcast, the Taoiseach apologised on behalf of the State. The following month – May 1999 – the Dáil debated the scandal of industrial schools, with Fine Gael's Alan Shatter delivering a damning indictment of the role of the State and the religious orders:

> It is time for us to acknowledge that Irish social policy relating to children has over the years been built on a bedrock of hypocrisy and deceit. The State,

26 April
In rugby's Heineken Cup, the prospect of an all Ireland final in Lansdowne Road is lost when Munster lose 13–12 to Toulouse in the first semi-final. Leinster also lose, 14–12 to Perpignan, in the second semi-final.

28 May
James Plunkett, the novelist and author of *Strumpet City* dies in Dublin at the age of eighty-three.

21 June
In Dublin, the Special Olympics opening ceremony takes place in Croke Park.

27 July
American icon and legendary comedian Bob Hope dies just two months after celebrating his 100th birthday.

15 August
Global oil production begins a four-year plateau (and subsequent decline) in the face of rising demand.

15 September
For the first time the All-Ireland football final is contested by two teams from the same province when Tyrone and Armagh meet. Tyrone win 0–12 to 0–9.

8 October
Film star Arnold Schwarzenegger is elected governor of California.

24 November
In Glasgow, Al Ali Mohmed Al Megrahi is sentenced to twenty-seven years for bombing Flight 103 over Lockerbie in 1988.

3 December
American troops capture ousted Iraqi president Saddam Hussein. He is found hiding in an underground chamber dubbed a 'spider hole'.

17 December
In Soham, England, Ian Huntley is convicted of the murders of ten-year-olds Holly Wells and Jessica Chapman.

which constitutionally committed itself to cherishing the children of the nation equally has over the decades placed her most vulnerable and destitute children in institutions in which they are brutalised and sexually violated …

Political soap box oratory about children's rights and their welfare has never been matched by the provision of the essential resources and comprehensive legislation required to provide our children with the protection to which they are entitled … The State, with its bureaucracy, must share the responsibility and blame for the scandalous events which took place within our institutions and have blighted the lives of so many placed in them during their childhood.

The State, church authorities and religious orders stand accused of hypocrisy and deceit. We now know that many of those who were in a position of authority in the Catholic church in the early years when I was a Member of this House and who railed at the evils of contraception, divorce and abortion lacked similar concern for the young children who were being buggered and abused by men and women in religious orders. We now know that those who stood on moral platforms and lectured society were moving abusive priests from one parish to another like pieces on a chess board, ignoring the fact that their sexual proclivities posed a risk to every child with whom they came into contact.

Priests were moved from parishes, not for the purpose of protecting children, but to cover up abusive conduct already known to have taken place, in order to protect the church. Reports of abusive conduct by those in religious orders and those employed by them were covered up by the State because of a false sense of its duty to the church, in gross violation of its obligation to protect the rights of children…

(*19 May 1999*)

The government had set up an inquiry into the legacy of abuse and also established a redress board to provide victims with compensation. Negotiations began with the religious orders to agree the amount they would contribute. The outgoing Minister for Education Michael Woods concluded the deal on his last day in office. The religious institutions would contribute cash, land and counselling services to the tune of €128 million and, in return, the government would indemnify the religious orders against any future legal actions and pay the remaining compensation bill. It was an appalling deal for the State, and, as Deputy Shortall pointed out in

> **"Priests** were moved from **parishes,** not for the purpose of **protecting children,** but to **cover up abusive conduct** already known to have taken place in order **to protect the church."**

Alan Shatter, 19 May 1999

June 2002, it let the religious orders off the hook:

> Will the Minister explain how this approach can help deal with the long running issue of child abuse in residential institutions given that it is essentially a cheap insurance policy for those perpetrators of abuse. It negates modern day thinking in terms of perpetrators taking responsibility for their actions. It is complete immunity for a very low price. Will the Minister explain how he can possibly justify that on behalf of the taxpayer?
>
> *(20 June 2002)*

Questions over the nature of the deal would continue for months as it emerged that the eventual compensation package would involve a sum in excess of €1 billion, funded by the State, with the exception of the €128 million contributed by the religious orders.

When the Dáil reconvened after the summer recess, the government concentrated on rerunning the referendum on the Nice Treaty which had been defeated in June 2001. With the ten applicant states depending on a Yes vote to proceed with the planned enlargement of the EU, the Taoiseach made an impassioned plea for a positive outcome:

> I speak in Dáil Éireann today not just as Taoiseach, or as a party leader, but as an Irish citizen. In the course of our national life, there are historic moments when we must move beyond politics. This referendum on the European Union is one such moment.
>
> We have reached a great crossroads – a turning point of enormous consequence for our people. Within weeks, the sovereign people of this Republic will cast a vote that will set our course far into the future. The result is awaited across Europe, within and without the Union. It will set new possibilities or new limits for Ireland and will form our national horizon. The choice we make, more than any other single action we take as a people in the next few years, will decide our standing in the world and decide whether Ireland succeeds and moves ahead in the right direction …
>
> *(10 September 2002)*

The referendum, held on 19 October 2002, saw a significantly increased turnout, up from 35 per cent to 49 per cent, and the treaty was passed by 63 per cent to 37 per cent.

1 January
Ireland takes over as president of the European Commission.

25 January
The second of two NASA rovers sent to explore Mars lands on the surface of the planet, where it will look for signs of water.

12 February
In San Francisco, marriage licenses are issued to same-sex couples in an act of civil disobedience.

28 February
Five people are killed in a bus crash on Wellington Quay in Dublin.

2 March
Cormac McAnallen, the Tyrone midfielder, dies in his sleep of an undetected heart condition at the age of twenty-four.

Despite the successful passage of the Nice referendum, clouds quickly gathered on the government's horizon. During the election campaign, Fianna Fáil denied that a downturn in tax receipts and an overrun in spending would result in cutbacks. However, within weeks of taking office, a range of expenditure adjustments indicated that not all was well. Reduced economic growth, under 2 per cent by year end compared to the near double-digit growth of previous years, led to a fall off in revenue, and the bright economic future touted so aggressively during the election campaign seemed far off.

McCreevy's budget in December contained none of the tax-cutting measures of previous years, and a new three-year, €100 million levy on the banks was introduced to provide additional income. The budget cutbacks had taken much of the gloss off the election victory. Before voters went to the polls in May, the government registered 61 per cent satisfaction in an *Irish Times*/MRBI poll. Eight months later, its satisfaction had plummeted to 31 per cent, the lowest level since 1997. Responding to McCreevy's budget, Fine Gael's Richard Bruton reflected the anger among much of the public:

> This budget is genetically flawed. Its genesis is in a fraudulent vision which was sold relentlessly in the run up to the general election. "Much done, more to do" – that was the slogan which was like a garland festooned everywhere one went. It was a reckless project designed with one thing in mind – to secure power again for those opposite. It was a project of self-preservation which resulted in spending growing at ten times the rate of growth of revenue generated by the Minister. However, this was all in the interests of the few and not in the interests of the public …
>
> This Government has for the most myopic reasons ensured that the truth about the reckless project in which we are engaged did not come out. That is why people feel angry, annoyed and frustrated. They know they were conned in the budget which resulted from two years of reckless spending. Ireland is not in economic crisis. The crisis we have today is a crisis of competence on the part of the Government.

> *(4 December 2002)*

The government's woes continued in 2003. The crisis in the health services, particularly in accident and emergency (A&E) units, continued, and the now-abandoned election commitment to eliminate waiting lists in two years was thrown

11 March
At least 170 people are killed after powerful explosions tear through three Madrid train stations during the morning rush hour.

27 March
The Irish rugby team win the Triple Crown in the Six Nations for the first time since 1985.

29 March
The smoking ban comes into operation in all workplaces, including pubs. The Irish government is the first in the world to implement a countrywide ban.

28 April
The CBS news program *60 Minutes II* shocks the world by broadcasting images of Iraqi detainees being abused at Abu Ghraib prison.

29 April
In America, production of the Oldsmobile ends. It is the oldest car marque in America.

11 May
Former international
rugby player and
coach Mick Doyle is
killed in a car crash
near Dungannon,
County Tyrone, at the
age of sixty-two.

at the government by its opponents at every opportunity. Added to this, a number of significant overruns in public projects saw millions being wasted and the delivery of essential infrastructure delayed. For many, the government seemed arrogant and out of touch, a theme Labour's Joan Burton picked up on when condemning new restrictions on the Freedom of Information Act:

> All through history, hubris has been a deadly disease of exaggerated pride and self-regard that takes hold of those who have been in power for too long for their own good. Its hallmark is overweening presumption – presumption was one of the sins in the old Catechism and is a fatal flaw in anybody who exercises power in a democracy. The current proposals on freedom of information have this hallmark in spades. The power elite that dominates this Government is showing many distinct signs that it has succumbed to this disease.
>
> *(26 March 2003)*

30 June
In Iraq, preliminary
hearings begin in
the trial of Saddam
Hussein for war
crimes and crimes
against humanity.

While deeply unpopular, the government did continue to introduce a range of reforms. A new fund to enable independent producers to avail of part of the television licence fee came into force; the Official Languages Act satisfied many Irish-language activists by placing an obligation on State bodies to communicate in the official language; and the plan to introduce a ban on smoking in public places was announced.

However, as with every administration, legislative activities rarely captured the public imagination, and the standing of the coalition continued to decline.

Finance Minister Charlie McCreevy attempted to restore the party fortunes in his December 2003 budget. In a relatively short speech, one idea stood out – the minister's decision to decentralise 10,300 civil and public service jobs to fifty-three locations outside Dublin. Decentralisation had long been advocated as a way of boosting the economy outside the capital. Previous schemes had seen sections of government departments decentralised, but McCreevy's plan was more ambitious and entire government departments and agencies would move, lock, stock and barrel.

4 July
In New York,
groundbreaking for
the Freedom Tower,
which is due to
open in 2011 ten
years after the 9/11
attacks, begins at
Ground Zero.

25 July
American Lance
Armstrong wins an
unprecedented sixth
consecutive Tour de
France cycling title.

Typically, McCreevy's initiative was announced without any consultation with employee representatives, and his grand plan met with significant obstacles and was effectively abandoned in 2008. For example, four agencies linked to the Department of Enterprise, Trade and Employment, involving a total of 917 staff, were selected for decentralisation in December 2003. In a parliamentary reply nearly three years later, it emerged that only eighteen people had actually relocated.

"All through history, hubris has been a deadly disease of exaggerated pride and self-regard that takes hold of those who have been in power for too long for their own good."

Joan Burton, 26 March 2003

27 August
At the Olympic Games in Athens, Cian O'Connor wins a gold medal in show jumping with the horse Waterford Crystal. However, he is stripped of his medal when it emerges later in the year that his horse has tested positive for a banned substance.

3 September
More than 200 people, mainly children, die after a three-day siege at a Russian school in Beslan School Number One comes to a bloody end.

26 September
The Luas 'Red Line', from Connolly Station to Tallaght, opens.

2 November
George W. Bush is elected President of the America for the second time, beating his Democratic rival by a comfortable margin.

As the local and European elections approached, the government announced its intention to hold a referendum on citizenship at the same time. As the law stood, any person born in Ireland was entitled to Irish citizenship, and this was copper-fastened in the amendments made to Articles 2 and 3 of the Constitution when the people overwhelmingly endorsed the Good Friday Agreement in 1998.

The government, citing an increase in the number of non-national women arriving in Ireland to give birth, sought to change the automatic right of children born in Ireland to citizenship. The legislation was introduced in the Dáil by Minister for Justice, Equality and Law Reform Michael McDowell in April 2004. Explaining his reasons for this surprise referendum – just two months earlier the Taoiseach had stated there were no plans to hold one – McDowell stated:

> Citizenship is the means whereby we become members of a moral, cultural, political, social, economic and legal community based on rights and duties established in law.
>
> Citizenship, then, is not just an entitlement to a passport with a particular symbol on its cover, although possession of a passport is undoubtedly an important attribute of entitlement to a particular citizenship. It is a complex of rights and obligations shared by people of a common nationality, and a symbol of the sovereign nature of the nation State.
>
> Governments have a duty then to safeguard the institution of citizenship to ensure that it continues to fulfil the requirements of its role as a manifestation of a nation whose people value membership of that nation …
>
> I have compiled sufficient information to provide clear and incontrovertible evidence that a disproportionate number of non-national mothers are giving birth to children in Dublin maternity hospitals and that a disproportionate number of non-national mothers are presenting to maternity hospitals at a late stage of pregnancy … I have been criticised for using the expression "citizenship tourism"… but that is precisely what we are faced with …
>
> *(21 April 2004)*

The proposal for the referendum produced a storm of protest from the opposition, with many seeing it as an attempt by the government to court popularity at the local and European elections by playing to latent fears about immigration, nevertheless, the referendum was decisively passed by 79 per cent to 21 per cent.

However, voters also used the opportunity to express their dissatisfaction with

Fianna Fáil, and the party lost eighty local-authority seats. Fine Gael and Labour picked up support, but it was Sinn Féin who made the largest gains, leading many to predict a substantial breakthrough for the party at the next general election.

The local and European elections also marked something of a success for Fine Gael leader Enda Kenny. For the first time since taking of the leadership of the party, he showed signs of connecting with voters. Fine Gael and Labour moved to capitalise on Fianna Fáil's poor election performance and the two parties announced a general-election pact at a meeting in Mullingar that would see the two parties fight the next election on a joint platform and provide voters with an alternative to Fianna Fáil–Progressive Democrats coalition.

The Taoiseach took heed of Fianna Fáil's poor electoral performance and changes were put in place to alter the public's perception of a right-of-centre, uncaring government. The most significant change was the appointment of Finance Minister Charlie McCreevy as Ireland's EU Commissioner.

When the Dáil reconvened following the summer recess, Ahern announced the departure of McCreevy and also the resignation from cabinet of two long-standing members: Minister for Agriculture Joe Walsh and Minister for Defence Michael Smith. Among the changes following the cabinet reshuffle, Brian Cowen became Minister for Finance and Tánaiste Mary Harney took up the Health portfolio.

Buoyed up by an impressive election result, Fine Gael leader Enda Kenny responding to the reshuffle, set his sights on his next electoral goal – the general election:

> It is clear that Fianna Fáil and the Progressive Democrats knew well before the summer elections that they had got it wrong. However, getting it wrong was not the problem, rather it was being found out. That meant being punished and hence the new leaf, the new look and the new veneer. The reason was naked political fear, a Fianna Fáil-Progressive Democrats phobia of losing power. Despite the pomp and circumstance which the House has just witnessed, any change is just cosmetic, a cheap veneer...
>
> When [they] vote in that election, now 100 weeks hence or less, they will not choose between candidates, parties or leaders but will choose the kind of Ireland they want to live in — an Ireland run for the short-term good of the parties under Fianna Fáil and the Progressive Democrats, or an Ireland run for the long-term good of the people led by Fine Gael and like-minded parties.
>
> (*29 September 2004*)

11 November
Yasser Arafat dies in hospital in Paris, aged seventy-five, bringing to an end more than forty years of rule over the Palestinian people.

26 December
Sea surges triggered by an earthquake under the Indian Ocean kill over 200,000 people in thirteen countries southern Asia.

2005

1 January
Cork becomes the European Capital of Culture for 2005.

16 January
Romanian Adriana Iliescu gives birth at the age of sixty-six, becoming the oldest woman in the world to do so.

20 January
Irish roads signs and regulations are changed to kilometres from miles.

16 February
The Kyoto Protocol that aims to slow down global warming takes effect but the US remains outside it.

The departure of McCreevy marked something of an image makeover for the government, and, to ensure that the electorate got the message that the government was compassionate and caring, the Taoiseach, in an interview with *The Irish Times* in November, declared himself a socialist. The claim roused the hackles of those on the left in Dáil Éireann, with Labour leader Pat Rabbitte enquiring:

> I want to ask comrade Taoiseach now that he has come out as a socialist how this will affect the ordinary lives of our citizens? Nothing has stretched credulity so much since the press conferences in Baghdad of "comical Ali". Will the Taoiseach say what this will mean in practice for ordinary people? How will it change the lives of ordinary people now that a true socialist leads the Government?
>
> (*16 November 2004*)

10 March
In London, the comedian Dave Allen dies in London at the age of sixty-eight.

2 April
Pope John Paul II, dies after twenty-seven years as pontiff, one of the longest reigns in papal history.

Not to be outdone, the following day, Socialist Party TD Joe Higgins also queried the Taoiseach's avowal of socialism:

> You can imagine, a Cheann Comhairle, how perplexed I was when I returned to find my wardrobe almost empty. The Taoiseach had been busy robbing my clothes. Up to recently the Progressive Democrats did not have a stitch left due to the same Taoiseach but we never expected him to take a walk on the left side of the street … He said: "I am one of the few socialists left in Irish politics." Immediately, Tomás Ó Criomhthaín came to mind, as he lamented the last of the Blasket Islanders: "Ní bheidh ár leithéidí arís ann". I then thought: "Good, Taoiseach. There are two of us in it and we will go down together."
>
> Sadly, I had to take a reality check. If this conversion was genuine we would have to go back 2,000 years to find another as rapid and as radical. Saul's embrace of Christianity on the road to Damascus stood the test of time but the Taoiseach's embrace of socialism on the banks of the Tolka hardly will.
>
> (*17 November 2004*)

16 April
In a decision welcomed by the IRFU and the FAI, the GAA agrees to open up Croke Park to allow rugby and soccer to be played in the stadium.

26 April
The last Syrian troops depart Lebanon, ending nearly thirty years of occupation.

The Taoiseach revelled in the attention and defended his claim by reeling off figures regarding government investment in health, education and social welfare. But he was later to launch an impassioned attack on the version of socialism espoused by Deputy Higgins and his Socialist Party comrades:

A national crisis, 28 April 2005. Despite Ireland's new-found wealth, demonstrations against ongoing bed shortages remained a constant reminder of social inequality.

Deputy Joe Higgins loves asking questions—but never wants to listen to answers. He would love to return to the days of … pathetic poverty when de Valera and Lemass built social houses, when no other houses were being built. People were living in council houses and had to emigrate because they had no jobs and no future … That is the great tradition Deputy Higgins and his merry warriors want to bring back … He has a failed ideology and the most hopeless policy pursued by any nitwit. He is a failed person who was rejected and whose political philosophy has been rejected. He will not pull people back into the failed old policies he dreamed up in south Kerry when he was a young fellow. Now go away.

(*21 June 2006*)

Unmoved by the great socialism debate, new Health Minister Mary Harney took steps to tackle the ongoing crisis in the health services. Despite significant increases in the health budget since 1997 and the launch of new services, such as the National Treatment Purchase Fund, the crisis in this sector, particularly in A&E departments, continued.

A slew of reports had suggested radical organisational reform, and one of

16 May
Scottish MP George Galloway appears before the US Senate committee to answer allegations of profiting from the Iraqi Oil for Food Programme.

23 May
In County Meath, five schoolgirls are killed and many others are injured in a collision between their school bus and two other vehicles.

25 May
After a sensational comeback to draw 3–3 at full time, Liverpool beat AC Milan 3–2 on penalties to win the Champions League.

31 May
W. Mark Felt is confirmed as 'Deep Throat', the Watergate whistleblower.

13 June
The Irish language is granted official status as a working language of the European Union.

Harney's first acts in her new role was to introduce the 2004 Health Bill, which abolished the health board system and established a new Health Services Executive (HSE) to deliver public-sector health care. Introducing the new legislation, the minister was confident it would lead to a greatly improved service:

> This is an historic piece of legislation. It provides for the most comprehensive reorganisation of our health services since 1970 which is long overdue and vital. It is a once-in-a-generation event. It is our generation's chance to put patients first in the design of the management of health services. It is our chance to put in place modern, effective management to make the best use of these tremendous resources we are applying to health and to get clear value and clear results for that money. It is our chance to create a system where money can follow patients and where outcomes can be measured. We are legislating for the start of the 21st century, for ten, 20 or 30 years in advance. There is no going back. We can no longer rely on outdated and ineffective legislation that may have met the needs of Ireland of the 1960s and 1970s …
>
> We do not need more than 58 separate health agencies. It has become a jumble and it has led to below-par results for patients and below-par value for money for taxpayers. Those are the two reasons we are proposing this legislation and the two ways Government policy should be judged: better outcomes for patients and better value for taxpayers' money. To achieve them, we badly need clarity of roles and accountability — political responsibility for the Minister and management responsibility for the management. The lines of responsibility and accountability are clear in this legislation …
>
> *(23 November 2004)*

In objecting to the legislation, Labour's Liz McManus highlighted the danger of the HSE becoming another bureaucratic entity, removed and unresponsive to patients and the community:

> I remember discussing proposals to create four health boards in the Dublin region and making the point that everyone acknowledged that the old Eastern Health Board was a monster but that there was a real risk that we are going to create four monsters instead of one … There is a real risk we will end up with a board that is unaccountable and untouchable, other than by way of its connection with the Minister, that there will not be proper oversight and

that it will not be open in the way modern society and the protection of patients demand.

(23 November 2004)

The HSE came into existence in 2005 and has failed to restore public trust in the health services. The executive continues to take tough decisions regarding the reorganisation and rationalisation of our health services, not least in respect of acute hospitals and cancer care, but there is little doubt that its job has been made harder by the constant criticism – some of it deserved, some not – that it has struggled to deal with since its inception.

> " We **do not** need more than **58 separate health agencies.** It has become **a jumble and it has led to below-par results** for patients and below-par **value for money** for taxpayers. "

Mary Harney, 23 November 2004

Finance Minister Brian Cowen's first budget in December 2004 continued with the new socially responsible approach the government was anxious to portray after the departure of Charlie McCreevy. Whereas McCreevy cut personal income-tax rates in four of his five budgets, Cowen took a different approach. Those earning the minimum wage were exempted from income tax and Cowen also increased spending on health, disability services and social welfare striking a notably differ-ent tone from the free-market bravura of the McCreevy era.

The Taoiseach and his ministers weren't the only people with finance on their minds in December 2004. On 20 December, more than £26 million sterling was stolen from the Northern Bank in Belfast. The PSNI and the British and Irish governments believed that the IRA was responsible, and the Peace Process, which

7 September
At Windsor Park in Belfast, the Northern Ireland soccer team beat England 1–0 in a World Cup qualifying match. It is the first time since 1927 that the team has beaten England at home.

1 October
Bombings in Bali kill twenty-five people and injure more than a hundred.

10 October
John Banville wins the 2005 Man Booker Prize for his novel, *The Sea*.

12 October
After a 0–0 draw against Switzerland, Ireland fail to qualify for the 2006 soccer World Cup.

14 October
Roy Keane announces his retirement as a player from international soccer. A month later, he leaves his club, Manchester United.

2006

9 January
Steve Staunton is appointed the new manager of the Repulic's soccer team. He will be mentored by Bobby Robson as International Football Consultant.

11 March
After 128 years, the last competitive rugby international is played at Lansdowne Road, the oldest rugby ground in the world. It is to be closed for redevelopment.

11 March
Slobodan Milosevic is found dead in his cell at the War Crimes Tribunal in The Hague.

had stalled largely over the decommissioning issue, was again in turmoil. Then, in January 2005, Robert McCartney, a father of two, was killed after a row in a Belfast bar. Again, IRA members were suspected of involvement in the killing.

Dáil Éireann turned its attention to Northern Ireland and the ongoing IRA involvement in criminal activities that contributed to the delayed implementation of the Good Friday Agreement, with Justice Minister Michael McDowell giving vent to the distinctly cooler reception that Sinn Féin was now experiencing in London and Dublin:

Democratic mandates, like democracy itself, are not capable of being taken hostage or of being transmitted like property by tiny groups to be used or abused by them in their future quest for power or influence. On the contrary, true republicanism can never be severed from the principle of democratic mandates, about which we hear so much. It is not a holy flame kept burning by some secret cult. The Irish Republic derives its authority from the strong voice of the people not from some ghostly whisper from history …

It is not possible to claim opposition to the use of violence by others if armed robbery, armed punishment beating — which is a euphemism for torture and mutilation — extortion, exiling under threat, attempted murder and murder fall to be viewed by one as things that are not crimes. One cannot hope to participate in the political process while one has those mental reservations …

No basis exists for anybody to claim they are being victimised by the unanimity and consensus that has emerged in recent weeks on these matters … On the contrary, as in the past, every opportunity is being offered to those who are democrats to take up the challenge of the mandate they have received and to contest the democratic process on equal terms with the rest of us.

(*9 February 2005*)

Sinn Féin's leader in Dáil Éireann, Caoimhghín Ó Caoláin, dismissed the widespread allegations surrounding the republican movement's involvement in criminal activities, asserting these allegations were motivated by electoral concerns:

As leader of the Sinn Féin Deputies, I wish to make clear our absolute refutation of all the false accusations of criminality made against our party … we reject criminality of any kind. I do not intend to use my limited time to address every false allegation thrown around this House and around the media. The charges do not relate to criminality, the IRA or even the peace process, they are about the party politics of this State. Charges are being made in a climate in which the old opponents of the peace process have come out of the woodwork … The current Minister for Justice, Equality and Law Reform was among the begrudgers at that time. His recent conduct shows that while he claims to have changed his mind, his heart is still back in the days of section 31, internment without trial and the demonisation of the entire Nationalist community in the North.

(*9 February 2005*)

Despite Ó Caoláin's robust denials, the new focus on criminality increased the pressure on the republican movement to deliver on decommissioning. In April 2005, Sinn Féin President Gerry Adams called on the IRA to lay down its arms and, in July, the IRA leadership issued a statement effectively declaring that the war was over and that arms would be put permanently beyond use. This paved the way for the St Andrew's negotiations in October 2006 that resulted in the restoration of the Northern Ireland Assembly and Executive, which had been suspended for the previous four years.

While 2005 was a momentous year in Northern Ireland, significant changes were also afoot south of the border. In June 2005, the Dáil debated the first reports from the Morris Tribunal. The tribunal was established in the months before the 2002 election, after Fine Gael's Jim Higgins and Labour's Brendan Howlin had pursued Minister for Justice John O'Donoghue over allegations of gross garda misconduct in Donegal. The damning reports from the tribunal revealed a litany of corruption, deceit and harassment, with many innocent victims, including the McBrearty and Shortt families, paying the price. Labour's Brendan Howlin compared the revelations in the reports to the gross miscarriages of justice in Britain during the 1970s:

This day has been a long time coming … more than six years of deep distress and unimaginable anguish for many individual citizens let down by the State have elapsed. More than that, their own State and its agent, the Garda Síochána grossly abused them.

The scale of the abuse of power outlined in the two Morris reports to date beggars belief. That it could have continued over such a period and involved so many individual gardaí of all ranks is both shocking and frightening … We

30 March
The novelist John McGahern dies from cancer at the age of seventy-one.

6 April
Paleontologists report the discovery of a fossil of Tiktaalik roseae, a so-called 'missing link' between fish and land animals.

23 April
At Lansdowne Road, 47,800 people watch Munster beat Leinster 6–30 in the Heineken Cup semi-final.

23 April
The 2006 census is held in the Republic.

23 April
Israeli prime minister Ariel Sharon is removed from office after four months in a coma.

20 May
Munster win the
Heineken Cup at
the third attempt
when they beat
Biarritz 19–23 in
the Millennium
Stadium in Cardiff.

21 May
In Dublin, armed
gardaí forcibly
remove thirty Afghan
refugees from St
Patrick's Cathedral
after a one-week
hunger strike.

25 May
Former CEOs
Kenneth Lay and
Jeffrey Skilling
are found guilty of
fraud and conspiracy
in connection with
the Enron scandal.

13 June
Colm Tóibín's novel
The Master wins
the International
IMPAC Dublin
Literary Award.

7 July
Dublin airport is
evacuated for the
second time in a
week when an
abandoned
package is found.

have our own scandal here and now, our Birmingham Six and Guilford Four and much more. Few issues matter more to the well-being of our citizens than good policing. For once, let this House be strong enough to do all that is required.

(17 June 2005)

Labour demanded the establishment of an independent commission to review policing in the State, much like the Patten Commission had done in Northern Ireland. The government rejected the idea; however, Minister for Justice Michael McDowell did introduce new legislation governing An Garda Síochána and while falling short of what many demanded, these reforms did represent a significant step forward in increasing the accountability of the State's police force.

The government was less open to radical reforming measures in relation to another issue gaining political significance: the environment and climate change. Improvements in some areas, such as recycling facilities and waste management had been introduced, but plans to introduce a carbon tax were scrapped by Charlie McCreevy in 2004. By 2005, the crisis presented by climate change was overwhelmingly accepted by the scientific and environmental communities. The government had published a climate-change strategy, but its solution concentrated on the purchase of emissions credits, rather than reducing net carbon emissions in Ireland, a policy that Green Party leader Trevor Sargent condemned:

> The irresponsibility of this Government has been shown in stark relief. In spite of feigned concern and crocodile tears … what the Government is doing is exacerbating the emissions problem. It is breaking agreements relating to the Kyoto Protocol and will punish the taxpayer for this inaction … The Government is soft-pedalling to favour the climate chaos villains, those who benefit from not paying their dues on the pollution issue … What we have opposite is a huddle of gangsters spending taxpayers' money in a carbon casino, plotting the most conniving scams to dodge even the woefully inadequate Kyoto targets.

(30 November 2005)

As preparations for the forthcoming election commenced, the 'green agenda' would play a key part of every party's election manifesto, confirming the move to the mainstream of environmental issues.

The battle lines for the general election had been established in 2004. Since then, political debate had settled into a predictable, if robust, clash between the two large blocs, with Fine Gael and Labour condemning the 'tired and jaded' government's failure to address health, crime and housing and honing in on massive overruns on capital and technological projects, while the government countered by highlighting its record of investment, reform and economic management since 1997, implying that the alternative 'slump coalition' could not be trusted.

In May 2006, an *Irish Times*/TNS mrbi opinion poll produced good news for the alternative government. Taken against a background of continuing deep public unease at the crisis in the health service, with Mary Harney admitting in March that conditions in A&E units were 'a national emergency', the polls revealed a resurgent Fine Gael at 28 per cent, just three points behind Fianna Fáil. More significantly, the combined support for Fine Gael and Labour, at 43 per cent, was substantially ahead of the 34 per cent recorded by Fianna Fáil and the Progressive Democrats.

As TDs prepared to return to the Dáil following the summer recess in September, Mary Harney surprised many colleagues by standing down as leader of the Progressive Democrats. In previous months, private tensions between Harney and Michael McDowell over the leadership of the party had developed into a very public spat. Now McDowell took over the mantle of leadership, and the ground on which the forthcoming election would be fought seemed fixed – until the developments at the planning tribunal rocked the political system.

On 21 September, *The Irish Times* broke a story that the planning tribunal was investigating payments made to Taoiseach Bertie Ahern. The investigation was triggered by an allegation of an alleged payment to Ahern by Cork-based property developer Owen O'Callaghan. In the course of this investigation, the tribunal asked Ahern to account for payments to his accounts in the early 1990s in an effort to rule out the possibility that these payments came from O'Callaghan. In the process, it unearthed a series of previously unknown loans and donations to Ahern.

Following a week of accusation, denial and speculation, the Taoiseach gave an interview to RTÉ's Bryan Dobson the day before the Dáil reconvened. Ahern explained that the money he received comprised loans and dig-outs from friends, given at a time when he was dealing with the financial consequences of his marriage break-up.

Despite the attempt to quell the controversy, the opposition put the revelations about the Taoiseach centre stage when the Dáil reconvened. Ahern, citing a previous incidence where allegations against him were found groundless in the courts, defended his integrity, while admitting to an error of judgement in accepting the cash, part of which was handed over after a dinner function in Manchester.

19 July
The warmest temperature in Ireland in the twentieth century – 32.3° C – is recorded in Elphin, County Roscommon.

19 July
Results from the 2006 census show that the population of the Republic is 4,234,925 million – the highest since the 1861 census. This makes the population of the whole island just under 6 million.

22 September
Europe win the Ryder Cup which is held a the K Club in Straffan, County Kildare.

10 October
Google buys YouTube for $1.6 billion.

15 November
Al Jazeera launches its English language news channel Al Jazeera English.

2007

There are few of us with the benefit of hindsight who would not change some of our past decisions … As I surveyed events of the past two weeks, I realised that my judgment in accepting help from good and loyal friends and the gift in Manchester, albeit in the context of personal and family circumstances, was an error. It was a misjudgment, although not in breach of any law or code of conduct at the time. It was not illegal or impermissible to have done what I did but I now regret the choices I made in those difficult and dark times. The bewilderment caused to the public about recent revelations has been deeply upsetting for me and others near and dear to me. To them, to the Irish people and to this House, I offer my apologies.

(3 October 2006)

Ahern's popularity had always been one of Fianna Fáil's strongest electoral cards, and now the opposition, particularly the putative alternative government of Fine Gael and Labour, sensed an opportunity to take some of the shine of the so-called 'Teflon Taoiseach', with Labour's Pat Rabbitte piling the pressure on the embattled Taoiseach:

To me the heart of the matter is this; did the Taoiseach do wrong? Is it remotely credible that moneys outstanding for 13 years, without repayment of any kind, can suddenly be categorised as loans? …

On the Manchester moneys, can we do more than highlight the absolute impropriety of a serving Minister for Finance accepting payment for a nixer outside the State? Never mind the "no law was broken" defence. By any standards, it was wrong. What does one say about this Government's standards when not a single Cabinet Minister can bring himself or herself to say that what happened at Manchester was wrong? One would believe in the tooth fairy if one believes that businessmen happen along to a function in a posh hotel to listen to any old Joe Soap lecture on the Irish economy and then organise an impromptu whip around to give him something for himself. In normal life one gets gifts from one's friends and one takes loans from strangers. Yet, Mr. Ahern says he got loans from his friends and took gifts from strangers.

(3 October 2006)

Opposition hopes that the revelations would mark a significant turning point and further erode support for the coalition were quickly shattered however. A TNS mrbi poll for *The Irish Times* published just ten days after the Dáil debate on the issue revealed a surge in support for Fianna Fáil, up eight points to 39 per cent since the previous poll. Fine Gael and Labour dropped 2 per cent and 4 per cent respectively in the poll. The combined support for the outgoing coalition was now a healthy six points ahead of the alternative. The opinion poll resulted in an immediate change of tack on behalf of the main opposition parties, which refrained from any questioning of the Taoiseach over his finances, despite further information regarding the purchase of the Taoiseach's house emerging.

> "In normal life one gets gifts from one's friends and one takes loans from strangers. Yet, Mr. Ahern says he got loans from his friends and took gifts from strangers."

Pat Rabbitte, 3 October 2006

In April 2007, on the eve of the general-election campaign proper, the sides were evenly balanced. Fine Gael enjoyed its highest opinion poll support in years, hitting 31 per cent just before the Taoiseach dissolved the Dáil, although Labour support had fallen back to 10 per cent. Fianna Fáil support was waning, down to 34 per cent and the alternative government had a 4 per cent lead over the outgoing Fianna Fáil–Progressive Democrat coalition as the campaign began.

The Taoiseach sought the dissolution of the Dáil at a dawn meeting, with the president in Áras an Uachtaráin on 29 April 2007. This unusual move prompted speculation that Ahern wanted the election out of the way before he began to give evidence to the tribunal, which had postponed its hearings for the course of the election. Further details regarding the Taoiseach's financial affairs hit the headlines, and the first half of the campaign proved disastrous for Fianna Fáil as questions about Bertie Ahern's purchase and refurbishment of a house and associated financial

30 January
Microsoft releases Office 2007 and Vista 2007.

3 February
The deadly H5N1 strain of bird flu is found at a Bernard Matthews turkey farm in England.

8 February
In California, the model and actress Anna Nicole Smith dies at the age of thirty-nine.

24 February
In an emotional game at Croke Park, Dublin, 83,000 people watch Ireland beat England 43–13 in the Six Nations Championship. It is the first time rugby has been played at GAA Headquarters.

1 March
In Paris, International Polar Year, a $1.5 billion research programme to study both the North Pole and South Pole is launched.

transactions dominated the political agenda. Fine Gael and Labour, still stung by the increased support for Fianna Fáil that followed the first revelations about the Taoiseach's finances the previous September, stayed out of the row and concentrated on their agreed strategy of urging the electorate to opt for a change in government, albeit a change that focused more on personalities than policy.

While the alternative coalition kept its powder dry, Tánaiste and Progressive Democrat leader Michael McDowell waded into the fray, threatening to pull his party out of government unless the Taoiseach made a full statement regarding the issues before the tribunal. The move backfired badly for the Progressive Democrats, with internal opposition to the stance taken by the party leader quickly finding its way into the public domain.

As the controversy raged, the historic return of devolved government in Northern Ireland, which saw Ian Paisley and Martin McGuinness take up the positions of First Minister and Deputy First Minister respectively, enabled Ahern to showcase his achievements in Northern Ireland, culminating in a landmark speech in Westminster halfway through the campaign.

Before his Westminster address, Ahern issued a lengthy statement regarding his tribunal travails and, immediately, Fianna Fáil moved to draw a line in the sand under the issue and to refocus its stalled campaign on the economy and the competency of the two government options before the electorate. In the final week of the campaign, following the television debate between Ahern and Kenny, there was a decisive swing to Fianna Fáil. The momentum behind Fianna Fáil continued until polling day and, despite its problems at the beginning of the campaign, Bertie Ahern was to record his third election victory in a row, leading his party to over 41 per cent of the national poll and returning seventy-eight TDs, a loss of just three seats. Fine Gael's election performance was also impressive, especially considering the drubbing it received just five years earlier, and it increased its Dáil strength by twenty seats, returning fifty-one TDs.

While the two major parties benefited from a contest that pitted two alternative coalitions against each other, the smaller parties lost out. Labour received 10 per cent of the national vote and returned twenty TDs to Dáil Éireann, the second election in a row where it had effectively stood still. The result was even worse for the Progressive Democrats, which lost six of its eight outgoing TDs, including Tánaiste and party leader Michael McDowell, all of which led to serious questions being asked about the future viability of the party.

Prospects of significant breakthroughs for both Sinn Féin and the Green Party

A new voice in politics, 2007. The Green Party provided a new voice in the Dáil and a new voice in government when it entered coalition with Fianna Fáil in 2007.

also failed to materialise. Sinn Féin – widely tipped to increase its parliamentary strength following an impressive performance in the 2004 local elections – struggled to gain 7 per cent support and lost a seat in the process. Likewise, expectations that the Greens would forge ahead in election 2007 proved unfounded: the party vote remained under 5 per cent.

In forming a government, Ahern employed the formula that produced his first administration following the 1997 election with a number of Independents and the two remaining Progressive Democrat TDs pledging their support. However, post-election negotiations also saw a new departure in Irish politics with the Green Party, after a somewhat tortuous talks process, entering coalition for the first time and taking two seats at cabinet – party leader John Gormley occupying the Environment portfolio and Dublin South TD Eamon Ryan becoming Minister for Energy, Communications and Natural Resources.

The Green Party's arrival in government buildings gave a new look to Ahern's third administration, although nearly half the cabinet appointed in June 2007 had been in office continuously for over a decade. While the price of power resulted in the Greens capitulating on prominent issues, such as the use of Shannon airport by the US military and the M3 motorway project near the Hill of Tara in County Meath,

27 June
Tony Blair, dogged by the unpopularity of the Iraq war, resigns after ten years as Britain's prime minister during which his Labour Party was re-elected three times.

30 June
A calendar blue moon occurs – whereby there is a second full moon in a single month – in the western hemisphere.

4 July
After 114 days in captivity, BBC journalist Alan Johnston is freed by his Palestinian captors.

21 July
The final book of the Harry Potter series, *Harry Potter and the Deathly Hallows*, is released. It sells over 11 million copies in the first twenty-four hours, becoming the fastest selling book in history.

21 July
Joe O'Reilly is found guilty of killing his wife Rachel at their home in Naul, County Dublin.

22 July
In golf, Padraig Harrington wins the Open played at the Carnoustie Golf Links in Scotland. It is his first win at a major championship.

27 September
In Burma, the military junta cracks down on protests led by Buddish monks.

5 November
The Writers Guild of America goes on strike, which will last for three months and severely affect US television programming.

17 November
After a 2–2 draw with Wales, the Republic of Ireland soccer team fail to qualify for the 2008 European championships.

the party was not slow to make its presence felt, introducing new energy-efficiency regulations for the house-building sector, pushing through environmentally driven reform of motor tax and providing enhanced supports for alternative-energy projects.

Yet, the issue that dominated so much of the election campaign – the Taoiseach's finances – managed to overshadow the new government's agenda. In September 2007, days before the Thirtieth Dáil reconvened after the summer recess, the Taoiseach gave evidence to the planning tribunal. In addition to the lodgements of cash from loans and dig-outs revealed twelve months earlier, the Taoiseach was questioned about the purchase and refurbishment of his house in Drumcondra. Ahern's explanations became increasingly tenuous as evidence regarding the movement of significant sums in cash, much of it in sterling, came to light.

When the Dáil met on 26 September, the Taoiseach, elected only four months earlier, faced a motion of no confidence from the opposition. Eamon Gilmore, who had replaced Pat Rabbitte as Labour leader, summed up the growing public doubts about Ahern's financial dealings in the 1990s now being unearthed at the tribunal:

It transpires that far from being eager to appear at the tribunal, the Taoiseach was often delaying and frustrating its work. It transpires that the total amount of moneys under discussion in these transactions comes to almost €300,000 in today's terms. These are substantial sums of money for which the Taoiseach cannot credibly account. Therein lies the kernel of the problem, his failure to offer a credible account?

After 18 hours of testimony, over four days, there are few who believe him. I do not believe him. I do not believe many of his own Deputies believe him and the public do not believe him either. I repeat that, after 18 hours of sworn testimony given in front of a panel of three judges, there is still no credible account of transactions involving large sums of money.

The people have a large reserve of common decency. They will insist on fair play and they will give a man time to account for himself. They also have a large reserve of common sense. They do not believe the bizarre and shifting tales that have been offered, of a former Minister for Finance who deals in briefcases full of currency, of men he never met before who suddenly give him cash, of wads of foreign currency … The issue is his failure to offer a credible account of himself and the political consequences that flow from that failure. The issue is that he is not believed …

(26 September 2007)

The government won the confidence vote, but Ahern's troubles at the tribunal were compounded by a series of controversies chiefly involving the health services. The government's standing took a further hit when news of a proposed double-digit pay hike in ministerial salaries hit the headlines at a time when there was growing concern about the economy.

The new year brought little relief for the government. Ironically, as the Taoiseach received glowing plaudits on the international stage – a visit to Tanzania in January demonstrated the tangible benefits of Irish overseas aid, which had increased fivefold since he took office, and an invitation to address the joint Houses of Congress in Washington confirmed his central role in bringing peace to Northern Ireland – his standing at home had rarely been lower. A January TNS mrbi poll in *The Irish Times* revealed that 78 per cent of people didn't believe Ahern's evidence to the tribunal. While his cabinet colleagues publicly rallied to the Taoiseach's defence, launching scathing attacks on the methods and motivations of the tribunal, privately some had doubts about his ability to continue in office.

When the Dáil reconvened after the Christmas recess, a motion of confidence in the tribunal was tabled by the opposition in response to attacks on the tribunal by senior Fianna Fáil members. Rejecting opposition claims that the Taoiseach's tribunal entanglement was deflecting the work of government, Fianna Fáil TD for Tipperary South Martin Mansergh accused the tribunal of persecuting the Taoiseach:

> I have no difficulty affirming confidence in the Mahon tribunal, although I do not subscribe to the doctrine that either courts or tribunals should be above and beyond criticism, either in this House or elsewhere. The Supreme Court has been quite critical of the tribunal. However, the Opposition parties do the tribunal no service by repeatedly attempting to pre-empt its findings, operating on the *Alice in Wonderland* judicial principle, sentence first, verdict afterwards.
>
> I do not much approve of political trials, but one cannot fail to note that, just as the beef tribunal was turned into a trial, first of Charles Haughey and then Albert Reynolds … similarly the Mahon tribunal about certain planning matters has ended up — one might wonder how — as a trial of Bertie Ahern, complete with a Ken Starr style special prosecutor … The 17th century French writer Nicholas Boileau once said: "Le vrai peut quelques fois n'être pas vraisemblable." The truth can sometimes be improbable …
>
> (*31 January 2008*)

6 December
The model Katy French dies at the age of twenty-four after collapsing on 2 December. It is believed her death is due to the use of illegal drugs.

13 December
EU leaders sign the Lisbon Treaty.

26 December
The singer Joe Dolan dies at the age of sixty-eight from a brain haemorrhage.

27 December
Pakistani politician Benazir Bhutto is assassinated two months after returning to Pakistan from five years in exile.

2008

2 January
After thirty-six years in business, the Burlington Hotel in Dublin closes with the loss of 400 jobs.

"Opportunity has replaced despondency, **peace** has replaced bloodshed and we have a new **beginning.** The **Irish people** did not surrender to the **common enemy** of despair. They have never **ceased to believe** that **better times** would come.**"**

Bertie Ahern, 7 April 2008

Despite Mansergh's loyal defence, the situation for the Taoiseach deteriorated over the following weeks as the veracity of his tribunal testimony became even more improbable.

Confidence within Fianna Fáil began to ebb, and, on the morning of 2 April 2008, the day the Dáil reconvened after the Easter break, Ahern, facing another return to the tribunal in the coming weeks, announced that he would resign a month later, on 7 May. Speaking in the Dáil only hours after his resignation announcement, Ahern reflected on the changes that his thirty years in Dáil Éireann had witnessed:

> The past 30 years have been times of great trials and great triumph for all of us on all benches of this House. For much of that time, the vision of a country that could one day prosper and be at peace seemed far off and almost impossible to maintain.
>
> Unemployment and emigration were harsh realities that made hope and optimism hard to sustain at times. The cloud of sectarian violence and political conflict hung over all of us and hung over the whole island …
>
> Opportunity has replaced despondency, peace has replaced bloodshed and we have a new beginning. The Irish people did not surrender to the common enemy of despair. They have never ceased to believe that better times would come. Time and again they looked to politics and to politicians — the people they chose to represent them in this House and elsewhere — to give leadership in the challenge of thinking about old problems in new ways. By brilliant innovation and hard lessons alike, this country has overcome a difficult past and shaped a new beginning …
>
> If there is any single achievement that this generation can boast of it is that it has realised the hopes bequeathed to it. We hand on confidence as our legacy and we leave tenacity as our testament. As we look forward to a new beginning in a new Ireland we have nothing to be complacent about. We have much to be confident in. This is a time of unparalleled opportunity in a country of great possibility …
>
> As I bring my time as Taoiseach to an end, in a month's time, I will recall that Ireland gave me the opportunity to be part of her history and now, at the end, I will submit to the verdict of history.
>
> *(2 April 2008)*

9 January
After days of heavy rainfall in the south-west of Ireland, serious flooding occurs in Fermoy and Mallow, with parts of Mallow under 1.3 metres of water.

10 January
Sir Edmund Hillery, credited with the first successful ascent of Mount Everest, dies aged eighty-eight.

13 January
Despite extensive protests, Aer Lingus completes its final flight between Shannon and Heathrow.

16 January
Wayne O'Donoghue is released from prison after serving three years for the manslaughter of his neighbour, eleven-year-old Robert Holohan, in January 2005.

On 7 May, in glorious sunshine, the Thirtieth Dáil met to elect Brian Cowen the twelfth head of government since the foundation of the State. Cowen had first entered Dáil Éireann in 1984 after winning a by-election caused by the death of his father Ber. Steeped in political tradition, Cowen's loyalty to the party and to politics had become one of his defining characteristics. In accepting the nomination as Taoiseach, Cowen set out his political vision, a vision centred on community, the common good and progressive change:

> One of the challenges we face today is to temper a rising tendency towards individualism within Irish society. We rightly have encouraged a culture of the individual taking personal responsibility for his or her well-being. We have reaped benefits from the more confident Ireland as presented by its most successful people forging new opportunities at home and abroad. Overdone however, this carries risks. Not correctly harnessed, this can sap the energy of our sense of community, which still is strong and visible in many ways. We must prioritise turning the benefits of individual flair to the benefit of the community as a whole.
>
> This is what the Government wants and needs. Its responsibility is to fuel the engine of community and to lead the charge away from the promotion of exclusive self-interest towards a superior value of a wider community interest. The pre-eminence of community and participation over self promotes social harmony and a better quality of life for all. This is what will allow us to develop a society of social inclusion.
>
> The ultimate test of our progress will be the extent to which we can mobilise all of the people to think and behave in a manner that puts the interests of society as a whole ahead of our own private interests. As Seán Lemass observed, all "national progress … depends … on an upsurge of patriotism" among the people. It is the job of government to lead on this issue but that of society as a whole to address. My Government will pursue this agenda to lead change.
>
> (*7 May 2008*)

Cowen's hoped-for upsurge in patriotism was short lived. Within five weeks of taking office, the Lisbon Treaty, supported by nearly all political parties in Dáil Éireann – with the exception of Sinn Féin – was rejected by the people in a referendum. The defeat of the treaty provoked a crisis in Ireland's relationship with the EU.

End of an era, 6 May 2008. Bertie Ahern waves to the media after tendering his resignation.

The rejection of the Lisbon Treaty also coincided with a rapid deterioration in the economy. In May 2008, the largest-ever annual increase in the live register was recorded and unemployment figures broke the 200,000 mark for the first time since 1999. The contraction in the construction sector, a key driver of Ireland's economic boom, was particularly marked and resulted in estimated growth for 2008 being set at just 1 per cent compared to the 3 per cent forecast in the budget the previous December. The declining economic situation resulted in a drastic shortfall in government revenues, with a €7 billion hole in the tax take predicated for 2008.

The changing fortunes in the Irish economy – matched with rising oil prices, increased inflation and lower consumer spending – have only served to confirm that the economic boom of the previous decade has come shuddering to a halt. The end of the Celtic Tiger era was at hand.

28 June
Paddy Canny, the all-Ireland champion fiddle player and founder member of the Tulla Céilí Band dies at the age of eighty-nine.

28 June
A syndicate of workers from County Carlow become the winners of €18,963,4111, Ireland's biggest ever lottery jackpot.

"We ordain that the elected Representatives of the Irish people alone have power to make laws binding on the people of Ireland ..."

Declaration of Independence, 19 January 1919

Conclusion

The political response to the economic downturn, the rejection of the Lisbon Treaty and the future direction of social policy will be debated, discussed and decided by Dáil Éireann, in the same way it has debated and discussed every political, social and economic change in fortune since 1919. However, today, there is a disconnect between those who are honoured to sit in parliament and the citizens who put them there through their democratic choice.

Now that the heady days of Celtic Tiger Ireland are waning and hard decisions regarding spending, taxation and social justice are upon us, our parliament will play a central role in the debate about where we go now as a society and as an economy. Whether Dáil Éireann also seizes this opportunity to chart its future as a modern parliament and takes the hard decisions needed to see that through remains to be seen.

In a debate on Dáil reform in 1996, Pat Upton, a Labour TD for Dublin South Central, identified the lowly position of backbench TDs within a parliamentary system dominated by the executive as a key problem, arguing that until this issue is addressed the concept of Dáil reform will remain largely academic:

> That relates to the concept of the ideal Government backbencher. The ideal one is a lady or a gentleman who has virtually no ideas or proposals and in the event of such backbenchers being contaminated by an idea, they will have the good sense to keep their mouths shut. Instead of concerning themselves with proposals, in an ideal world they would sing as best they could the party song, whether it was good, bad or indifferent. That may be something of a dramatisation or an exaggeration of Irish politics, but there is a fair degree of truth in it. Unless we are prepared to address some

of these matters, we will continue to have Dáil reform for many years to come because the end product will remain unsatisfactory.

(*9 October 1996*)

While Upton's comments referred specifically to government backbenchers, his criticism aptly describes the status of many TDs on either side of Dáil Éireann. Parliament has failed to develop a role or identity separate from government. Party loyalty is the all-important principle in Dáil Éireann to the exclusion of all else, with the result that parliament has largely failed to foster a system whereby the Dáil exercises a role as a watchdog of the executive, regardless of which parties are in power. An exception can be found in the work of some Dáil committees, notably the Public Accounts Committee and the sub-committee it formed to undertake the DIRT inquiry, but examples of this remain rare and, compared to other parliaments, particularly Westminister from where so much of our parliamentary culture emanates, the record is poor.

The emasculated role of parliament within our system of government facilitates the time-honoured tradition of the TD as a messenger boy or girl, toiling away at constituency concerns in the knowledge that this work reaps rewards at the ballot box.

The close relationship between public representatives and their constituents is more pronounced in Ireland than in any other European democracy and, while often derided, it has many benefits. The fact that every member of the national parliament knows the rate of a weekly social welfare payment or has experience of the chaos that often arises in hospital A&E units is of immense value. TDs are often the advocates for those who need a voice and this experience feeds into debate and formulation of policy at a national level. However, our electoral system and our political culture can lead to a complete distortion of the relationship and reward a TD who deals solely with the symptoms of policy failure but punishes a TD who attempts to address the causes of these problems through parliamentary work.

Reform is a much-overused term these days, and hardly a week goes by without politicians of all hues referring to public-sector reform, or health-service reform or a general dollop of 'root and branch' reform in any number of sectors. Perhaps their calls would carry more weight if they attended to the urgent reforms needed a little closer to home in the national parliament.

For instance, it has been six years since the Supreme Court ruling that severely restricted the ability of parliamentary committees to investigate many issues of public concern, yet legislative or constitutional change to reassert this important function of parliament has yet to be initiated. Likewise, while the Taoiseach now answers questions from party leaders on current issues of the day, no facility exists for ministers to field questions in a similar manner. Such an initiative was announced in February 2002 but remains to be implemented. In addition, while the Dáil has conferred substantial policy-making and enforcement powers on a range of new State agencies in recent years – analysis suggests there are more than 800 such bodies in existence but, remarkably, no one knows for sure – parliament has yet to devise a system of scrutiny that ensures these organisations are accountable to the legislature for the decisions they take and the citizens' money they spend.

That said, it is not just our much-maligned politicians who need to reassess their attitude to parliament. The media and we, the voters, also have a role. Elements of the media often deride the role of parliament, bemoaning the long holidays and questioning the work rate of TDs, while at the same time wilfully ignoring the work that takes place in the Dáil chamber, Seanad Éireann and in the committee rooms.

As citizens, we also are only too willing to dismiss the activities of Dáil Éireann, denigrating the role that TDs play in devising solutions to national issues and bemoaning their attachment to parish-pump politics. At the same time, opinion polls confirm that in choosing our elected representatives their constituency record is the most important factor in deciding who we vote for. The number of hard-working, talented TDs who took their parliamentary role seriously – often while their competitors in a constituency assiduously attended funerals, fixed potholes or claimed to secure medical cards – and subsequently lost their seats is proof of the double standard that voters often apply to their TDs.

As Dáil Éireann enters its ninetieth year, the achievements of the parliament are many. Few other nations born of such turmoil as Ireland witnessed between 1919 and 1923 have survived and managed to build a stable democracy. That democracy has proved resilient, often at times of great strain – such as during the Emergency and the Arms Crisis. However, a modern democracy cannot look to the past. Our country and our world is changing rapidly, and Dáil Éireann must prove adept at responding to that change over the challenging years ahead.

Acknowledgements

This project would not have been completed without the patience, generosity and support of numerous colleagues and friends. Firstly, to Ciara Considine in Hachette Books Ireland who first suggested the idea and to her colleague Claire Rourke whose guidance, good humour and professionalism have been invaluable.

Many people gave sound advice, timely criticism and were available for lengthy discussions in various public houses as the project evolved, including Ronán O'Brien, Ivana Bacik, Tony Heffernan and Ross Higgins and to them I am eternally indebted, however any errors, omissions, prejudices and slanders are my own work.

Thanks are also due to my family, especially my mother Pauline and my father Peter, for their unflinching support and belief and to Geraldine Abberton for her kindness, patience and love.

And finally to my friend Finbarr O'Malley, without whom this book wouldn't have seen the light of day, and to whom this work is dedicated.

Photograph Permissions

The author and publisher would like to thank the following for allowing the use of their copyrighted material in *Creating Ireland*.

Getty Images: Topical Press Agency/Getty Images: viii • Hulton Archive/Getty Images: 4; 68 • Sean Sexton/Getty Images: 11; 15 • Hulton Archive/Illustrated London News/Getty Images: 25 • Walshe/Getty Images: 34 • Walshe/Topical Press Agency/Getty Images: 42; 50 • Keystone/Getty Images: 56; 135; 141; 168 • Haywood Magee/Picture Post/Getty Images: 85 • Haywood Magee/Getty Images: 90 • Tony Linck/Time Life Pictures/Getty Images: 92; 96 • Time Inc./Time Life Pictures/Getty Images: 116 • Alex Bowie/Getty Images: 155 • Central Press/Getty Images: 172 • Sahm Doherty/Time Life Pictures/Getty Images: 225 • Peter Muhly/AFP/Getty Images: 307

National Library of Ireland: 18; 30

The Irish Times: 58; 104; 112; 151; 234; 281

RTÉ Stills Library: 158

Photocall Ireland: 185; 199; 205; 208; 250; 256; 260; 276; 291; 301

Maxwell's Dublin: 194

The author and publisher have endeavoured to contact all copyright holders. If any images used in this book have been reproduced without permission, we would like to rectify this in future editions and encourage owners of copyright not acknowledged to contact us.